CW00517657

SUNNINGDALE

The Search for Peace in Northern Ireland

SUNNINGDALE

The Search For Peace In Northern Ireland

NOEL DORR

Acadamh Ríoga na hÉireann
Royal Irish Academy
Dublin 2017

Sunningdale: the search for peace in Northern Ireland

First published 2017

Royal Irish Academy, 19 Dawson Street, Dublin 2
www.ria.ie

Text © 2017 Noel Dorr

ISBN 978-1-908997-64-7 (Hardback)
ISBN 978-1-908997-65-4 (pdf)
ISBN 978-1-908997-66-1 (epub)
ISBN 978-1-908997-67-8 (mobi)

British Library Cataloguing in Publication Data. A CIP catalogue
record for this book is available from the British Library.

Editor: Maggie Armstrong
Typesetter: Datapage International Ltd
Indexer: Brendan O'Brien
Project manager: Helena King

Printed by CPI

Contents

Introduction

In 1970 I was a middle-level diplomat in the Irish embassy in Washington D.C., where I had served for nearly six years—a good deal longer than the usual posting in our foreign service.

Without telling my embassy colleagues, and without taking—I hope—from my work in the embassy, I had managed to pursue courses in Georgetown University simultaneously with my life as a diplomat. This was made somewhat easier by the fact that lectures in the graduate school normally took place in the evenings.

In late June of that year, my double life came to an abrupt halt. The ambassador passed me a letter from the Administration Division of the Department of Foreign Affairs in Dublin. I was to be transferred home and to report for duty in Dublin 'with imme-diate effect'. What exactly did this mean, I asked? Since it was many years since this ambassador had served at home he was inclined to take instructions from that distant authority rather more literally than one more closely acquainted with its vagaries might have done. 'Immediate' he said, reflectively. 'I think that must mean immediate'.

In retrospect now, I can see that it was probably time for me to come home although I did not take it well at the time. One of the hazards of diplomatic life is that of 'going native' after a long time in a particular post. It was beginning to happen to me. In May 1970, a month before my transfer to Dublin, a colleague in the

Irish consulate general in New York in the course of a phone call asked my views on the 'current political crisis'. We had spoken for half a minute before I realised that we were at cross-purposes: I was talking in American terms—about the events at Kent State University in Ohio where on 4 May the National Guard had shot dead four unarmed students who were part of a group protesting against the Vietnam War and the bombing of Cambodia; he had meant 'the Arms Crisis' at home, which led the taoiseach, Jack Lynch, to sack two ministers in his government who were accused of the illegal importation of arms destined for Northern Ireland.[1]

I did in the end allow myself some leeway in regard to timing—but only a little. One Monday morning in early July, just two weeks after I had received the letter, I reported for work at Iveagh House in Dublin.

The situation in Northern Ireland was deteriorating seriously at the time. In June there had been rioting in Belfast and Derry and five men had been shot dead. On 3 July more were killed and a 34-hour curfew was imposed on the whole of the Lower Falls. Jack Lynch's government in Dublin was trying to cope with the aftermath of the so-called Arms Crisis, and the Department of Foreign Affairs was not at that stage well organised to play the part it began to play later in regard to Northern Ireland. So it was reasonable to think that, although I was still relatively junior, the reason I had been recalled at such short notice was that an extra hand was needed in one or other section of the department at a difficult time.

If that was so there was no great evidence of it on those first days after my return. My initial impression was that the system did not quite know where to put me. In due course I was assigned to the Press and Information section where I had responsibility for handling visiting journalists. Northern Ireland had now become a subject of wide international interest and the London-based correspondents of many foreign news media had begun to travel there, and then on to Dublin, in order to cover the story. My job was to ensure that they were briefed on the Irish government's view and to set up a series of appointments—with ministers, opposition spokespersons, academics, Irish journalists and so on. This gradually developed into writing a ministerial speech from time to time and, later, on occasion, some input into policy issues.

During the initial months after my return I was far from content. Apart from the obvious difficulties of adjusting to life in Ireland after eight years abroad, my thoughts were still very much on the student half of my life in Washington. I had a small amount of money saved—though not enough. But if I took my courage in my hands, I thought privately, perhaps I could find some way of giving up my post in Foreign Affairs and returning to Georgetown to finish my studies. After that, who knows?

The dream of taking that other road did not fade easily. But as the weeks and months went on the situation in Northern Ireland became steadily worse. I was more and more drawn to think that none of us on the island of Ireland could escape some kind of moral responsibility for a conflict that was beginning to consume the north and spill over into the south. So I too, as an official in the Department of Foreign Affairs in Dublin, was in some way involved. A pretentious idea, one might say, for someone who occupied quite a modest position at the time, but it carried me through the early months of disillusion which followed my precipitate recall home.

I did not know it then but the same thought was to stay with me through much of the rest of my career. Sometimes I had quite different responsibilities in other areas of the Irish foreign service. Nevertheless, I seemed to be drawn back, in various ways, and at different times over the next 25 years, to some degree of involvement as an official in the efforts by successive taoisigh and ministers in Dublin to respond to the conflict in Northern Ireland. This extended over quite a lengthy period—from 1970 when London tended to dismiss Dublin's views as those of an outsider, through the Anglo-Irish Agreement of 1985, to the mid-1990s when the British and Irish governments, notwithstanding some disagreements and tensions, were working closely together to steer the 'peace process'. It covered the terms of office of six taoisigh—Jack Lynch, Liam Cosgrave, Charles Haughey, Garret FitzGerald, Albert Reynolds and John Bruton—and eight ministers for foreign affairs. Of these only the late Garret FitzGerald has written at length about the events of his time in office.

I retired from the foreign service in 1995, just three years before the historic Good Friday Agreement of 1998.

A landmark in the early period was the Sunningdale conference of December 1973—the first joint initiative in relation to Northern Ireland by the British and Irish governments, working with those democratically-elected parties in Northern Ireland willing to participate. In the short-run it did not succeed. But I have always been intrigued by the acerbic comment of Seamus Mallon, one of the most active and important political figures over this whole period: the 1998 Agreement, he said, was 'Sunningdale for slow learners'. By implication that was an accusation addressed to all those who helped to bring down the Sunningdale settlement, and in particular perhaps to supporters of the Democratic Unionist Party (DUP) and Sinn Féin, the two main parties who share power in the executive. If they had been less politically intransigent, and if those who were engaged in violence had been prepared to end it at that time, could everything that was agreed in 1998 have been achieved 25 years earlier at far less cost in human suffering? A haunting question indeed. In the nature of things we have to accept that there can be no definitive answer. But I do think that Sunningdale was important. Although it did not succeed in its immediate objective, I believe that it marked an important turning point in the approach of both the British and the Irish governments to the problem of Northern Ireland. Furthermore, ideas and concepts that were developed around the time of Sunningdale—on issues such as power-sharing and north-south relations—remained relevant and some were drawn on as building blocks in the settlement achieved eventually in Northern Ireland some 25 years later.

In this book I want to look back at the Sunningdale conference and its outcome, at the short life of the new political institutions, and at some of the reasons why this initiative, born in hope, did not succeed. My main focus will be on how the policies of the Irish government—or rather, two successive Irish governments—in relation to Northern Ireland evolved over the years 1969 to early 1974. However, I want to look also at what I see as a significant change in the attitude of the British government over those years, which helped to make Sunningdale possible.

In 1969, at a time of serious troubles in Derry and Belfast, British ministers in London rejected advice from the Irish minister for external affairs, Dr Patrick Hillery, on what they insisted was a matter internal to the United Kingdom. In August 1971 the British prime minister Ted Heath, responding publicly to the taoiseach Jack Lynch, refused to 'accept that anyone outside the United Kingdom can participate in meetings designed to promote the political development of any part of the United Kingdom'. Yet a short time later Heath invited Lynch and Brian Faulkner, the Northern Ireland prime minister, to a meeting at Chequers where the situation in Northern Ireland was discussed over two days; and in 1973, little more than two years later, he agreed to the setting up of a Council of Ireland linking north and south, in which the British government would have no direct involvement.

This new approach, in my view, implied a radical change of attitude on the part of the British government. Over the previous half-century the assumption in London had been that 'the Irish Question' had been settled when the island was divided in 1920–21. At the time 'the Troubles' broke out in the late 1960s, relations between Dublin and London were good but even so, as Dr Hillery was told bluntly by ministers in Harold Wilson's Labour government, there was a limit to how far the affairs of Northern Ireland could be discussed with 'outsiders'. Heath, who was Wilson's Conservative successor, came, eventually, to see things differently, and, in a Green Paper in late 1972, his government acknowledged explicitly that there was an 'Irish Dimension' intrinsic to Northern Ireland which would have to be taken into account in any settlement of the conflict there. As I see it, this was a tacit recognition that 'the Irish Question' had not been fully resolved in the 1920s: unresolved issues in the Anglo-Irish relationship still at play in Northern Ireland were an underlying source of much of the conflict there; and the British and Irish governments had a shared responsibility to work together to resolve them.

This change of approach by the British government was evident at the Sunningdale conference in December 1973; and the extent to which the two governments worked together at that time prefigured the close cooperation between them which, notwithstanding many tensions and difficulties, developed in later years, and which now provides a firm basis for the present settlement in Northern Ireland. My interest here is in the events that led up to this change of approach and the part which two successive Irish governments—led respectively by Jack Lynch and Liam Cosgrave—may have played in helping to bring it about.

I will focus particularly on political and constitutional issues and concepts. This does not mean that I overlook economic, social and religious aspects of the conflict. Nor do I in any way want to ignore the appalling violence and suffering that took place over the 30 years of 'the Troubles'. It has always seemed to me, however, that it is a sense of insecurity on the part of people of both communities and the resentments, hopes and fears to which that insecurity gives rise, that has kept tensions alive and been the prime driver of conflict over several generations in the divided society of Northern Ireland.

I cannot claim that what I offer will be a full account either of the period or of the role of the Irish government, still less of that of its British counterpart. Memory, I know, is fallible and selective and it fades with the years. So I have checked and supplemented my recollections as best I could by drawing on documents wherever possible—some in the National Archives of Ireland, some from the British National Archives in Kew, and from the Public Record Office of Northern Ireland in Belfast, and some in my own possession. But this will be essentially a personal view of events, issues and ideas as seen by one Irish official over that five-year period and I hope it will be read as such. I should also acknowledge that I may be prone to the 'professional deformation' of the civil servant who can sometimes see a continuity of ideas where each successive government is certain that its policies are new and distinctive.

I am aware too, of the important part played by political leaders in Northern Ireland, especially those of the SDLP such as Gerry Fitt, John Hume, Austin Currie and Paddy Devlin. John Hume's far-sighted political thinking, sustained over decades and always rejecting violence, was of particular importance. So, too, particularly at a later stage in the years after Sunningdale, was the part played by Seamus Mallon. But theirs is another story. I will not dwell on it here at any length—there are others who could recount it much better.

Leaders of the Unionist and Alliance parties at that time would no doubt have their own, quite different, narrative of the events covered in this book. Brian Faulkner, the leader of the Ulster

Unionist Party at the time, set out his views in an autobiography published shortly after his death;[2] and a very distinguished former Northern Ireland civil servant, Sir Kenneth Bloomfield, who worked closely with him as secretary to the Northern Ireland executive, has written extensively and well about the period—albeit from a viewpoint rather different to mine.[3]

The central figures in the story I recount in this book are Jack Lynch and his successor as taoiseach, Liam Cosgrave. Each of the two, in their rather different ways, did much to bring home to the British prime minister, Ted Heath, and his government the importance of the 'Irish Dimension' and the role of the Irish government in bringing about a settlement. Liam Cosgrave, too, at the Sunningdale conference, and in the months that followed, was able to establish a good personal and working relationship with Brian Faulkner, leader of the Ulster Unionist Party and head of the Northern Ireland executive. In a more auspicious time and circumstances, that might have proved a solid foundation for the settlement which they and others agreed in December 1973. Another major figure in these events was Garret FitzGerald, who became minister for foreign affairs some nine months before Sunningdale and whose ideas and energy did much to shape the government's approach to the Sunningdale conference. He has written at length about the events of the period in not just one, but two, autobiographies.[4]

I write as a former official. Of course, I was only one among many—from the Taoiseach's Department and the Department of Justice as well as Foreign Affairs—who worked with political leaders at that time. Dermot Nally, secretary to the government, who, sadly, is no longer with us, played a central role then and later. So, too, did my former colleague in Foreign Affairs, Sean Donlon, who travelled regularly and extensively in Northern Ireland and maintained contact with a wide range of opinion there, as did some other of his colleagues. Their work was invaluable in keeping the Irish government fully informed in its efforts to work towards a peaceful political settlement. Sean has offered me helpful comments in writing this book; and talking to him about these far-off events in which we were both involved reminds me again that mine is only one narrative, one part of a complex story.

If I seem to refer too much in what follows to what I myself thought, or said, or did, I apologise in advance to our political leaders at the time and to those of my colleagues who were also deeply involved in these events and contributed greatly to the effort to find a solution. They may well have rather different memories of those years which it would be interesting to read. Sadly, however, some who were centrally involved are no longer here, and those who are do not seem inclined to write about that time. So this is my effort to recount the story as I recall it many years on.

A final thought: I recall how Eliot's Prufrock described his own modest role:

> ...an attendant lord, one that will do
> To swell a progress, start a scene or two,
> Advise the prince; no doubt an easy tool,
> Deferential, glad to be of use,
> Politic, cautious, and meticulous.[5]

Was I really like that? I would hope not; and I hope, too, that my former colleagues never thought of me like that then, or remember me like that today.

NOTES

[1] The two who were sacked by Jack Lynch on 6 May 1970 were Charles J. Haughey, Minister for Finance and Neil Blaney, Minister for Agriculture and Fisheries. A third minister, Kevin Boland, resigned in protest. (Another, Micheál Ó Móráin, the minister for justice, had resigned two days earlier at Lynch's request.) Haughey and Blaney, together with Captain James Kelly; John Kelly, a Belfast republican leader; and Albert Luykx, a Belgian businessman resident in Ireland, were brought before the Irish courts but charges against Blaney were dropped and, later, after further court hearings, all of the others were cleared. Charles Haughey returned to office as minister for finance in Lynch's 1977 government and he succeeded Lynch as taoiseach in December 1979.

[2] Brian Faulkner, *Memoirs of a statesman* (ed. by John Houston) (London, 1978).

[3] Sir Kenneth Bloomfield, Head of the Northern Ireland civil service 1984–91, author of *Stormont in crisis* (Belfast, 1994) and *A tragedy of errors: the government and misgovernment of Northern Ireland* (Liverpool, 2007).

[4] Garret FitzGerald, *All in a life: an autobiography* (Dublin, 1991) and *Just Garret: tales from the political front line* (Dublin, 2010).

[5] T.S. Eliot, 'The lovesong of J. Alfred Prufrock', in *Collected poems, 1909–1962* (London, 1974).

CHAPTER 1

History and its consequences

Those who cannot remember the past are condemned to repeat it, according to Santayana.[1] Is that perhaps also true of those who remember it only too well, as some say we do in Ireland? Whatever about repeating the past, we have certainly not been averse to recounting it. So I ought to be wary, in this first chapter, of delving too deeply into history for explanations of the conflict that tore Northern Ireland apart for over 30 years. There are, after all, other ways to understand it: one could, for example, focus on economic, social or political aspects or talk about religious differences. In my view, however, it is best understood as an unresolved residue of the long and complex historic relationship between Britain and Ireland. For that reason I feel I must start with some account of that relationship and the unsolved issues in the relationship that troubled the island of Ireland up to recent times.

This is not easy to do—or at least to do briefly. For one thing, it is difficult to give an account of what happened at any one point in Irish history without starting just a bit further back to explain how things came to be as they were. There is also the caustic comment that the problem in Northern Ireland has been, not so much finding agreement on the future as agreement on the past; and any Irish reader, north or south, may well have his or her own—possibly quite different—view of whatever history I may recount. So I would ask the reader to take this first chapter as an attempt to give some idea of Ireland's troubled past—and its bearing on the present—to a well-meaning outsider who knows nothing of the intimacy of our quarrels. Those who already know the story all too well may prefer to move directly to the next chapter where I begin to recount the events from 1969 onwards, which are the main focus of my attention in this book.

In Ireland, over time, two different senses of what I would call 'community identity', offering two opposed agendas for the future, crystallised out of the centuries-long interaction between the two islands. The complexity of the so-called 'Irish Question' in the late-nineteenth and early-twentieth centuries was due in part to the fact that whatever decision was taken on the future relationship between Britain and Ireland could also determine definitively the respective positions of the two main communities in Ireland—that is, whether one would be a minority in an autonomous Ireland or the other a minority in the larger entity of the UK. The effect of the settlement of 1920–21 was to divide the island into two separate entities—Northern Ireland with a devolved parliament within the United Kingdom, and the Irish Free State which is now the Irish republic. But this division resolved the issue only in part. The contention between unionist and nationalist agendas remained, bottled up now in a new form, and it has been played out over years since then in the narrower ground of Northern Ireland.[2]

What do I mean by 'community identity'? Something more than religious differences—though religion can play a part, and did in Ireland. The broader concept I have in mind is not easy to define. I am talking about the sense of relationship and community that develops among a particular population: a sense of continuity over time; a sense that they have a common history. Or, perhaps, it would be more correct to say that they have a shared narrative about the past, passed on from generation to generation.

'Narrative', in the sense in which I use it here, is very different from the more objective, balanced account we are entitled to hope for from the historian. The kind of narrative I have in mind is necessarily selective. It is the story a community tells itself about its past, an account of the griefs, the trials and the triumphs that shaped it and gave it a sense of a common identity. For them it is simply 'our history'—but it is actually the result of a selective weaving together of aspects and events of the past which are seen as having helped to constitute the community and which, as such, the community has chosen to remember. It is epitomised in the easy, unselfconscious use of 'we', the first person plural: in talking about the past people will speak of 'our ancestors' and 'our forefathers'; and looking forward, they will express their hopes for 'our children' and 'our children's children'.

It is this sense of continuity stretching back into the past, and the projection of that continuity into the future, which makes the term 'imagined community', used by Benedict Anderson in his study of the origins of nationalism, particularly apposite.[3] For Anderson, an 'imagined community' is a kind of proto-nation. But I would suggest that the term can be applied in recent history to both unionists and nationalists in the island of Ireland even though only the latter aspired to the establishment of a separate sovereign state.

To talk of just two 'communities' in the island of Ireland, it may be said, is to simplify grossly—Irish history is much more complex than that. That is true of course. But, it is still true, broadly speaking, that the division of Ireland nearly a century ago was an effort to deal with the fact that the turbulent currents of Irish history had left us with two differing narratives about the past and a contention between two sharply different agendas for the future of the island. One, the majority tradition in the island, largely but by no means exclusively Catholic, was shaped by a narrative that depicted the Irish as a people, supposedly of 'Celtic' origin, who in earlier times had assimilated successive invaders; a people who, following Norman, and later, English, conquest, had been subjected for centuries to oppression but whose aspiration to nationhood had never been extinguished. The other, a minority, substantially but not exclusively Protestant, drew on a very different narrative and looked to a different agenda for the future in which Ireland would remain part of the United Kingdom. In the north-east in particular, a strong sense had developed of a distinctive local Protestant community which traced its origins to settlers from Scotland and England which, in the bloody wars of the seventeenth century, had withstood attack, and even attempted massacre, from the native Irish whom they had displaced. It was a community that celebrated annually—as it still does today—the notable part played by its forebears in sieges and battles that ensured the Protestant succession to the throne in England and consolidated the liberties achieved in the 'Glorious Revolution' of 1688; a community that, in the early twentieth century, was determined, by force if necessary, to maintain its place in the United Kingdom—which it saw as both the assurance of its liberties and its guarantee against being pressed into the position of a minority in a majority Catholic Ireland.

This is a very broad-brush presentation; and it is not the whole story. To focus as I have done on the Protestant/unionist community in the north-east is to overlook some quite strong unionist sentiment elsewhere in the island, among some Catholics as well as Protestants, in the years before Irish independence; and I know that there are other aspects, such as differences in social and economic status, to be considered, although I will not discuss them here. I will limit myself to a very brief and necessarily selective account of some events in the nineteenth and early-twentieth centuries that form a background to the division of Ireland and which still underlie the contention between the unionist and nationalist/republican agendas in Northern Ireland today.

Until the end of the eighteenth century Ireland as a whole had been, nominally at least, a separate kingdom under the British crown. It was governed from Dublin through a Protestant, largely Anglican, 'ascendancy', and an Irish parliament, which was ultimately subordinate to the authority of the parliament in London. Its laws and legal system, the so-called 'Penal Laws', discriminated against both the Catholic majority in the island and also, for much of the century, against the 'Dissenters'—mainly Presbyterians—who were now strongly established as a community in the north-east around Belfast.

Two related events, which occurred just a few years apart at the close of the eighteenth and the start of the nineteenth centuries, did much to determine the subsequent history of the island. It could indeed be said that they did much to shape the two differing narratives about the past into two alternative agendas for the future.

One was the 1798 Rebellion organised by the 'United Irishmen', a radical reform movement, initially called the 'United Irish Society', which had been established in Dublin and Belfast in 1791.[4] In those years Enlightenment values and egalitarian ideas drawn from the American and the French Revolutions had gained support, particularly among Belfast Presbyterians, and to a lesser extent also elsewhere in Ireland. A Dublin Protestant, Wolfe Tone, a leading figure in the United Irishmen, who is seen today as a founding figure of the separatist Irish republican tradition, proclaimed it as his aim 'to break the connection with England, the source of all our ills'; his means to that end would be 'to unite Protestant, Catholic and Dissenter' throughout the whole island of Ireland. The rebellion inspired by these ideas, which broke out in several parts of the country in 1798, drew together, for a time, to temporary common purpose, both radically-minded Presbyterians in Belfast and somewhat more sectarian-minded Catholic rebels elsewhere. It received some limited support from revolutionary France, and a small French military force landed to help the rebels in the west. However, the rebellion failed and it was suppressed harshly and with considerable bloodshed. Nevertheless, the ideas that inspired it lived on through the nineteenth and twentieth centuries, and they are still seen as of seminal importance by Irish republicanism, and indeed all who retain a hope for Irish unity in the Ireland of today.

The second major event occurred two years later, in large part as a reaction to the first. The British prime minister, William Pitt, had been alarmed by the rebellion and the role France had tried to play; and he was aware of the growing pressure for what came to be called 'Catholic Emancipation'. So in 1800 he decided that the best—and the safest—way to pacify Ireland and to grant relief to the Catholic majority from their disabilities, was to end the autonomy of the Irish parliament and establish a new United Kingdom of Great Britain and Ireland. An Act of Union was pressed through both parliaments and came into effect on 1 January 1801. Henceforth there was to be a single parliament for both islands with a specified number of seats allocated to Ireland. While the emergence in the twentieth century of an independent Irish state was to mean an end to the Union of two islands as established in 1801, 'the maintenance of the Union', in the more limited sense of ensuring that Northern Ireland will remain part of the United Kingdom, continues to be of fundamental importance to the unionist community in Northern Ireland today.

In the nineteenth century Belfast became an industrial centre; and the area around it grew relatively prosperous. So for part of the Irish population the Union of 1801 could be said to have had positive consequences. For Irish nationalists, however, the decision by the Irish parliament, unrepresentative though it was, to agree to its own abolition, had been fundamentally wrong: they believed that 'the Union' had been pushed through by corrupt means and they wanted to see it reversed. But a mass 'Repeal' campaign in the 1840s, led by Daniel O'Connell, the hero of 'Catholic Emancipation', had no success.

It became evident as the nineteenth century went on that Pitt's hope that the union of the two kingdoms would lead to 'the tranquillity and improvement of Ireland' was far from being realised. 'Catholic Emancipation', which was part of his plan, was achieved only in 1829. The Great Famine in the late 1840s was a major disaster, made worse, unintentionally, by the laissez-faire policies of the British administration at the time. There were lesser famines at times; widespread agitation over land issues; and sporadic attempts at rebellion. The most serious of these was the campaign conducted by the secretive Fenian organisation, which continued the militant tradition of Irish republicanism in the latter part of the nineteenth century. They had strong support in Irish-America and also, to an extent, links back to the tradition of the Ribbonmen and other secretive groups that had been involved in militant action on land issues in rural areas earlier in the century. After an abortive attempt at rebellion in Ireland, and even an attempted invasion of Canada from the United States in the 1860s, some Fenians turned in the 1880s to a dynamiting campaign in Britain, which included attempts to blow up the Mansion House in London and Liverpool Town Hall in 1881, and the detective department at Scotland Yard in 1884. This could, perhaps, be seen as the precursor of the tactic of extending bombing campaigns to Britain adopted by the IRA in more recent times.[5]

Religious differences also became sharper in the years after Catholic Emancipation was achieved. The Roman Catholic Church, which had been discreet and quietist in the eighteenth century, became more publicly assertive of its position as the largest religious denomination in Ireland. It embarked on a programme of building churches, schools and hospitals, as well as on what has been called a 'devotional revolution' in matters of religious practice.[6] This was quite understandable but an unfortunate side-effect was that it contributed to an accentuation of confessional differences and a tendency, by some nationalists at times, to seek to equate their 'Irishness' and their nationalism with Catholicism. The response, in the words of one historian, was that 'faced with the rising tide of Catholic influence and power, the Protestant community closed ranks'.[7] This, in turn, had long-term consequences, particularly in the area that is now Northern Ireland. Evangelical religious impulses too came to the fore there in the early-nineteenth century;[8] and the radical, egalitarian ideas which had animated many Belfast Presbyterians who took part in the United Irishmen rebellion of 1798, and which had been a vital strand in the origin of the republican tradition, were no longer in evidence. In the words of the historian A.T.Q. Stewart, 'almost everyone has tended to assume, like the United Irishmen themselves, that because unity was proclaimed it was also in some way achieved'. This did not prove to be the case. Religious differences had now become more prominent. As another respected historian, Roy Foster, puts it:

> With the development of organized Catholic politics, the differences between Anglicans and Presbyterians in Ulster became less important: the evangelical fervour of the 1850s, and the Catholic triumphalism of the same decade, reinforced their common Protestantism. So did the economic conditions of Ulster life.[9]

In the 1880s the Irish Parliamentary Party in the House of Commons, led by Charles Stewart Parnell, a Protestant landowner, pressed the case for Home Rule for Ireland, which had been made initially in the early 1870s by another Irish Protestant MP, Isaac Butt.

Although the party had taken a democratic path and pursued its aim by parliamentary means, it was also thought to draw some measure of support from the militant Fenian movement and its former members. The aim of the party was no longer the simple repeal of the Act of Union which O'Connell had campaigned for some 40 years before: the aim now was to secure a local parliament for Ireland which would exercise certain devolved powers and a limited measure of autonomy within the broader framework of the United Kingdom. Home Rule, or the 'Irish Question', as it came to be known, was to be a matter of great contention in British politics for more than a generation and the issues that emerged were to shape the history of the island of Ireland down to the present. They have lost none of their potency, or their complexity, in Northern Ireland today.

The outcome of a General Election that took place throughout the United Kingdom in 1885 created a favourable opportunity for Parnell and his party to advance their demand for Home Rule. Neither the Liberals with 335 seats, nor the Conservative Party with 249, gained an overall majority in the House of Commons and neither could form a government on its own. The Irish Parliamentary Party with 86 seats held the balance; and it promised its support to the Liberal leader, William Gladstone, in return for a commitment that when he became prime minister he would support Home Rule for Ireland. He kept to that commitment for the rest of his political career—not only for political advantage but also because he had personally come to believe that the Act of Union had not worked well as a definitive settlement of the relationship between Britain and Ireland.

In its demand for Home Rule, the Irish Parliamentary Party had the strong support of a substantial majority of the Irish population. This was evident at successive elections, even though the franchise at the time was quite limited. But a substantial, though smaller, part of the population in Ireland, including some large landowners, was strongly opposed to it and committed to the maintenance of the Union.[10] The opposition to Home Rule was not solely Protestant, or based solely on religious reasons, though it was substantially so; nor was it confined to the north-east, though it was strongest there. It was particularly strong in Belfast which, by now, was a relatively prosperous industrial city. The mood there had changed greatly since radical Presbyterians in the United Irishmen had played a leading role in the rebellion of 1798. Older memories and traditions drawn from the troubled seventeenth century were now much more potent, and religious differences sharper. The substantial Protestant population in Belfast and the surrounding counties had no wish to be 'forced out of the Union' and left as a minority in a largely Catholic Home Rule Ireland which they feared would be quite unsympathetic to their interests. Belfast's merchants and manufacturers, too, were concerned for economic and business, as well as for religious, reasons to maintain the full integrity of the Union. The Conservative Party in England, now in opposition in the House of Commons, strongly opposed a step that they believed could lead to the break-up of the Union, and even perhaps, in time, of the Empire. Partly on constitutional principle and partly for political advantage they committed themselves to full support for unionists in Ireland in their opposition to Home Rule.

In introducing the Home Rule Bill in the House of Commons on 8 April 1886, Gladstone noted that for many of the years since the Act of Union there had been 'repressive legislation of an exceptional kind against Ireland' on the statute books. The problem, as he saw it, was 'how to reconcile imperial unity with diversity of legislation'; his aim was that 'the mainspring of law in Ireland' would be felt by the people to be Irish.[11] The Home Rule Bill that he presented was quite a limited measure. It provided for a one-chamber Irish 'legislature' modelled on the general synod of the Church of Ireland. It would comprise two 'orders' (corresponding very approximately to 'Lords' and 'Commons'), which might meet separately or together. It would have power over a variety of domestic matters in Ireland but, although there would no longer be Irish representation in the House of Commons, the Westminster parliament would be sovereign and would remain the supreme legislative authority for Ireland as for other parts of the United Kingdom.[12]

It is interesting now to note that, in introducing this limited Home Rule measure, Gladstone also showed an awareness of what he called 'the state of opinion in that wealthy, intelligent, and energetic portion of the Irish community which…predominates in a certain portion of Ulster'. However, he insisted that he had to act in accordance with the wishes of the majority population in Ireland since 'five-sixth of its lawfully-chosen representatives are of one mind in this matter'. But he was also prescient in foreseeing—perhaps even inviting—the division that was ultimately to occur:

> Various schemes, short of refusing the demand of Ireland at large, have been proposed on behalf of Ulster. One scheme is that Ulster itself, or, perhaps with more appearance of reason, a portion of Ulster, should be excluded from the operation of the bill… there may be others.

None of these schemes seemed to him to be justified at that point, either on its merits or because of the support it would achieve. But things might change: if a plan were 'given practical form and… found to be recommended by a general or predominating approval', it would, 'at our hands, have the most favourable consideration, with every disposition to do what equity may recommend.'[13]

In spite of Gladstone's strong advocacy, the Bill was defeated in the House of Commons on 8 June 1886, by 341 votes to 311, and he resigned as prime minister. In 1893, at the end of a long career, and now in his last term as prime minister, he made another effort to resolve 'the Irish Question' by introducing another Home Rule Bill framed in terms that differed in some respects from that of 1886. This Bill too was defeated in parliament—this time it passed through the House of Commons but was defeated in the House of Lords.

Notwithstanding the fall, and the subsequent early death, of its leader, Parnell, and the internal party divisions that followed, the Irish Parliamentary Party continued to press the case for Home Rule. The issue came to a head in the years before the First World War. In 1911 the Parliament Act had curtailed the power of the House of Lords to block legislation as it had been able to do with the Home Rule Bill in 1893. In 1912 the Liberal government of the day, led now by Asquith, introduced a third Home Rule Bill in the House of Commons. The Bill was to apply to the whole of Ireland, notwithstanding a formal proposal to Cabinet by Lloyd George and Winston Churchill on 6 February 1912 'that Ulster, or those counties in which Protestants were in a clear majority, should be given an option to contract out of the Bill as introduced'. However, Asquith told the king that the Irish leaders should be warned that the government felt 'free to make…changes, if…it becomes clear as the Bill proceeds that some special treatment must be provided for the Ulster counties'.[14]

Once again the measure was strongly opposed by unionists in Ireland, led by Dublin-born Edward Carson, and their efforts to block it had very strong support from the Conservative Party in Westminster. Some prominent public figures, including leading lawyers, even supported the view that there was a right of resistance to what they saw as fundamentally illegitimate proposals by the government.[15] Opposition was strongest in Ulster where Carson, speaking at a mass rally to launch the anti-Home Rule campaign on 25 September 1911, said '[w]e must be prepared…the morning Home Rule passes, ourselves to become responsible for the govern-ment of the Protestant province of Ulster'.[16] That opposition found eloquent expression in Ulster's Solemn League and Covenant, a document signed by some 250,000 people on 28 September 1912.[17] In 1913 Unionist leaders in Ulster, meeting in the Ulster Unionist Council,[18] approved the setting up of a 'provisional government' which met for the first time in July 1914.[19] They also established an Ulster Volunteer Force (UVF) which had a headquarters staff and was organised into county divisions as well as regiments and bat-talions and 'altogether enrolled about 90,000 men'.[20] In the Spring of 1914, the UVF imported a substantial quantity of arms from Germany in preparation for possible armed opposition to Home Rule. By then, as Roy Foster puts it, 'the Ulster leaders (Carson apart) had moved perceptibly towards demanding a way out for Ulster rather than an end to Home Rule for all Ireland.'[21]

In November 1913 nationalist leaders in Dublin supporting Home Rule followed the unionist example by establishing the Irish Volunteers, a force which, in turn, in July 1914, also imported a much smaller quantity of arms from Germany. There was now a serious political and constitutional crisis over Home Rule and two armed militias with opposing aims in Ireland. One of these could count on the main opposition party in the House of Commons to support its militant stance; and British army officers based at the Curragh near Dublin, when informally consulted, indicated that if Home Rule legislation were adopted they would be unwilling to enforce it.

The war that broke out in Europe in September 1914 changed the situation radically. At that point, faced with a new and even greater crisis, the House of Commons agreed to pass the Home Rule Bill into law as the Government of Ireland Act 1914. However, a Suspensory Act passed at the same time provided that the Home Rule Act would not come into operation for a year—a period that could be further extended from time to time, by Order in Council. This was in fact done at regular intervals during the war years. It was also widely understood at the time the Home Rule Act was passed that it could be subject to further amendment and that some arrangement—whether temporary or permanent—would probably be made to exclude Ulster, or part of it, from its operation.[22]

Satisfied that a Home Rule Act had been passed at last—albeit subject to important conditions—many Irish nationalists volunteered to join the British forces in the war. Some 200,000 did so eventually and it is estimated that somewhere between 30,000 and 40,000 died. A more militant minority of Irish nationalists, however, prominent among whom were members of the secret Irish Republican Brotherhood, planned to use the opportunity of the war to organise a rebellion, which broke out at Easter 1916. The rebels seized a number of buildings in Dublin; proclaimed the establishment of an Irish republic; and held out for a week before surrendering. Initially this Easter Rising appeared to have little public support. That changed greatly however when, following the imposition of martial law, sixteen of the leaders were executed. This was seen by nationalist Ireland as a draconian response; and that, as well as widespread opposition to the threat that conscription would be extended to Ireland in 1917, greatly strengthened support for a more militant form of nationalism in Ireland.

In the latter part of 1917 and early 1918, an 'Irish Convention' in Dublin brought together representatives of the Irish Parliamentary Party, unionists and a wide variety of other parties and interests. Sinn Féin refused to attend, there was a conflict between southern and northern unionists, and the convention was unable to reach agreement.[23] In December 1918, a month after the end of the war, a General Election was held throughout the United Kingdom. Unionist candidates retained considerable support in the north-east. In the rest of Ireland, however, the greater part of the electorate deserted the older Irish Parliamentary Party, which they had supported for two generations in its efforts to achieve Home Rule. Instead, they returned a large number of Sinn Féin party candidates who had pledged that if elected they would not take their seats in Westminster but would set up an independent Irish parliament instead. Some of the successful Sinn Féin candidates who had been active in the Easter Rising were still in custody but a month after the election those who were free to do so met in Dublin in January 1919 and formally declared themselves to be the national parliament of Ireland (the Dáil). One of their first acts was to issue the Irish 'declaration of independence'. It recalled the 'Proclamation of the Republic' at the start of the Easter Rising three years before and went on:

> Now therefore, we, the elected representatives of the ancient Irish people in national parliament assembled, do in the name of the Irish nation, ratify the establishment of the Irish Republic and pledge ourselves and our people to make this declaration effective by every means at our command.[24]

Sporadic guerrilla attacks on the Royal Irish Constabulary, the armed police force, were already beginning to occur. Two and a half more years of guerrilla warfare lay ahead as its supporters fought to establish, and gain recognition for, the newly proclaimed Irish republic. In the meantime, the British government, a coalition led now by Lloyd George as prime minister, continued to press ahead with the pre-war Home Rule agenda—which meant seeking to implement the Home Rule Act that had been passed but suspended in 1914—while at the same time doing all they could through the use of force to suppress the guerrilla insurgency that was now widespread in many parts of Ireland. In 1920 a Government of Ireland Act, which if adopted would put a 'Home Rule solution' in a new form into effect, was passed into law. It provided for the division of Ireland into two new entities—a six-county 'Northern Ireland' and a twenty-six county 'Southern Ireland'. Both were to remain within the broader framework of the United Kingdom but each would have internal autonomy—in effect Home Rule— through its own local parliament; and the two were to be linked for matters of mutual interest by a 'Council of Ireland', which might, if both agreed, eventually take steps to develop further towards Irish unity.

This was much less than Irish unionists had wanted: for two generations now unionists throughout the island had opposed Home Rule and sought to maintain the whole island of Ireland as an integral part of the United Kingdom. However, the Act was accepted by unionist political leaders in the new six-county area. They could count on majority support there, even though that area would also include a substantial nationalist minority opposed to the scheme; and Home Rule for that area seemed tolerable precisely because unionists would be in the majority. So the parliament of the new entity of Northern Ireland was duly elected on 24 May 1921 and formally opened by King George V in June of that year.

By that stage, however, a Home Rule solution seemed completely irrelevant to Irish nationalist opinion throughout the island—as indeed the British government must have known. The public had been radicalised by the Easter Rising and by the executions of rebel leaders that followed; a democratically elected parliament—the Dáil—had issued a declaration of independence which ratified the Republic proclaimed in 1916; and the guerrilla campaign to put it into effect had widespread, though by no means universal, popular support. So the new 'Home Rule' entity of 'Southern Ireland' provided for in the Government of Ireland Act never came into being and the fighting continued.

Eventually in June 1921 a truce was agreed between the British and the republican forces. Following inconclusive exchanges over the following months between Prime Minister Lloyd George and Eamon de Valera, who had been elected president by the Dáil, negotiations between an Irish delegation and British government ministers were eventually opened in London on 11 October, 'with a view to ascertaining how the association of Ireland with the community of nations known as the British Empire may best be reconciled with Irish national aspirations.' Two months later, on 6 December 1921, the negotiations concluded with the signature by both sides of 'Articles of Agreement for a Treaty between Great Britain and Ireland, dated the sixth day of December 1921'—more generally known now as the Anglo-Irish Treaty.

The Treaty established 'the Irish Free State'—initially the whole island—as a dominion within the British Empire (later to evolve into the Commonwealth) with the same status as the other dominions—that is to say Canada, Australia, New Zealand and South Africa. The king was still to be head of state but in many other respects 'dominion status' amounted to substantial independence for the new entity. The Treaty also provided, however, that the newly established 'parliament of Northern Ireland' might opt out within one month. If it did so then 'Northern Ireland' would continue being a part of the United Kingdom with its own devolved parliament and the new 'Irish Free State' would comprise the 26-county area only, that is the present area of the Irish republic.[25]

The signature of the Treaty by the Irish negotiators was a subject of great controversy on the Irish side. It led to a split between those who saw it, in the words of Michael Collins, as 'freedom to achieve freedom' and those who saw acceptance of dominion status and a continuing role for the king as a betrayal of the republic that had been proclaimed in 1916 and ratified by the Dáil in January 1919. The Dáil approved the Treaty by a relatively small majority but in 1922 the dissension about its terms erupted into an open civil war between pro- and anti-Treaty forces which ended with the defeat of the forces opposed to the Treaty in 1923. The Irish Free State came into existence formally in December 1922. It was recognised internationally and it was admitted to the League of Nations in 1924.

To the British prime minister Lloyd George the 1920–21 settlement which divided Ireland must have seemed the only practical solution to 'the Irish Question' of the late-nineteenth and early-twentieth centuries. As he saw it, he faced an apparently intractable dilemma: the nationalist majority in the island wanted an independent Irish republic and supported those using force to achieve it; and a substantial unionist minority concentrated in Ulster had shown clearly before the war that they were equally willing to use force to oppose Home Rule and defend the Union. On 14 October 1921 during the Anglo-Irish Treaty negotiations, Lloyd George told Michael Collins and Arthur Griffith in response to their arguments for Irish unity:

> Attempts have been made to settle the Irish problem since 1886 on the basis of autonomy...We tried from 1911 to 1913. Ulster defeated Gladstone, Ulster would have defeated us...We could not do it. If we tried the instrument would have broken in our hands.

Any attempt to use force to achieve an independent united Ireland would, he argued, lead to a religious civil war in the island.

> I am glad that De Valera has come to the conclusion which we favoured that force is not a weapon you can use. It would break in your hands. We should have a terrible civil war and you would draw in men from all parts into the vortex of the whirlpool...It would resolve itself into a religious war.[26]

Faced with two contending agendas for the future of Ireland, Lloyd George cut the Gordian knot—perhaps I should say the unionist 'not'. The settlement he and his coalition government put in place in 1920–21, by dividing the island, gave something to each of the two main political forces in Ireland but not all that either had sought. The response to Irish nationalism's demand for separation was not to be a republic but an 'Irish Free State' with the substantial, but still partially limited, independence that went with dominion status; and the response to unionists was to create a new area of 'Northern Ireland' in which they formed a local majority and which was given the option of remaining within the United Kingdom with its own 'Home Rule' parliament. At the time this may have seemed to be a pragmatic effort to accommodate nationalism and Unionism separately in the island. Each, it could be said, would have their own territory; the border between them would be worked out through a Boundary Commission; and Irish nationalists could retain some undefined hope of eventual unity through a Council of Ireland.

The logic underlying such an approach required that there be a sufficient degree of homogeneity and acquiescence in each of the two parts of the island to allow each to achieve a reasonable degree of stability and eventually provide a basis for practical cooperation between them. But the newly created area of Northern Ireland was not homogenous; and the situation there was complicated further by sharp religious differences that intensified division. Northern Ireland now had a unionist majority. But it also included a very substantial, largely Catholic, nationalist/republican community that resented and contested the settlement that had created the area and left them, as they saw it, a new and seriously disadvantaged minority within its narrow artificial borders. The largely Protestant unionist majority in the area acquiesced in the settlement, even though it was less than the united Ireland within the United Kingdom that unionists had originally wanted. And, ironically, the forceful opposition of unionists to Home Rule for the whole island had culminated in the acceptance by Northern unionists of a Home Rule parliament for the area they now controlled. But they too were still fearful, since they knew that Irish unity, if it were ever to come about, would reverse their position and make them a minority in an independent Ireland. The result was sullen disaffection on one side and active discrimination on the other. The two played off against each other: disaffection, amounting to 'disloyalty', seemed to justify discrimination against the minority; and that, in turn, provided further justification for their disaffection.

The devolved government and parliament of Northern Ireland followed the Westminster model in which the party with a majority in the House of Commons formed the government, while the 'loyal opposition' could hope that if their party gained a majority it would be their turn to form the government after the next election. But in the Northern Ireland parliament there was no such rotation of power over its whole life of 50 years. Normal politics focused on social and economic issues never developed because the existence of the border that had made one community a majority and the other a minority remained the central issue in every election. The opposition, the Nationalist party, representing a deeply disaffected minority that resented the very existence of Northern Ireland, could hardly be described as 'loyal'. Indeed, for most of the life of the Stormont parliament it did not even accept the role of official opposition; and the Unionist Party, which did not welcome Catholics as members for most of its history, always had a parliamentary majority—which meant that it was permanently in government. Meanwhile, British politics developed a convention under which Westminster, having devolved substantial power to the local parliament and government in Stormont, seldom if ever intervened in the domestic affairs of Northern Ireland.

On the southern side of the border, the Irish Free State, which later became the republic, was, if anything, too homogenous after partition took effect. It was predominantly Catholic, conservative, inward-looking and lacking in a healthy cultural and religious diversity. And it started life, not with the religious/civil war between nationalism and unionism Lloyd George had warned the Irish Treaty negotiators about, but with its own disastrous internal civil war over acceptance of the limited settlement he had offered. One consequence was to leave a legacy of antagonism and bitterness to its politics for several generations. Nevertheless, the Free State stabilised over time and went on to achieve greater independence, within the Commonwealth in the 1920s and 1930s, and, from the late 1940s onwards, as a republic outside the Commonwealth. In building the institutions of a new state, however, it inadvertently consolidated division in a variety of practical ways while paying lip service to the ideal of Irish unity, grumbling from time to time about the 'wrong' of partition, and futilely seeking international support to redress it.

This position of rhetorical assertion and practical acceptance was given subtle expression in a new Constitution in 1937. In convoluted language it enunciated a claim of principle in Article 2 and then drew back and limited the claim to all-Ireland jurisdiction in practice in Article 3. In the meantime, the IRA, now a still militant minority movement, which claimed to act in the name of the independent, united Irish republic proclaimed in 1916, rejected the whole settlement of 1920–21. It asserted a right to use force to achieve Irish unity and engaged sporadically in futile campaigns of violence that included a bombing campaign in England in 1939 and cross-border attacks on police barracks in Northern Ireland in the late 1950s.

If it had indeed been possible in 1920–21 to divide the island of Ireland into two reasonably homogenous parts, then perhaps over time unionism in the north and nationalism in the south might have achieved a reasonably stable accommodation with each other as neighbours. And Anglo-Irish relations too could then have developed in a much more positive way than was the case over the following decades. But the effect in practice of the way Ireland was divided was that there were now, not just two, but three parts in an uneasy relationship in the island—the majority and minority communities in Northern Ireland and the new Irish state to the south.

It is only fair to acknowledge that, whatever its defects, the 1920–21 settlement did bring a measure of stability to Ireland for close to 50 years. But at a cost—which weighed most heavily on the minority in Northern Ireland. The settlement left the contention between the unionist and nationalist agendas for the future unresolved, though concentrated now in 'the narrow ground' of Northern Ireland.[27] Over half a century neither unionism nor nationalism/republicanism in Ireland proved capable of the kind of enlightened and generous political approach that would have been a necessary—though perhaps not a sufficient—condition for implementation of its particular agenda. The unionist majority in Northern Ireland never seemed able to deal with the newly created and deeply disaffected nationalist/republican minority in that area in such a way as to co-opt them into full acceptance of what had been done. Nor have the nationalist majority in the island ever been able to offer such welcome and assurance to unionists as to induce them to consider Irish unity—either as a unitary state or as a federation or confederation of the two political entities in the island. And so both agendas have remained in contention—most acutely within Northern Ireland because the eventual outcome would determine which of the two communities in that narrower area would end up definitively in a minority position. Worse still, the sporadic and wholly ineffectual IRA violence of earlier decades, followed by three more recent decades of sustained violence in Northern Ireland, aggravated unionist fears and deepened sectarian division.

In the early 1960s, after four decades of relative immobility, the first stirrings of change began to be felt in Northern Ireland. In 1963 Terence O'Neill, a moderate unionist, well-meaning if somewhat patrician in character and outlook, became leader of the Unionist Party and prime minister. Unlike his four predecessors since 1920 he could see something at least of the dangers ahead. He began to reach out in a variety of small ways to the Catholic/nationalist minority who at the time numbered about 35 per cent of the population; and he also embarked on a cautious programme of reform.

Notwithstanding a cold relationship at political level there had always been practical cooperation between north and south in Ireland—albeit always on a somewhat uneasy basis. New ground was broken in 1965 when the taoiseach Seán Lemass travelled north to meet Prime Minister O'Neill in Stormont. O'Neill made a return visit to Dublin shortly afterwards. Jack Lynch, who succeeded Lemass as taoiseach, also met with O'Neill. These were the first such meetings between leaders north and south since the 1920s. O'Neill's tentative efforts at modernisation and reform, and these relatively cordial 'hands across the border' encounters, gave rise to some cautious optimism in the mid-1960s.

However, O'Neill's attempts at reform were opposed by conservative elements in his own Unionist Party. More radical protest on the streets was led by Rev. Ian Paisley, a forceful figure who potently mixed religious fundamentalism with political activism and later founded and led his own Democratic Unionist Party. Opposition took a violent turn for a time as the paramilitary Ulster Volunteer Force, founded in 1965, was involved in three killings in 1966. In an effort to rally public support for his reform programme, Prime Minister O'Neill addressed the public on television in December 1968. He warned solemnly that 'Ulster stands at the crossroads'. But the outcome of an election which he called a few months later left his position in his own party weaker than before. In the months after the election bombs exploded at electricity stations and reservoirs that supplied Belfast. The IRA were blamed at first but it emerged later that year that the UVF were responsible. As O'Neill's support slowly crumbled he felt he had no option but to resign. He was succeeded by Major James Chichester-Clark, a conservative landowner who was no more successful in implementing a badly-needed programme of reform and seemed much less willing to try.

By the late 1960s a new generation of leaders had begun to emerge among the nationalist community in Northern Ireland. Educational reform in the United Kingdom as a whole in the period after World War II had opened up new opportunities for young people who would never otherwise have aspired to university education; and the civil rights movement in the United States with its unofficial anthem 'We shall overcome', as well as events in Paris and elsewhere in 1968, offered heady examples of what protest might seek to achieve. Instead of arguing futilely as their predecessors had done for Irish unity, the protesters focused on demanding their full rights as citizens of the United Kingdom. But some marches for civil rights in 1968 and 1969 met with a repressive response.

Under these new pressures, Northern Ireland fractured along a fault-line which, arguably, had been built into it from the outset. Efforts at reform were slow and inadequate—too little, too late. Communal violence, with a strongly sectarian aspect, broke out in Belfast and Derry and oppressive policing left the Royal Ulster Constabulary (the RUC) largely discredited as an impartial police force. The IRA, practically moribund for a decade, began to re-emerge and claim a role as defenders of the minority community. In August 1969 the British army was introduced onto the streets of Belfast and Derry in a quasi-policing role 'in aid of the civil power'. It was welcomed at first by the embattled minority but in the absence of substantial change and reform it gradually came to be seen as defending the status quo. It soon came under attack by the IRA—which in December 1969 split into two rival organisations—the so-called 'Officials' and 'Provisionals'. Loyalist paramilitaries, too, were now engaged in violence—often of a deeply sectarian character—claiming to be responding to the violence of the IRA and defending their own community. The two main loyalist paramilitary organisations were the UVF, who were already active since 1966, and a new and larger organisation, the Ulster Defence Association (the UDA), which was established in 1971. A conflict had now begun which was to last for most of the next 30 years.

NOTES

[1] George Santayana, *The life of reason: reason in common sense* (New York, 1905), 284.

[2] 'The narrow ground' is a phrase borrowed from the title of a book by A.T.Q. Stewart, *The narrow ground: aspects of Ulster, 1609–1969* (London, 1977).

[3] Benedict Anderson, *Imagined communities: reflections on the origin and spread of nationalism* (London, 1983; 2nd edn, 1991), 6.

[4] Alvin Jackson, *Ireland, 1798–1998: war, peace and beyond* (Oxford; 2nd edn, 2010), 12–13.

[5] Charles Townshend, in *Political violence in Ireland: government and resistance since 1848* (Oxford, 1983), describes this as 'a new and distinctly political form of terrorism, a strain of modern revolutionary or "agitational" terror', 159.

[6] Led by Cardinal Cullen, Archbishop of Armagh and, later, Dublin. See Patrick J. Corish, *The Irish Catholic experience: a historical survey* (Dublin, 1985), 212, and, more generally, all of Chapter 7. The phrase 'devotional revolution', as used in this context, is generally attributed to Emmet Larkin, 'The devotional revolution in Ireland, 1850–75', *American Historical Review* (77) (June 1972), 625–52.

[7] Corish, *The Irish Catholic experience*, 217.

[8] Stewart, *The narrow ground*, 99.

[9] R.F. Foster, *Modern Ireland, 1600–1972* (London, 1988), 387–8. In the view of Nicholas Mansergh, at the time of the first Home Rule Bill of 1886 the exploitation by party leaders of religious prejudices caused a more definitive hardening of religious differences 'especially where there existed, as in Belfast, a substratum of economic competition'. See Mansergh, *The Irish question, 1840–1921* (Toronto; 3rd edn, 1975), 209.

[10] 'The earliest and most active Irish opponents of home rule were members of the old protestant landed ascendancy in the north and south. They were landlords who for years had occupied a dominant, and they thought, responsible role in Irish society': Patrick Buckland (ed.), *Irish unionism, 1885–1923* (Belfast, 1973), 23.

[11] T.C. Curtis and R.B. McDowell (eds), *Irish historical documents, 1172–1922* (London, 1943; 2nd edn, 1977), 289.

[12] Alvin Jackson, *Home Rule: an Irish history, 1800–2000* (London, 2003), 57–8.

[13] Curtis and McDowell, *Irish historical documents*, 290–91. See also Mansergh, *The Irish question*, 214–15.

[14] Nicholas Mansergh, *The unresolved question: the Anglo-Irish Settlement and its undoing, 1912–1972* (New Haven and London, 1991), 50 (citing the Asquith papers in the Bodleian Library in Oxford). Ronan Fanning in *Fatal path: British government and Irish revolution, 1910–1922* (London, 2013), 64–5, quoting from the biography of Asquith by Roy Jenkins, cites the following from Asquith's report to the king: 'if in the light of such evidence or indication of public opinion, it becomes clear as the Bill proceeds that some special treatment must be provided for the Ulster counties, the Government will be ready to recognise the necessity either by amendment of the Bill, or by not pressing it on under the provisions of the Parliament Act'.

[15] 'At heart, mainstream British unionism was convinced that no government could legitimately end (or seriously dilute) unionist Ulster's citizenship within the United Kingdom.' (Among the legal figures who took this view were MacNaghten, a lord of appeal from Northern Ireland, and the great English jurist A.V. Dicey.) Paul Bew,

Ideology and the Irish question: Ulster unionism and Irish nationalism, 1912–1916 (Oxford, 1994), 51–3.

[16] Bew, *Ideology and the Irish question*, 21, citing A.T.Q. Stewart, *Sir Edward Carson* (Dublin, 1981), 73.

[17] Curtis and McDowell, *Irish historical documents*, 304, say 471,000. Paul Bew in *Ireland: the politics of enmity, 1789–2006* (Oxford, 2007), 368, says 'a quarter of a million'; Foster, *Modern Ireland*, 'nearly 250,000', 466.

[18] Founded in 1904–5. See Buckland, *Irish unionism*, 201–2.

[19] Buckland, *Irish unionism*, 207.

[20] Buckland, *Irish unionism*, 225–6.

[21] Foster, *Modern Ireland*, 470.

[22] 'Asquith and the Liberal government were publicly and irrevocably committed to partition once Asquith offered the exclusion of the six north-eastern counties of Ulster in the House of Commons on 9 March 1914'—Ronan Fanning, *Fatal path*, 135.

[23] Jackson, *Home Rule*, 177–85. Nicholas Mansergh, *The Irish Question*, 238.

[24] Curtis and McDowell, *Irish historical documents*, 318–19.

[25] *Documents on Irish foreign policy*, volume I, *1919–1922* (Dublin, 1998), 1; Curtis and McDowell, *Irish historical documents*, 322–6.

[26] Keith Middlemas (ed.), *Thomas Jones: Whitehall diary*, volume III (London, 1971), 129–30.

[27] Stewart's term—see above.

CHAPTER 2

An 'internal situation'

It is not easy to pinpoint the exact starting date of 'the Troubles' in Northern Ireland—to use a euphemism for the conflict borrowed from an earlier era in Irish history. The events of the 1960s that I described at the end of the previous chapter were, as we can now see, ominous signs of a gathering storm. The storm finally began to break with the repressive police reaction to a civil rights march in Derry in October 1968 and the police mishandling of an ambush attack by loyalists on a People's Democracy civil rights march at Burntollet in January 1969.

Following these events, the 'marching season' later in 1969 promised to be difficult and dangerous. The Irish minister for external affairs, Frank Aiken, went to New York in late April to brief the UN secretary general. In a press conference afterwards he spoke of his hope for 'the restoration of Irish unity' by peaceful means but he also made it clear that his focus was not on ending partition but on civil rights in Northern Ireland and the need for reform.

Nationalists were particularly apprehensive about the annual Apprentice Boys march which was to take place in Derry on 12 August. Large numbers from outside were to march and it looked as if up to seventy bands might take part instead of the usual seventeen. The concern of the Irish government about what lay ahead was conveyed strongly to the British government on 1 August when Dr Patrick Hillery, who had replaced Frank Aiken as minister a few months previously, had an unpublicised meeting in London with Michael Stewart, the foreign secretary in the Labour government.[1] The issue of Northern Ireland had been touched on, very briefly, during a short courtesy call that Hillery had made on Stewart in Brussels a week previously but there had been no serious discussion. Now, however, according to the Irish side's note of the meeting, Hillery told Stewart that Derry was a 'powder keg'; he asked that the parade be banned, or at least limited to the normal size and sensitively policed; and he suggested that the British government send observers. Stewart was far from receptive—better, he said, to control the parade rather than ban it; responsibility lay with the Northern Ireland government; and, in any case, 'there is a limit to the extent to which we can discuss with outsiders—even our nearest neighbours—this internal matter.'[2] The British record is less detailed but it does say that Stewart 'reiterated that we regarded the matter as one for our internal jurisdiction'. He also wanted to regard the meeting as 'a normal one between foreign ministers', so the press was to be told that other matters such as Nigeria and European integration were also discussed.

On both these points Stewart was following the advice in a briefing note from his officials:

> Although Dr. Hillery is no doubt genuinely concerned about the situation in Northern Ireland, he probably hopes, as a result of this meeting, to establish that the government of the Irish Republic has a right of consultation in Northern Ireland matters. It is important that he should be left in no doubt that this is not the case.

> It would be helpful, particularly to the Home Office and the Northern Ireland government, to bolster this point by insisting that the meeting is a normal one between Foreign Ministers and that subjects other than Northern Ireland should be discussed even if only briefly.[3]

The apprehension that Hillery had expressed to Stewart proved fully justified in the event. Thousands of loyalists from other parts of Northern Ireland came to swell the numbers in the Apprentice Boys parade in Derry on 12 August. Stone-throwing broke out between nationalist youths and marchers. The police used batons in an effort to force the stone-throwers back to the Bogside area. The rioters threw petrol bombs; the police responded with tear gas. There were demonstrations in sympathy in Belfast on 14 August. Rioting broke out there too and soon took a sectarian character. Shots were fired. The police used armoured cars and fired machine gun bursts. People were driven from their homes and houses were burned. In the face of these events, and accusations about the partisan behaviour of the police, the British government decided to deploy troops, and British army units began to appear on the streets for the first time—in Derry on 14 August and in Belfast a day later. They were welcomed initially by the Catholic minority who felt besieged and had lost all trust in the police. A subsequent judicial enquiry by Mr Justice Scarman showed that 10 people had been shot dead, 154 wounded and 745 injured; 1,800 families were displaced—five-sixths of them Catholic.[4]

In their initial response to these dramatic events, neither the British nor the Irish governments showed much understanding of the deeper realities of Northern Ireland. The Labour government in Britain, and its senior civil servants, had at least had the foresight in 1968/69 to plan quietly for the possibility that they might have to resume active responsibility for Northern Ireland at some point. Ronan Fanning, in a detailed account of the respective reactions of the British and the Irish governments to the events of 1968–69 in Northern Ireland notes that

> Harold Wilson's government had been getting 'early and explicit warnings' of a recrudescence of violence in Northern Ireland since 1965–6...[By February 1969] British ministers had already subjected the crisis to a rigorous analysis, which included the preparation of a draft Bill for the introduction of direct rule in Northern Ireland.[5]

the home secretary advised the prime minister that 'the overall plan for suspending the Northern Ireland Constitution and replacing it by direct rule from London has also now been worked out in detail'; it was his intention 'to have this ready in final shape' before the Northern Ireland election on the 24th.[6]

In phone conversations, and during a meeting in early August, the home secretary, Jim Callaghan, also warned the Northern Ireland prime minister, Chichester-Clark, that

[in] the event of the continuing use of troops Her Majesty's Government would have to assume some sort of control of the circumstances in which the troops were used. This would mean in some senses assuming responsibility for Northern Ireland affairs.[7]

The Irish government, to say the least, was poorly prepared for what was to happen. As we now know, the taoiseach Jack Lynch over several years had the benefit of steadying advice on a personal and private basis from Ken Whitaker, the secretary (general) of the Department of Finance who had been active in arranging the meetings of Lynch himself, and his predecessor Seán Lemass, with the Northern premier, Terence O'Neill, which I mentioned in the previous chapter. This continued even after Whitaker moved from the Department of Finance to become the governor of the Central Bank. Donal Barrington, one of the leading figures in the discussion group Tuairim, in the 1960s, and later a Supreme Court judge, also carried considerable influence with Lynch, then and later.[8] But otherwise Lynch could count on few sources of reliable advice as the situation across the border became more and more alarming. Neither of the two government departments that were later to play an important role, the Department of the Taoiseach or the Department of External Affairs, had a section, or even any individual, assigned specifically to the Northern Ireland issue. Nor had there been much new thinking on the matter for years.

Michael Kennedy in his study of the archives looked at the responses of twenty senior Irish diplomats abroad in September 1969 to a secret request from the secretary of the Department of External Affairs, Hugh McCann, for their personal views as to what policy the government should adopt in relation to Northern Ireland. All 'foresaw eventual Irish unity' and they were 'overwhelmingly in favour of a federal solution to partition.' This, Kennedy notes, 'had been government policy for many years' and it was provided for, indirectly, in Article 15.2 of the 1937 Constitution.[9] But, he concludes, '[i]t was clear as the replies came in to McCann in Iveagh House that most senior External Affairs officials knew little about Northern Ireland or its population, nationalist or unionist.'[10] I should add, however, that McCann himself, who had been secretary of the department for a number of years, was a source of sensible advice, when necessary, to his minister and to the taoiseach: prior to his appointment as secretary he had been ambassador in London and his good working relationship with Sir John Peck, who was appointed British ambassador in Dublin in 1970, was to be helpful at times in sorting out misunderstandings between Dublin and London over this difficult period.

I can confirm from personal experience that Dublin was ill-prepared to respond to the events of August 1969. I was home on leave at the time—on holidays in my mother's house in the west of Ireland—and I was called back to the department in Dublin for a few days. My mother had no phone—in the Ireland of the time most houses did not—and the message was conveyed to me via the gárda barracks by an elderly gárda who knocked on my mother's door. My aunt who lived nearby and saw him standing there was startled—she feared that some close relative had died. His reply was reassuring to her, but for me somewhat deflating: 'Ah no, it's just that the young fella is wanted in the department'. I read now that Ken Whitaker, who was on holidays in Connemara, received a message by a similar channel asking him to contact the taoiseach.[11] But he was a considerable personage—the governor of the Central Bank being consulted personally by the taoiseach on matters of high policy was one matter, whereas I was a relatively low-level first secretary home on leave from the embassy in Washington, called in by my colleagues to Iveagh House merely 'to give them a hand for a few days'.

As I remember it the mood in Dublin at the time was one of high emotion. There was indignation linked with apprehension about the dramatic events in Northern Ireland and a widespread feeling that 'something simply must be done' to protect the minority in Northern Ireland. But there was no great clarity about just what that ought to be. We know now that there were serious differences of view within the Cabinet—this became clear at the time of the Arms Crisis nine months later.[12] At the time, as officials working to put together some kind of sensible response to the requirements of the government, we could hardly have been fully aware of this although I think we did have at least some sense of the excitable atmosphere around the Cabinet table—and not only there. In an interview with Ronan Fanning many years later Hillery described it vividly: '[he] likened one of the subsequent emergency Cabinet meetings to "a ballad session…They were all talking patriotic".'[13]

The government met several times during the week following the march, including Saturday, which was most unusual; and it took a number of decisions—most of them a response to public emotion rather than measures likely to have any real effect. In a television address on 13 August, the day after the events that followed the Apprentice Boys march in Derry, the taoiseach, Jack Lynch, said that it was clear that 'the Irish government can no longer stand by and see innocent people injured and perhaps worse'.[14] He announced that Irish army field hospitals would be sent to the border to treat injured persons who might not wish to go to hospitals in Northern Ireland; and he said that Ireland would apply immediately to the United Nations for the urgent despatch of a peacekeeping force to the six counties of Northern Ireland. In fact the government, through the embassy in London, first asked the British government to seek such a force. The request to do so was refused—the response from the Foreign Office was that events in Northern Ireland were an internal matter and a UN force was not necessary or appropriate.

On 15 August the minister for external affairs, Dr Hillery, went again to London. In the absence on holidays of the foreign secretary, he met two British ministers—Lord Chalfont, a Foreign Office minister, and Lord Stonham of the Home Office. The discussion was blunt enough at times as Hillery recalled his warnings about the parade at his meeting with the foreign secretary on 1 August. In addition to calling for more urgency about reforms he asked now for the disarming of the B Specials.[15] He again asked the British government to seek a UN peacekeeping force or, alternatively to agree to a joint British-Irish peacekeeping force for Northern Ireland, since, he said, '[t]he continued presence of [British] troops could provide extremists from both sides with pretexts for intervention'. The British ministers acknowledged his concern. But they said that the UN had no competence in the matter; and they rejected any suggestions that the government did not have the situation under control or that there had been attacks by the police on the people of Derry. Lord Chalfont in particular was definitive in rejecting any substantive role for the Irish government:

> It is a situation with tragic implications but Northern Ireland is part of the United Kingdom and we are confident that we can deal with the situation. We cannot undertake to consult your Ministers. We will consider as useful normal diplomatic consultations, but we could not undertake to consult the Irish government on how to solve a problem which is essentially a problem of the United Kingdom. But we will take careful note of what you said.

He repeated this position several times:

> It would be entirely improper for me to agree with a representative of a foreign government to take action in our domestic sphere.

And again:

> I cannot undertake on behalf of Her Majesty's government to enter into consultations with you about this problem.

This is not a situation in which the citizens of Ireland are involved.[16]

The British record of the meeting is equally categorical:

> *Lord Chalfont* said that it would be quite wrong for him to agree with the representatives of a foreign government what action Her Majesty's government should take in the domestic sphere.

> *Lord Chalfont* repeated that we could not have consultations with the government of the Republic on the affairs of Northern Ireland.

A telegram that same day from the Foreign Office to the British embassy in Dublin summarising the outcome of the meeting repeats this position:

> Lord Chalfont...emphasised that Northern Ireland was part of the United Kingdom and that he could not engage in ministerial discussions with the Irish Republic about our domestic affairs.[17]

Since the request for a joint British-Irish peacekeeping force had been rejected in London, as they must have known it would be, the government decided to 'take it to the UN'. The Department of External Affairs prepared a memorandum that examined the various ways in which this might be done. I contributed in a very minor way to the discussion among my colleagues who were working on this document. As I recall it my main concern—based on what I knew of the UN where I had attended several General Assembly sessions—was to inject a note of caution about the idea that anything much could be achieved. After presenting various options, the memorandum suggested that an approach to the General Assembly seemed to be 'the most profitable course'. It added that this did 'not exclude...raising with the Security Council the question of a peace-keeping force'. But it recognised that 'such action has practically no prospect of success'; and it concluded:

> The main value of such an approach would be the attempt to ventilate the question in that forum and the attendant publicity.[18]

The government decision was to take the matter to the Security Council and, within hours of the conclusion of the Cabinet meeting that Saturday, Dr Hillery was on his way to New York to ask the Council to send a peacekeeping force to Northern Ireland.

It was evident that his task was going to be very difficult. UN peacekeeping was still evolving at the time but it was an established principle that a peacekeeping force could not be sent to a territory without the consent of the government concerned;[19] and it had already been made clear to Hillery in London that the British government would not agree to accept a UN peacekeeping force in Northern Ireland. Furthermore, the UK was a permanent member of the Security Council with great influence and a right of veto—though that might not apply if Ireland made its request for a UN force under the part of the charter that deals with the 'Peaceful Settlement of Disputes'. In retrospect it is surprising that the department allowed its new minister to travel to New York to handle such a difficult issue with no officials from Dublin to help him en route—a further indication, perhaps, that it was not well organised at the time to deal with the new demands the Northern Ireland issue was to make, demands that were to increase greatly over the decades that followed.

In the event, Dr Hillery did not succeed in his overt mission. Not only did he not get the peacekeeping force he had been sent to seek—he was not able even to get Ireland's request placed on the agenda of the Council for discussion. But, with the tacit acquiescence of the UK representative, Lord Caradon, he was given a full opportunity to state his case in a lengthy speech to the Council during a procedural debate on whether or not the matter should go on the agenda. A month later, when the annual session of the General Assembly opened, Ireland asked initially to have the question listed for debate but, in the event, it did not press the matter. In a preliminary discussion in the committee which was to decide the agenda, Dr Hillery agreed to 'reflect on' an assurance given by the UK representative Lord Caradon that there would be urgent reform in Northern Ireland. And there the matter was allowed to rest.

By then, after my two or three days of 'helping out' in Iveagh House, I had returned to my post in the embassy in Washington and had been again assigned from there to New York for three months as a member of the delegation to the General Assembly. After the drama of his Security Council appearance a month before, my colleagues and I who were in the room at the UN at the time were a bit surprised that Dr Hillery did not press more strongly to have the issue listed for discussion in the General Assembly. It became clear that the government had decided to let the matter go at that stage. It was wise to do so. The initial resort to the Security Council in August had helped to an extent to channel public emotion and defuse tension at home. A prolonged debate in the General Assembly a month later would have generated considerable noise, as some member states would have been glad of the opportunity to attack the UK. But it would have done nothing to reduce—and might well have increased—the tension in Northern Ireland, which had already begun to diminish somewhat since the high drama of August; and it was most unlikely to have resulted in the establishment of a UN peacekeeping force. However, Dr Hillery's representations to British ministers at his meetings in London in August, which seemed to have been fruitless at the time, could perhaps be said to have produced one result: as a follow-up to the Hunt Report of October 1969 the B Special force was disbanded in May 1970.[20]

The refusal to enter into consultations with the Irish government about what they saw as an internal problem of the UK, conveyed to Hillery at his meeting with Stewart, the foreign secretary, on 1 August and repeated by Chalfont on 15 August, remained the official British position for several years. It was a formula, a position of principle of the British government, to be publicly reiterated on occasions when tensions with Dublin were high or when the Irish government sought actively to assert a role. Stating it publicly at such times could help to reassure unionists, as could the standard assertion that 'the border is not an issue'. The underlying implication was that 'the Irish Question' had essentially been settled in 1920–21; reform within Northern Ireland would be sufficient to restore stability; and the republic, an independent country though a close neighbour, had no role to play. That said, it was a principle that was not—indeed could not—be sustained in practice, given the historic background, the realities of Northern Ireland and the evident need for security cooperation across a 250-mile porous border.

However, the 'hands-off' reaction of the Foreign Office ministers to the Irish government's concern about events in Northern Ireland was not universal in the British governmental system even in the weeks after the rebuff to Hillery. At official level, there were some in the Foreign Office, such as Oliver Wright (who had been appointed UK representative in Northern Ireland), who saw it as essential to open up the lines of communication between Westminster and Dublin and Westminster and Belfast and keep them open.[21] Another was Kelvin White of the Western European Department who, following a committee discussion, prepared a draft paper in September on 'Our Relations with the Irish Republic'. The paper outlined various ideas. One which 'after some thought' he decided not to include was a paragraph on a Council of Ireland. Others, which 'would (if pursued)…need very careful presentation both privately to governments and publicly to the press and other media', included, surprisingly enough, 'a federal solution', with 'Stormont surviving much as it is now but with Westminster's powers transferred to Dublin.'[22] By 15 December 1969, a version of the paper, approved 'in general outline at departmental level' in the Foreign and Home Offices and described 'partly as contingency planning and partly as a method of clearing our own minds', was circulated to the British ambassador in Dublin and to Oliver Wright. White was not a particularly senior figure and it would be going too far to think of it as anything like a set of serious policy proposals but it is interesting that some of the ideas mentioned were even being talked about at all at this early period.

At ministerial level, the home secretary, Jim Callaghan, who had responsibility for Northern Ireland at the time, was concerned to maintain contact with Dublin, though very cautious about being seen publicly to do so. This is clear from a series of exchanges with the Foreign Office and the prime minister which he initiated in the Autumn of 1969.

Following a visit to Northern Ireland on 27 August, during which he pressed the Stormont government to commit itself to further reform and to set up the Scarman tribunal (see above), Callaghan began to discuss with his officials how it might be possible, over time, to find ways to involve the Irish government. The deputy under-secretary in his department, Waddell, informed his opposite number in the Foreign Office, Sir Edward Peck, in a letter on 5 September that

> the Home Secretary has spoken of the need to develop long-term policies involving the Republic as well as Northern Ireland, and I think we might profitably exchange views about this. We have also been asked to consider a specific suggestion that a non-political conference might be arranged between North and South in an attempt to build up better relations through discussion not of common problems but of each other's problems.[23]

Nothing came of the latter suggestion. However, Callaghan, who had known Jack Lynch when they were fellow finance ministers, took a very positive view of Lynch's Tralee speech of 20 September (to which I will refer further in Chapter 4). On 23 September he sent a note to the prime minister, Harold Wilson. In it he said that he had reproved the Northern Ireland prime minister, Chichester-Clarke, for his negative public response to the speech and had made it clear to him that 'foreign relations were the responsibility of the United Kingdom Government'. He also told Wilson that he had seen the British ambassador in Dublin, Sir Andrew Gilchrist, that afternoon

> and explained that we were aiming to have all the legitimate civil rights grievances met by the end of the year and then to try to lift on to a different plane the whole

complex of relations between North and South and between the South and the United Kingdom.

On 29 September Wilson's private office replied to the Home Office that the prime minister had seen the minute and agreed with the line Callaghan had taken with Chichester-Clarke. There was no comment on Callaghan's reference to lifting relations 'on to a different plane'.[24]

The Foreign Office duly followed up on Callaghan's discussion with the ambassador: in a telegram of 25 September, it sent him some points from the record of his discussion with the home secretary to use in meeting Lynch. The telegram said that

> [t]he Home Secretary was most impressed by Mr. Lynch's statesmanlike speech over the weekend. He considered that his speech showed a complete strategic understanding of the necessities of the situation.

However, the telegram went on, the first step was the reform programme in Northern Ireland and Callaghan was concerned that 'the prospects of success would be greatly prejudiced if the reform programme was seen to be linked with a greater role for the government of the Republic'. So Lynch 'should feel free to make full use of the diplomatic channel to communicate with United Kingdom Ministers'. He could be assured, however, that the UK government's active interest in Northern Ireland affairs was not a temporary one

> and when the reform programme had been set firmly under way, say by Christmas, it would be possible to consider leading the Government of Northern Ireland down the next path. The Home Secretary said he saw some value in a semi-judicial three-way guarantee of human rights but recognised that this was an idea that needed a great deal more thought.

Callaghan also hoped that when the reform programme was under way Lynch would be prepared to cultivate relations with Chichester-Clark.[25]

These exchanges suggest that while the home secretary's immediate focus was, understandably, on reform in Northern Ireland, he accepted that a time would come when the Irish government should have some role. But he also believed that any public acknowledgement of this before then could lead to an outcry from unionists, further destabilise Northern Ireland and make implementation of his reform programme more difficult.

Ambassador Gilchrist was unable to pass on the message to Lynch at that point, but the idea behind it was still of interest in London. This interest now extended to senior levels in the Foreign Office and even to the foreign secretary, Michael Stewart, notwithstanding his formulaic rejection of Hillery's representations at the beginning of August. In a letter of 20 October, Sir Denis Greenhill, Permanent Under Secretary at the Foreign Office, explained to his opposite number at the Home Office, Sir Philip Allen, that the message containing Callaghan's reflections had not been delivered.

> In the event Mr. Lynch stayed away from Dublin and that particular message could not be passed. But he knew the message existed, and there are indications that the Irish are still looking for links with us.

Greenhill said that the Foreign Office saw 'considerable advantage in resurrecting the original message'. The foreign secretary 'would like to be associated with the message'; and he thought also 'that No. 10 should be informed'.[26]

At this point Ambassador Gilchrist in Dublin suggested that, instead of a message to Lynch, there should be an 'inspired' parliamentary question. The Foreign Office, however, in agreement with the Home Office, did not like the idea of any kind of public statement.

> It would make public a link between Westminster and Dublin. Hitherto our essential aim has been to keep Dublin relaxed while not exciting Protestant extremists in Ulster by being seen to be talking to Dublin. The time for a more open policy of links with Dublin must surely come, but the timing will be largely governed by events in Northern Ireland, and that time has yet to come.[27]

On 5 November Callaghan resumed his initiative and addressed another minute to the prime minister. In it he said that Lynch had 'taken a very statesmanlike position over Northern Ireland in recent weeks'; and the foreign secretary and he both judged that 'it would be useful to go to particular pains' to let Lynch know that 'we greatly appreciate the way in which he is now approaching the situation'. Enclosed with Callaghan's minute was a message which, if the prime minister agreed, he would, 'in association with the Foreign Secretary', pass on to the taoiseach, through the ambassador in Dublin. The prime minister's response, conveyed through his private secretary the next day, took a more cautious approach. He agreed that such an initiative was desirable but he wanted its form to be reconsidered.

> For our Ambassador to hand over a message from the Home Secretary would not be in accordance with precedent and would carry the risk that Mr. Lynch would feel that he now had direct access to the Home Secretary on Northern Ireland matters. This could cause difficulties in the future.

One alternative would be to treat it as a message from the government, 'conveyed by the Ambassador on the basis of a normal instruction from the Foreign and Commonwealth Secretary'. Alternatively, 'if it were thought that there would be advantage in making it a personal message to Mr. Lynch, the prime minister would feel that he should send it himself.'[28]

However, the home secretary and the Foreign Office felt it better to keep the long-delayed message informal, as originally intended. So the ambassador was instructed to convey the main points informally to Lynch as though they were views expressed to him, the ambassador, by the home secretary: he was 'to avoid giving what you say the dignity of a Government to Government message'. The points, to be conveyed, were, for the most part, those in the earlier version of 25 September but there was now no mention of Callaghan's thoughts about 'leading the Government of Northern Ireland down the next path' when the reform programme was under way.

On 19 November Gilchrist reported to the Foreign Office that he had spoken, as instructed, to Lynch that day. In doing so he had 'amplified a point' in his instructions

> by saying that our current programme of reforms in the North was founded on quite other motives than a desire to bring about a united Ireland: but that neither was it designed to impede or prejudice any legitimate movement of opinion which might develop towards that end.

The taoiseach, the ambassador said, accepted this. Otherwise he made 'little direct comment', though he agreed generally about the need for caution in public statements. However, he expressed considerable concern to Gilchrist about the reform programme in the north, where, he said, 'the Stormont men were letting Callaghan down and badly.'[29]

So this, at last, was the outcome of Callaghan's initiative of more than two months earlier. It was, to say the least, something of an anti-climax. No doubt the taoiseach appreciated hearing that Callaghan took a positive view of his recent speeches. For the rest, he had been told that the reform programme in the north might be jeopardised if it appeared to be linked with a role for the republic; and that he should use 'the diplomatic channel to keep in touch.' He can hardly have attached any great importance to hearing points of this kind from the ambassador on this particular occasion. He would certainly have had no idea that he had been given a message that was the culmination of two and a half months of exchanges within the British government involving the home secretary, the foreign secretary, the prime minister and their senior officials.

Callaghan, to be fair, was well-intentioned; and he seems in his thinking to have been ahead of his colleagues in that Labour government in recognising, at least in internal discussion, that there would be a 'need to develop long-term policies involving the Republic as well as Northern Ireland.' But not just yet. He may have reproved Chichester-Clarke but he still depended on him to get the reform programme through and he could not afford to be seen publicly to develop links with the republic until it was well under way. Notwithstanding Wilson's concern not to allow the taoiseach to 'feel that he now had direct access to the Home Secretary on Northern Ireland matters', Callaghan might in time, given the opportunity, have brought his colleagues in government along with his aim of lifting 'on to a different plane the whole complex of relations between North and South and between the South and the United Kingdom.' However, it was not to be. Callaghan— and Labour—lost office in June 1970 and were replaced by a Conservative government with Ted Heath as prime minister. Reginald Maudling, a rather less understanding politician, took Callaghan's place as home secretary with responsibility, among other things, for Northern Ireland.

The formal refusal of a role to the Irish government in regard to the affairs of Northern Ireland had not changed, notwithstanding Callaghan's more open position in internal exchanges; and there did not seem to be much prospect that it would be changed by the new Conservative government. On the contrary, it was asserted very strongly by Prime Minister Heath in an angry public statement in August 1971, as I will recount in Chapter 5. But Heath, too, came to a deeper understanding of the Northern Ireland problem and this led him to take a very different approach in preparing for, and during, the Sunningdale conference of December 1973. How and why that happened is one of my main themes in this book.

NOTES

[1] I have written about these events in greater detail elsewhere. See my chapter in Michael Kennedy and Deirdre McMahon (eds), *Obligations and responsibilities: Ireland and the United Nations, 1955–2005* (Dublin, 2005), 253–80 and Noel Dorr, *Ireland at the United Nations: memories of the early years* (Dublin, 2010), chapters 10 and 11.

[2] The National Archives of Ireland (hereafter cited as NAI), TSCH 2000/6/657 and DFA 2000/5/38. The Irish side's note of the meeting. [In this book documents archived from the Department of the Taoiseach have the prefix TSCH and documents from the Department of Foreign Affairs the prefix DFA.]

[3] The National Archives (Kew, London) (hereafter cited as TNA), FCO 33/757 (FCO is an abbreviation for Foreign and Commonwealth Office.) The British record is a typed

draft with various manuscript amendments. There does not appear to be any cleanly typed text on this or other related files.

[4] *Violence and civil disturbances in Northern Ireland in 1969: report of tribunal of inquiry* (Belfast, HMSO, April 1972, Cmd. 566). See also Brian Feeney, *A short history of the Troubles* (Dublin, 2010), 27.

[5] Ronan Fanning, 'Playing it cool: the response of the British and Irish governments to the crisis in Northern Ireland, 1968–69', *Irish Studies in International Affairs* 12 (2001), 57–85: 58.

[6] Fanning, 'Playing it cool', 64, citing from the archives of the Public Record Office, PRO PREM 13/2842/1-3, Callaghan to Wilson, 17 February 1969.

[7] Fanning, 'Playing it cool', 72.

[8] Tuairim (the Irish word for 'opinion'), founded in 1954, was an intellectual movement of importance in Ireland in the 1950s and 1960s, which provided a forum for the discussion of ideas and policies. Donal Barrington was a founding member, as was Garret FitzGerald, who was subsequently minister for foreign affairs and, later, taoiseach. See Tomas Finn, *Tuairim, intellectual debate and policy formation: re-thinking Ireland, 1954–75* (Manchester, 2012). Donal Barrington was later a member of a 'think tank' that Lynch, who was then in opposition, established in the mid-1970s: Dermot Keogh, *Jack Lynch: a biography* (Dublin, 2008), 403.

[9] Article 15.2 of the 1937 Constitution allows provision to be made by law for 'subordinate legislatures'.

[10] Michael Kennedy, '"This tragic and most intractable problem": the reaction of the Department of External Affairs to the outbreak of the Troubles in Northern Ireland', *Irish Studies in International Affairs* 12 (2001), 87–95.

[11] Keogh, *Jack Lynch*, 176; Anne Chambers, *T.K. Whitaker: portrait of a patriot* (London, 2014), 279.

[12] See Introduction, n.1.

[13] Fanning, 'Playing it cool', 73. In similar vein, John Walsh in *Patrick Hillery: the official biography* (Dublin, 2008), 210, quotes from a private note composed by Hillery after a government meeting in the Autumn of 1969 which is now in the UCD archives: 'A government meeting is not a ballad singing session'.

[14] John Lynch TD., *Speeches and statements on Irish unity and Anglo-Irish relations, August 1969–October 1971* (Dublin, 1971), 2. Popular memory has it that Lynch said that the Irish government could no longer stand *idly* by (emphasis added) but it is clear from television footage of the time, and other sources, that he did not use the word 'idly', although this word had indeed appeared in a draft prepared for him by the Department of External Affairs. (See Fanning, 'Playing it cool'.)

[15] The B Specials were an almost entirely Protestant auxiliary armed local police force which was greatly disliked by the nationalist minority who saw it as partisan and provocative.

[16] NAI TSCH 2000/6/658. Copy also in possession of author.

[17] The British record and telegram no. 92 of 15 August 1969 are on TNA file FCO 33/757.

[18] NAI TSCH 2000/6/657.

[19] The United Nations secretary general, U Thant, withdrew the United Nations emergency force from the Sinai in 1967 when the government of Egypt withdrew its consent.

[20] *Report of the Advisory Committee on Police in Northern Ireland, October 1969* (Belfast, HMSO, Cmd. 535).

[21] TNA FCO 33/758. Wright letter to Waddell of Home Office, 23 September 1969.

[22] First draft is on TNA FCO 33/758; final version on TNA FCO 33/760.

[23] TNA FCO 33/758.

[24] TNA FCO 33/759.

[25] Telegram no. 121 on TNA FCO 33/758. The speech was Lynch's Tralee speech of 20 September 1969 (see Chapter 4).

[26] TNA FCO 33/759. Greenhill to Allen, 20 October 1969.

[27] TNA FCO 33/759. Submission by Kelvin White, through Morgan, to Sir Edward Peck, Deputy Under-Secretary FCO (cleared by White with Langdon of the Home Office), 24 October 1969.

[28] TNA FCO 33/759. Callaghan minute of 5 November and response of 6 November 1969 from Gregson, the prime minister's private secretary, circulated in FCO and to Home Office.

[29] TNA FCO 33/760. Telegram from Gilchrist, 19 November 1969.

CHAPTER 3

Briefing the media

In July 1970 I was transferred back to Dublin from the embassy in Washington and assigned to the Press and Information section in Iveagh House. As I explained in the Introduction, part of my job there was to help and brief visiting journalists. By then Northern Ireland had become a story of considerable international interest to news editors in the UK, in Europe and in North America. Some of the journalists I dealt with were from the UK; others from Europe or the US. Quite a number were the resident London correspondents for various news media around the world. From London they usually covered British affairs and they also had ready access to a UK government view of what was happening in Northern Ireland. But as the conflict there intensified they were encouraged by their news editors to get over to Belfast and Derry from time to time to see for themselves. The 'view from Dublin', too, now became part of the story so we had a steady stream of visiting journalists for whom meetings and facilities had to be arranged. Con Howard, our active—and unconventional—press attaché in the embassy in London, did much, during extended lunches and otherwise, to encourage their interest.

When the Troubles began there were no full-time British correspondents based in Dublin but shortly after I took up my new assignment the BBC, *The Times* and the *Financial Times* all appointed resident Irish correspondents.[1] All three were serious and responsible journalists—which is not to say that their coverage of Irish affairs and Irish government policy was always favourable. But over time their reporting did help to improve understanding of our position in Britain. The Soviet news agency, Tass, too, appointed a resident correspondent in Dublin for the first time.[2] He was pleasant and affable. I cannot vouch for how he covered Ireland for the Soviet news media—we did not have an embassy in Moscow at the time—but I would guess that much of what he reported back on Irish affairs was destined for readers in Moscow closer to the Kremlin than to the Russian public.

My return to Dublin came a short time after the Arms Crisis of May 1970 which I touched on in the Introduction. The taoiseach, Jack Lynch, had sacked two of his ministers, Charles Haughey and Neil Blaney. They subsequently faced charges of seeking illegally to import arms—'for the defence of the minority in Northern Ireland'—though ultimately neither was found guilty. Two other ministers resigned—one at Lynch's request. The shock waves of all this were still reverberating through the political system. However, our minister, Dr Hillery, had remained loyal to Lynch during the crisis so the shock of what had been one of the most severe crises in government since the foundation of the state was not felt so directly by us in the Department of External Affairs.

As a first secretary in the department I was not particularly senior at the time but because so much of our work with news media at home and abroad related to the problem of Northern Ireland I was drawn increasingly over the next few years into policy issues and speech-writing from time to time for the minister and the taoiseach. On occasion, as part of our press work, we brought small groups of journalists over from London for a few days and arranged for them to meet a range of persons prominent in public life—ministers, journalists, economists and others, including, quite often, spokespersons for the main opposition parties. The programme in such cases usually included a lunch hosted by the taoiseach at which he would speak frankly and informally and answer questions. His apparent affability and ease with people usually came across quite well to the visitors on such occasions.

In that early phase of the Troubles, policy on Northern Ireland was not always very clear or coherent. The Irish government, to an even greater extent than the British government, had been taken aback by the outbreak of serious conflict in Northern Ireland in 1969/70 and it was not well prepared to respond to what was happening. In the mid-1960s there had been relatively cordial reciprocal visits and talk of greater cooperation between two successive taoisigh—Lemass and Lynch—and the Northern Ireland prime minister Terence O'Neill. But now Northern Ireland seemed to be coming apart along the old fault-line. While pressing the Irish government for greater cross-border cooperation on security and extradition, the British government still regarded it as not entitled to have any political role in relation to the north.

In the south—I use the term for convenience only—the reactions to the developing conflict in Northern Ireland were complex and they ranged across a wide spectrum. The old argument that partition had been wrong and unjust from the start and that Ireland should be united, still carried weight; and the plight of the minority as a community under attack aroused strong public emotions, which were reflected at political level in the rash actions of several ministers during the Arms Crisis. There was no substantial public support for the IRA campaign of violence: and some of its more sectarian aspects in particular came to be widely deplored and condemned. But underlying this was an ambivalence about their declared aim of seeking to bring about Irish unity, their claim to be inheritors of the older Republican tradition of 1916 and even 1798, and the role they had begun to assume for themselves as defenders of minority areas under attack. Many people resolved this ambivalence for themselves by saying that they supported the aims of the IRA but not its methods. The initial response of the Northern Ireland authorities to the civil rights movement was seen as repressive; and Orange marches were seen as provocative and triumphalist. But here too there was an underlying tension between the professed aim of Irish nationalism of persuading unionists that they were 'fellow Irishmen and women' who might eventually accept Irish unity, and the immediate welling-up of sympathy and fellow-feeling for Northern Catholics forced to endure such provocations under unionist majority rule. Even the terminology was a problem—should it be Protestant/Catholic? unionist/nationalist? majority/minority?—and vaguer terms like 'identity', 'aspiration', 'community' came into common use in speeches and statements. Public anger flared up at particular actions of the security forces; and, as I will recount later, there was universal outrage at occasional harsher actions of the British army such as those in Derry on Bloody Sunday in 1972. There was deep resentment, too, at the portrayal of the Irish government in sections of the British press as 'soft on terrorism' and the taoiseach Jack Lynch as weak and ineffectual. Cross-border security cooperation was accepted in principle but it was sometimes very patchy in practice; and it did not extend to extradition for actions claimed to be 'political offences'. The argument of successive Irish governments—a tenuous one at best—was that that would have run counter to Article 29.3 of the Constitution, which states that 'Ireland accepts the generally recognised principles of international law as its rule of conduct in relations with other states'.[3]

All in all, a complex situation, to say the least—and not a very clear message to communicate. So far as we were concerned, two things were very much needed in those early years of the Troubles—greater clarity about government policy; and an improved capacity on our part to communicate that response and make it more widely understood. It took some time before either could be achieved. In the chapters that follow I will look at how the Irish government gradually developed a more coherent policy approach to the Northern Ireland problem. In the present chapter my concern is with our dealings with the press.

It was clear that as the crisis in Northern Ireland deepened it was important to make every effort to ensure that the policies and position of the Irish government were fully understood and not misrepresented; and it is true that there was much to criticise in the policies of the Northern Ireland and British governments at the time. The Irish government in speeches and statements wanted to direct attention forcefully to what was wrong in the north; and it was pressing the British government strongly for reform. But the government also had to make it clear at all times that it was strongly opposed to the campaign of violence; and that it would not make common cause with the IRA. On the contrary, it was prepared to act against it with determination in its own jurisdiction. This, as I said earlier, was a complex message to communicate to foreign news media who sometimes saw what was happening in Northern Ireland as a 'freedom struggle', and indeed even to news media in Britain who sometimes saw the Irish government as tolerant of, if not secretly complicit with, the IRA. An over-simplistic and polemic approach in press releases and publicity material that did not take this fully into account would give a skewed impression of government policy and would be counter-productive.

I recall two temporary expedients in the matter of press and publicity to which the government resorted in the early days. I suppose I am a bit defensive, perhaps even biased, since I was working in that area in Foreign Affairs for part of that time. But I still think neither was well-advised. Both probably originated with suggestions from 'other voices' to the taoiseach that the official government structures in this area—what was then the Government Information Bureau, and the diplomatic and consular missions of the Department of Foreign Affairs—were weak and ineffective in their press and information work. They were indeed. But the answer was to strengthen them and make them work properly—not to set up new structures with a looser mandate which would make them much less amenable to policy direction by the government. The phrase 'loose cannon' comes to mind.

One of the two temporary measures to which I refer occurred while I was still based in the embassy in Washington and on temporary assignment to the UN delegation in New York. It probably originated with George Colley who was minister for industry and commerce at the time. Public relations officers were borrowed by the government from up to about a dozen semi-state bodies and sent at short notice as temporary press attachés to various Irish embassies and consulates abroad. No doubt they were well-intentioned and I know they did their best. I doubt, however, if they were briefed adequately and regularly on the complexities of Irish government policy at the time; and the arrangement was brought to an end after a few months. The historian Dermot Keogh described it rather tartly in his biography of Lynch as 'yet another example of rushing into making decision(s) that proved counter-productive.'[4]

I was involved to an extent myself in the second of the two expedients I mentioned. This was the appointment of an agency called Markpress to undertake information and publicity work on behalf of the Irish government in 1971/72. Markpress was in fact largely a one-man operation that was based in Geneva and run by an American called H. William Bernhardt. He had done a great deal, through the distribution of harrowing pictures and otherwise, to gain world attention for the widespread suffering caused to the population in Biafra by the war that followed its attempt to secede from Nigeria in 1967; and there were some who caught the ear of Jack Lynch with a proposal that his agency could do something similar to highlight what was wrong in Northern Ireland. The minister for foreign affairs, Dr Hillery, was emphatically not one of them.

Markpress was retained by the government at a very substantial fee; and a 'steering committee' that reported back to the Taoiseach's Department was set up.[5] It comprised some people from outside the public service; one or two others from semi-state bodies; Eoin Neeson, the director of the Government Information Bureau; and myself. Before I went to the first meeting of the steering committee, Dr Hillery, who had a strong sense of the need for a coherent government policy on the north and disapproved of the taoiseach's decision to employ Markpress, gave me a very clear instruction—'your job is to see to it that they do no harm'. Since he was a medical doctor I assume he had in mind the Hippocratic injunction to doctors *primum ne nocere*, which loosely translates as 'first of all, don't do any harm to the patient'. I felt that I could not admit to the other members that I had been given this instruction by my minister. So I had a somewhat uncomfortable year or two on the committee. Some of its members proposed that Markpress should be free to make its own decisions on what to publicise without implicating the taoiseach in any way; and some suggested, for example, that Markpress should 'plant stories' to embarrass the British government' in continental countries by highlighting its past attitudes to torture by French forces in Algeria or to concentration camps in wartime Germany.[6] I don't know how well I carried out my instructions but I don't recall that either of these ideas—or some others which were equally exhilarating perhaps, but also quite alarming—were ever carried through.

To be fair to Markpress I don't think they had any role in a public relations debacle for the Irish side which occurred in September 1972 when Jack Lynch met the British prime minister Ted Heath during the Olympic Games in Munich. It appears that the meeting itself was reasonably positive—notwithstanding some of the strains in Anglo-Irish relations at the time. Drawing on the Lynch papers, Dermot Keogh in his biography gives a detailed account of the meeting.[7] Heath did press for greater security cooperation but, according to Keogh's account, he also said 'he was keen on talks with Lynch "and those who were critical of such talks in Northern Ireland would have to lump it"'. But, as I remember it, in briefing the press afterwards Heath's press secretary, Sir Donald Maitland—who served in later years with distinction as a British diplomat—depicted the meeting as one where Lynch had been more or less 'beaten roundly about the ears' by Heath for what he called the failure of the Irish government to cooperate whole-heartedly on security issues. Lynch, it seems, had no press 'minder' to brief the news media on his behalf—or if he had, it seemed that it was not done effectively. So the image that took hold in the media was that of a schoolboy taoiseach who had been sharply reproved by the British prime minister. It was an image that lingered a long time in the memory of Irish ministers and officials; and it became vivid for them again in planning for the press arrangements whenever a new Summit meeting was under consideration.

Over the course of 1972 and early 1973 enthusiasm for Markpress gradually waned and the contract with the agency was finally ter-minated when a new government took office in 1973. During that same period, Dr Hillery, who had always been opposed to the idea of a semi-detached agency like Markpress having a role bearing in any way on policy formation, asked me to draft proposals for a properly organised Press and Information function in the Department of Foreign Affairs. He told me that in doing so I should have a relatively free hand and said that the agreement of the Department of Finance would not be a problem. I did what he asked and, within a short time, the Press and Information section of the department where I worked and the press work of the embassy in London were strengthened and press attaché posts were created in our missions in Washington, New York, Paris and elsewhere.

I said earlier that our press attaché at the embassy in London, Con Howard, was unconventional. That was something of an understatement. He was an 'ideas man', given to inventive, creative proposals that included among many other things, the establishment of the annual Merriman Summer School in County Clare—which Séan MacRéamoinn memorably termed 'a lark in the Clare air'. But, after the initial idea was launched, Con's detailed 'follow-through' was sometimes a little uncertain. Perhaps I might conclude this account of the Press and Information section at Iveagh House with an account of an event in which Con and I were involved. It had all the aspects of a disaster at the time but in retrospect it has taken on something of a softer, mellower, glow.

In mid-1971, at Con's suggestion, we arranged to bring a group of the lobby correspondents from Westminster to Dublin for briefing on the viewpoint of the Irish government. The 'Westminster lobby' at the time was a closed and very select group of journalists from various British news media who covered the British parliament.[8] They enjoyed the privilege of 'unattributable briefings' from the prime minister's press secretary, which often resulted in news stories about what 'sources at Westminster' were saying or thinking. Our section in Iveagh House had been provided with funds to cover the costs of such visits as part of our 'information campaign' so I made the necessary arrangements and the group duly came over to Dublin in early September. After some days of official commitments in Dublin, which included a briefing over lunch by the taoiseach, meetings with other ministers and opposition leaders, we took them out of Dublin for a short tour in the west and south in the hope of winning them over further. After a tour of the Burren and an overnight stay in Lahinch, we ended up on a Saturday night in a hotel in Killarney.

By this time the initially reserved lobby group had relaxed somewhat. They were due to return to their sheltered lives in Westminster on Monday. Over a convivial dinner in Killarney Con had one of his bright ideas—we would take them on Sunday, their final day in Ireland, to see Skellig Michael. Not only that—he proposed that we hire a helicopter for the purpose. I felt that my job was to bring Con's good ideas down to earth, or close to earth, without stifling his undoubted creativity. And in those days hiring—or even finding—a helicopter in Killarney on a Saturday night was stretching things a bit too far. We did manage to arrange for a bus and so the next morning, we and the visiting group set off together for Portmagee where we arranged with a local boatman to take us out to the Skellig.

I blame myself in part for what happened next. I had never been in that part of Kerry before and did not know much about the Skelligs: I had a vague idea that those high, craggy islands where the beehive cells of early Irish monks cling to the rock, were at most perhaps half a mile out from shore. The boat was small, with room for about fifteen people. It had, not a cabin, but a kind of half shelter or housing around the wheel at the front and otherwise was open to the elements. As we chugged down the long channel from Portmagee to the sea I began to have serious misgivings. My concern grew greater as we reached the open waters of the Atlantic. It had been fine when we left but now the wind had begun to rise; the water became increasingly choppy; and the spray came over the side of the boat. Our guests, the lobby correspondents from London, grown very silent, sheltered as best they could in the small area in front beside the wheel. Somewhat quixotically I left the space to them and, in my light summer clothing, crouched in the stern where the spray over the side was strongest. Things were not going well.

And there was a further problem. Before we left Killarney, one of the visiting journalists—the lobby correspondent for the *Yorkshire Post*—said he had a difficulty that meant he would have to stay behind. He had done a story for his paper about the briefing the taoiseach had given the group over lunch in Dublin and he had to phone it in to his paper that Sunday afternoon for the following day's paper. The call would have to be made some time between 2 p.m. when the 'copy-taker' at the *Post* would come on duty and 7 p.m., which was the deadline for copy for the next day's paper. Con reassured him: he could make the call from the phone in the lighthouse on the Skellig. Cheered by this, the journalist decided to join us on the trip.

When I think about it now I am still amazed at Con's powers of persuasion. Anyone old enough to remember the creaky, uncertain phone system in Ireland at the time will recall that it could sometimes take an hour or two to make long-distance calls to Dublin from many parts of rural Ireland. The odds on landing on a rocky crag in the Atlantic, getting to the lighthouse, persuading the keeper to allow the phone—if indeed the lighthouse had one—to be used, getting through to Yorkshire reasonably quickly while the boat waited, and dictating a political news story to someone at the other end on a Sunday afternoon had to be extremely long. As the wind rose, the weather deteriorated and the sea grew rougher, the odds against it all happening as planned became astronomical.

Skellig Michael, that pyramid of rock also known as the Great Skellig, is, in fact, some eight miles out in the Atlantic. We reached it at last. The wind, we were told, was now Force 5 and rising; there was a heavy swell, and the boatman told us that there was no hope of landing. There was nothing for it but to round the Skellig, and then battle our way back through the waves and the spray with our nervous cargo of political correspondents. No one spoke: the only sounds were the chug of the engine, the rising wind and the slap of the waves against the side of the boat as it ploughed through what were now heavy seas. We landed eventually and regained the bus. But my memory of when and how is something of a blur. I was told afterwards that, drenched with spray and in my very light clothing, I was almost in a coma. My next reasonably lucid memory is of our group around a blazing fire in the Glenbeigh Hotel being thawed out with hot whiskies before going in to a good dinner prepared by Ernie Evans, the owner and a chef of great distinction at the time. I was soaked and I did not have a change of clothing with me. So the hotel kindly lent me a pair of trousers. It was large—it appears that it belonged not to Ernie himself but to his brother, a man of ample proportions, so ample that my memory, exaggerated perhaps, is that I had to fold the waist band twice around myself to keep it in place.

And what of our friend who had become increasingly frantic about the call he had been told he could place to Yorkshire from mid-Atlantic? Apparently we had dropped him off as the bus passed through Cahirciveen in the hope that he could find a working phone from which to convey his thoughts on Jack Lynch's briefing to the eager readers of Monday's *Yorkshire Post*. At this remove

I cannot remember if he was successful. Neither do I recall much about subsequent events. I assume we got the group back to the hotel in Killarney and back to Dublin next day for their flight home to London and the calmer waters of the House of Commons lobby.

On the face of it, as a PR exercise, the whole thing had been a disaster. But, I was assured, for our British guests the sharper edges of what had happened began to blur over time into warmer memories, recounted at dinner parties for years, of their intrepid Irish adventure in the wild Atlantic. So their visit worked out well after all. But then the person who assured me of this was our indomitable press attaché in London—so as I say this I remember Con and I begin to wonder.

NOTES

[1] John Simpson, now the distinguished BBC chief foreign correspondent, was the BBC representative; Denis Taylor was correspondent of *The Times*; and Dominick Coyle the correspondent of the *Financial Times*.
[2] Yuri Ustemenko.
[3] See Chapter 18.
[4] Keogh, *Jack Lynch*, 189.
[5] There are numerous files on Markpress in the National Archives, for example TSCH 2003/16/549 and 562 and the series 2003/16/480–485.
[6] I have confirmed my memory of discussions in the committee from a note I wrote in October 1972.
[7] Keogh, *Jack Lynch*, 358–60.
[8] By courtesy at that time one Irish correspondent, Aidan Hennigan, London correspondent of the *Irish Press*, was also admitted to membership of the lobby.

CHAPTER 4

Jack Lynch, 1969–70

It took quite some time after the events of 1968/69 for the Irish government to develop a sensible and coherent policy on Northern Ireland. In retrospect this is understandable—or at least explicable. A few short years before there had been a degree of optimism in the air as Lynch followed his predecessor, Seán Lemass, in 'hands across the border' meetings with the Northern Ireland prime minister, Terence O'Neill. But as the skies darkened in Northern Ireland—with a repressive response to some civil rights marches, reluctance to implement reforms, police partisanship, killings, and eventually the British army brought onto the streets as a protective force—the Irish government had difficulty in finding the right response to what was becoming an increasingly chaotic situation. Public emotion was high in the south; and there were many, including some government ministers, who pressed for a vigorous and assertive government policy directed ultimately to 'ending partition' and, in the immediate term, 'to protecting the minority in the North'. There was even some wild talk at one time of the possibility of a cross-border incursion to Derry or Newry by the Irish army—which, needless to say, would have been completely disastrous.

The British government at this stage still held to the formal position that the Irish government was an 'outsider', 'a foreign government', as the foreign secretary, Michael Stewart, and Lord Chalfont respectively told Hillery in August 1969.[1] However, outsider or not, the taoiseach and his government were subjected to increasing criticism from London on security matters: there was talk of the need to deal with 'IRA training camps in the Republic' and of the possibility of 'hot pursuit' if persons responsible for an attack in the north fled across the border to the south. So it could be said that, to that extent at least, the British government seemed to accept—in security practice if not yet in political principle— that the south had some role to play.

In 1969 and early 1970 Lynch still had several ministers in his government who took a hard-line approach to events in Northern Ireland, and he had to compromise with them at times if he was to maintain at least a façade of unity in his Cabinet. Even after he sacked two ministers during the Arms Crisis of May 1970,[2] he must still have wondered whom he could trust. And he did not have strong civil service backup: at the time the Troubles started neither his own department nor the Department of External Affairs had staff assigned to deal with the issue of Northern Ireland on a full-time basis. Both departments moved to remedy this deficiency in the early 1970s; and from then on they both, along with the Department of Justice, worked closely together. The need for continuing close cooperation between these three departments in particular will be obvious on reflection. Because of its fundamental importance as an issue, which, potentially at least, raises a question of the very identity of the state, the taoiseach and his department have to have a central role in dealing with Northern Ireland. But Northern Ireland is also a long-standing issue in Anglo-Irish relations—and, it was to become so in relations with the US and the EU. So the minister for foreign affairs and his department must also be deeply involved. Besides, foreign affairs officers who have served abroad have developed a particular experience in dealing with, and reporting on, political issues elsewhere, which they could draw on in dealing with Northern Ireland. And, since many of the issues that arise relate to cross-border security cooperation and—even more fundamentally, to the security and public order of the state—the minister for justice and his/her department, too, must have an important role.

Jack Lynch had become taoiseach in 1967 when Lemass stepped down—a compromise candidate between the two rivals Charles Haughey and George Colley. He came across as decent and affable—a sporting hero with six All-Ireland medals to his credit. As his political opponent Liam Cosgrave said when he died, 'Jack Lynch was a gentleman. At one time he was the most popular politician in Ireland since O'Connell'.[3] Lynch had a soft-spoken persona, non-threatening and emollient even to the point of apparent weakness when under pressure. This drew the listener in and subliminally invited a response of sympathy and support rather than opposition or censure. This was most evident, to the chagrin of his political opponents, in the tea and sympathy he was plied with by nuns when he visited their convents as he toured the country during election campaigns.

Lynch began, I think, as a conventional Irish nationalist of moderate views who probably knew little of Northern Ireland and even less of the unionist population there. He must have come close to being overwhelmed by the onrush of events in 1969/70. Some critics saw him as weak, but a tougher attitude, less affable than the face he normally maintained, showed through on rare occasions. In dealing with the conflict in Northern Ireland he may have faltered at times but in general he held up well and showed courage in his response, as he had done in his youth on the sports field. He deserves enormous credit for holding firm against the plot by some of his ministers to import arms 'for the defence of the minority in Northern Ireland'—an adventure that could have had disastrous consequences. In this and in other ways he did much to uphold the democratic institutions of the state during what could have been one of the most serious crises in its history.

Dr Patrick Hillery, as his minister for foreign affairs, and, after the Arms Crisis, Des O'Malley as his new minister for justice, strongly supported him in this; and during the turbulent years that followed, when events in Northern Ireland were generating strong emotion, all three showed courage and good sense in standing against violence and developing a more sensible approach to the conflict across the border.

In 1969–70 the Department of External Affairs (as it still was) began, gradually at first, to develop some greater expertise in relation to Northern Ireland.[4] This started with Eamonn Gallagher, from Letterkenny in Co. Donegal, who was a first secretary at the time.[5] He was transferred home from the embassy in Paris in July 1968. Finding himself assigned to an area of work in the department which did not seem to draw fully on his talents, he began, on his own initiative, to travel to Northern Ireland from time to time at weekends. Through connections of his family in Letterkenny he arranged to meet John Hume at Hume's home in Derry in August 1969.[6] He then extended his contacts further, meeting frequently with, among others, activists such as Austin Currie, Seamus Mallon, Ivan Cooper, Paddy Devlin, Gerry Fitt and Paddy O'Hanlon, all of whom were to be prominent in the Social Democratic and Labour Party (SDLP) which was founded on 21 August 1970.[7] On his return to Dublin after these visits he reported—unasked at first—on his discussions, and generally at that stage without identifying those to whom he had spoken.

Gallagher's reporting style was clear and trenchant. The reports he submitted to the secretary of the department, Hugh McCann, were passed on to the minister, Dr Hillery, and then to the taoiseach. They gave a realistic picture of what was happening on the ground and they helped to cut through some of the uncertainty that had characterised the government's initial response to events in Northern Ireland in 1969 and early 1970. Undoubtedly both the views and the analysis he offered in these reports were deeply influenced by the thinking of John Hume, who was already a significant figure and whose approach and ideas were to be of central importance to successive Irish governments throughout the Troubles, though he was careful always to maintain a non-partisan attitude in relation to the politics of the south. Hume also proved very successful in building support for a non-violent, democratic approach to the problems of Northern Ireland among leading political figures in the USA and Europe. There is some reason to think, too, that in these early years of the Troubles he and Lynch between them, with Gallagher acting as a kind of travelling intermediary, had been influential in encouraging the coming together of diverse figures on the nationalist side to establish the SDLP as the voice of the minority in the north.[8]

In Spring 1970 Gallagher's unorthodox role as a 'free-lancer' was formalised: he was promoted to counsellor and he became head of a new section dealing with Northern Ireland within the Political division, which was headed at the time by Sean Ronan. The new section initially comprised a first secretary, Joe Small, and two new third secretaries, Donal Kelly and Jim Brennan. In August 1971 Sean Donlon, who was then the consul general in Boston, and who was later to play a very prominent part in relation to Northern Ireland issues, joined the new section—temporarily at first and then on a more permanent basis.[9] His initial task was to assemble material for a complaint by the Irish government alleging breaches of the European Convention on Human Rights following the introduction of internment in Northern Ireland.[10] His remit broadened in time and he was the first of a succession of Foreign Affairs officials who were assigned to travel regularly in Northern Ireland over the following years (see Chapter 13).

If diplomats can be categorised somewhat simplistically as either realists or idealists, Eamonn Gallagher fell very definitely on the realist side of the line: he was highly intelligent, a good negotiator, 'hard-nosed' as the phrase has it, and he would have been very good at poker—though I am not sure if he actually played.[11] He had a strong and self-assured personality and, after his first meeting with Hume, his contacts in Northern Ireland were so good that he became the department's acknowledged expert on what was happening there. He also became an important adviser and speech-writer for Jack Lynch on Northern Ireland and Anglo-Irish rela-tions. The particular role this gave him in relation to the taoiseach ruffled feathers in his own department on occasion, and did not always make for an easy relationship with his own minister. While Lynch drew for advice on other sources too, notably Ken Whitaker, Gallagher's role in the development of Irish government policy was very important in 1970 and 1971. In early 1972 his influence with Lynch began to diminish—perhaps because the part he was play-ing had become too widely known.[12]

In early 1972 the Department of Foreign Affairs took further steps to organise itself to deal with Northern Ireland issues. For the first time it set up a separate 'Anglo-Irish division' headed by an assistant secretary, Bob McDonagh, something it should have done much earlier.

The new division had three sections—Anglo-Irish Political, Cultural, and Press and Information (where I worked at the time).[13] Eamonn Gallagher continued in his role as head of the Anglo-Irish Political section within the division until mid-1972. At that point he was promoted to assistant secretary, moved away from Northern Ireland issues, and took over a new area of responsibility as head of the EEC division of the department.

While Lynch's role as taoiseach was central, Dr Hillery, who was minister for foreign affairs from mid-1969 to the end of 1972, was also actively involved in the Northern Ireland issue—particularly in the early years of his term in office. As his biographer puts it he was

> a leading advocate for peaceful constitutional change in Northern Ireland once the crisis broke in August 1969...His consistent objectives were to re-establish peace within the North and secure justice for the Catholic minority...He promoted more intensive engagement with Northern nationalists than any Irish foreign minister since the foundation of the state. Hillery also led the way in promoting diplomatic contacts between the two governments in the first two years of the crisis.[14]

A dramatic signal of Hillery's wish for 'more intensive engagement with Northern nationalists' was his surprise visit to the Falls Road in Belfast in July 1970. It was quietly arranged by Eamonn Gallagher who also drove him there. At the time tensions were high because of a curfew imposed for nearly two days following serious sectarian conflict, including gun battles in which six people were killed. The British government were concerned—ostensibly for security reasons—that Hillery, as minister, had not given advance notice of the visit but in some ways that for him was the point: as well as showing concern for Northern nationalists, he had wanted to establish that a visit by an Irish minister to Belfast was nothing out of the ordinary. In occasional meetings with the British foreign secretary, Sir Alec Douglas-Home, over 1970 and 1971, Hillery also felt that he was 'establishing the right of the Irish government to be heard in Whitehall'. He found Sir Alec better informed and more willing to listen to the Irish case than some of his colleagues in government. 'The Foreign Secretary readily discussed the progress of the reform agenda in the North and acknowledged the legitimacy of the Irish government's concerns.' Sir Alec even mentioned 'the prospect of "a solution of the Constitutional problem at some distant date."' But, his biographer goes on, 'Hillery's efforts to secure more rapid reform within Northern Ireland had little immediate influence on British policy'.[15]

From 1971 onwards Hillery became more and more preoccupied with the intensive negotiations over Ireland's application for EEC membership and his role as lead negotiator took up a great deal of his time. He signed the Accession Treaty, along with the taoiseach, on 22 January 1972; and then he led the government's campaign in the referendum on ratification which followed in the Spring of 1972. By that time the taoiseach had taken full control of government policy on the north. As Hillery's biographer puts it:

> Lynch increasingly took the leading role in Anglo-Irish relations from 1971 onwards, as the turmoil within the governing party subsided and his hold on power became more secure.[16]

Up to then Lynch's own department, in contrast to Foreign Affairs, had remained relatively small[17] but in late 1972 Lynch took a step that was to prove of great importance—he brought in Dermot Nally, who was then in the Department of Local Government, and appointed him to the post of assistant secretary to the government. Dermot was an outstanding and hardworking public servant; and over the next twenty years, in addition to his functions, first as assistant secretary and later as secretary to the government, he played a major part as adviser to successive governments and taoisigh on both Northern Ireland and European affairs.[18]

At a meeting on 28 May 1970, following a submission by the minister for external affairs, the government decided to set up an 'Interdepartmental Unit comprising representatives of the Departments of External Affairs, the Taoiseach and Finance'. Its remit was 'to keep in touch with all aspects of Anglo-Irish relations having a bearing on the Six Counties'; it was to arrange for studies of long-term solutions, to advise on contacts in the north and in Britain, to guide and direct information activity abroad, and to act as a 'clearing house' for the activities of other departments.[19] The IDU, as we called it, was chaired by the Taoiseach's Department—for a time by Dan O'Sullivan, Secretary to the Government, and later by Dermot Nally. It met quite frequently, and gave advice and prepared extensive working papers and proposals for the taoiseach and ministers. As I recall it now, in retrospect, its work could be described as probably useful, but certainly not always central, to government decision-making in Dublin. I attended meetings—very occasionally at first, but more frequently in late 1972 and early 1973.

It is possible, I think, to identify several different phases in the evolution of Irish government policy on Northern Ireland as enunciated in some of Lynch's more important statements and actions over the years 1969 to early 1973.

During an initial phase in 1969 his response to the crisis that was erupting in Northern Ireland was not always well judged. It was undoubtedly coloured by the make-up of his Cabinet at the time, which included some ministers whom he sacked during the Arms Crisis of the following year.[20] In the television address on the day after the events in Derry on 12 August 1969 that I referred to in Chapter 2, he said that the only permanent solution was the re-unification of Ireland and that it was the intention of the government

> to request the British government to enter into early negotiations with the Irish government to review the present constitutional position of the Six Counties of Northern Ireland.[21]

He moderated his approach somewhat over the following months. His statements and speeches maintained the idea of eventual Irish unity as the long-term solution but developed it in a more carefully thought-out and irenic way. Unity, he said, could be achieved only by agreement and not by force; it would have to be based on mutual respect; it might have to come in stages; and some kind of federal arrangement between north and south could be a possibility. In responding on 28 August, for example, to a declaration by the British and Northern Ireland governments that 'the Border is not an issue', he said that the Irish government 'agree that the Border cannot be changed by force'. But, he added, 'it is and has been their policy to seek the re-unification of the country by peaceful means.' After speaking of the need for a police force that was 'respected and accepted', he went on:

> Nothing must be left undone to avoid a recurrence of the present troubles, whether in five or fifty years, but to continue to ignore the need for fundamental constitutional change, so clearly necessary, could only have such a tragic result.

The ultimate solution would not 'easily or expeditiously come about'. However, the Irish government were prepared to explore every reasonable prospect including discussing with the British government the possibility of 'a solution along Federal lines' achieved through intermediate stages.[22]

These ideas almost certainly reflect the advice of Ken Whitaker who, as we now know from his biographer, was an important influence on Lynch over this whole period. Whitaker had a good personal relationship with Lynch—first as secretary of the Department of Finance and from 1969 on as governor of the Central Bank. The advice he gave was always moderate and reasonable; it looked forward to eventual Irish unity, possibly in stages, but insisted that it could be achieved only with mutual respect, by agreement and without the use of force.

Whitaker had already put the case for such a policy privately to Lynch a year previously. In 'A Note on North-South Policy' of 11 November 1968, he argued that, having long since, and rightly, abandoned the use of force to undo partition '[w]e were, therefore, left with only one choice, a policy of seeking unity in Ireland by agreement in Ireland between Irishmen.' This would have to be a long-term policy that would require 'patience, understanding and forbearance and resolute resistance to emotionalism and opportunism.' We should be open 'to explore all

kinds of possibilities—confederation, federation, external association, condominium, the Benelux arrangement, the political
principles involved in the EEC'. For financial and other reasons
'a very special formula may have to be found'.[23]

However, the British ambassador in Dublin, Sir Andrew
Gilchrist, often a less than sympathetic observer of Irish government policy, was not very impressed by Lynch's thoughts on 'a solution along federal lines'. He reported to the Foreign Office that
Lynch 'and almost the whole Irish political establishment' regarded
'the prospect of an immediate and complete union of Ireland with
genuine horror.' What Lynch had in mind, he said, was the transfer
of certain Catholic areas to the south.

> A truncated Northern Ireland would be administered
> by a Stormont-like body which would somehow be
> represented in Dublin and somehow subject to it, no
> members from the area being represented in the Dáil:
> certain Catholic areas including the great prize of
> Londonderry would be integrated with the Republic:
> the truncated 'Unionist' area would retain all its eco-
> nomic links with the UK, continuing to benefit as at
> present from British subsidies, social security etc.[24]

Some three weeks later, on 17 September, however, Gilchrist
reported that he had had an hour-long 'straight-forward and
friendly' discussion with the taoiseach at the taoiseach's suggestion.[25]
The report is interesting because Lynch seems to have met the
ambassador on his own, with no official present, and he is perhaps
more likely to have been expressing his own views rather than
drawing on prior briefing by officials. Lynch praised what
Callaghan was doing on civil rights in the north. He said that he
himself had shown restraint through the period of stress, and had
enforced restraint on his Cabinet and party; 'and he intended his
own next speech to be more mild and helpful than any he had
made so far.' However, he went on, 'I was not to imagine from this
that the Irish Government could be told by Chichester-Clarke or
by Stewart or by Chalfont to keep its nose out of the affairs of
Northern Ireland...No Irish Prime Minister could do less and

survive, given the feelings about the unity of Ireland in the Republic today.' He accepted that the south was incapable of taking over the north in the foreseeable future and financial and social adjustments would be necessary in the south.

> But however long the period of adjustment the South would never abandon the right, a right enhanced by recent events, to say its say over Northern affairs and to try to make its views effective. What was needed was for some degree of consultation with Britain to be conceded.

In passing, it is interesting to note that the minister for finance, Charles Haughey, who was to be dropped from his Cabinet by Lynch some eight months later, and who was to succeed Lynch as taoiseach in 1979, also asked the British ambassador to call to see him at his house a short time later to discuss Northern Ireland. Haughey was even more assertive about Irish unity than Lynch had been. According to the ambassador's report to the Foreign Office on 4 October:

> He began with a firm combative statement of his own position. There was nothing he would not sacrifice, including the position of the Catholic Church (with all the related social legislation) in order to get a united Ireland. From now on the South could not turn aside from this objective, not for a moment. If, of course, Britain wanted Ireland back in the Commonwealth, he would accept that. If Britain wanted access to Irish bases, or if NATO wanted to occupy bases, he would accept that.

If he was combative, Haughey was also prescient. He thought 'further trouble...would soon put an end to [Northern Ireland prime minister] Chichester-Clark'; and he said that 'the assumption of direct power by Britain was inevitable and necessary'.[26]

I have suggested that Whitaker's influence can be detected in the taoiseach's statement of 28 August. It was even more evident in a speech delivered by Lynch in Tralee on 20 September 1969 that attracted considerable attention for its relative moderation at a time when emotion generally ran high. It was indeed one of the most notable policy statements by the Irish government in this early period of the Troubles in Northern Ireland.[27] Whitaker prepared the draft at Lynch's request and Lynch used it with only minor modifications. Whitaker's biographer is in no doubt about both the importance of the speech and the authorship. Modifying the more strident notes of Lynch's August broadcast, in 'clear and simple' terms Ken laid out the basis of the new policy.[28] The speech touched on the historic basis for Irish unity; ruled out the use of force; emphasised the principle of consent; and looked ultimately to 'a free and genuine union of those living in Ireland based on mutual respect and tolerance.' It also referred again to the possibility of 'a solution on federal lines' and envisaged that there could be 'intermediate stages in an approach to a final agreed solution.'[29] Whitaker's role in drafting this speech would probably have been known to an inner circle at the time but I doubt if many were aware of the extent to which he continued on a personal basis to advise Lynch during these first few years of the crisis.

Some months later Whitaker went further: on 24 November 1969 he wrote to Lynch enclosing a four-part study entitled 'The Constitutional Position of Northern Ireland'. He had prepared it with the help of some of his senior colleagues from the Department of Finance.[30] This document too was reasonable and moderate in tone. According to the Introduction:

> The terms of reference were to study the constitutional position without attempting to propose solutions. This has been interpreted as not precluding a review of policies and an examination of how policy may or should develop in the future.

The paper is in four parts: (1) the historical development of the present position; (2) the pro-partition views; (3) the anti-partition case and the development of present policy; (4) how the views may be expected to evolve and whether there is scope for a common meeting ground between north and south.

The fourth and final part of the paper was headed 'Possible Reconciliation between North and South'. It set out a number of preconditions—economic, social, cultural, religious, political and so on—'for a 32-county set-up' and then outlined a variety of possible structures for eventual Irish unity. Three of these—a federation or a confederation of north and south, or a condominium under which Britain and Ireland would exercise joint authority over Northern Ireland—foreshadowed the three main options put forward fifteen years later in the Report of the New Ireland Forum. The paper then touched on a number of possible ways of linking north and south, though it made no explicit mention of a Council of Ireland, an idea that was to gain great prominence a few years later. The two that came closest to the idea of a Council, without mentioning the word, were 'An EEC or Benelux Type of Arrangement', involving an agreement for gradual economic integration of north and south over a fixed period; and a looser 'OECD/ Council of Europe type Agreement' providing for cooperation, consultation and co-ordination of policies' and 'institutionalising existing *ad hoc* meetings between the two sides'. Under the latter heading the paper suggested that '[a] permanent subcommittee of the Anglo-Irish Committee to deal specifically with North/South matters might be a possibility';[31] and also that '[m]eetings of Parliamentarians on the lines of the Council of Europe would have obvious advantages'.

While the paper does not spell out explicitly the need for consent of a majority in Northern Ireland, it seems to imply this in saying that 'any structure would have to be agreed between North and South'. The final paragraph of the paper offers the following conclusion:

> *Summary*: The basic problem in any solution is to reconcile the interest of the North in being economically close to Britain with a loosening or severance of the political links between them. Closer links between the South and Britain would go some way to solve the problem but would pose important political questions

for the South. In a wider grouping such as the EEC the problem is considerably reduced.

Pending developments on the EEC front slow progress must be accepted. As a first step the confederation solution...or the Council of Europe arrangement appear to be most worthy of further examination.

Over the following years Whitaker, in frequent correspondence, continued to provide advice to Lynch. He also met, and corresponded privately with, a very wide range of contacts that he had developed in Northern Ireland, many of them liberal unionists; and, notwithstanding the deteriorating situation on the ground in Northern Ireland, he continued to promote ideas that might eventually advance the long-term aim of Lynch's Tralee speech—a free and genuine union of those living in Ireland based on mutual respect and tolerance.'

Speeches and statements by Lynch in 1970 drew to a considerable extent on Whitaker's advice, especially in emphasising that Irish unity could be achieved only by agreement and not by force, but this is not to say that Whitaker's approach always prevailed. Sometimes the political demands of the moment seem to have required Lynch to take a more robust approach. It is safe to say, for example, that the following highly emotive passage from his address to the Fianna Fáil Árd-Fheis on 17 January 1970 is unlikely to have been drafted by Whitaker:

> Partition is a deep, throbbing weal across the land, heart and soul of Ireland, an imposed deformity whose indefinite perpetuation eats into the Irish consciousness like a cancer. As I have said, it is impossible for true Irishmen, of whatever creed, to dwell on the existence of Partition without becoming emotional.[32]

To be fair, Lynch went on to say that 'emotionalism and the brand of impetuous action or demands that it leads to cannot possibly solve, or even help in dealing with such a problem.' He again referred to peace as 'the only path to re-unification';

and spoke of 'trust, goodwill and brotherhood'. Later that year in an address to the General Assembly of the United Nations, he spoke of

> a fund of goodwill between Ireland and Britain, derived from a surer and deeper understanding of each other, reached through quiet diplomacy and personal conversation.[33]

Whitaker's more moderate voice reasserting itself once again in these formulations, one might think.

I suggested earlier that Jack Lynch was modest about the extent of his own direct knowledge of Northern Ireland; and I believe that Anthony Craig, author of a recent book on the early years of the Troubles, who had the benefit of a long interview with Eamonn Gallagher in 2008, is right to say that he was very much influenced by his advisers.[34] In 1969 and for part of 1970 the strongest influence was probably Ken Whitaker. Whitaker had a degree of access to his taoiseach and a willingness to use it that was quite exceptional in a civil servant at the time. I knew nothing of this and I wonder now if my seniors did. My own sense as a middle-level official after my return to Dublin in mid-1970 was that the main source of policy advice to the taoiseach between then and early 1972 was Gallagher, whose regular contact with John Hume and others on his travels north continued to give him a particular authority on Northern Ireland issues. This personal memory of Gallagher's role accords well with Craig's view that by early 1970

> Jack Lynch had changed his policy with regard to Northern Ireland. Instead of trying to create an alliance with unionism, a principle that had guided Lemass's trips to Stormont and one characteristic of Ken Whitaker, Lynch was now refocused on allying with London. A London-Dublin alliance, alongside links with the emergent SDLP, became the typical aim of Dublin governments up until 1974. As a policy this was the brainchild of Eamonn Gallagher and the

Department of Foreign Affairs, as Ken Whitaker was gradually sidelined from Northern Ireland affairs after September 1969.[35]

However, I think that this view may under-state Whitaker's continuing role as a friend and source of advice to Lynch, while to speak of 'allying with London' rather than 'building closer relations with' it, seems to me somewhat overstated. I also wonder now whether this was solely Gallagher's idea or whether, in urging this approach on Lynch, as he undoubtedly did, he may have been reflecting ideas that derived ultimately from Hume.[36] In any case I believe that Craig was probably right in his overall judgement about those years: 'the truth is that Lynch continued for a time to listen to both Gallagher and Whitaker, taking from each what he felt best suited to the situation he faced.'[37]

In succeeding chapters I will recall memories of Gallagher's role as policy adviser. That role lasted for a relatively short time but some aspects of the approach he advised Lynch to take were to prove influential long after he himself had moved on to other things. I believe it is not too much to say that some of those ideas were still of importance a quarter of a century later in the shaping of the present settlement in Northern Ireland.

NOTES

[1] See Chapter 2.

[2] For details see Introduction, n. 1, and also Chapter 3.

[3] Keogh, *Jack Lynch*, 450.

[4] At the end of 1971, on the initiative of the minister, Dr Hillery, the government decided to change the name of the department from 'External Affairs' to 'Foreign Affairs'. See Walsh, *Patrick Hillery*, 170. Curiously, the Irish version of the name, 'Roinn Gnóthaí Eachtracha', was left unchanged.

[5] The Irish Department of Foreign Affairs follows international practice in the titles of various grades in its diplomatic service. 'First secretary' equates to 'assistant principal', and 'counsellor' to 'principal', in home departments.

[6] See Sean Donlon's essay 'John Hume and the Irish government', in Sean Farren and Denis Haughey (eds), *John Hume: Irish peacemaker* (Dublin, 2015), 83–93: 85. Also Fanning, 'Playing it cool', 80.

[7] See essay by Paul Arthur in Farren and Haughey, *John Hume*, 52.

[8] A thought suggested to me by my former colleague Sean Donlon.

[9] Sean Donlon was later to become, successively, head of the Anglo-Irish division, ambassador in Washington, and secretary general of the department. He has given a very good account of these events, and of the seminal importance of John Hume's thinking from 1964 onwards, in his essay in Farren and Haughey, *John Hume*, 83–93. I am grateful to him also for the detailed information in this paragraph which fills out my own fading memory of the establishment of new structures in the Department of Foreign Affairs to deal with Anglo-Irish issues and with Northern Ireland.

[10] I deal with this in greater detail in Chapter 12.

[11] A few years later when, as a senior official in the commission, he led for the EEC side in the Euro-Arab dialogue negotiations, Eamonn Gallagher was quoted as saying, facetiously, that his background knowledge of the world of cattle-dealing in Donegal had been helpful in preparing him for the task.

[12] I will deal with Eamonn Gallagher's approach in greater detail in Chapter 9.

[13] I had worked with Bob McDonagh earlier—in 1960, when he was a very senior, and I a very junior, third secretary. In the mid-1970s he was appointed secretary of the department and later served as a senior ambassador in several important posts abroad.

[14] Walsh, *Patrick Hillery*, 255.

[15] Walsh, *Patrick Hillery*, 264–5.

[16] Walsh, *Patrick Hillery*, 255.

[17] Charlie Haughey expanded it greatly when he became taoiseach in 1979.

[18] A colleague, Wally Kirwan, worked closely with Dermot in those years. He later became assistant secretary in the department and worked on Northern Ireland and EEC issues over many years.

[19] NAI TSCH 2001/6/549.

[20] See Introduction, n. 1.

[21] Lynch, *Speeches and statements*, 3.

[22] Lynch, *Speeches and statements*, 6–7.

[23] NAI TSCH 2001/8/6 (Papers of Jack Lynch) (accessed from CAIN, the online archive maintained by the University of Ulster for material dealing with conflict and politics in Northern Ireland; accessible at: http://cain.ulst.ac.uk/).

[24] TNA FCO 33/758. Telegram of 29 August 1969 from Ambassador Gilchrist to FCO.

[25] TNA FCO 33/758. Telegram of 17 September 1969 from Gilchrist to FCO.

[26] TNA FCO 33/759. Telegram of 4 October 1969 to the FCO.

[27] As I recounted in Chapter 2, the home secretary, Jim Callaghan, was particularly impressed and he asked the British ambassador, Gilchrist, to pass on his commendation on the speech to the taoiseach.

[28] Chambers, *T.K. Whitaker*, 283.

[29] For the draft as sent to Lynch see Keogh, *Jack Lynch*, 202–5. For the speech as delivered see Lynch, *Speeches and statements*, 9–12.

[30] NAI TSCH 2001/8/6 (Papers of Jack Lynch). In his letter he describes the paper 'as revised by Maher, Murphy and myself'. The two colleagues were Denis Maher and Kevin Murphy (who, after retirement from finance, served later as the ombudsman). I am grateful to Professor John Coakley for drawing this document to my

attention; see also Chambers, *T.K. Whitaker*, 286–7. I do not think that in preparing the paper Whitaker consulted with other departments. However, the paper must have been copied subsequently to External Affairs, since I have a stencilled document circulated internally in the department in late 1969 that is substantially similar, though not wholly identical to it.

[31] I assume this refers to the meetings of officials from Dublin and London in the late 1960s, following the Anglo-Irish Free Trade Area Agreement of 1965, mentioned in D.J. Maher, *The tortuous path: the course of Irish entry into the EEC, 1948–73* (Dublin, 1986), pages 255–6.

[32] Lynch, *Speeches and statements*, 16.

[33] Lynch. *Speeches and statements*, 35.

[34] Anthony Craig, *Crisis of confidence: Anglo-Irish relations in the early Troubles, 1966–1974* (Dublin and Portland, Oregon, 2010), 60.

[35] Craig, *Crisis of confidence*, 60.

[36] A thought reflecting a discussion with my former colleague Sean Donlon, who, in subsequent years, was an important channel for Irish governments' contact with John Hume.

[37] Craig, *Crisis of confidence*, 60–1.

CHAPTER 5

Summit at Chequers, 1971

In the previous chapter I suggested that Whitaker's influence can be seen in speeches by the taoiseach that ruled out the use of force, emphasised the principle of consent and looked forward in the longer term to drawing Northern unionists towards accepting 'a free and genuine union of those living in Ireland based on mutual respect and tolerance'. Eamonn Gallagher's policy advice did not run directly counter to this but his approach was more pragmatic, tough-minded and directed to the immediate future. While Whitaker looked towards better relations with unionists, Gallagher saw an assertive approach to the Dublin-London relationship as the key. In his view, a united Ireland was the only real solution in the long-term but his advice to Lynch emphasised two immediate objectives in dealing with the British government: asserting a political role for the taoiseach and the Irish government, and showing that parliamentary and governmental institutions based on the 'winner-takes-all' Westminster model were completely unsuited to the divided society of Northern Ireland. This approach undoubtedly reflected the thinking of John Hume, as I suggested at the end of the last chapter. Indeed it is quite possible to go further: the concept of a sharing of power in new institutions, in particular, may have originated with him and been developed by Gallagher through his regular contacts with Hume and his role as adviser to Lynch at this period.

No one in Dublin or the north would have known it at the time but, as the archives now show, the possibility of a united Ireland, though improbable, was not ruled out in principle in some high-level British thinking at this period. The Conservative leader, Ted Heath, had replaced Harold Wilson as prime minister following the election of June 1970. On 19 April 1971 Northern Ireland was the main topic at the first of what was to be a series of occasional 'think-ins' Heath held with a small group of trusted advisers comprising Sir William Armstrong, Sir Burke Trend, Lord Rothschild and Robert Armstrong. The minutes of the discussion, prepared by Robert Armstrong, allow us a glimpse of their private thoughts at this relatively early stage in the Troubles.

The meeting identified three possible policy options.

- Direct rule: there would be a case for this if the security forces 'were precluded by the present political system in Northern Ireland from taking types of action which they thought could improve law and order significantly'. It might also be forced on the British government by 'political or other developments in Northern Ireland'. However, it could not be a lasting solution; it could well lead to greater rather than less bloodshed, since the Protestant community would certainly oppose it. 'They would see the British government as siding with the Catholics and even with the IRA, and would fear direct rule as a precursor to handing them over to the Republic'.
- Pull out and leave Northern Ireland, 'in effect leaving Northern Ireland to work out its own destiny either in independence or in fusion with the rest of Ireland'. This 'would probably precipitate civil war in Ireland, and it would be a breach of oft-repeated pledges by Westminster Governments not to change the constitutional position of Northern Ireland without the agreement of the Northern Ireland Parliament'.
- Continue 'on broadly the present lines'.

In passing, almost in a throwaway fashion, comes the comment:

> The only lasting solution would lie in bringing about unification of all Ireland. Before the resignation of Lord O'Neill it had been possible to believe that events were moving quietly in that direction. Recent developments had, however, created a sharp set-back to those hopes.

As a practical matter, however, the meeting concluded that if the first two options—direct rule and a 'pull-out'—were ruled out, then there was 'no alternative but to continue much as at present'. The prime minister 'agreed that we should go ahead with talks with the Taoiseach and that those talks might well include an examination of what the Republican government [*sic*] could do to help to deal with the IRA.'[1]

Jack Lynch in Dublin, of course, knew nothing of the inner thoughts of Heath and his advisers in those days. Advised by Gallagher, Lynch's concern was to assert a role for Dublin in relation to Northern Ireland. In August/September 1971, he did so in practice in a very blunt—and public—exchange of messages with the British prime minister. This led to a high level of animosity in Anglo-Irish relations for a short time but the aim, which was to have the British accept some Dublin involvement beyond mere cross-border security cooperation, was achieved, so it is worth outlining what happened in some detail.

A month previously, on 11 July, the 50th anniversary of the 1921 truce, the taoiseach had called more strongly than before for Irish unity by agreement. His speech at the Garden of Remembrance in Dublin was addressed in particular to Britain and to the unionist majority in Northern Ireland and it was couched in generally positive terms.

> Whatever happened thereafter in Ireland, whatever the mistakes made, whatever the goals unreached…on 11th July, 1921…Britain had finally been brought to agree to recognise the Irish nation…But there still

remains the division of Ireland. As long as it lasts the North remains unable to contribute its skills, its resources to the Irish nation—and the whole country is the poorer for that.

He recognised that progress towards Irish unity would be gradual.

The national majority have the primary duty and responsibility if they wish to make progress towards the achievement of Irish unity by agreement. They must come to terms with the fact that the process will be slow, sometimes frustrating and sometimes painful.

Jack Lynch quoted the poet John Hewitt to the effect that the Northern unionists 'have rights drawn from the soil and sky'; and he added '[t]here are many different kinds of Irishmen, there are not two separate Irelands'. He spoke positively of 'the friendly relations which exist between the peoples of Ireland and Britain'. He said it was unwise of Britain 'to continue the kind of guarantee to the North [in the Ireland Act 1949] which makes intransigence a virtue and silences reason'; and he asked the British government 'to declare their interest in encouraging the unity of Ireland, by agreement, in independence and in a harmonious relationship between the two islands.'[2]

The speech, with its emphasis on the theme of Irish unity, was undoubtedly drafted by Eamonn Gallagher. Ken Whitaker, in a letter afterwards to Lynch, commended it but also expressed worry that it might be interpreted as implying that Westminster support would be withdrawn from the north.[3] The Northern Ireland prime minister, Brian Faulkner, thought it 'unhelpful and ill-considered'.

I suppose I should admit here that while I had nothing to do with the rest of the speech I did have some small input in that I supplied the brief quotation from John Hewitt. I had recently discovered his work and I particularly liked his poem *The colony*, from which it was drawn. The poem is an allegory—overtly about Roman settlers in Gaul but obviously directed by implication to a community much closer to home. I am tempted to quote here a few more lines from the final section.

we are changed
from the raw levies which usurped the land,
if not to kin, to co-inhabitants

for we have rights drawn from the soil and sky;
the use, the pace, the patient years of labour,
the rain against the lips, the changing light,
the heavy clay-sucked stride, have altered us;
we would be strangers in the Capitol;
this is our country also, nowhere else;
and we shall not be outcast on the world.[4]

It had been a turbulent year in Northern Ireland up to then. In February the first British soldier was killed. In March Brian Faulkner succeeded Chichester-Clark as prime minister. In July the SDLP withdrew from Stormont after their demands for an enquiry into shootings in Derry were rejected. The sky darkened further on 9 August when internment without trial was introduced in Northern Ireland. It was done in a ham-fisted and one-sided way: all but one of the 342 persons interned were from the minority community even though loyalist organisations had already been implicated in scores of killings. Gunfights and rioting followed; barricades were erected; houses on both sides of the community divide were burned. As Bew and Gillespie's *Chronology of the Troubles* describes it:

> Two thousand Protestants were left homeless, while 2,500 Catholics left Belfast for refugee camps set up in the Republic…By 12 August twenty-two people had been killed and up to seven thousand people (the majority Catholics) left homeless as houses were burned to the ground.[5]

Lynch had been given no advance notice that internment was to be introduced. However, the British ambassador in Dublin had asked him some days before whether the government would introduce it in the south if it were to be introduced in the north. Lynch's response was an emphatic 'no'; and he warned the ambassador that, if it were introduced in the north, the consequences could be cata-strophic.[6] On 9 August, the day internment was introduced, Lynch issued a strong statement in which he said that the introduction of internment was 'deplorable evidence of the political poverty of the policies' pursued in Northern Ireland. It was 'an attempt to main-tain a regime which has long since shown itself incapable of just government and contemptuous of the norms of the British demo cracy to which they pretend allegiance'. He called for 'a conference of all the interested parties…in order to obtain a new form of administration for Northern Ireland'.[7] The government sent the minister for foreign affairs, Dr Hillery, to London. He was received there by the home secretary, Reginald Maudling, on 11 August but his talks with Maudling had little effect.

Lynch was now under severe pressure at home. On 12 August, following discussions with political leaders of the minority in Northern Ireland, he issued a more detailed statement saying that the introduction of internment without trial was 'seen to be a delib-erate decision by the Stormont administration to attempt the out-right repression of the minority'. The Irish government, he said, had acted with 'responsibility and restraint' over the previous two years. It would not wish now to cause an escalation of an already grave situation and it would not support any armed activity 'which will inevitably cause further suffering and death'. The best way to ensure that 'the subjection of the minority in the North to unjust law, biased administration and institutional violence' would end was 'through determined political action.' However, he said, the main concern of the Northern Ireland government appeared to be 'to meet the wishes and demands of the most extreme elements within the unionist community'. In these circumstances, 'as an immediate objective of political action, the Stormont Government should be replaced by an administration in which power and decision-making will be equally shared between unionist and non-unionist'.[8]

One week later Ted Heath summoned the new Northern Ireland prime minister, Brian Faulkner, to London. They met at the British prime minister's country residence at Chequers on 18 and 19 August. The foreign secretary Sir Alec Douglas-Home, the home secretary Reginald Maudling and the defence secretary Lord Carrington were also present. Jack Lynch was not invited to join the talks although it had been agreed earlier that he and Heath would meet in late October, when it might be expected that the main focus would be on both countries' negotiations for EEC membership. On Gallagher's advice, Lynch deliberately waited until the afternoon of the second day when the talks had almost—but not quite—concluded: he then sent a telegram to Heath and released the text immediately to the news media even before it was received by the British government. This was most unusual. The normal channel for such communications at head of government level would have been through the Department of Foreign Affairs and the Irish embassy in London. In this case the message was sent through the postal service as an ordinary telegram.[9] The telegram spoke of 'the failure of internment and of current military operations as a solution to the problems of Northern Ireland.' It said to Heath that it must now be obvious to him that 'solutions require to be found through political means' and they should be 'based on the principle of immediate and full equality of treatment for everyone in Northern Ireland irrespective of political views or religion'. If policies of seeking military solutions continued, Lynch said, he intended to support the passive resistance campaign being pursued by the non-unionist population. If, however, there was agreement to 'a policy of finding solutions by political means', he was prepared to attend

> a meeting of all the interested parties designed to find ways and means of promoting the economic, social and political wellbeing of all the Irish people, North or South, without prejudice to the aspiration of the great majority of the Irish people to the re-unification of Ireland.[10]

This message from across the Irish Sea had the effect of a missile lobbed at the Chequers talks at a time and in a way calculated to have maximum disruptive effect. It was a clear assertion by the taoiseach that he and the Irish government had to have a role; it was backed by a veiled threat that the Irish government could create difficulties by supporting passive resistance in Northern Ireland;

and in a sharp break with normal diplomatic usage, the text was deliberately released to the news media before it had time to reach the prime minister to whom it was addressed.

Heath was stung by this. As his biographer, quoting the British ambassador in Dublin, puts it, 'understandably Mr. Heath and Mr. Maudling [the home secretary] were not amused.'[11] This was an understatement, to say the least. Later that same evening Heath sent an angry reply by way of rebuttal of Lynch's message. The reply set out seven numbered points. The first point set the tone for the rest:

> Your telegram of today is unjustifiable in its contents, unacceptable in its attempt to interfere in the affairs of the United Kingdom and can in no way contribute to the solution of the problem of Northern Ireland.

Heath's angry tone continued through the remaining six points. Lynch should know that the principle of equality of treatment for everyone in Northern Ireland was the accepted policy of the British government and that it was being fully implemented: the military operations were designed solely for the defence of the people against terrorist activities, 'many of which originate in, or are supported from the Republic'. Point 4 was categorical in rejecting a role for the Irish government in the affairs of Northern Ireland:

> While I naturally welcome contacts with you as the head of a friendly government, and while Mr. Faulkner and I have often made clear our desire to see greater co-operation between all governments concerned in promoting the mutual prosperity and wellbeing of the peoples of Northern Ireland and the Republic, I cannot accept that anyone outside the United Kingdom can participate in meetings designed to promote the political development of any part of the United Kingdom.

Heath's message went on: 'your reference to supporting the policy of passive resistance' was 'calculated to do maximum damage to the cooperation between the communities in Northern Ireland which it is our purpose, and I would hope would be your purpose, to achieve.' He deeply regretted that, although a meeting between them had already been arranged (for October) 'to discuss the whole range of matters of common interest' to both countries, Lynch had 'publicly taken up a position so calculated not only to increase the tension in Northern Ireland but also to impair our effort to maintain good relations between the United Kingdom and the Irish Republic.' The final paragraph was a direct riposte to Lynch's deliberate release of the text of his message:

> Since the text of your telegram was given to the Irish press before it was received here, I am also releasing the text of this message to the Press.[12]

Was this response by Heath no more than an immediate—and understandable—flare-up of anger, a temporary set-back to an improving relationship? It was certainly that—in part at least. But his fourth point, as quoted above, seems to go beyond the emotion of the moment. It is a publicly stated principle, a reversion to the standard formula I referred to in Chapter 2: he refuses to accept that 'anyone outside the United Kingdom'—in this case the Irish government—could 'participate in meetings designed to promote the political development of any part of the United Kingdom', which, in this case, was to say Northern Ireland.

Lynch responded to Heath's message in a relatively low-key way, suggesting in a long-suffering tone that he had been misunderstood. He regretted that Heath had interpreted his message in the way he did. He had hoped that Heath would have accepted his offer 'to participate in discussions among all those concerned to find an amicable solution to the problems of Northern Ireland'. His message was 'solely intended to try to bring the present unrest to an end and to begin again the promotion of economic, social and political progress.' No one who had examined the situation could accept that the Troubles in Northern Ireland had originated in any way from the south. Heath had asserted that military operations were a necessary prelude to restoring harmony between the communities and that they were solely for defence of the people against armed terrorists. On the contrary they were driving them further apart. Over the previous twelve days the republic had received 'many thousands of refugee women and children mainly from Catholic ghettos in Belfast'. The fact that internment had been 'so patently directed' at the non-unionist community did not encourage belief in the assertion that the principle of equality of treatment for everyone was accepted, and being implemented, by the governments of the UK and of Northern Ireland. As to Anglo-Irish relations, Lynch said he had spoken frequently on that subject and had attempted to set relations on a path that promised 'hope, progress and an ultimate final settlement, by agreement and through peaceful means only, of the age-old "Irish Question"'. He concluded,

> Mr. Heath's assertion that what is happening in Northern Ireland is no concern of mine is not acceptable. The division of Ireland has never been, and is not now, acceptable to the great majority of the Irish people who were not consulted in the matter when that division was made fifty years ago… I remain convinced that the time has arrived for all those who can contribute to a peaceful solution of current problems in Northern Ireland to come together to discuss constructively how this can be achieved.[13]

On 23 August the taoiseach met elected leaders of the Northern Ireland opposition. A statement after the meeting said it had been agreed that all should work towards the objective of obtaining equality of treatment for everyone in Northern Ireland and that this objective should be pursued by non-violent political means. However, 'in stating this immediate objective there is no departure from the intention of the great majority of Irish people to achieve the unification of Ireland'.[14]

The exchanges between Heath and Lynch had raised the temperature in Anglo-Irish relations very considerably. However, the *coup de telégramme* produced its intended effect. A short time later Heath invited Lynch to meet him at Chequers. The meeting took place on 6 and 7 September just over two weeks after the angry exchanges of 20 August.

The brief prepared for the taoiseach before the meeting is couched in quite tough and trenchant terms.[15] I would have expected that such a document would have been prepared by Eamonn Gallagher but I am inclined now to doubt very strongly that this was the case here. The document was certainly not written with the clarity I would expect from Eamonn. Under the heading 'Breakdown Points', it lists three specific issues on which the taoiseach can 'break'—which is to say walk out of the talks. One was a continuing insistence by Heath 'that the IRA is the problem' (presumably what was meant here was 'the sole problem'). The second a refusal by Heath 'to give credence to the Taoiseach's main speech about the final inviolability of the present system of government in the North'. (I presume that the intention here was to refer to the possibility that Heath would insist that the existing system of devolved government at Stormont could not be changed). And the third a refusal by the (British) government to release John Hume, Ivan Cooper and others if they were jailed as a result of a court case that was to take place a few days later. The briefing note adds that there 'would probably be a number of other points… at which Mr. Lynch can close the meeting'; and it ends with a rather extraordinary conclusion:

> The main point to be kept in mind at all times is that Mr. Heath is in considerable difficulty and that a walk out by the Taoiseach on any ground that may prove to be reasonable, whatever the consequences in the short term might be, will distroy [sic] Mr. Heath in due time.

Another paper in the taoiseach's brief for the meeting was entitled 'What the Taoiseach should ask for'. It lists three points at the outset. I quote them here in full because, in contrast to the oddity of the other document I have just mentioned, they seem to me to reflect reasonably well the taoiseach's general policy approach at that time.

(1) The Unionist monopoly of power must disappear. This implies a form of government or administration which will enable consensus to be reached across a central band of opinion from moderate unionism to moderate non-unionism.

(2) The British government should indicate publicly that it is in favour of Irish reunification by agreement.

(3) An all-Ireland Council should be set up which would work towards bringing the two parts of Ireland into harmony. This Council might include an advisory role for the British government but should, in principle, be bilateral as between Dublin and Belfast while perhaps bringing in London at technical levels where necessary.[16]

Points 1 and 3 here can be seen as a first outline of principles that were to be developed more substantially under a new Irish government two years later and worked out further in negotiation with the British government and three Northern Ireland parties—Unionist, Alliance and SDLP—at the Sunningdale conference in December 1973. I will suggest in later chapters that even though Sunningdale failed, these two principles remained relevant in all subsequent efforts to resolve the Northern Ireland problem up to and including the Good Friday Agreement of 1998. Point 2 was not one that Heath, or his successors, would be prepared to accept—even though there was a more open tone to British statements in later years, no British government, then or later, was prepared to become an open 'persuader for Irish unity', as the phrase had it.

At the Chequers talks on 6 and 7 September 1971, Lynch was accompanied by the Irish ambassador in London, Donal O'Sullivan, while Heath had with him the secretary of the Cabinet, Sir Burke Trend.[17] The foreign secretary, Sir Alec Douglas-Home, and the home secretary, Reginald Maudling, joined the party for lunch. After the acrimonious public exchanges across the Irish Sea little more than a fortnight previously it was to be expected that the atmosphere, in the opening stages of the meeting at least, would be frigid.[18] But—even taking account of Ambassador O'Sullivan's judiciously bland tone in his lengthy report of 9 September on the meeting—this does not appear to have been the case.[19] In the latter stages of the two-day meeting, however, that is on the afternoon of 7 September, there were signs that the acrimony of a few weeks before had not entirely dissipated. Lynch expressed considerable disappointment that so little that he could present at home as a positive outcome seemed to be emerging from the talks. He declined to endorse a proposal for talks between the Northern Ireland parties chaired by Reginald Maudling, the home secretary. Heath in turn became irritated at this response. Nevertheless, Heath's willingness to discuss all aspects of the Northern Ireland issues, expressed several times in the opening stages, seems to me now, in retrospect, to mark an important turning point in the Anglo-Irish relationship.

This was most evident in the early stages of the meeting when, according to the ambassador's report, Heath told Lynch that the

> Taoiseach and he should feel free to go over the whole ground on the Northern problem. [He] was anxious that the talks should take place now rather than in October as the situation in the North had become very much graver…Nothing was to be regarded as excluded from the scope of the discussion but what would be said to the press later was a matter for the two of them.

On the face of it this was a remarkable change. Less than three weeks on from his categorical public refusal on 17 August to accept that 'anyone outside the United Kingdom' could participate in meetings on Northern Ireland, Heath was now saying that he wanted 'to go over the whole ground on the Northern problem' with Lynch: nothing was 'to be regarded as excluded'. How is the change to be accounted for?

In part, I suggest, it shows that, in resorting to a standard British formulaic response to Lynch's public and deliberately discourteous telegram in mid-August, Heath had succumbed to a flash of anger. Now, however, he was beginning to apply his mind seriously to the Northern Ireland issue and perhaps also beginning to accept the idea of an 'Irish Dimension'—a term he would not have used at the time but which became current later following its use in the Green Paper of 1972. There was also, no doubt, a pragmatic acceptance that he ought to talk to another head of government who, like him, was engaged in negotiating for membership of the EEC. Furthermore, Heath was well aware that Lynch had faced down and sacked hardliners from his government little more than a year before. Even if he thought the demands of the Irish government excessive, he may have understood that Lynch was as reasonable in his approach to Northern Ireland as any Irish leader at the time could be expected to be—and certainly better than any likely alternative. Indeed one of the briefing notes prepared for Heath said so explicitly: 'Mr Lynch…remains the best Irish Prime Minister in sight.'[20]

Over the two days of talks, Lynch dwelt on the fact that Northern Ireland was an artificially created territory that would always have a unionist majority. He spoke again about a possible reformulation of the British guarantee which he had called for in his Garden of Remembrance speech of 11 July. He acknowledged that, initially, the introduction of the British army on the streets had had a calming effect, and that reform had seemed to be effective but, lately, he said, it was more a matter of form than of substance. Internment was wrong, one-sided and badly handled; and he expressed concern about the number of guns in unionist hands. The IRA drew on popular support because the minority looked to them for protection. If that could be ended it would help eliminate the bombing. The elected representatives of the minority had now withdrawn from Stormont and they were determined not go back unless three conditions were met: (1) Release of all internees and prosecution of any who could be charged; (2) Establishment of a commission to administer the area; and (3) A quadripartite meeting involving representatives of the British and Irish governments, Brian Faulkner as leader of the Unionists, and representatives of the parliamentary opposition in Northern Ireland.

Heath's tone over the course of the lengthy discussions suggests that he may have come some way towards accepting Lynch's argument about the monopoly of power by the Unionists. He wanted to give the minority full assurance about their rights but 'in a democratic way'. He acknowledged their right to advocate the reunifica-tion of Ireland but not by violent means.

Towards the end of the meeting, according to the ambassador's note, Heath raised the possibility of a tripartite meeting between himself, the taoiseach and Brian Faulkner, 'but made it clear that he would not want to go to Mr. Faulkner on this if the Taoiseach were not satisfied about a meeting.' Lynch said that 'he would not favour a move on these lines.' Faulkner, he said, was on record as not favouring such talks. Faulkner, he added, unlike Heath and Lynch himself, was not the head of a sovereign government and tripartite talks would give him status. Lynch, in turn, then threw out the idea of bilateral talks in which Heath would have Faulkner with him, while he, Lynch, would be accompanied by a represent-ative of the Northern minority. Heath's response was that 'this would be extremely difficult'.

No formal statement was issued at the end of the meeting.

In the days following Lynch's return to Dublin there was some confusion about whether or not Heath had offered further tripart-ite talks. 'Downing Street sources' said that he had, while the taoiseach's view, according to press reports, was that no such offer was made and that in any case 'Mr. Faulkner had repeatedly said he was not interested in such talks.' Lynch himself seems to have been doubtful about the idea. However, the issue was eventually clari-fied. Heath invited Lynch to another meeting later that month at which the Northern Ireland prime minister, Brian Faulkner, would also be present and the taoiseach accepted.

Anthony Craig sees this episode as 'a trick of political oppor-tunism' and 'a subtle masterstroke by Heath', which played on 'Lynch's image outside Fianna Fáil as "Honest Jack"'; he says that 'it brought Jack Lynch into talks with Faulkner without the SDLP'; and he adds that '[f]or Lynch, the opportunity to talk to Heath and Faulkner without the SDLP was not ideal, but would not harm his reputation as a statesman.' He also mentions Eamonn Gallagher's reflection in an interview some 37 years later that 'a tripartite meet-ing was still better for the Republic's long-term interests than a series of summits exclusively between Heath and Faulkner.'[21]

Be that as it may, it was agreed that a tripartite meeting between Heath, Lynch and Faulkner should take place at the end of September. All in all, Lynch was entitled to feel that the missile which, on Gallagher's advice, he had directed at the Heath-Faulkner talks in mid-August, had been well aimed.

NOTES

[1] TNA, Prime Minister's Office Files (hereafter cited as PREM) 15/611. William Armstrong, Treasury Permanent Secretary, became head of the Home civil service in 1968; Burke Trend was the Cabinet secretary; Robert Armstrong, who wrote the minutes, was Heath's principal private secretary and, later, Cabinet secretary; and Lord Victor Rothschild, variously described as scientist, wartime hero and head of the British branch of the banking family, was director of Heath's think tank—the Central Policy Review Staff. The 'Lord O'Neill' referred to was Terence O'Neill, who resigned as Northern Ireland prime minister on 28 April 1969. Philip Zeigler, in *Edward Heath: the authorised biography* (London, 2010), mentions the comment about a united Ireland briefly but in a context (p. 309) that could imply that the meeting took place in 1972 during planning for direct rule, though a footnote does mention '19/4/71'.

[2] Lynch, *Speeches and statements*, 60–6.

[3] Keogh, *Jack Lynch*, 302–3.

[4] 'The colony' in Frank Ormsby (ed.), *The collected poems of John Hewitt* (Belfast, 1991), 76–9.

[5] Bew and Gillespie, *Northern Ireland*, 37. See also Feeney, *A short history of the Troubles*, 37.

[6] Keogh, *Jack Lynch*, 306.

[7] Lynch, *Speeches and statements*, 73.

[8] Lynch, *Speeches and statements*, 74–6.

[9] In his memoir *Dublin from Downing Street* (Dublin, 1978), Sir John Peck, who was British ambassador in Dublin at the time, expresses puzzlement about this. He says (p. 131), 'But for reasons we could not fathom his telegram was not sent through the Department of Foreign Affairs and the Irish embassy in London but as an ordinary telegram through the Irish and English postal services.' In his biography of Lynch, Keogh writes that 'For a reason yet to be explained, this telegram was sent by the normal route and did not get to Heath until after Faulkner had left for Belfast. Lynch made the text public' (Keogh, *Jack Lynch*, 314). I can confirm that Eamonn Gallagher told me and some others at the time that the decision to handle the message in this unusual way—timing, channel and immediate publication—was taken deliberately for tactical reasons.

[10] Lynch, *Speeches and statements*, 77–8.

[11] Keogh, *Jack Lynch*, 314, quoting from Peck, *Dublin from Downing Street*, 130–1.

[12] Lynch, *Speeches and statements*, 78–9.

[13] Lynch, *Speeches and statements*, 79–81.

[14] Lynch, *Speeches and statements*, 82.

[15] NAI DFA 2003/17/30, part 1

[16] NAI DFA 2003/17/30, part 1.

[17] Robert Armstrong, Heath's principal private secretary (later Lord Armstrong of Ilminister) and Sir John Peck, the British ambassador in Dublin, joined the group for coffee at the start but do not appear to have been present for the more formal meeting that followed.

[18] Heath's briefing note observed that 'It would do Mr. Lynch no harm were it to be reported that he had contended vigorously with the Prime Minister'. TNA, Cabinet Office Files (CAB) 133 407.

[19] Ambassador O'Sullivan's report is on NAI DFA 2007/58/36. The British record is on TNA CAB 133 407.

[20] TNA CAB 133 407.

[21] Craig, *Crisis of confidence*, 102.

CHAPTER 6

Chequers II

The second British-Irish summit within a month duly took place at Chequers on 27 and 28 September 1971. In a briefing note before the meeting Eamonn Gallagher advised the taoiseach that it would be enough to look for 'a single step' towards Irish unity from this meeting:

> So far as the question of Irish unity goes the Taoiseach is bound to raise it as a future eventuality. It is consistent with his general policy however to get there step by step. All that he needs from Chequers II, therefore, is a single step. Perhaps this could be encompassed through the creation of an Economic and Social Council of Ireland designed to harmonise the economic and social conditions of the country North and South. Possibly such a Council could be sub-parliamentary in the initial stages. This could be made to be palatable more easily than could a Parliamentary Council. It seems to me out of the question that a Parliamentary Council could be given any real functions—apart altogether from the question of how it could be formed. A sub-parliamentary Council,

on the other hand, could be more easily formed, could have real functions and stand some chance of being acceptable to the Northern majority.

The taoiseach, the note said, should also raise 'the need to provide bi-polar structures in the north designed to respond to the bi-polar nature of the Northern community'—in effect some form of 'power-sharing'. He should emphasise this since it was an issue where the British government could be 'pushed' and Faulkner 'would have to yield considerably'.[1]

Neither of the two points that Gallagher's note suggested the taoiseach might raise was wholly new.

The concept of a sharing of power in Northern Ireland had been advocated by John Cole, Deputy Editor of the *Guardian* in 1969, and discussed at some length by Dr John Whyte in a pamphlet published by the New Ulster Movement in June 1971.[2] The taoiseach himself had told the Dáil on 12 August 1971 that 'as an immediate objective of political action, the Stormont government should be replaced by an administration in which power and decision-making will be equally shared between unionist and non-unionist'.[3]

The second idea—the creation of some kind of structured link to harmonise economic and social conditions between north and south—harked back, though in a limited way, to the Council of Ireland envisaged in the Government of Ireland Act 1920. I will look back in more detail in Chapter 11 at what was envisaged at that time and also why such a Council was never established. The former home secretary, Jim Callaghan, who was now in opposition, had again raised the idea of a Council in a speech in the House of Commons shortly before the meeting I refer to here. However, the Irish government was cautious in its approach to the idea at that stage, although as I noted in the previous chapter, the idea of an all-Ireland Council with a harmonising role had been included in the taoiseach's brief as one of three points which, the brief suggested, he might look for at his Chequers meeting with Heath on 6–7 September 1971. Lynch did not pursue the point at the meeting. Indeed he had told the Dáil a few weeks previously that the kind of all-Ireland Council that Callaghan had suggested, 'without any real powers or known or overt functions', would not last long. But, he added, 'that is not to say that the idea of a Council of Ireland and other ideas expressed here and elsewhere should not be re-examined.' He noted that he himself had floated the idea of an economic council some weeks before. 'It may be that giving representatives both North and South the opportunity of working together in a formal way would expand the scope of their functions and further bring about efforts to reconcile views North and South'.[4]

Lynch's cautious approach to the idea of some kind of Council of Ireland may well reflect the advice Eamonn Gallagher was giving to him at this stage. I am not sure that the reference to 'an All-Ireland Council' in Lynch's briefing note for the Chequers Summit of 6 September came from Gallagher but it is true that, now, in his briefing note for this second Chequers meeting, Gallagher was now suggesting a 'sub-parliamentary' economic and social council might be a possibility. However, he saw the latter, not as part of a long-term settlement of the Northern Ireland problem but primarily as something that the taoiseach would be able to point to after the meeting as a step towards Irish unity. I do not believe that Eamonn would have been particularly enthusiastic about the kind of substantial Council of Ireland with executive functions which the Irish government began to plan for in the latter part of 1972 in response to the recognition of the 'Irish Dimension' in the British Green Paper. By then, however, Eamonn's influence as adviser to Lynch had already waned, and at about that time he moved on from his role in relation to Northern Ireland issues and was promoted to become head of the EEC division in Foreign Affairs. (I will deal with his views in more detail in Chapter 9.)

Gallagher's present briefing document concluded on a fairly sobering note.

> I am satisfied that the Taoiseach is entering into a most difficult political period. It could be, with a great deal of luck and skill, a fruitful period but only if it is understood that unity is a long way off. The condition of the North is treacherous at present; I consider that those who believe that unity can result from further violence are politically insane.[5]

The meetings at Chequers—'Chequers II' as we called it at the time—lasted for two days. Heath and Lynch held bilateral discussions on both mornings. Faulkner joined the talks only after midday on both days. This was, presumably, a face-saving concession to the concern that Lynch had expressed at the meeting on 6 September about the difference in status between his position as head of a sovereign government and that of Faulkner as head of 'a regional administration'. However, it can be seen now that this apparent consideration by Heath for Lynch's wishes was balanced by the fact that he held a private meeting with Faulkner at Chequers, at 9.45 p.m. the night before. At that meeting Heath had with him the home secretary, Reginald Maudling, and the defence secretary, Lord Carrington, as well as the Cabinet secretary, Sir Burke Trend. Faulkner was accompanied by the Northern Ireland Cabinet secretary, Sir Harold Black. The meeting lasted an hour and 45 minutes. Heath held another separate meeting, lasting half an hour, with Faulkner on the afternoon of the second day of the talks after Lynch had left. I doubt if Lynch and his officials knew at the time that his own meetings with Heath were 'book-ended' by private meetings, before and afterwards, between Heath and Faulkner.

The way in which Heath opened the discussion when he met Faulkner separately on Sunday night, 26 September, could suggest indeed that his purpose was to collude with Faulkner about the handling of the meeting with Lynch on the following morning. He proposed that they 'run over the main points…of current concern…including civil disobedience, security and the problem of persuading Mr. Lynch to get the opposition back to Stormont'. He then went on:

> It was clear that Mr. Lynch, in originally rejecting the invitation to tripartite discussions, had misjudged the situation; and it was significant that he had subsequently had to back-pedal. By agreeing to come to Chequers, he had implicitly accorded to Mr. Faulkner the status of Prime Minister which he had previously denied him; and the fact that the Social Democratic and Labour Party (SDLP) had rejected him as their spokesman had made it impossible for him to maintain this claim also,

despite the fact that he had sought to sustain it during his earlier visit to Chequers. Against this background it was not impossible that the tripartite meeting could effect a new breakthrough...[i]t would be necessary to make a determined effort on the following day to get Mr. Lynch to endorse and support the discussions which were now proceeding under the Home Secretary's chairmanship.[6]

However, in the course of the private talks, Heath disagreed with Faulkner on a number of points and sometimes sharply rebutted something Faulkner had just said. For example, when Faulkner said that 'there were plenty of Catholics in the UDR', Heath said that 'on the contrary the ratio of Catholics to Protestants was steadily dropping'; when Faulkner said that 'the introduction of any minority representative into the Northern Ireland government itself would be liable to be regarded as an unacceptable constitutional innovation', Heath said that 'he could not necessarily accept this'; and when Faulkner suggested that the trade unions 'might oppose the introduction of a Catholic as a sectarian move', Heath's response was blunt:

> If the introduction of a Catholic would be regarded as a sectarian move, that was because we were dealing with a sectarian problem. The Unionist Party itself was a sectarian party.

Many of the concerns raised by Faulkner related to the arrangements for guarding police stations; the need, as he saw it, to supply automatic weapons to the RUC, and the advantages of allowing the 'local expansion of the UDR'. In response to Faulkner's request that he define the objectives of the tripartite meeting on the following day, Heath said that he felt that

> they must be prepared to discuss anything and everything without prejudice; and they must do all they could to involve the other parties in Ulster in the discussion of constitutional developments. For that

reason he and Mr. Faulkner must press Mr. Lynch very hard to use his influence with the opposition… He and Mr. Faulkner must therefore try to get Mr. Lynch to say what he regarded as a fair deal for the minority. His suggested fifty/fifty commission was wholly undemocratic: and this had been made clear to him during his last visit to Chequers. But he must be induced to say what he would regard as a reasonable solution within the basic framework of the Northern Ireland Constitution. It might also be useful to discuss with him the relationship between the two parts of Ireland and the possible scope for a bipartite or tripartite body to discuss all-Ireland topics, which would probably have to be limited to economic issues at the outset but could subsequently be enlarged if all the parties agreed.

Faulkner 'concurred'—on condition that the body would consist of representatives of governments, not parliaments, 'since on the latter hypothesis the Republicans would have a majority' and that it would be advisory, and not executive.

While it would not do to exaggerate the degree of new thinking on Heath's part at this early stage, it seems to me that this outline of his approach to the talks with Lynch on the following day is interesting—even remarkable—when contrasted with his angry, and public, refusal just over a month previously to accept a role for 'anyone outside the United Kingdom' in relation to Northern Ireland. He will now want Lynch to say 'what he would regard as a reasonable solution' (still, of course, 'within the basic framework of the Northern Ireland Constitution'); he will want the taoiseach to use his influence to help get the opposition—that is to say the SDLP—back to Stormont; and he is open to the idea of a 'bipartite' (north-south) or 'tripartite' (north, south and UK) body which would deal with economic issues at first but which might subsequently be 'enlarged' to other issues. A long way indeed from the rebuff to Hillery by British Labour ministers in 1969.[7]

Faulkner's responses to what Heath had said about 'the permanence of the Protestant majority at Stormont' are also of interest.

His starting point, which, as I mentioned above, Heath did not accept, was that 'the introduction of any minority representative into the Northern Ireland government itself would be liable to be regarded as an unacceptable constitutional innovation.' In other exchanges Faulkner applied the term 'republican' very broadly to anyone who favoured Irish unity—as, for example, when he referred to 'Republicans such as Nationalists or the SDLP'; and he seemed to rule out as possible participants in government even those who, while advocating Irish unity, accepted that it could be achieved only with majority consent:

> It would, of course, be out of the question to have Republican Catholics in the same Cabinet as Unionists. But a non-Unionist Catholic might be a possibility—although he had not consulted his colleagues on this point. One thing about which he was quite clear was that there was no room for Mr. Hume or Mr. Fitt; he would rather go than contemplate that possibility…He must also make it clear that it would not be possible to include in the Cabinet individuals who professed to respect the principle that there could be no change in the status of Northern Ireland until the majority so wished but nevertheless felt free to advocate publicly a 32 County government.

The meeting concluded at 11.30 p.m. with a brief exchange about the Orange Order. Faulkner said it was only 'a minor element' which his party could do without; and in an oddly-phrased and rather defensive attempt at vindication he added that '[t]here was nothing in the terms of the party's constitution which required it to be a sectarian party.'

The meeting between the prime minister and the taoiseach began at 10.45 a.m. on the following [Monday] morning. Heath was accompanied throughout by the Cabinet secretary, Sir Burke Trend and, for part of the time, by his principal private secretary, Robert Armstrong.[8] Lynch had with him the Irish ambassador, Donal O'Sullivan, while two advisers, Sean Ronan[9] and Eamonn Gallagher, were available for consultation. Brian Faulkner, together with Sir Harold Black, the Northern Ireland Cabinet secretary, joined the discussions at noon. On the Irish side a detailed note of the discussions in which the taoiseach participated was prepared by Ambassador O'Sullivan two days later.[10] The British record covers Heath's two bilateral meetings with Faulkner and his bilateral meetings with the taoiseach as well as the tripartite meetings between Heath, Lynch and Faulkner.[11]

The summary that follows is a composite in that I draw as appropriate on both the Irish and the British accounts of the discussions, which are now available in the respective archives.

It would appear from both accounts that there was no longer any of the acrimony between Heath and Lynch that had characterised their public exchanges in mid-August: that would seem to have been dispelled at their earlier bilateral meeting on 6 September. Their talks at this second meeting in three weeks, and indeed the three-way discussion when Faulkner joined them at noon, were not exactly cordial, and there was quite substantial disagreement at times, especially in the closing stages, but the talks could at least be described as amicable in the sense that all three of the main participants come across as apparently reasonable people obliged, to their regret, to disagree on some fundamental issues.

A particular theme of the talks on Heath's side was his persistent attempt to get Lynch to persuade the SDLP to take part in preliminary talks which the home secretary, Reginald Maudling, was trying to get under way at the time. The background to this is that some months earlier, John Hume had demanded an impartial enquiry into the shooting dead by the British army of two men in Derry. When this was not forthcoming, the SDLP decided on 16 July to withdraw from the Stormont parliament. They called for a campaign of civil disobedience; and they set up what they called 'An Assembly of the Northern Irish People'. This did not turn out to be a very successful initiative: the 'Assembly' was to meet for the first time in Dungiven Castle, Co. Derry on 26 October 1971 and it met only twice in all. At the time of the talks in Chequers, however, the SDLP was carrying its withdrawal to the extent of refusing flatly to come to the talks proposed by Maudling. The introduction of internment some seven weeks previously, the botched way in which it had been handled, and the deaths and displacements that followed, would have made it very difficult politically for them to do so.

Heath opened the bilateral discussion with Lynch on Monday morning, 27 September, by speaking about the Maudling talks proposal and the refusal of the SDLP to participate. The problem, he said, was how to get them 'off the hook'. In the meantime Faulkner was working on proposals in a Green Paper to give the minority a greater voice. The British government had not yet taken a position on these proposals. Heath suggested that in their discussions he and Lynch should concentrate on matters of disagreement. He saw two stages—first, get the minority representatives into the Maudling talks; and second, discuss with them the changes to be made in Northern Ireland. As to internment, an advisory appeals system was now in place and the International Red Cross and a parliamentary delegation from Westminster had been invited to inspect the detention centre.

The taoiseach said his position remained unchanged—reunification must remain a central objective of policy. He hoped that, without prejudice to that ultimate objective, their discussions could find some way forward, not least by way of his original initiative for closer economic cooperation between north and south. He had given the SDLP a general account of his discussions with Heath earlier in the month. They remained adamant on ending internment and they thought the functions of the proposed Advisory Committee, which was to scrutinise individual cases, were too limited. Could it, he asked, be given the right to decide? Lynch said he wanted to be helpful. However, he was not in a position to speak for the representatives of the minority community in the north—they had made it plain that he was not their spokesman—and he could seek to be helpful only in a way that would be acceptable to them. A continuation of permanent unionist government in the north would certainly not be acceptable to the minority. What was urgently needed was a re-structuring of Stormont that would give minority representatives a position in decision-making and in power, as of right, and not merely by grace and favour. He stressed this matter again at several points in the discussion. He also saw internment as an important stumbling block. He wondered if it might be possible instead to have Special Courts of the type that existed in the south?

Much of the bilateral talks on each of the two mornings turned on Heath's continuing effort to have Lynch accept the need to persuade minority representatives, as a first step, to take part in the exploratory talks that Maudling was organising. Lynch was not prepared to do so and he was unwilling to have that emerge as the main outcome of their present meeting. The minority representatives, that is the SDLP, were, he said, 'very adamant in their stance.' He could not see them departing from it. They must be seen to be effective and unless their position could be strengthened there was a risk that even moderate people in the north would begin to look more to the IRA.

Two of Lynch's interventions are of some particular interest in retrospect, in that, though none of the participants could have known this at the time, they seem now faintly to foreshadow some aspects of the settlement that was eventually to be reached many years later. One came after Lynch had commented that Paisley's influence had been growing, even among moderates. Heath said that 'Paisley had been putting around the idea that he could do a deal with Catholics'. Lynch responded that 'if Mr. Paisley were Prime Minister and offered Catholics seats in government, they might accept.' The other came towards the close of the bilateral meeting, just before Brian Faulkner joined the discussion. It also led on to a more ominous exchange about the possibility of civil war. According to the British record, following a reference to the possibility of proportional representation,

> *Mr. Lynch* suggested that there might be a case for a more radical approach—e.g. the Prime Minister from the majority party, the Deputy Prime Minister from the minority. There was also the possibility of some form of all-Ireland Council to promote co-operation between the Republic and Northern Ireland. All sorts of ideas could be put forward and discussed. But already there was talk of civil war if the situation did not improve. He hoped very much that it would not

come to this; but he was disturbed to be told privately by the Protestant clergy that they were fast losing control over their own flock.

The prime minister said all these thoughts should be pursued. But, if law and order broke down in the North, the South would be involved sooner or later.

Mr. Lynch agreed. But the South had had one civil war and did not want another.

Ambassador O'Sullivan's account of the exchange on civil war is more explicit and perhaps more ominous.

The Taoiseach [said]…[t]here is talk of the imminence of civil war and, if there is no improvement in the situation this could happen. Some of the Protestant clergy in the North are losing influence over their flocks and are fearful of the consequences. A group of these clergymen came to see him recently but they did not want it known that they met him. Mr. Heath said that if the worst were to happen in the North, the trouble could probably not be confined within the area. He realised that if there were to be a massacre of the minority, it would be very difficult for the Taoiseach to stand by. The Taoiseach said that he does not in any circumstances want to see Ireland involved in another civil war. Some of the effects of the last one still remain.

Faulkner, together with the Northern Ireland Cabinet secretary, Sir Harold Black, joined the talks at noon.

Heath, welcoming both the other participants, said that public opinion had clearly endorsed the tripartite meeting. 'It was no small thing that the three Prime Ministers could meet and seek practical steps to relieve the tension and promote some forward move…they should all speak with complete frankness'. There was, he said, a good deal of common ground. They were all agreed in opposing the use of violence for political ends. 'Both Ireland and Britain are affected by the violence in the North'.

The taoiseach agreed. However, the existence of the IRA was a by-product of the situation in the north. The settlement of 50 years before had polarised the two communities in the area. Even with reforms, the method of government there was not working and the two communities were now further apart. Internment had been a grave mistake. What was urgently needed was a change in Stormont that would allow minority representatives to participate as of right in decision-making and in power. He was not their spokesman but he had seen them two days before and they had confirmed that their stand on internment had not changed.

> He himself was under some political pressure. Even by undertaking to meet Mr. Faulkner he was thought to have gone too far in acquiescing in the existence of Stormont. But continuing violence created so terrible a prospect in human terms and so grave a threat to political stability that he felt he must do anything he could to ease the tension. But for this there must be some change at Stormont.

Brian Faulkner spoke at length, then and again on the following day, about his plans for reform. He could not agree that there was an urgent need for constitutional change but he was considering such reforms as election by proportional representation, the setting up of strong Parliamentary Committees, two of which would be chaired by minority representatives, a broadening of the Senate and the House of Commons, and giving the chairpersons of certain local authorities seats in the Senate. Involvement of the SDLP in the Cabinet would, however, be out of the question—they differed from the majority on fundamentals; they did not represent the majority of Catholic opinion; they had said that they would not serve in the same Cabinet as unionists; and if it were to happen, then people like Paisley and Craig, who were also in opposition, would seek to be included. Heath said he understood Faulkner's position on this point—it would be very difficult to include the

SDLP in the administration since their objective is to bring it down. Heath did however make a distinction:

> There must surely be people who, while in principle favouring a united Ireland, would say that, so long as the majority preferred to remain in the United Kingdom, they were prepared to work the system. That was a different position from those who believed in a united Ireland and were not prepared to work the existing system even though a majority still favoured the union. He did not see how people of the latter kind could participate in government in Northern Ireland.

In a discussion on security issues Lynch again criticised the handling of internment—the longer it lasted the worse the situation would become. He rejected Faulkner's claims that substantial amounts of gelignite from the south were being used to make bombs in Northern Ireland; and he was not prepared to commit himself to some kind of tripartite arrangement to consider border security and traffic in arms and explosives. In his turn, he pressed Faulkner on the large number of gun licences in the north—he asked that licences be withdrawn and issued, where necessary, on a more limited and careful basis.

When the bilateral talks resumed on the morning of the second day, Heath offered Lynch a draft press statement prepared overnight by his advisers.[12] At this point the discussion became sharper. Lynch said the draft was unacceptable. According to the British record, he went on:

> It reflected no more than the offers of further constitutional change which Mr. Faulkner had suggested... [It] assumed that the minority were to remain excluded from effective participation in the government of Northern Ireland; and this would not be acceptable to the elected representatives of the minority community. Indeed, it would positively weaken their position; and by giving further advantage to the IRA, it would bring the prospect of civil war significantly nearer.

He referred to other problems and objections. Internment remained a stumbling block, as did allegations of brutality by the troops. He was convinced that the evidence would sustain a charge of infringement of the European Convention on Human Rights. He had done all he could to control access to gelignite—there was no point in establishing a tripartite mechanism on this (as proposed in the British draft statement) though UN observers on the border might be useful if both governments agreed. The draft statement was slanted—not deliberately, but insofar as it endorsed the position of the Unionist government. If nothing better than this was to emerge from their meeting, 'he must be free to say publicly that no acceptable basis for progress had yet been found, although of course he would go on trying to find one.'

Ambassador O'Sullivan's report brings out some other points. It notes that Lynch objected to phrases in the draft which, he said, put Stormont on a par with the two sovereign governments and also suggested that Northern Ireland was a democracy; he could not accept a paragraph that would appear to commit him to the Maudling proposals—he could not see them getting anywhere; and he thought it premature to think of setting up an Economic Council of Ireland until there was satisfactory progress on other matters including the re-structuring of Stormont. Most of the reforms, he said, were more a formality than a reality. Their talks on the previous day had shown that Faulkner was intent on maintaining and strengthening Unionist rule. His proposals would isolate the minority further and if they went ahead they could drive the area closer to civil war.

Heath did not agree with Lynch's view that Faulkner's proposals were designed to strengthen the Unionist government. He repeated that it would be very difficult to have in government people who thought the area should not exist.

> Mr. Fitt had already said publicly that he would not enter that Government unless it were accepted that he was there as of right. But how could you have a compulsory coalition? How could you have a system in which people said that they would not accept an invitation from the Prime Minister to serve in his Government but insisted

on being there as of right, regardless of their compatibil-
ity with the rest of the Government?

Lynch responded that it was a fact that the minority representatives
were not prepared to talk at that point and he pressed for 'some
dismantling' of the roadblock of internment. The time might come
when Faulkner and the British government might have to talk to
the IRA instead of to the Irish government. The judgement of their
talks would be that they had achieved nothing—but he stressed
that in this he was concerned about peace and not about his own
political position.

After further exchanges, Lynch said he 'could not hold the
ground which he had been holding if he had to subscribe to this
draft statement.' Heath 'asked him what, in that case, he could
accept'. Lynch suggested confining it essentially to saying that
they now understood each other's views better. He recalled that
he had had reservations about this tripartite meeting which the
discussions had not removed. After further exchanges he suggested an adjournment to allow him consult his advisers and
prepare a new draft statement. This revised draft was circulated
before the lunch, which was also attended by the home secretary, Reginald Maudling and the defence secretary, Lord
Carrington.

The meeting resumed after lunch. The Northern Ireland
prime minister, Brian Faulkner, joined the talks and the discussion turned to the new Irish draft for a communiqué, which
had been circulated before lunch. Faulkner said he was disappointed that 'it said so little'. He also regretted that there was
no reference to the tripartite working party on border security
and the control of gelignite which he had proposed. After some
further exchanges a few verbal changes were agreed.[13] It was
also agreed to include a passage from the original British draft
about further tripartite meetings, and also a final paragraph,
separate from the main text, about close communication
between the British and Irish prime ministers 'on all subjects
affecting the future of Anglo-Irish relations'. Then, as the
ambassador's report says somewhat laconically, '[t]he Taoiseach's
draft was otherwise regarded as acceptable'. The meeting

concluded after some further general discussion and the statement was duly issued.

In my view the text of the statement is important so I will quote it here in full.

> During the last two days we have discussed the situation in Northern Ireland in all its aspects. We have done so fully recognising that each of us remains committed to his publicly stated position on the constitutional status of Northern Ireland; and we have been concerned to see whether, without prejudice to those positions, we can find some agreed means of enabling all the people of Northern Ireland to live in the conditions of peace and stability which any democracy should ensure to its citizens without regard to their religious or political conviction.
>
> We are at one in condemning any form of violence as an instrument of political pressure; and it is our common purpose to seek to bring violence and internment and all other emergency measures to an end without delay.
>
> We also recognise that to bring violence quickly to an end and to resume economic, social and cultural progress means must be found to establish harmony and co-operation between the two communities in Northern Ireland. Our discussions in the last two days have helped to create an atmosphere of greater understanding between us and it is our hope that the process of political reconciliation may go forward to a successful outcome.
>
> We agree that our meeting has served a significant and useful purpose in present circumstances, and we believe that further such meetings may have a helpful part to play in the future.

Mr. Heath and Mr. Lynch agreed to keep in close communication with each other, personally, through their ministerial colleagues and at official level, as might be appropriate, on all subjects affecting the future of Anglo-Irish relations. In this respect the meeting between the two prime ministers scheduled for the autumn to discuss a range of subjects, including the Anglo-Irish Free Trade Area Agreement and the applications of both countries for membership of the European Communities, will be held on dates to be announced later.[14]

It is evident from Ambassador O'Sullivan's report in which he says that 'the Taoiseach's text was otherwise regarded as acceptable' that the joint communiqué issued at the end of the meeting was essentially drafted by the Irish side although in several paragraphs it does draw on the text of the initial British draft. This is also clear from the wording of the three texts—the initial British draft, the Irish draft and the final statement issued—which are reproduced in full in the British record.

I can confirm this from personal recollection. Sean Ronan, who, along with Eamonn Gallagher, had been the taoiseach's adviser at Chequers, told myself and one or two other Foreign Affairs colleagues about the meeting in the course of an informal discussion over coffee in Iveagh House next morning. Looking back on a short note that I scribbled for myself afterwards I see that Sean said that 'they [the British side] more or less left the drafting up to us'. He also mentioned several small textual changes that were made to the taoiseach's draft; and he added an interesting detail—apparently Heath disliked the French term 'communiqué' and preferred to use the English word 'statement'. He also said that the text could have included reference to a 'Council of Ireland'. Heath and Faulkner favoured this but Lynch rejected it. My note continues:

The view was that this could come as part of a package but not otherwise. The Council would have no real function…The general conclusion seems to be that the significance of Chequers is the acceptance of a role for

Jack Lynch a scant few weeks after Heath's rebuff to him. There is still however...speculation that maybe some significant things re internment etc. were agreed *sub rosa* and their significance will become clear in a few weeks.[15]

It may seem surprising at first sight that the taoiseach should have rejected the idea of a north-south body. His briefing document had proposed he should look for something of the kind, albeit as 'a sub-parliamentary body'; and in one of his interventions on the opening day of the Summit he had spoken of 'the possibility of some form of all-Ireland Council to promote cooperation between the Republic and Northern Ireland' (as mentioned above). Furthermore, as I mentioned at the start of this chapter, he had himself earlier floated the idea of an economic council and he had referred to the idea again when speaking in the Dáil on 6 August 1971. It is clear, however, that at the Chequers meeting he was not rejecting the concept of a Council as such. It was rather that he thought he would be open to criticism if such a body were announced in a statement in which he felt he had so little else to show as a successful outcome to the meeting. As the ambassador's note puts it, he thought it was 'premature...until such time as satisfactory progress has been made in other directions including the re-structuring of Stormont'. As to the cryptic reference in my note to other things that might have been agreed *sub rosa*, I don't think anything of the kind ever emerged.

As I mentioned earlier, Heath and Faulkner exchanged views at Chequers for a further half-hour after the Irish side had left. Some of their comments on the earlier discussions with Lynch present may be worth a brief mention here.

Heath said to Faulkner that internment 'was now a front-line issue at Westminster'. Whitehall and Stormont must keep in closer touch. When Maudling wondered 'what Mr. Lynch's terms for helping us really were', Faulkner's answer was 'the end of internment and something which would bring the opposition back to Stormont'. Heath did not think his terms were so specific. Lynch, he said, had been relatively helpful in regard to explosives and gelignite because he was 'very well aware of the danger to himself if the IRA took over.' Heath added, rather caustically:

> As regards the SDLP, however, he [Lynch] could not go further than saying that we must give them whatever they want. But if we were prepared to do that, we should not, of course, need Mr. Lynch himself!

Faulkner suspected that 'the SDLP were more basically Republican in their sympathies and objectives than they would like us to believe…What they really wanted was the end of Stormont.' When Heath suggested broadening the Stormont Cabinet, Faulkner's response was that he was considering whether, if he could find a suitable candidate, he might bring in a Catholic as a minister without portfolio.

At first sight, Lynch's two days of discussion at Chequers II might seem to an outsider to have achieved very little. Lynch had reservations from the outset about the format of the meeting, which he felt would give 'status' to Faulkner, who was not the head of a sovereign government; and even as the meeting on the second day was drawing to a close he must have felt that he was getting nowhere in pressing for a radical re-structuring of Stormont that would bring minority representatives into government and end the Unionist monopoly of power. Heath, for his part, could not achieve his aim of getting Lynch to support Maudling's efforts. He seemed to be just beginning to come to grips with the whole problem; and it is clear that his thinking had not yet evolved far enough to allow him to contemplate replacing the Unionist government at Stormont with an arrangement for structured power-sharing, a concept he was to accept and endorse later in the Sunningdale Communiqué of December 1973. Faulkner continued, if not to fight, at least to argue, for his corner, putting a good face where possible on the monolithic structure of government at Stormont and reluctantly conceding, where he had to, that it might be broadened, though only to a minimal degree.

Nevertheless, in my view these meetings over two days mark an important—I would even say a historic—point, even though neither side may have fully grasped that at the time. The importance lay not in what was agreed—that was minimal—but in the very fact that the taoiseach, whatever his initial reservations, had been involved in two full days of discussion of Northern Ireland, first with Heath, and then with Heath and Faulkner; and, especially, in what was said in the joint statement issued when the meetings concluded. I would argue that this episode has to be seen now, in retrospect, as the first explicit public acceptance by a British prime minister that, beyond facilitating cross-border security cooperation, the taoiseach and the Irish government had a part to play at the political level in relation to Northern Ireland. In that sense it was the first step on a new path—a path which, notwithstanding many vicissitudes and considerable turbulence at times, was to lead eventually through the Sunningdale conference of 1973, the Anglo-Irish Agreement of 1985 and the Downing Street Declaration of 1993, to the extraordinarily close cooperation between the taoiseach Bertie Ahern and prime minister Tony Blair that played a major part in bringing about the Good Friday Agreement of 1998.

If this seems to go too far, then I suggest that a comparison of the statement from the Chequers meeting with Dr Hillery's exchanges with the Labour government ministers, which I mentioned in Chapter 2, and Heath's own flat public refusal, in response to Lynch's egregious telegram of 20 August 1971, to accept that 'anyone outside the United Kingdom [could] participate in meetings designed to promote the political development of any part of the United Kingdom', will help to make the point.

It is true of course that, as I mentioned in Chapter 4, the then foreign secretary, Sir Alec Douglas-Home, a naturally courteous old-style Tory aristocrat of Scottish origin, was prepared to listen sympathetically to the minister for foreign affairs Dr Hillery, at several meetings in 1970–71. But this did not involve any change in the formal position of the British government. Now a British prime minister had discussed the Northern Ireland situation 'in all its aspects' with Faulkner and Lynch together, at several meetings, over two days; and he and Lynch had announced publicly that they had 'agreed to keep in close communication with each other…on all subjects affecting the future of Anglo-Irish relations'. By implication this had to include the issue of Northern Ireland. Furthermore, certain of the exchanges at the meeting could suggest that, though his thinking had not yet gone very far, Heath was already beginning to cast around for some new approach to the Northern Ireland question.

One of Heath's biographers recognises the importance of this change of attitude—he describes it as 'the first acknowledgement by a British government of an 'Irish Dimension to the Ulster problem'.[16] But curiously, Sir John Peck, the British ambassador in Dublin at the time—who was otherwise a perceptive and sympathetic observer—did not seem to do so. In his book written some seven years later, his comment on the two Chequers meetings Lynch attended that September was 'that it would be an abuse of the English language to describe the talks as negotiations', though, to be fair, he did find 'one glimmer of hope' in the agreement between Heath and Lynch in the final paragraph of the 27 September statement: 'to keep in close communication with each other'.[17]

The divergence of view about the meeting of 27–8 September, and the importance or otherwise of the statement issued when it ended, runs through other accounts of these events. Lynch's biographer, Dermot Keogh, sees the previous meeting of 6–7 September as a success but he passes quickly over the tripartite meeting in late September. In her 2007 book on Fianna Fáil, Catherine O'Donnell finds it 'not surprising that the statement issued on behalf of the three participants to the talks reflected the fact that little agreement was reached.'[18] In his account of Anglo-Irish relations in the early years of the Troubles, Anthony Craig says that '[p]redictably the tripartite meeting at Chequers a few weeks later between Heath, Lynch and Faulkner was not a success.' Lynch, he notes, pressed for an end to internment while Heath and Faulkner pressed the issue of the movement of arms and explosives across the border. 'Agreement was never really a possibility at the meeting as nothing had been put forward initially to discuss.'[19]

On the other hand, Sir Kenneth Bloomfield, who was deputy Cabinet secretary in Northern Ireland at the time, and who had a long and deep involvement in these issues over many years, takes what I consider a more perceptive view. He sees the very fact that such a meeting took place as important and, contrary to Craig, he attributes the initiative for the meeting to Lynch.[20]

The offer of a tripartite meeting, along lines earlier suggested by Lynch, showed a distinct and significant shift in the British attitude.

There was, Bloomfield says, no common ground on the border or on constitutional issues.

Nevertheless, the unprecedented tripartite meeting could be regarded as the first tacit recognition of the so-called 'Irish Dimension' acknowledged in the discussion paper of 1972.[21]

Since Bloomfield himself had some involvement in the drafting of that document—the Green Paper—and may perhaps even have coined the very phrase 'Irish Dimension', this seems to me to be a particularly significant comment from someone in a good position to judge. Garret FitzGerald, who was then in opposition, also took a more positive view—though he focused on the first of the two meetings between Heath and Lynch, that of 6–7 September rather than on the statement of 27–8 September. He thought that it 'marked a significant advance on the British side since it recognised the Irish government's legitimate interest in a situation threatening the security of both parts of the island.'[22]

I think both Garret FitzGerald and Ken Bloomfield are right in this; and now, in the longer perspective of history, we can see what those involved could not see at the time—the significance for the future of this first public acknowledgement by a British government that the Irish government had to have a role in resolving the problem of Northern Ireland beyond that of cross-border security cooperation.

NOTES

[1] NAI DFA 2003/17/30, part 1.
[2] I am grateful to Professor John Coakley for pointing out to me that both John Cole and John Whyte had argued earlier for some kind of sharing of power arrangements for Northern Ireland. Dr Whyte's pamphlet, *The reform of Stormont: a new Ulster movement*

publication, was accessed on 27 September 2016 at: http://cain.ulst.ac.uk/othelem/ organ/num/num71a.htm. John Cole's advocacy of something of the kind in the *Guardian* in 1969 is referred to in Brian M. Walker, *A political history of the two Irelands: from partition to peace* (UK, 2012), 124. Of course, the British government itself also had some experience, though limited success, in trying to handle divided societies in territories under British rule elsewhere. However, neither the way it dealt with Cyprus in the late 1950s and early 1960s, nor its handling of India in the 1930s and 1940s, provided a very good example of how to address the problem of Northern Ireland.

[3] Lynch, *Speeches and statements*, 76.

[4] Dáil statement of 6 August 1971. Lynch, *Speeches and statements*, 69.

[5] NAI DFA/2007/58/36.

[6] TNA PREM 15/487. Record of a discussion with the prime minister of Northern Ireland held at Chequers on Sunday, 26 September 1971, at 9.45 p.m.

[7] See Chapter 2.

[8] As Cabinet secretary himself more than a decade later, Robert Armstrong was to play a prominent part in Anglo-Irish relations, including negotiation of the 1985 Anglo-Irish Agreement.

[9] Assistant secretary, Department of Foreign Affairs.

[10] NAI TSCH 2003/13/7.

[11] TNA PREM 15/487.

[12] The text of this initial British draft statement is at Annex A on pages 34–5 of the British record. The Irish 'counter-draft' is Annex A on pages 37–8. The final text of the joint statement that was issued is Annex B on page 38. I think there is some confusion in Ambassador O'Sullivan's record of these texts. On page 31 of his report, he describes the initial British draft as 'Annex A'. On page 39 he says, 'The Agreed Communiqué is attached as Annex B'. However, there is only one annex to his report in the file (NAI 2003/13/7). It is identified on top in what I take to be his handwriting as 'Annex B'. This is actually the initial British draft and not the text of the statement as issued.

[13] It was agreed to reverse the order of the words 'violence' and 'internment' and to add the phrase 'and all other necessary measures'.

[14] British record (Annex B), 38; see also Lynch *Speeches and statements*, 84–5.

[15] Taken from a brief personal note I made, dated Wednesday, 29 September 1971.

[16] John Campbell, *Edward Heath: a biography* (London, 1993), 428.

[17] Peck, *Dublin from Downing Street*, 134.

[18] Catherine O'Donnell, *Fianna Fáil: Irish republicanism and the Northern Ireland Troubles, 1968–2005* (Dublin and Portland, Oregon, 2007), 37.

[19] Craig, *Crisis of confidence*, 99–104. Craig's view is that 'in a trick of political opportunism' Heath 'bounced' Lynch into the tripartite meeting of 27–8 September. After the meeting of 6–7 September Heath 'twisted the interpretation of what was discussed at the meeting (where Lynch had told Heath that tripartite talks without the SDLP were unacceptable) by releasing a statement that evening publicly offering a summit. This put Lynch in a tight position'. Once the offer had been made public Lynch could hardly refuse lest he be blamed for 'having stalled in its infancy, a potential political solution' (102).

[20] I am not sure he is correct in this.

[21] Bloomfield, *A tragedy of errors*, 136.

[22] FitzGerald, *All in a life*, 99.

CHAPTER 7

Bloody Sunday

In his public speeches and statements through 1971 and 1972, and in occasional briefings over lunch or dinner for groups of visiting journalists whom we brought over from time to time from London, the taoiseach continued to talk about issues such as the need for reform of abuses and an end to discrimination in Northern Ireland; his concern about the number of guns, licensed and otherwise, held in Northern Ireland; the fact that the Irish government were acting against the IRA in their own jurisdiction; and his hope for eventual unity in Ireland. From August 1971 onwards, on Gallagher's advice (which no doubt reflected also the thinking of John Hume), he began also to press the point that the type of parliamentary democracy based on the Westminster model that was established in Northern Ireland under the Government of Ireland Act 1920 was completely unsuited to a divided society. The case made for this at the time was broadly as follows.

At Westminster the basic political framework is accepted by all parties; the party that gains a majority at an election forms the government; and while it is in office the government of the day has a virtual monopoly of political power. A particular government may at times enjoy a long period in office but it is always open to effective challenge and when there is an election the contest at the polls is a real one. The opposition—even the smaller opposition parties—accept the way the system works. They are sometimes spoken of as 'the loyal opposition' because they are loyal to the fundamental framework—'the queen in parliament'; and though they are out of power for the moment the main opposition party know that there is always the possibility of a change of government at the next election.

In Northern Ireland, in contrast, the very existence of the polity to be governed was contested from the outset. And not only that: the 1920 Act, by determining the extent of the area, had also determined its political character and the proportions that the respective sections of its divided community were to bear to each other. The consequence was to leave an area split between a substantial minority who resented the settlement that made them a minority and looked to the day when they would form part of the majority in a united Ireland, and a newly established unionist majority who feared that this might happen eventually, and for that reason felt their position under constant threat. The politicisation of religious differences, and a belief that the minority were a threat to the whole settlement, ensured the cohesiveness of the unionist population. At every election the underlying issue on which voters felt they were voting was the existence or otherwise of the border that had made one community a majority and the other a minority in the area. The outcome was always predictable. Unionists were a majority of the population and the Unionist Party, which, for much of its history, did not welcome Catholics to membership, always formed the government—there had been no change in that for half a century. There was discrimination against the minority at local government level but Stormont elections were fair enough to allow the government at Stormont to claim, rightly, to be 'the constitutionally and democratically elected government'. The problem was that it always had been, and always would be, a Unionist government. That was not due to an abuse of the Westminster-style system of parliamentary democracy—it was rather an inevitable consequence of the way that system operated in a deeply divided society such as Northern Ireland.

There was a further consequence, the argument went, for the Unionist Party itself. Because it was seldom if ever subject to effective challenge at the polls it was unbeatable as a party. But its party leaders were not: in the 1960s and early 1970s when reform was imperative, each party leader in turn had to face a challenge from his own party's right wing. When the minority became active in airing their grievances, right-wing unionists, who saw this disaffection as subversive, were likely to demand sterner security measures—to restore normality as they saw it. There was no effective countervailing pressure from an opposition party to demands of this kind. So each Unionist Party leader faced a choice: either to meet the demands of his own party's more extreme wing or be displaced eventually by a successor who would do so. The result was that O'Neill was replaced by Chichester-Clark, who was replaced in turn by Brian Faulkner.

I cannot claim to have had any great share in devising the new policy approach in Dublin, which pointed out the flaws in this kind of political structure. However, I had some share in helping to formulate and promote it in regular briefings for visiting journalists and then, in late 1971, in a lengthy paper that set out the argument as I have just outlined it. It was entitled 'Stormont: An Assessment'. This was a purely internal document at first but at some point the department decided that it ought to be published as a pamphlet for distribution in appropriate quarters in Britain. The question was how to do this to best effect. The department decided to press an organisation in London called 'The United Ireland Association (Britain)' to take on the role of nominal author, and publisher, of the document. This Association was a remnant of an earlier era— the late 1940s and early 1950s I think—when Irish government policy was more loudly and actively 'anti-partitionist'. One of the stalwarts of the Association of the time, Tadhg Feehan, had later been found a place as an attaché at the Irish embassy in London—a position which he still occupied in the early 1970s. The department pressed Tadhg, and Tadhg in turn pressed the association, such as it was at the time, to undertake sponsorship and nominal authorship of the pamphlet. They agreed to do so—with some reluctance, as I recall, since the analysis it offered pointed in a reasoned way to the need for a reform of the political institutions of Northern Ireland and did not at all make the kind of vigorous arguments against partition itself that they would have liked. However, they agreed, under pressure, to stand over it if some more overtly anti-partitionist language were added here and there. So the final paragraph—the last sentence of which was somewhat out of tune with the document that preceded it—was made to read as follows:

> We are encouraged by the interest in the problem shown by all the political parties in this country. We believe that all must now see the need for institutional change. But beyond this we would welcome a declaration from each of them that they would accept the peaceful reunification of Ireland as the only long-term solution to the Anglo-Irish problem.

In the event the pamphlet was widely distributed in political and other circles in Britain and a second printing became necessary— an extra 6,000 to add to the original run of 5,000. It was also given a somewhat more limited distribution in the US through the embassy in Washington and parts of it were even read into the Congressional Record by a friendly congressman. Did it have any effect? Perhaps—I can't really say. It did at least contribute in a small way to the effort to show that the political institutions at Stormont were unsuited to the kind of society that existed in Northern Ireland.[1]

From the Autumn of 1971 there was a notable improvement in personal relations between Heath and Lynch. Both the UK and Ireland were negotiating in parallel for EEC membership during this period and to that extent, at least, in areas beyond Northern Ireland, their interests were beginning to converge. In a speech in October 1971 Heath spoke of both Lynch and Faulkner as 'men of proven resource, moderation and good will';[2] and Lynch and he met on several occasions between then and the end of January 1972. On 6 December they had a relatively short meeting at the House of Commons where Lynch looked for an end to internment in Northern Ireland and also pressed Heath to take a political initiative. The tone was reasonably cordial. When Lynch once again raised the issue of Irish unity Heath responded that it was 'a rightful aspiration' but it was opposed by the Unionist majority and he was not prepared to tell other people what they ought to want. The two met again at the residence of the British ambassador in Brussels on 23 January.[3] On the previous day, 22 January, Heath and Lynch, together with the Danish and the Norwegian prime ministers, had taken the historic step of signing the respective Acts of Accession of their countries to membership of the EEC. (Following a referendum in September 1972, however, Norway did not become a member.)

In the previous chapter I suggested that the statement issued after the meeting on 27–8. September 1971 between the three heads of government—Heath, Lynch and Faulkner—had been an important first step towards acceptance by the British government that the Irish government had to have a role in the effort to find a solution to the problem of Northern Ireland. But it was no more than a very short step on a long and very bumpy road. The sky darkened further in Northern Ireland and the road became notably bumpier in late 1971 and early 1972. September saw the establishment of the UDA—the Ulster Defence Association—a loyalist paramilitary force which at its peak in 1972 had a membership of nearly fifty thousand. Fifteen hundred additional British soldiers had to be sent to Northern Ireland in October. In November 1971 the Report of the Compton Enquiry was issued. It had been established by the home secretary on 31 August to enquire into allegations that the security forces had been responsible for 'physical brutality' towards a number of those arrested and interned on 9 August. It found that there had been 'a measure of ill-treatment' in some cases but not 'physical brutality'.[4] Prime Minister Heath considered the report 'unbalanced'; opinion in Ireland saw it as a 'whitewash'.[5] In early December a UVF bomb in McGurk's bar in Belfast killed fifteen people—the largest loss of civilian life in a single incident in Northern Ireland until the Omagh bomb of 1998.[6]

Two months later, on Sunday 30 January 1972, an event occurred that was to have great long-term consequences: during a civil rights march in Derry thirteen people were shot dead by the soldiers of the Parachute Regiment.

The killing caused outrage among the nationalist community—and among the public in the south. There were protest marches across Dublin over the following days and the government proclaimed Wednesday, 2 February a day of national mourning. That was also the day of the funeral in Derry of those who had been killed on the Sunday. An estimated 25,000 people attended, including six ministers of the Irish government.

My memory of the early days of that week is of an eerie, gloomy atmosphere where the weather seemed to match the public mood. In the Department of Foreign Affairs on the Monday I was present at a meeting where the secretary and senior officials considered what policy advice to offer to the minister and the taoiseach. There was a strong view that the Irish ambassador in London, Donal O'Sullivan, should be recalled 'for consultations'. In the language of diplomacy this is a well-established signal of very serious tension between two governments, but one that stops short of the final step, the breaking off of diplomatic relations. Nothing of the kind had ever happened before in British-Irish relations.

On the national day of mourning, Wednesday, 2 February, the third day after the killings in Derry, a very large protest march—perhaps up to 30,000 people—began to converge in the early afternoon on the chancery of the British embassy on Merrion Square. Factories and other places of work had closed for the day and civil servants were allowed time off to attend religious services though only those in certain departments availed of the permission to do so.[7] This left many people free to take part in the protest. There were also many participants from north of the border—some of whom were evidently ready to express their outrage in a very forceful fashion. A strong force of gardaí tried to protect the embassy but as militants among the large and belligerent crowd pressed forward the gardaí were pushed steadily back and a number were injured. Some in the crowd who must have come equipped to do so began to throw petrol bombs over the heads of the beleaguered gardaí at the building behind, which then caught fire.

In diplomatic practice the premises of one state's embassy in another state are inviolate and the receiving state has an obligation to ensure that both the embassy and its staff are protected if they should come under attack. The British ambassador had been summoned urgently to London on the previous day to meet with the prime minister and other ministers.[8] In his absence the chargé d'affaires at the embassy was in urgent touch with the Department of Foreign Affairs to seek adequate protective measures. I was not directly involved but I was aware that, as the situation escalated, the demands from the embassy were being pressed with increasing urgency. I remember believing, naively as it turned out later, that the duty of the government to respond and to protect the embassy by all available means simply had to be carried through at all costs. That would have meant calling out the army. I am not sure whether a decision to the contrary was taken at a high level—presumably by the taoiseach—on the basis that that was the more prudent course, or whether there was simply a failure to take any decision. In any event the army were not turned out, the attackers gradually over-whelmed the gardaí who tried valiantly to protect it, and the embassy went up in flames.

I left Iveagh House to walk home about 6.30 that evening in a very worried mood. As I came to the corner of Leeson Street and Fitzwilliam Street I could see in the distance the throng outside the embassy so I walked down towards it as far as I could until I was halted by the crowd as I came closer to Merrion Square. I could see the flames from there as the fire in the embassy burned unchecked. An ambulance was parked between the door of the embassy and the outnumbered gardaí. Close beside me, about 100 yards away from the embassy and some yards short of the edge of the crowd, a number of firemen from the Dublin Fire Brigade stood by their vehicles—a large ladder-truck and another fire tender. I exchanged a few words with them. They told me that they had been told not to go down any further. Some other passers-by added that they had been threatened that if they did so they would be 'wrecked'. A fire-man said to me ruefully that it was the first time that they had ever stood by and watched a house in flames without doing anything. I left the scene and went home deeply depressed and ashamed at what I had seen happen.

Later that evening I heard Conor Cruise O'Brien, who had so often warned of the dangers of wider conflict in Ireland, say on BBC radio that he had changed his position since the previous week: Britain, he said, should now set a date for withdrawal of its troops from Northern Ireland. In London over the following days he argued for this when he met in succession with the home secretary, Reginald Maudling, and the opposition leaders, Harold Wilson and Jeremy Thorpe. The swirling emotions of the time had evidently shaken even one who had been notable for trying to cool the more dangerous passions of Irish nationalism. Writing six months later he acknowledged that in the first flush of emotion caused by what he still characterised as murder, he had over-reacted to an extent.[9] In government little more than a year later he was again acutely aware of the dangers that setting a date for withdrawal of British troops would pose and sharply critical of anyone who proposed it.

On Thursday, 3 February, the morning after the dramatic events of the national day of mourning, the eerie, gloomy atmosphere of the early days of the week had lifted. So too had the national mood. It is not easy to admit it even now but it was evident that the burning of the British embassy, outrageous and unacceptable as it was, had had a cathartic effect: oddly the catharsis seemed to extend even to the weather. Prudence had clearly over-ruled principle in the taoiseach's decision—or was it a non-decision—not to call in the Irish army to defend the embassy premises when the gardaí, notwithstanding their best efforts, proved unable to do so. At the time that seemed to me to be quite wrong. Emotion was high but I thought that not to do everything possible to prevent a foreign embassy from being attacked and burned by an outraged mob reflected very badly on our capacity as a civilised democratic state. But thinking about it now, I have to consider what the consequences might have been had the army been used, and had Irish soldiers been obliged to open fire at some point. In the volatile mood of the time this might have compounded the effect of the Derry shooting and drawn the Irish government, and 'the South', directly into the conflict in Northern Ireland to an extent beyond anything that actually happened over the following years. There were already some siren voices that suggested that full-scale civil war—the ultimate disaster, as I thought of it—was not to be feared: there was already virtual civil war in the North, so the argument went, and widening the conflict now would 'clear the air' and prepare the way for the ultimate settlement in Ireland.

If that seems exaggerated perhaps I can quote from a very worried private note I wrote to myself two days later, the evening before another protest march which was to take place in Newry on Sunday, 6 February:

> Are we heading towards civil war—real civil war? It is clear that the Unionist regime in the North is breaking up. Or rather that the North is coming apart, clearer than ever after Derry on Sunday. Something really new is coming. The optimists, who are dominant (Eamonn Gallagher on Thursday at lunch with Edward Behr of *Newsweek* for example), believe it will be a united Ireland. The pessimists (Conor Cruise O'Brien until recently at least) that it will be civil war. The *New Statesman* and the *Economist* seem ready to contemplate the latter. Who is right? I don't know. But what if it *is* civil war? Does one get off the juggernaut? If so when? and how?

The Newry march passed off peacefully. But the sense of foreboding remained. I see from another worried note to myself which I scribbled some six weeks later that Liam de Paor, a respected commentator and academic, said on the Irish language TV programme *Féach* that civil war (in Ireland) was likely: it would be complex; and he did not see how it could be averted.

There was a further increase in tension and a surge in violence in Northern Ireland in the weeks and months following Bloody Sunday. On 9 February William Craig, Minister for Home Affairs, launched 'Ulster Vanguard', which was to be an umbrella group for the right wing of unionism. On 18 March he told a rally of 60,000 people that 'if and when the politicians fail us it may be our job to liquidate the enemy'; and he spoke of the possibility of a provisional government in Northern Ireland.[10] The IRA, which had been split into 'Officials' and 'Provisionals' since December 1969, stepped up their violence. The Officials were first with a 'spectacular'—an attack for the first time on the British mainland. On 22 February they detonated a car bomb outside the barracks of the Parachute Regiment in Aldershot. As an act of revenge for Derry, and what they would have liked to think was a heroic blow for Irish freedom, their success was limited, and their callous incompetence great: the death toll was seven—they murdered five cleaning women, a gardener and a Catholic chaplain. On 25 February they tried to murder John Taylor, Minister of State for Home Affairs. On 4 March a bomb placed by their rivals, the Provisional IRA, at the Abercorn Restaurant in Belfast killed 2 and injured 130 people; on 20 March a no-warning car bomb in Lower Donegall Street in Belfast, complemented by a hoax call that misled shoppers into moving towards the area, killed 6 and injured more than 100.[11]

The gloom was deepening.

NOTES

[1] NAI DFA 2003/17/32 contains two copies of the pamphlet and a copy of the distribution list in the UK, as well as a copy of the extracts from the text, which were read into the Congressional Record (Extension) by Congressman Jonathan Bingham of New York. See also NAI DFA 2002/19/500.

[2] Campbell, *Edward Heath*, 429.

[3] Report of the meeting is on NAI DFA 2003/12/22. See also Keogh, *Jack Lynch,* 324.

[4] *Report of the enquiry into allegations against the security forces of physical brutality in Northern Ireland arising out of events on the 9th August 1971* (November 1971; HMSO, Cmnd.4823). The Introduction, Terms of Reference and Summary can be accessed at: http://cain.ulst.ac.uk/hmso/compton.htm (30 September 2016).

[5] 'Official inquiries: what the Compton and Parker reports found', *Irish Times*, Saturday, 25 July 2015.

[6] Bew and Gillespie, *Northern Ireland*, 43. The largest loss of life attributable to the Troubles on a single day in Great Britain or Ireland occurred on 17 May 1974, when bombs exploded by loyalists in Dublin and in Monaghan killed a total of 33 people.

[7] NAI TSCH 2003/16/504 (accessed on CAIN).

[8] Peck, *Dublin from Downing Street*, 1–8.

[9] Conor Cruise O'Brien, *States of Ireland* (London, 1972; 2nd edn, 1974), 264–5. His later book *Memoir: my life and themes* (Dublin, 1998), 334–7 repeats the same account and adds the following: 'So I calmed down and reverted to my former view, which has been my view ever since, that, whatever difficulties might attend the presence of British troops in Northern Ireland, their withdrawal would be followed by the far greater disaster of full-scale civil war.'

[10] Bew and Gillespie, *Northern Ireland*, 46.

[11] Bew and Gillespie, *Northern Ireland*, 46–7.

CHAPTER 8

Direct rule

In the week after Bloody Sunday in Derry, there was shock among the public in Britain too—but nothing like the high emotion felt in Ireland. Considering that there had been no such lethal use of troops against protestors on the streets of a city in the United Kingdom since the Peterloo Massacre of 1819, an outsider unfamiliar with Northern Ireland and with the intimate paradoxes of the Anglo-Irish relationship might find it odd that the great wave of emotion and outrage that swept Ireland carried nothing like the same overwhelming force on the British mainland. But the prime minister and his government did realise the full seriousness of what had happened. As one biographer of Heath puts it:

> Bad as the situation had been before, 'Bloody Sunday' was the shock which convinced Heath and his senior colleagues that they must take an urgent grip of Northern Ireland before it slid uncontrollably into civil war. 'It was the most awful two days of my life', Carrington told a friend. With the EEC Treaty safely signed, Heath now 'sent for all papers and made it a top personal priority'— at any rate until the miners' strike diverted his attention.

Ever since the British army was brought onto the streets in 1969 there had been difficulties about the division of responsibility for security between the British and Stormont governments. Heath was now persuaded that Westminster must take full and direct responsibility. But more was needed.

> Heath was convinced that only a dramatic new policy initiative could bring peace. Over the next few weeks he began to examine the options. Changing the border? Regular plebiscites? Power-sharing? Proportional representation?[1]

The need for a new initiative led to a flurry of activity in Whitehall, which came to a head in March. Prompted by Robert Armstrong, who had had a word with the queen's private secretary, Sir Michael Adeane, Heath wrote at length to the queen on 9 March to keep her informed about his thinking about a new political initiative in Northern Ireland:

> The essentials of such an initiative would be that there should be no change in the status of Northern Ireland as part of the United Kingdom, without the consent of a majority of the people of Northern Ireland, but that changes should be made in the form of Government of Northern Ireland which would give the minority parties the assurance of an active and permanent share in the decisions which shape the Government and the future of the Province.

> The situation is one of great complexity, because of the difficulty of finding a solution that will commend itself to so many different and disparate shades of opinion.

The queen received the letter aboard the royal yacht H.M. Britannia, at sea between the Maldives and the Seychelles. Her assistant private secretary, Martin Charteris, in a reply of 16 March thanked Heath on her behalf and agreed with Heath about the complexity of the situation: 'It is hard to believe that a more complicated and intractable problem could exist.'[2]

On 10 March the Cabinet secretary, Burke Trend, in a summary for the prime minister of points on Northern Ireland to be discussed at the Cabinet meeting that morning, began with a question.

> Are the Cabinet sufficiently in agreement to enable us to start moving? In particular, do they endorse the policy which seems to offer the least scope for objection— namely, that we should ask Mr. Faulkner to agree to the transfer of law and order to Westminster, holding ourselves free, if he refuses, to say that we then have no option but to move straight to direct rule?

He also told Heath:

> The need to secure [? simultaneously] a hard and firm agreement with Mr. Lynch about the action which he will take in the South to match our action in the North. This, too will take a little time; and it pre-supposes that we know how much action on his part we would regard as adequate.[3]

In another minute on 13 March, he told the prime minister '[s]ome form of political initiative is now inevitable. Public expectation has been too far aroused, and speculation has become too widespread, to enable the government to remain inactive any further.'

However, one important Cabinet member, the foreign secretary, Sir Alec Douglas-Home, was unhappy about the direction things were taking, as he told Heath in a two-page note that day.

> I really dislike Direct Rule for Northern Ireland because I do not believe that they are like the Scots or the Welsh and doubt if they will ever be. The real British interest would I think be served best by pushing them towards a united Ireland rather than tying them closer to the United Kingdom. Our own parliamentary history is one long story of trouble with the Irish.

'Would it be possible', he asked,

> if we have to agree to a prorogation to give a time limit
> (say six months) for an agreed political solution with
> notice that if it is not agreed we would impose our
> own solution and require a general election for the
> Stormont Parliament to be held upon it?[4]

There had been a number of exchanges between Heath and
Faulkner, by phone, letter and in person, in February and March.
At the request of the Cabinet Office, the Home Office on 17 March
submitted a summary of Faulkner's various proposals. These
included periodic referenda on the border; a solemn and binding
agreement by the republic to recognise the government of
Northern Ireland; treating the whole of Ireland as a 'common law
enforcement area' for the purpose of arrest warrants; and consideration of a Bill of Rights and a 'joint Irish Inter-Government
Council', with equal membership from north and south but with
no powers, to discuss matters of mutual interest, particularly economic and social issues. However, Faulkner had 'specifically
rejected' 'any place in government for representatives of the
minority community': he said it would be 'wrong in principle and
unworkable in practice'. He had also rejected the transfer of law
and order powers to Westminster, any change in the internment
policy while violence continued and 'the transfer to the Republic
of any part of Northern Ireland.'[5]

In a telegram of 14 March the Foreign Office told the British
ambassador in Dublin that, as the prime minister needed to talk
further to Faulkner 'as a prelude to final decisions', he would invite
Faulkner to meet him in London the following week. Before then
he would have liked to have a further talk with the taoiseach but
there would be difficulties about their being seen to meet at that
stage and such a meeting could hardly be kept secret. So, the telegram said, could the ambassador advise on whether Lynch would
allow Erskine Childers to go to London instead?[6] If he would,
Childers could visit London 'on private business', or 'for St.
Patrick's Day'; or the UK government, with Irish Air Force

cooperation, could provide an aircraft to fly him to the RAF base at Benson and a car to take him to Chequers to meet Heath. This did not happen.

More ominous for the Irish government, had they known about it, was the thought behind a letter of 15 March from Robert Armstrong to the Cabinet secretary, Burke Trend.

> At some stage in the next week or two it will be necessary for there to be contact with Mr. Lynch about an initiative in Northern Ireland. The Prime Minister has it in mind that it may be necessary to be able to say to Mr. Lynch that the success of the government's initiative will depend on certain action being taken by Mr. Lynch's government; and that, if that action is not taken, the British government might well be forced by the pressure of public opinion here to take certain action against the interests of the Irish Republic which they would not wish to have to take.

> The Prime Minister would be grateful for an urgent report, by close of business on 17 March, on action of this kind which the British government could take. Examples of the sort of thing he has in mind are: restrictions on entry by Irish nationals into Britain, the re-introduction of identity cards for Irishmen in this country, restrictions on the right of Irishmen to vote in this country, and action in the fields of trade or agriculture. It might also be necessary to indicate that the British Army would need to feel free to pursue terrorists across the border. The Prime Minister would be grateful for an examination of the doctrine of 'hot pursuit' and of what would be involved in the pursuit of terrorists across the border.[7]

It is not clear just what action Lynch would be asked to take. Presumably it would be to increase cross-border security cooperation. But then, as the Cabinet secretary had dryly commented in

135

the note to the prime minister on 10 March that I mentioned above, that 'pre-supposes that we know how much action on his part we would regard as adequate'.

Two days later, the Cabinet Office responded to Armstrong's letter with an eight-page paper, which incorporated the views of relevant departments and examined in detail the various potential sanctions mentioned by Heath. It concluded:

> If sanctions against the Republic are to have any effect, they would need to be short, sharp and painful. Of the possibilities discussed above, action on immigration controls seems the only one likely to hurt the Irish without doing even more damage to ourselves—even if for EEC reasons it could in any case be only temporary. It must nevertheless be realised that any sanctions of this kind are likely to hurt us as well, and that it would be open to the Irish to seek to retaliate, both by refusing to buy our goods and by presenting us internationally as bullies picking on smaller and poorer countries.[8]

The Foreign Office in a letter on the same day responded to Armstrong's enquiry about 'hot pursuit'. It suggested that British troops, if fired on from across the border, could return fire, using 'the argument which we believe to be sound, though it is certainly not to be found in legal textbooks,' that they were acting lawfully in self-defence, but it distinguished this from 'deliberate incursion into Irish territory by official British forces'; that would be more dubious, both legally and politically.[9]

According to his letter of 9 March to the queen, Heath was now contemplating 'a political initiative which could be acceptable to majority opinion in Northern Ireland and at the same time to a great body of moderate opinion on both sides of the border'; 'no change in the status of Northern Ireland as part of the United Kingdom, without the consent of a majority of the people of Northern Ireland'; and changes in government in Northern Ireland to give 'the minority parties the assurance of an active and permanent share in the decisions which shape the government and the future of the Province'. In retrospect all three points can be seen as an outline of ideas that were to emerge in the Green Paper six months later—an 'Irish Dimension', assurance on 'status' and power-sharing. To this extent one could say that the arguments that the taoiseach, Jack Lynch, had been pressing on him were having an effect although, behind the scenes, and unknown to Lynch, Heath was still of a mind at this stage to approach the issue with—to borrow a phrase—a positive initiative in one hand and possible sanctions against Dublin in the other.

Notwithstanding the doubts of several of its members, the Cabinet approved Heath's proposals unanimously in mid-March.

> Westminster would take over responsibility not just for security on the streets but the whole apparatus of law and order—the judicial system and the prisons as well as the police. Internment would be phased out, plebiscites held on the border and discussions initiated with the SDLP to establish 'community government'. None of this would be negotiable: it would be presented to the Northern Ireland government as a *fait accompli* which they must accept in total or else resign.[10]

Some British ministers still had hopes that Brian Faulkner might agree to remain in office as prime minister of Northern Ireland even though the responsibilities of the government there were about to be greatly diminished. But facing an ultimatum that he had not expected, Faulkner felt betrayed. After nearly ten hours of talks at Downing Street, he announced his resignation. On 24 March 1972 Prime Minister Heath told the House of Commons that the Stormont government would be suspended and direct rule introduced. Planning for this had already been in place for some time.[11] On 26 March William Whitelaw, a heavy-weight politician and a senior member of the Cabinet, was appointed to the newly created post of secretary of state for Northern Ireland.

The suspension of the Northern Ireland parliament 51 years after it was opened by King George V was met by large-scale unionist protests. Vanguard, led by William Craig, organised a 48-hour strike which stopped public transport and cut power supplies; and some 100,000 people attended a protest rally outside Stormont. However, none of this could stop what was about to happen. The Northern Ireland parliament met for the last time on 28 March; the legislation proroguing it passed through the House of Commons in an all-night sitting; and it became law on 30 March 1972.

'Direct rule' meant that political power and decision making in Northern Ireland now rested with a British Cabinet minister, the secretary of state for Northern Ireland, and his/her department, the Northern Ireland office. The Northern Ireland civil service continued in being—though now under the direction of the secretary of state rather than Stormont ministers. Legislation in regard to Northern Ireland, which had previously been a matter for the Northern Ireland parliament, was now dealt with at Westminster, where it was usually put through, without discussion, under the procedure known as 'Orders in Council'.

From the outset both Heath and the newly appointed secretary of state, William Whitelaw, made it clear that in principle direct rule was intended to be a temporary arrangement that would last only until a better political structure for Northern Ireland could be worked out in consultation with all those concerned. They could not have known then how long that would take. A possible alternative approach might have been to cease treating Northern Ireland as a distinctive entity with its own devolved government and instead to integrate it as fully into the United Kingdom as, say, Yorkshire or Devon. Even though some individual politicians talked about this on occasion it was not an approach favoured by any British government, then or later.

A historian might perhaps see this as a policy that dated back as far as Gladstone's Home Rule Bill of 1886, which had stepped back from Pitt's policy in 1800 of creating a single, integrated United Kingdom of Great Britain and Ireland (albeit with an Irish administration centred in Dublin Castle). Although Home Rule had, in the event, not come into effect, the recognition it implied of the distinctive character of Ireland, as such, had been carried through into Lloyd George's 1920–21 settlement. The new Irish Free State went its own way towards eventual full independence. But even that part of the island that was to remain within the UK was treated as distinctive—for the following 50 years it remained the only part of the United Kingdom that had its own devolved parliament and government. So, ironically, as the historian Alvin Jackson has pointed out, that part of Ireland where opposition to Home Rule had been most entrenched was the one part to achieve and operate it for half a century.[12]

Now, in 1972, the British government had come to accept that the particular political structures established in Northern Ireland by the 1920 Act were clearly unsuited to that divided society. But its underlying belief that the area should have devolved government—which is to say some kind of Home Rule—remained. So, if full integration of Northern Ireland into the United Kingdom was ruled out, if the existing system of government at Stormont modelled on Westminster was no longer acceptable, and if Irish unity continued to be rejected by unionists, as it clearly was, then British policy had to be directed towards devising some kind of more equitable and balanced political institutions in Northern Ireland to which power might again be devolved by Westminster. That was a task that was begun at Sunningdale but it was not successfully achieved for several decades. Some might say it has still to be completed in a fully satisfactory way.

NOTES

[1] Campbell, *Edward Heath*, 430. The Carrington quotations are from the *Sunday Times* of 26 March 1972.
[2] Letter and reply are on TNA PREM 15/1004.
[3] TNA PREM 15/1004.
[4] TNA PREM 15/1004. According to Zeigler, *Edward Heath* (310), Hailsham and Carrington were also opposed.
[5] TNA PREM 15/1004.
[6] The tánaiste (deputy prime minister) and minister for health.
[7] TNA PREM 15/1004. One must assume that the measures in question would apply also to Irishwomen.
[8] TNA PREM 15/1004.

[9] TNA 15/1004, letter of 17 March 1972 from Johnny Graham, the principal private secretary to the foreign secretary.

[10] Campbell, *Edward Heath*, 431.

[11] At least since February 1969. See Chapter 2, which refers to Fanning, 'Playing it cool'. Craig, *Crisis of confidence* (93), mentions a draft bill to suspend the Northern Ireland parliament produced by a ministerial committee on 17 March 1971.

[12] Jackson, *Home Rule*, 'In the end, the paradox is not simply that the Unionists won Home Rule; it is rather that they were burdened by a form of Home Rule that they themselves had subverted' (200).

CHAPTER 9

How policy is formed

In March 1972 the taoiseach was invited to contribute an essay on the Northern Ireland problem to the prestigious American journal *Foreign Affairs*. His own department was then of modest size and the request for a draft was referred to the Department of Foreign Affairs, where it ended up in the Press and Information section where I was still working at the time. It may be of interest to recount how a draft was eventually prepared for the taoiseach as an example of one of the various ways in which government policy on Northern Ireland gradually evolved during a very difficult period.

When the request arrived a senior colleague who was head of the Press section at the time responded with a memo saying that if we were to prepare a draft in the section it would first be necessary to have clear directions on government policy. This was not unreasonable: in the White House, for example, policy is set from the top and there is usually a clear distinction between those who make or advise on policy and the speech-writers, the 'wordsmiths', who shape the elegant rhetoric in which it is presented. But our system—in those days at least—worked somewhat differently. It was never very likely that a memo asking for clear direction on policy would elicit a particularly helpful response.

Historians may find this strange, perhaps—in principle, they would think, policy should always be determined at political level; and it did indeed always require political approval. But this does not mean that it always had to come downward in the first instance by way of directive or instruction, or that it had to be based solely on formal position papers submitted and approved at government level. In my experience policy was often developed also in a creative interaction between the person who had been asked to prepare a draft speech and the political leader who could choose to modify and adapt it, or to accept and deliver it. I wonder if that is not the case also in other administrations. Sometimes of course a taoiseach or minister would give a clear enough indication of what he or she wanted a speech to say. But at other times it was up to the person doing the draft to try to think through what the situation required. I do not mean of course that the speech-writer was free to write what he or she wished or that a speech-writer worked in a wholly policy-free vacuum: there were previous speeches and statements, answers to parliamentary questions (themselves drafted by civil servants and approved by ministers) and subsequent, more spontaneous, Dáil exchanges to draw on; and the good speech-writer would have what the Germans call *Fingerspitzengefühl*—a finger-tip feel, or better still, perhaps, a pen-tip feeling, for the position of the taoiseach or the minister. But something more was needed for a really good draft speech—a small additional touch of imagination, something that advanced policy a bit but still within the limits of what the speaker would be willing to accept. That is to say, at best the aim of the speech-writer should be to offer the speaker something that the speaker would approve, and that he or she would be glad to have said once he or she had said it.

I should perhaps add a point that may be obvious on reflection. In their efforts to respond to what was happening in Northern Ireland in those years, successive Irish governments were struggling to develop policy on an issue of great complexity, an issue rooted in history, an issue that not only affected the security of the state but ultimately raised questions as to its very identity. The conflict there had re-opened dramatically the settlement of half a century earlier; and it was a conflict to which no lasting solution was in sight, then or for many years afterwards. In view of all this it is perhaps understandable that Irish government policy, like that of the British government, evolved slowly, with occasional untidiness, and sometimes in response to immediate events, rather than in a carefully worked out way or in a linear sequence.

As it happened, within days of the request from the taoiseach for a draft for his article for *Foreign Affairs*, my senior colleague was moved to a post elsewhere and I took his place. The file with the request for a draft was now on my desk; time was short; and there seemed to be nothing for it but to try my own hand at the assignment. I did so in the hope of providing for the taoiseach a moderate and reasonable account of his position which might also advance policy a bit further if that could be done.

When the draft was finished it still had to get past my more senior colleague Eamonn Gallagher, whose direct line of advice to the taoiseach made him, in effect, the gatekeeper of official policy at the time. So I sat down across a desk from him in his room on a Thursday evening in late April 1972 to work through the text. We began to discuss it, sentence by sentence, about 7 p.m. Neither of us got up until we had finished, some time after 1 a.m. During those six hours we argued about this and that part of the wording. On some aspects of the history, and on the argument that Irish unity was the only real solution, Eamonn insisted on a somewhat more assertive formulation than the more emollient text I had offered in the draft. We finished at last, however, with an agreed text that was submitted that Friday afternoon to the secretary of the department, Hugh McCann. He cleared it and sent it over to the Taoiseach's Department on Monday. A week later it came back, approved by the taoiseach, and we sent it off to New York. It duly appeared in the July issue of *Foreign Affairs*.[1] In the following weeks, the government had it translated into French, German and Italian and published in pamphlet form for distribution abroad.

The article began by situating the problem of Northern Ireland in the wider context of British-Irish relations and it outlined the history of relations between the two islands at some length from the seventeenth century onward. It went on to suggest that Lloyd George's 1920–21 settlement could be seen as an attempt to divide Ireland on confessional lines. That may have seemed to be a pragmatic approach but, as an answer to the complexities of the so-called 'Irish Question', it had not worked well. The resumption by the British government of direct rule in Northern Ireland now was a positive step, since it recognised that new structures were needed. However, approaches such as re-partition, population shifts or full integration should be ruled out—they would, if anything, aggravate the problem. The Northern Ireland issue could not be seen in isolation: as an answer, or part of the answer, to the older 'Irish Question', it had proved to be inadequate. But in the overall Anglo-Irish relationship today Northern Ireland was a problem for which there was a solution. What was needed was to work towards a new settlement that would encourage 'reconciliation between all the peoples of both islands'. Such a settlement should encourage Irish unity but should not attempt to impose it by force. Obtaining unity would be a difficult process: there would have to be a growth of trust and reconciliation on all sides.

Since there was already much talk in those years about the confessional nature of the Irish Constitution and the so-called 'territorial claim' in Articles 2 and 3 as obstacles to reconciliation in Ireland, the concluding section of the draft proposed a different approach. A united Ireland would not be an Ireland in which the present state in 'the South' took over 'the North' and assimilated it into its existing structure. The negotiation should be about a new Ireland with a completely new Constitution worked out together by all those who were to live under it. Then, in an effort to push official policy a bit further, the text had the taoiseach offer some additional thoughts on what such a new Constitution might be like.

> Parnell said in 1886 that 'the best system of government for a country [is]…one which requires that government should be the resultant of all the forces within that country'. I think something similar is true of the final working out of a Constitution and system of government for a new Ireland. These are matters best worked out by the representatives of all those who are to live under the new structures. A philosopher or a constitutional lawyer may advise or draft a constitution; but he should not, I think,

attempt to write the final version, at least not in a situation like ours in Ireland, where the building up of trust and the overcoming of fears are so important.

The Constitution of the new Ireland would have to be a written one, with firm and explicit guarantees for the rights and liberties of all who live under it. I would tend to favour the view that these guarantees should relate to the individual citizen rather than to institutions as such. The Constitution makers should perhaps take a 'minimal' approach, i.e. not start from broad philosophical assumptions but, instead, try to piece together an agreement on what is necessary for government to function while ensuring rights and liberties to the individual.

Though neither Eamonn nor I knew this at the time, it appears that Ken Whitaker, who by then was governor of the Central Bank, 'was given sight of the text before publication' but not invited to make any suggestions. After seeing it Whitaker wrote to Lynch describing it as an 'admirable statement of your views', but he favoured 'a slightly different ordering of the priorities': he would have liked some stress on the immediate need for a regional administration in Northern Ireland to allow people to work together while leaving the door open to the 'new Ireland' concept; a statement that a united Ireland might take many years to achieve, though a start could be made without delay; and, rather than a 'phasing out' of the British subsidy, something to say that it should be maintained until a united Ireland was achieved.[2] The biography of Ken Whitaker, on the other hand, does not mention this letter to the taoiseach: it touches on some points from the article—unity by consent, a positive relationship with Britain and the possibility of a new Constitution guaranteeing explicit rights and liberties; and it adds that the article 'reflected many of Ken's views and drew substantially on his advice.'[3]

It is interesting to see from this that Whitaker, while sharing the idea of a united Ireland as a long-term aim, would have wished the taoiseach to envisage a 'regional administration' in Northern Ireland as an immediate step. For much of the previous year we had been trying to impress on the British government that a devolved government like Stormont, based on the 'winner-takes-all' Westminster model, was not suited to the divided society of Northern Ireland. And I know that, following the British Green Paper of October 1972, and not long after the taoiseach's article was published, we were working in the IDU on ideas and proposals for an alternative approach that would include a new type of Northern Ireland administration as well as a Council of Ireland. This had also been a theme of the 1971 pamphlet on Stormont which I mentioned in Chapter 7. In view of all this, I find it very strange that for some reason the two ideas of a Council of Ireland and some new type of partnership government in Northern Ireland were not mentioned in the taoiseach's text; and, if I omitted to refer to both these points in my draft, that Eamonn Gallagher did not add something about them during that long night of debate between us. The text focuses on Irish unity as the eventual long-term solution. It does envisage—but only in the most general terms—a 'phasing-in' period that would allow north and south to bring their economies into closer harmony.

I know that Eamonn himself felt strongly that a united Ireland was the only real solution and he had very definite views on what needed to be done. This is evident from a nine-page analysis paper entitled 'Towards a general settlement?' he wrote on 21 April 1972, shortly before we worked on the draft for the taoiseach, a month after Stormont was prorogued and shortly before Dr Hillery was to meet the newly appointed Northern secretary, Willie Whitelaw.[4] The paper gives a good idea of his thinking, and, I imagine, of the advice he would have been giving to Lynch at this relatively late stage before his influence waned and he moved on to other things.

The paper starts from the view that Northern Ireland was in 'a constitutional limbo': the British government, by proroguing Stormont, had unilaterally 'swept away' the Unionist belief that its constitutional position under earlier British enactments had virtual Treaty status; and no one really believed that a Stormont parliament and government were likely to be recreated after twelve months—'if ever'. The 'trouble-making potential of Northern Ireland' was much too great to be contained indefinitely through the procedures of direct rule; and it was difficult to see how the Unionist Party could accept 'the restoration of a Stormont Parliament and Government, without police powers, and with built in participation in Government for the minority.' Since the buffer of a local parliament and government had gone and could not successfully be reconstituted, it seemed reasonable to suppose that the British could be 'nudged towards considering a more general settlement'.

One possible option—integration into the UK—was not on: British public opinion was not interested; it would not bring permanent peace; the minority would reject it; and it would re-define the issue 'unequivocally' as an Anglo-Irish and colonial question. Instead, 'Britain should decide, in her own interest, that she should encourage Irish unity'. The 'myth of the Northern majority' had to be re-examined because the unionist population did not form a majority in either UK or Irish terms.

> The objective of [Irish] Government policy is Irish unity—not unity *eventually* nor unity *ultimately*. The words 'eventually' and 'ultimately' merely represent potential time-scales. They do not qualify the objective, govern it, reduce it or do anything else to it.

'In order to make it possible to obtain a majority for Irish unity in the North' it was hoped 'as a matter of tactics—indeed good common sense' to win over a sufficient number of unionists by persuasion. But persuasion must not be a sole policy: it could also include 'political, economic, social etc. pressures from London.' It was doubtful if an interim period would be available to cool passions and win over significant sections of the unionist population.

> The gun has been out for several years in the North and the genie of Irish nationalism is also out of the bottle. Neither can readily be suppressed…Essentially the Northern minority—not the majority—hold the key to Irish unity.

The paper went on to make a number of suggestions for 'present and future' Irish government policy leading to negotiations for a general settlement. Three of these are of particular interest here, as they bear out the view that what he would call his 'realist', and others his 'hard-line', approach was quite out of sympathy with the way Irish government policy was to develop under Jack Lynch and his successor, Liam Cosgrave, over the following years.

One was that, while receptive and cooperative in relation to common north-south concerns e.g. an Economic and Social Council of Ireland, Carlingford Lough Commissioners, 'these should be regarded as peripheral matters of no great consequence. There are much bigger fish to fry'. A second was that, in the absence of real British moves towards Irish unity, the government should not be drawn into 'something in the nature of a common law enforcement area—a recent Faulkner idea.' Heath and his colleagues repeatedly asserted the right of the north to remain separate from the rest of Ireland. But

> it is the Irish assertion that this right has not been granted by the Irish people as a whole and has no validity. It follows from this that military repression of the minority, whether conducted by Mr. Faulkner during his primacy or by Mr. Whitelaw now, can be seen as the use of force to prevent a solution to the Irish problem in accordance with Irish views of the matter;

The third was that

> ideally, it would be best if all parties in the North were to accept Mr. Heath's initiatives and operate them more or less agreeably for some years. The analysis above indicates that this is unlikely. If the analysis is correct it could be a mistake to strive to have the minority work the initiatives.

The paper concludes that 'an early opportunity should be taken to ask the British Government to negotiate the conditions of Irish unity in independence.' Britain should be prepared to negotiate about a financial settlement and to put pressure on unionism 'to accede to an Irish Parliament and Government'; Dublin should accept that a suitable (new) Irish Constitution and institutional changes would be necessary; and an Anglo-Irish Convention covering such matters as dual citizenship and 'cultural association' should be considered.

He expressed somewhat similar ideas in several long discussions I had with him—at the beginning of May 1972 just after we had finished working on the draft for the taoiseach, again in mid-June just before the article was published, and again in mid-July. As I look back now on some personal notes I made after these discussions I see that Eamonn believed that there had been very little clear thinking in Dublin so far about the situation in Northern Ireland. For about a year he had been advocating to the taoiseach what he called 'a total policy'. Whitelaw, the Northern Ireland secretary, he said, could not win by placating each side in turn. Britain simply must face up to unionism and outface the UDA; and the Irish government had to be ready and willing to do so itself, by force if necessary. We had to prepare for that. If Britain threatened to pull out, and communal fighting developed, we would inevitably be drawn in. Militant unionists would try to consolidate their hold on the six counties but this would not be possible—they simply could not win. There was talk of 'persuading Northern Protestants' but how could you do that? The minority in Northern Ireland would not 'go back in their box again'. 'The revolving door of history is now open and no Taoiseach could back away'. The minority would not 'wear', and would not let the Irish government 'wear', any solution that did not allow for Irish unity. This, for him, was the crucial point: he saw unity as the eventual solution but I had the impression that if the minority were to accept that Northern Ireland should remain part of the United Kingdom, then he could probably accept it too. I should stress also that he did not want to see a direct confrontation between the Irish government and unionist militants but he believed that could happen. The best way to ensure that it did not happen was to be well prepared to deal with it in case it did.

At bottom, he said, articles such as the draft I had just done for the taoiseach for *Foreign Affairs* were very logical, very sensible and they put the British on the spot. But they had nothing to do with the reality. After a second such discussion I summarised his views for myself as follows. There must not be full integration of Northern Ireland into the United Kingdom—Irish unity had to be the goal. The British government must see that, commit themselves to it and encourage it. Unionists could attempt a backlash against the Catholic minority but the British could not allow that. Nor could Britain simply pull out, because of the reaction there would be in Europe to such a course of action. If, however, it were, nevertheless, to do so, then the Irish government would have to cope with the situation, forcefully if necessary. The government should prepare in advance for that eventuality. That was the best way of ensuring that it would never happen—but if it did happen, and the government were ready for it, they would be strong enough to win through.

I argued strongly with Eamonn each time. I found his belief that the Irish government and Irish nationalism might have to engage in a forceful confrontation with militant unionists deeply disturbing. Apart from anything else there could be no certainty that if they did so they would be successful; and, even supposing that this might eventually lead in some way to unity, how could a united Ireland achieved in this way ever be peaceful and stable? His answer was that the unionist population was not homogenous and the forces that militants among them could muster would not be effective—they could barely hold east of the Bann. Independence—so-called UDI—for Northern Ireland, was simply not feasible. The unionists, deserted by Britain, having no other way out, and nothing else to look for, would settle for Irish unity. Unionists, he said, must make up their minds: either they are Irish, in which case they must accommodate to the majority; or they are 'colons', that is settlers originally from elsewhere, in which case 'there is the ferry'.

What was my reaction to all this? I have to say first that Eamonn deserves considerable credit for his earlier policy advice to the taoiseach. The British government were gradually coming to accept the two main points that he continued to emphasise: first, that a parliament and government based on the Westminster model were not suited to a divided society—some better political structures had to be found; and, second, that the Irish government could no longer be treated as an outsider—it had to have a role in finding a lasting solution. But I also have to say that I thought the view he put to me several times over these months in 1972—that the government should prepare for the possibility of a direct and forceful confrontation between unionism and nationalism in Ireland—rather frightening, and I still do. My belief was, and still is, that such a confrontation could become, in effect, a kind of civil war—a danger that Lloyd George had warned the Treaty negotiators about in 1921; it would be a betrayal of everything the better angels of Irish history had hoped for over the centuries; and 'preparing for it' could risk increasing the possibility that it would happen. I wanted no part of anything of the kind, and if his view were to become official policy I would want out.

Am I being unfair to Eamonn's memory in writing here in this way about the views he expressed at that time? After all he was not advocating this kind of forceful confrontation—on the contrary, his belief, contrary to mine, was that preparing for it in advance was the best way to avert it.[5] Nor did he share the wilder ideas of some at the time who said that since the north was virtually in a state of civil war already, the problem could be resolved once and for all if the south were to join in. Indeed, in his briefing note for Lynch's Chequers meeting with Heath in late September 1971, which I quoted from at the start of Chapter 6, he was quite categorical: 'I consider that those who believe that unity can result from further violence are politically insane.'

I think now that in our discussions, and in his advice to Lynch, he was simply being cool and analytical—a clear-eyed realist, as he would see it. But might it also be possible that, having debated long and hard with me over some of the formulations in the *Foreign Affairs* draft, he was simply continuing the exchanges in an argumentative mood provoked by my 'softer' approach? Perhaps. But I don't really think this was the case—after all, he spoke to me on similar lines on three separate occasions over a period of two months following the publication of the taoiseach's article in *Foreign Affairs*.

That still leaves a question for me—should I recount his views here or should I let them rest unremembered? I have decided, with some hesitation, to record here what he said. He had after all been a close adviser to the taoiseach in that period, and he told me several times that he had been recommending this kind of 'total policy', as he called it, to Lynch over the previous year. If Lynch was disinclined to take that advice, and if, as I believe, it was partly because he thought Gallagher's views too 'hard-line' that, by mid-1972, he was turning elsewhere for advice, then that too should be recorded to Lynch's credit. I see from my final personal note of 13 July, after the last of my three intensive arguments, that the taoiseach did not use Eamonn's draft when he spoke in the Dáil on the adjournment. Furthermore, in his speech Lynch referred to the possibility of a re-structured regional parliament in Northern Ireland to replace Stormont. This suggests to me that, while he might continue, formally, to see Irish unity as the ultimate aim, he was already veering away from the 'unity is the only solution' theme that Eamonn's approach had imposed on the initial draft of the *Foreign Affairs* article—and accepting instead Ken Whitaker's view that it was urgent to stress

> the immediate need for a form of regional administration that would enable the whole community to live and work together in peace, while leaving the door open to an approach, by majority consent and possibly gradually, to the 'new Ireland' concept.[6]

There is one more reason for recalling Eamonn's views now more than four decades later. The fact that someone who, in September 1971 had referred to those who sought Irish unity through violence as 'politically insane', was advising, eight months later, that the government should be prepared to confront militant unionists by force if necessary, may help to show the fraught atmosphere of the time, the dangers and the uncertainties of the situation, and some of the roads Ireland might have taken in those years in the early 1970s but, thankfully, did not.

In late July and early August, following the publication of the *Foreign Affairs* article, Heath and Lynch had relatively cordial diplomatic exchanges. These included a reply from Lynch to a letter of 30 July from Heath, which was delivered in person to Heath on

1 August by the Irish ambassador in London. In it Lynch told Heath that 'Northern Ireland had been discussed "searchingly among ourselves" and, referring to his recent article in *Foreign Affairs,* he said the principal underlying view was that "the door to Irish unity by agreement must be unlocked."' In delivering the letter to Heath, Ambassador O'Sullivan made a number of points, one of which was that '[t]here could be no solution without the Irish Government playing an adequate role—not necessarily with full publicity'.[7] But over the next few months the situation on the ground in Northern Ireland continued to deteriorate. There was one brief glimmer of hope in late June when, following contacts behind the scenes by John Hume, and feelers put out by Whitelaw, there was a brief ceasefire followed by talks between the British government and representatives of the Provisional IRA.[8]

The talks began with a preparatory meeting on 20 June 1972 between Philip Woodfield, Deputy Secretary of the Northern Ireland Office and two IRA representatives, 'Mr. David O'Connell and Mr. Gerard Adams.' They met for over three hours in a private house near the Donegal border. According to Woodfield's note on the meeting, which is now in the British archives,[9] he had been armed with a written authorisation from Whitelaw to discuss three points. At the outset P.J. McCrory, a solicitor brought along by the IRA representatives for this purpose, examined the authorisation and declared it 'authentic'. He then withdrew. Woodfield then started by outlining the IRA position 'as reported to the Secretary of State.'

> The IRA were prepared to call an indefinite ceasefire if they could be satisfied that the Secretary of State would accept the demand of certain convicted prisoners for 'political status'; that he would immediately order the cessation of all harassment of the IRA; and that he would be prepared after the ceasefire had been shown to be effective to meet representatives of the Provisional IRA.

These were in fact the three points he had been authorised to discuss. The two IRA representatives 'did not directly challenge the accuracy of this as their position.'

On the first point, Woodfield, though unwilling to accept the term 'political status', said that the substance of what they sought was already virtually the case; and the hunger strike on the issue had just been called off. The second point, 'harassment', was, he said, vague but Whitelaw could give an assurance that there would not be raids, searches and arrests of wanted persons. On the third point, Whitelaw would agree to meet IRA representatives ten days after the ceasefire, provided, in his judgement, that it was effective. In response the two IRA representatives said they would need some time 'to give advance warning down the line' about the ceasefire. They wanted Whitelaw to send them a letter setting out in writing his response to the three questions. Woodfield said that this would be 'politically wholly impossible' since Whitelaw would have no control over the use that might be made of it. 'They saw the validity of this'. It was 'eventually proposed that Mr. McCrory...should be invited to call at a convenient place and see a written statement by the Secretary of State covering the three points'. The IRA side, summarising the three points, dropped 'the reference to the polit-ical prisoners' and introduced a new proposal for a liaison between a member of Whitelaw's staff and an IRA representative in order to make the ceasefire work. (Woodfield mentions that Whitelaw had instructed him, if possible, to obtain just such an arrangement, but he made no comment on the fact that the IRA side had now made it a condition for a ceasefire.) They agreed to the use of a form of words dictated by Woodfield that would say 'We are ordering an indefinite ceasefire to take effect from...in the confident belief that the Secretary of State will make an exceptional response to this exceptional measure as he has said he will do in his public state-ments.' As the meeting concluded Woodfield suggested that 'it would make it much easier if Mr. McStiofain [sic] were not included' in the delegation for the meeting with the secretary of state after the ceasefire was announced. They said they could not arrange to exclude him but he might or might not attend.

At the end of his report, Woodfield said that the atmosphere at this 'first encounter with the Provisional IRA' was 'informal and relaxed'.

> There is no doubt whatever that these two at least
> genuinely want a ceasefire and a permanent end to

violence...Their appearance and manner were respectable and respectful...Their response to every argument...was reasonable and moderate. Their behaviour and attitude appeared to bear no relation to the indiscriminate campaigns of bombing and shooting in which they have both been prominent leaders.

In the event the Provisional IRA did announce a ceasefire, six days later, on 26 June. Eleven days later, on 7 July, the RAF flew six leaders of the Provisional IRA over to London for the promised meeting with Whitelaw which was held in a house in Cheyne Walk in Chelsea. Notwithstanding Woodfield's suggestion, the delegation was led by the chief of staff, Séan MacStiofáin. It emerged later that at a meeting which MacStiofáin chaired in Dublin the week before it had been agreed that 'the only purpose of the meeting with Whitelaw was to demand the declaration of intent to withdraw.'[10] Brian Feeney in his brief history of the Troubles describes what happened next.

> [O]n 7 July, Whitelaw secretly met IRA leaders, including Gerry Adams and Martin McGuinness, in London...The meeting was a fiasco. The IRA delegation, led by chief-of-staff Séan MacStiofáin, made impossible, peremptory demands, including a British withdrawal from Ireland, to be completed by 1 January 1975, and an immediate amnesty for all political prisoners, internees and all those on 'wanted' lists. Whitelaw and his advisers concluded they could not do business with the IRA. Two days later the truce collapsed in an exchange of gunfire in west Belfast, amid recriminations between the IRA and the British Army.[11]

The brief hope raised by the ceasefire had been snuffed out.

On 13 and 14 July four British soldiers and five civilians were killed. In Belfast, on 'Bloody Friday', 21 July 1972, twenty-six IRA bombs killed eleven people. Some bodies were so badly mangled that their body parts had to be collected in plastic bags.

One hundred and thirty were injured, some very severely.[12] On 31 July in 'Operation Motorman', thousands of British troops smashed the barricades which had created 'no go areas' in Belfast and Derry and re-asserted government control. Two young men were shot dead in gun battles in Derry; and IRA car bombs in Claudy killed eight people. On 22 August an IRA bomb at the Customs post in Newry killed nine people, including three of the bombers.[13]

As the toll of death and injury continued on the streets in Northern Ireland and the Ulster Vanguard leader, William Craig talked of his ability to mobilise 80,000 men in opposition to British policy, there were two weak and unsuccessful efforts at political initiatives, in September 1972. The SDLP in a policy document called for joint sovereignty by the two governments over Northern Ireland and a declaration of intent by Britain about working for Irish unity; and the Northern Ireland secretary, William Whitelaw, convened a conference of Northern Ireland parties at Darlington in England to consider possible options. The SDLP refused to attend because of internment and the three parties that did attend—the Ulster Unionists, Alliance and the Northern Ireland Labour Party—could not reach agreement on the future governance of Northern Ireland.[14]

There was a considerable improvement over a year or more in the relationship between Heath and Lynch. But there was still a potential for things to go wrong as was evident from the reaction in Dublin to what was seen as a hostile press briefing about 'security co-operation failures' after what had seemed a relatively amicable meeting on 4 September during the Munich Olympic Games.[15] But at that meeting Heath also said that 'he was keen on talks with Lynch "and those who were critical of such talks in Northern Ireland would have to lump it"'. He had also assured Lynch 'that he was prepared to "make special arrangements through the Foreign Office to keep the Taoiseach informed, in which it would be open to the Taoiseach to inject his views or make proposals"'.[16] This suggestion, and even the language used, might perhaps be seen now as a first—and very tentative—move towards the eventual formal acceptance by the British government in the Anglo-Irish Agreement of 1985, thirteen years later, that the Irish government would have a right to put forward 'views and proposals' in relation to Northern Ireland

and that 'determined efforts' would be made by the two govern-ments to resolve any differences.

Lynch and Heath met again in Paris for a private discussion, late at night, at the close of a Summit meeting in Paris on 21 October 1972. There were no note-takers or other officials present. According to the note that Lynch himself prepared after his return to Dublin, he spoke to Heath about the worsening situation since the Darlington conference and 'the need for maintaining political ini-tiative or better still providing a new one'. He said he understood why Whitelaw had gone ahead with that conference but that it was far from representative and only unionist proposals had been dis-cussed there. He hoped the proposed Green Paper would reflect a much wider range of opinion. It should not be limited to generalit-ies about equal treatment for minorities but should be very specific, not only about fair treatment in social and political spheres but in security matters also, because of the disillusionment among the minority about their treatment by the British army, especially in West Belfast. Lynch also expressed disappointment at the British handling of the press after their Munich meeting. Heath told him, in response, that he had seen and approved the Green Paper (actu-ally, in error, he said 'White Paper') before he left for Paris. It would be specific about 'no integration' (of Northern Ireland into the UK) and no return to the status quo before March 1972. Lynch asked for some idea of Heath's long-term thinking but Heath would not go beyond referring to the forthcoming Green Paper and the legisla-tion that would follow.

It is interesting that, after their meeting, Heath seems to have felt that, cautious as he had been, he had still gone too far in talking about the forthcoming initiative. In a 'PS' to his note on the meet-ing, Lynch records that the British ambassador in Dublin (Sir John Peck) called to see him on the afternoon of 23 October to convey an urgent personal message from Heath 'to the effect that the prime minister felt he had been too oncoming about the Green Paper, its contents and time of publication' when they spoke in Paris on the night of 21 October. Lynch reassured the ambassador that Heath had said nothing significant (beyond the points summarised above); and, he said, 'I had told the Prime Minister that I would confine my comment to the Press on our talks to my pressing for quadripartite talks and his reluctance to agree.' The ambassador said that 'he had seen it [the Green Paper] himself but not soon enough to have it altered before it went for printing. Some parts of it, he thought, would be to our liking—other parts perhaps not.'[17]

Just about a week later, at a very dark moment towards the end of the bloodiest year of the Troubles, the British government published the Green Paper to which Heath had referred. It was entitled *The Future of Northern Ireland: A Paper for Discussion*.[18] Some accounts of the time pass over this event briefly. Heath's authorised biography does not even mention it.[19] Another biography makes a throwaway reference to it in a sentence or two.[20] In my view, however, the publication of this document was one of the most important events of those years. It marked a turning point in the policy of the British government on the Northern Ireland problem; and the approach it set out in broad terms became the basis for all subsequent cooperation between the two governments in working towards a political settlement. I will deal with this at greater length in the next chapter.

NOTES

[1] John M. Lynch, 'The Anglo-Irish problem', *Foreign Affairs: An American Quarterly Review* 50 (4) (July 1972), 601–17.
[2] Keogh, *Jack Lynch*, 344.
[3] Chambers, *T.K. Whitaker*, 304.
[4] NAI DFA 2003/13/16, accessed through CAIN. So far as I can now recall, I knew nothing of this paper at the time.
[5] Gallagher's view reflected a well-known Latin adage—*si vis pacem, para bellum*—if you want peace, then prepare for war.
[6] Whitaker's letter of 21 June 1972 to Lynch—see n. 2 above (Keogh, *Jack Lynch*, 344).
[7] Keogh, *Jack Lynch*, 348–9.
[8] For Hume's role in relation to the ceasefire and subsequent talks, see the chapter by Sean Donlon on 'John Hume and the Irish government', in Farren and Haughey (eds), *John Hume*, 87.
[9] TNA PREM 15/1009. Woodfield's note on the meeting, marked 'Top Secret', was seen and initialled by Heath on 28 June. Woodfield was accompanied at the meeting by a colleague, Frank Steele.

[10] Patrick Bishop and Eamonn Mallie, *The Provisional IRA* (London, 1987), 178, quoting from an interview by the authors with Martin McGuinness in 1985–6.

[11] Feeney, *A short history of the Troubles*, 40.

[12] Bew and Gillespie, *Northern Ireland*, 54, say there were 26 bombs. Feeney, *A short history of the Troubles*, 41, says 22.

[13] Bew and Gillespie, *Northern Ireland*, 55.

[14] Bew and Gillespie, *Northern Ireland*, 55–6.

[15] I have referred to this in Chapter 3.

[16] Keogh, *Jack Lynch*, 358–9 (drawing on the Lynch papers).

[17] Copy of Lynch's note is in my possession; there is also a copy on NAI DFA 2003/13/10.

[18] *The Future of Northern Ireland: A Paper for Discussion* (London, 1972, SBN. 11 700498 7). From here on I will refer to this as 'the Green Paper'.

[19] Zeigler, *Edward Heath*, Chapter 15, 'Ulster'.

[20] 'The Unionists reacted violently to a Green Paper Whitelaw published after Darlington proposing local government elections by proportional representation', Campbell, *Edward Heath*, 546.

CHAPTER 10

The Green Paper

As I suggested in previous chapters, Jack Lynch, on the advice of Eamonn Gallagher, had pursued two main policy objectives in the years 1971 and 1972: establishing a role for the Irish government in relation to Northern Ireland, and convincing the British government that a parliament and government modelled on Westminster were wholly unsuited to such a deeply divided society. The statement issued after the tripartite summit between Heath, Lynch and Faulkner at Chequers in September 1971, which did not seem so significant at the time, can be seen in retrospect as a step towards the first of these objectives—acceptance by Britain that the Irish government had to be involved in the effort to find a settlement. By mid-1972 there was also some movement in relation to Lynch's second policy objective in the sense that the reintroduction of direct rule from Westminster, after more than half a century of devolution, cleared the way for an effort to devise political structures better suited to a divided community like that in Northern Ireland.

The Green Paper published by the British government at the end of October 1972 was an important public step further in this direction. It gave a clear indication for the first time of the probable direction that future British policy would take; and it seemed to point towards the creation of new structures that would go a long way towards meeting both of the main policy objectives the Irish government had been pursuing over the previous eighteen months. It was still characterised as simply 'A paper for discussion' but I believe it is not too much to describe it as one of the most important developments in British policy in relation to Northern Ireland for 50 years.

I will outline the main points in the Green Paper below. First, however, I want to refer to a very far-sighted internal paper, prepared by the Northern Ireland civil service, which is now in the Public Record Office in Northern Ireland. From internal evidence, I believe it to have been an influential contribution to the internal debate that must have preceded the publication by the British government of the Green Paper two months later.

The internal paper was one of three such 'secret' papers prepared by a 'Future Policy Group' of permanent secretaries chaired by Sir David Holden, who was head of the Northern Ireland civil service at the time. It is headed 'Political Settlement: The "Irish Dimension"'; and it was forwarded to the secretary of state for Northern Ireland on 8 September under cover of a letter from Sir Harold Black, the former Northern Ireland Cabinet secretary.[1] Sir Kenneth Bloomfield, who was later himself head of the Northern Ireland civil service, clearly had substantial input to its preparation, and possibly also to the Green Paper that followed. In his memoirs, published eighteen years later, the then secretary of state, William Whitelaw, pays 'a tribute to all who worked on it' and he adds 'Ken Bloomfield in particular…was a most valuable adviser.'[2] In his own book *A tragedy of errors*, Bloomfield himself refers to the work of the Policy Group:

> A great deal of my own time was spent preparing 'What if?' papers for this Group. What were the considerations bearing upon such options as power-sharing government, 'total integration' into the United Kingdom, more structured relations with the Irish Republic, and so on? These reports were not only made available to the Secretary of State but were also discussed with him fully across the table.[3]

The particular paper I refer to was one of three—the other two considered the issues of devolution and full integration of Northern Ireland into the UK respectively. However, in the light of later events, it is this paper that now seems most interesting and perceptive.

In his covering letter Sir Harold Black says, 'we are wholly persuaded that no settlement will "stick" for more than a brief period if it does not tackle the fundamental and underlying problem of the relationship between the United Kingdom and Ireland, of which the Northern Ireland problem is an aspect.' The paper itself quotes Jack Lynch's *Foreign Affairs* article, which it describes as 'of the greatest relevance'. It points out that the 1920 Act which created Northern Ireland 'did not envisage the creation of an international frontier but the establishment of devolved institutions in two parts of the United Kingdom, and with the possibility of unity by agreement very much in mind'. The paper then goes on to advocate a political settlement for Northern Ireland that ought to have an external as well as an internal dimension. It would take the form of

> a re-definition of Northern Ireland's present constitutional status and possible future course to be embodied in new, internationally-registered Treaty arrangements between the United Kingdom and Ireland. We believe that it should be a primary objective of HM Government's policy, using every means of influence and even pressure which can be exerted upon the Irish Republic to secure the Republic's commitment to such arrangements. They should be based on recognition of the reality of the situation: that Northern Ireland at present has a majority wishing to be associated with the United Kingdom and a minority wishing to be associated with a united Ireland. In recognition of this the *present* status of Northern Ireland should be defined as that of a part of the United Kingdom, *but* a part enjoying a special relationship with the Irish Republic by virtue of common interests etc. This special relationship should be acknowledged at once by the establishment of a joint

Council for co-operation and consultation but without—in the first instance—major executive functions. [Emphasis in the original.]

Most remarkable of all, for a document prepared by senior Northern Ireland civil servants at that time and discussed with the secretary of state, it goes on to say that

[t]he re-definition of constitutional status [of Northern Ireland] should proceed from this to set out an acceptable means for movement towards Irish unity in stages, *subject to consent at each stage.* This would again represent an acknowledgement of reality—that unity can never be achieved unless the people of Northern Ireland can be convinced that it is in their interests; that even in calmer times people will not take such a vital decision without knowing the 'terms of entry'; and that if unity is ever to come about at all, it must be in a staged, orderly way. [Emphasis in the original.]

Of course, ministers and officials in Dublin knew nothing of this paper at the time. But, looking back now, it seems clear to me that some of the ideas in the paper, and in particular the recognition of the 'Irish Dimension', must have had an important influence on the British government's Green Paper which was published two months later. Perhaps the same hands can even be detected at work in parts of both documents—although of course the Green Paper stopped well short of the proposal for some kind of staged progress towards Irish unity which had been outlined by the Northern civil servants.

The Green Paper itself began with a very open analysis of the problem as well as a summary of proposals put forward by the different parties in Northern Ireland. This was helpful but the real importance of the document lay in three significant points that followed in the body of the text.

First, it made it clear that the British government was open to possible Irish unity—but only if this were achieved by consent:

No United Kingdom Government for many years has had any wish to impede the realisation of Irish unity, if it were to come about by genuine and freely given mutual agreement and on conditions acceptable to the distinctive communities.[4]

In itself this was not new—Lloyd George had spoken in somewhat similar terms to the Treaty negotiators in 1921.[5] But restating it clearly in this document in the circumstances of 1972 was important. The phrasing—'on conditions acceptable to the distinctive communities'—is also of interest in that it could imply that not just the consent of a majority but the consent of each of the two main communities in Northern Ireland would be necessary if there was to be a united Ireland.

Second, it acknowledged, in effect, that the Westminster 'winner takes all' parliamentary model was not well suited to a local parliament in a divided society. This view, which had been pressed by the Irish government over the previous eighteen months, was most clearly put in the following paragraph:

A Northern Ireland assembly or authority must be capable of involving all its members constructively in ways which satisfy them and those they represent that the whole community has a part to play in the government of the Province. As a minimum this would involve assuring minority groups of an effective voice and a real influence; but there are strong arguments that the objective of real participation should be achieved by giving minority interests a share in the exercise of executive power if this can be achieved by means which are not unduly complex or artificial, and which do not represent an obstacle to effective government.[6]

This requirement, which was later to be called 'power-sharing', came to be accepted as a necessary element all in future attempts at a settlement from Sunningdale in 1973 up to and including the Good Friday Agreement of 1998.

Third, it introduced for the first time an important new concept—the 'Irish Dimension'—picked up, as we can now see, from the internal Northern Ireland civil service paper I mentioned above. The Green Paper presented this as an acceptance of realities: north and south shared some common difficulties and opportunities; an element of the minority continued to see itself as part of the wider Irish community; and 'powerful influences which regard[ed] the unification of Ireland as unfinished business' had to be taken into account in the search for stability in Northern Ireland. The phrase itself was defined only to the extent of saying that

> [w]hatever arrangements are made for the future administration of Northern Ireland must take account of the Province's relationship with the Republic of Ireland: and to the extent that this is done, there is an obligation upon the Republic to reciprocate.[7]

The 'Irish Dimension' in the Green Paper may well have been intended as a vague general phrase that would please the minority in Northern Ireland—and the Irish government—without unduly alarming the majority. But, whatever the original intention, it came to be an essential concept to be recognised, fleshed out and given substance in subsequent attempts at a settlement. The Council of Ireland envisaged in the Sunningdale Agreement of December 1973, the role for the Irish government provided for in the Anglo-Irish Agreement, the north-south negotiations in the so-called 'second strand' during the Brooke-Mayhew Stormont talks of the early 1990s and the north-south ministerial council established under the 1998 settlement, were, each in their time, a way of acknowledging it and seeking to give it institutional expression.

I call this Green Paper, and particularly the recognition of an 'Irish Dimension', a turning point for several reasons.

First, whether or not this was the explicit intention, it could be seen in some ways as a kind of 're-legitimation' of the Irish nationalist agenda by the British government in an official document for the first time since the Treaty. By this I mean that it was at least a tacit acceptance that the old 'Irish Question' of the late-nineteenth and early-twentieth centuries had not been settled definitively in 1920–21.

The Green Paper showed that the British government was now coming to accept that what had once been a contention between the unionist and nationalist agendas for the future of the whole island of Ireland now remained bottled up and still unresolved in the narrower ground of Northern Ireland.

Second, it followed that the Irish government would have to have a role in the effort to reach a stable settlement—not as a foreign government that maintained an untenable 'claim' from outside on Northern Ireland but because there was an 'Irish Dimension' intrinsic to Northern Ireland itself. Any settlement of the conflict there 'must also recognise Northern Ireland's position within Ireland as a whole', and find a way to take the 'Irish Dimension' of the problem there into account.[8] The phrasing was vague and general but it was clear enough that something more than routine cross-border exchanges was contemplated.

A third point was also clear. If the 'Irish Dimension' were to be accommodated in a settlement in Northern Ireland then the republic would have to reciprocate. One obvious implication of this was that the south would have to play its part in any structure that might be set up between north and south. But something more would be required. If the minority were to share in devolved government in Northern Ireland, and some kind of organic link were to be established with the south, then it would be necessary for the Irish government on its side to provide reassurance to the unionist community against their fear of being pushed or slid against their will into a united Ireland. It may not be too much to see a further implication in the phrase about the republic having to reciprocate. The drafters of the Green Paper probably did not have this in mind, but in retrospect the phrase can be seen as implying that change in the north, and some rapprochement between north and south, would be facilitated if there were also some changes in society and attitudes in the republic—a foreshadowing, perhaps, of something like the reforms envisaged in the 'constitutional crusade' Garret FitzGerald called for a few years later.

Be that as it may, the three main ideas in the Green Paper— partnership government of some kind in Northern Ireland, some arrangement or structure to accommodate the 'Irish Dimension', and a guarantee to the unionist community on the 'consent' issue—describe in broad outline the elements that were found by the two governments to be necessary in all of their subsequent efforts to resolve the Northern Ireland problem; and, in a more fully developed form, they are essential parts of the settlement arrived at eventually in 1998.

Jack Lynch responded very positively to the publication of the Green Paper. This is hardly surprising, since the ideas I have just mentioned reflected quite well the kind of approach he had been urging on Heath and his government for several years previously. I still have a copy of a scribbled note in Lynch's own handwriting setting down the main points he wanted to have included in a statement that he proposed to make in the Dáil very early in November. The note was passed to me, through our minister Dr Hillery, with a request—at short notice—for a speech, which I duly drafted. It may be of interest here to include the text of Lynch's note since the points he made show his personal thinking in the days immediately following the publication of the Green Paper.

> The Green Paper discusses structures that make a solution possible and that would guarantee rights (economic etc.) and protection of the minority. Welcome positive steps to this end. Reconciliation in NI is a sine qua non. Hope Green Paper produces it. To no one's benefit to let situation drift and especially to let any opportunity offered in the Green Paper slip. No reasonable suggestion will be met with negative response. That will be attitude of government. If we neglect opportunity to build on whatever offers there may not be another and situation may be taken over by extreme factions.

> Support the setting up of regional assembly in which minority would have fair representation in it and in decision making. Support also the idea of Ireland Council if it is worthwhile and evolutionary (evolutionary might be expressed in a different way). Assuming that the proposals in document set us on

the right road we must do everything to move forward and insure [sic] that no faction will do anything to divert or impede us.

Insofar as Green Paper points the way to a solution in all Ireland context we welcome (or some phrase less enthusiastic). Structures that existed hitherto made this impossible. Similarly lack of (acceptable) structures would make it impossible. Political evolution inherent in it.[9]

The Green Paper also touched on a proposal which the Irish government, and the political leaders of the minority in the north, found less welcome. This envisaged that '[t]he wishes of the people of Northern Ireland on their relationship to the United Kingdom and to the Republic will be ascertained by a plebiscite early in the New Year' (that is in early 1973). This proposal, however, cannot have come as a surprise. Prime Minister Heath had spoken publicly of the idea six months previously. Speaking of the 'consent principle' in the House of Commons on 24 March 1972, the day he announced the prorogation of Stormont, he said

[t]his government, and their predecessors, have given solemn and repeated assurances that the position of Northern Ireland as part of the United Kingdom will not be changed without the consent of the people of Northern Ireland. We have decided that it would be appropriate to arrange for the views of the people of Northern Ireland to be made known on this question from time to time. We, therefore, propose in due course to invite Parliament to provide for a system of regular plebiscites in Northern Ireland about the Border, the first to be held as soon as practicable in the near future and others at intervals of a substantial period of years thereafter.[10]

Heath had also mentioned the proposed plebiscite to Lynch at the meeting in Paris on 21 October 1972 that I referred to in the previous chapter. In the next chapter I will touch on the implementation of this provision on 8 March 1973, for the first and only time to date.

I have depicted the publication of the Green Paper at the end of October 1972 as a positive and important development—though I accept that this is clearer now than it may have seemed at the time. In other respects, however, the year 1972 was grim enough. Bew and Gillespie in their chronology describe it bluntly as '[t]he most bloody year of the Troubles': 470 people were killed; 1,853 bombs were planted and 18,819 kilograms of explosives were found.[11]

Relations between the British and Irish governments, and personally between Heath and Lynch, were now reasonably good—they had certainly improved considerably since the angry exchanges of August 1971. And both countries, along with Denmark, were preparing to take up membership of the EEC as from 1 January 1973. This was important for many reasons—not least because, over time, it greatly improved both personal and working relations between the two governments—though the full effect of this was felt only after Lynch lost office in March 1973. In later years British and Irish ministers—not just foreign ministers but ministers from many other departments also—got to know each other well as they attended regular meetings of the Council in Brussels and Luxembourg. Not only that, they learned to work well together, where, as often happened, they had interests in common, since they were the only two common law countries in a community where the legal traditions of all other member states derived from the Napoleonic Code. The taoiseach of the day and the prime minister, too, as heads of government of EEC member states, saw each other from time to time, initially at special Summit meetings, and then in a more routine and more structured way as members of the European Council established in December 1974. Over the years all of this was to have a considerable ameliorative effect on Anglo-Irish relations—including in particular relations in regard to Northern Ireland. In late 1972, however, all that was still in the future.

Towards the end of 1972 the taoiseach was invited to speak at the Oxford Union, the prestigious debating society in Oxford University. The invitation came from Philip McDonagh, an Irish student at Balliol College, who had been elected president of the Union for that year.[12] Philip is a son of the late Bob McDonagh, who was head of the Anglo-Irish division in Foreign Affairs at the time. The taoiseach travelled to Oxford on Thursday 23 November. Philip's father, Bob, travelled with him, and I, too, was among the officials from the taoiseach's own department and from Foreign Affairs who were with him on the trip. After an early dinner with Philip and the other officers of the Union, the taoiseach went on to speak in the formal debate. His speech was very well received. His mild, affable, non-threatening persona came across well. I see from a short note I made later that I thought that, although his voice was low and he was not a particularly inspiring speaker, he was good at careful articulation of policy.

After Oxford, Lynch went on to London. In the course of an off-the-record briefing for the press at the Irish embassy next morning he mentioned the question of Irish unity. When asked what he thought might be a possible timetable for its achievement he said 'a date like 1999 or 2000' might be set as a target: that would help to concentrate minds in the interval on 'working it out'.[13]

On the evening of Friday, 24 November, Lynch had a working dinner with the prime minister in 10 Downing Street. The foreign secretary Sir Alec Douglas-Home, the Cabinet secretary Sir Burke Trend, and Robert Armstrong, Ted Heath's principal private secretary, were also present. Lynch was accompanied by the Irish ambassador, Donal O'Sullivan.

In his report on the meeting the ambassador makes clear that, although Heath and Lynch did not agree on all points, '[t]he atmosphere throughout was most cordial'.[14] Lynch, in an opening statement, referred to the disabilities suffered by the minority in the north over 50 years; he expressed satisfaction at the British Green Paper which ruled out UDI,[15] integration of the north into the UK and a return to Stormont; and he welcomed the concept of the 'Irish Dimension', which should be given meaningful expression. He was, he said, greatly encouraged by the statement that any solution for the north must be acceptable to the republic; he welcomed the idea of a Council of Ireland, which should be strong and should have evolutionary possibilities; and he said that if there were to be a Northern Ireland assembly it should have a multi-party executive. However, he continued to object to the proposed border poll as well as to the stark nature of the proposed questions. Re-unification would continue to be 'the ideal for the overwhelming majority of the Irish people' and there must be full scope for the legitimate expression of this idea by the Northern minority.

Heath, responding, was glad to see that there was a considerable meeting of minds between them on many issues. The UK still had to consider the timing and content of the proposals to be made in the forthcoming White Paper. However, he was committed to the border poll. He thought the role of the proposed Council of Ireland on economic and social matters could be important 'in the context of the Common Market'. He said initially that while he could not agree to 'negotiations' on the Council with the Irish government, there could be 'consultation, discussion and contact'. Lynch was disappointed at this. However, returning to the issue later, and approaching it in another way, Lynch asked whether there could be early meetings between officials on both sides to contribute towards a suitable proposal? Heath agreed to this suggestion. In a discussion on security, Lynch confirmed his resolve to deal with the IRA; he spoke of new legislative proposals that would be introduced in a few days; and he gave details of the work of the Special Criminal Court. He said he was disappointed at the tendency of the British side to blame him for not doing more. Heath 'indicated understanding'.

As it happened, a crisis that was beginning just before Lynch left Dublin for Oxford developed further that evening and intruded on the discussions with Heath at this point. On 19 November, RTÉ broadcast an interview that Kevin O'Kelly, a respected journalist, had done with the IRA leader Séan Mac Stiofáin. The government were outraged: the Broadcasting Act, in their view, required RTÉ not to broadcast interviews with IRA members. The gardaí arrested Mac Stiofáin, who went on hunger strike. When he appeared in court on 24 November, O'Kelly was asked to identify him. He refused to do so and he was sentenced to three months' imprisonment for contempt of court. Mac Stiofáin was also convicted and sentenced to prison where he continued his hunger strike though only for a short time. The government were dissatisfied with the response they had received from the RTÉ Authority about the affair, and on the evening of Friday, 24 November the minister responsible, Gerard Collins, sacked the whole Authority.[16]

According to the ambassador's report Heath was very interested in what had been done. He admitted that he had his problems too and 'would wish at times to be able to take the same forthright action against the BBC'. This is accurate, no doubt. But it misses the full flavour of the occasion as often recounted years later to myself and other colleagues by Robert Armstrong, Heath's principal private secretary, who was present, and whom we got to know well during the negotiations for the Anglo-Irish Agreement of 1985, when he was the Cabinet secretary. News of the dramatic and unprecedented step taken by the government in sacking the RTÉ Authority actually came through while the taoiseach was in discussion with Ted Heath at Downing Street. Lynch was called out to take a phone call from his minister in Dublin who conveyed the news of what had just been done. Robert's story was that when Lynch returned to the room and told Heath in a low-key, almost off-hand way, Heath was amazed at first at what seemed to him to be such a daring move. He then turned to Armstrong and, with a mischievous glint in his eye, said 'Do you think I could do that to the BBC, Robert?'

The taoiseach and his delegation returned to Dublin in the early hours of Saturday morning. My recollection is that in those days, before there was a 'government jet', Aer Lingus had put on a special flight. We arrived in Dublin airport at about 2 a.m. As I remember it, the airport was bleak and deserted but for two government ministers, George Colley and Gerard Collins, who had come out to greet the taoiseach and brief him on what had been an eventful day at home. After talking with them, and while we waited in the VIP lounge for our baggage, the taoiseach called over Bob McDonagh and myself to give us a more personal account, in confidence, of his discussions at dinner with Heath earlier that evening. He said his meeting with Heath over the working dinner earlier that evening had been 'the best so far'. He had briefed Heath on what the government was doing on security and had asked him 'to lay off' the tendency on the British side to be constantly critical on these matters.

He had also emphasised to Heath that 'there would have to be discussions if the "Irish Dimension" was to mean something'. He had 'thrown out' to Heath the idea that there should be what he called 'disownable'—that is to say highly confidential—'talks' between British and Irish officials on these issues in the near future, for which, he seemed to imply, we should be ready. Heath had responded, 'why not?'[17]

Bob McDonagh, as head of the Anglo-Irish division in Foreign Affairs, and Ambassador O'Sullivan, subsequently met twice in London with British officials from the Foreign and Commonwealth Office and the Northern Ireland Office—on 1 and 22 January 1973; and documents were exchanged between the two meetings. However, the meetings were low-key and, from an Irish viewpoint, the documents were disappointing. The British at that stage seemed to envisage a consultative council only, with no specific functions prescribed in advance. They argued that they could not impose a strong Council of Ireland on unionists, since it would be necessary for unionists to agree to take part. So it was better to start on a limited basis and provide for possible evolution later.[18]

After the taoiseach's return home from Oxford and London, the government, in an effort to tighten up on security, introduced a Bill amending the Offences against the State Act. The Bill, among other things, would allow the belief of a senior officer of the gardaí that an accused was a member of the IRA to be introduced in evidence in a court case. It was opposed initially by the two main opposition parties, Fine Gael and Labour, and it might well have been defeated. However, two bombs exploded in Dublin on 1 December 1972. Two people were killed and more than a hundred were injured. Fine Gael, reacting to the public emotion aroused by this, abstained in the Dáil vote; the Bill passed through both Dáil and Seanad and was immediately signed into law.

A referendum that was held a week later was also relevant to the Northern Ireland problem. The government had come to believe that the reference in the Constitution to 'the special position of the Roman Catholic Church as the guardian of the faith of the great majority of the Irish people' was sectarian in tone, and that the removal of the whole article that included this reference could help in promoting reconciliation. The referendum took place on Thursday 7 December and the proposal to remove the provision was adopted: the vote was 84 per cent in favour and 16 per cent against.[19] There was some subdued unease at the time on the part of other religious denominations such as the Church of Ireland and the Jewish Congregations, who had also been named in the article now to be deleted. Even though it spoke of the 'special position' of the Roman Catholic Church, they had valued the fact that they too had been given explicit recognition by name in the Constitution. The initiative was well-meaning but it was quickly forgotten; and it had little or no effect on the situation in Northern Ireland.

NOTES

[1] Memo and enclosure of 8 September 1972: 'Political settlement: "the Irish Dimension"', from H. Black addressed to secretary of state. Public Record Office of Northern Ireland (PRONI), DCR/1/126. I am very grateful to Professor John Coakley for bringing this document to my attention.

[2] William Whitelaw, *The Whitelaw memoirs* (London, 1989), 108.

[3] Bloomfield, *A tragedy of errors*, 31.

[4] Para. 77.

[5] On 14 October 1921 when he said, 'We begin with (1) no force and are left with the only alternative (2) persuasion without any pressure from us…Use persuasion and we will stand on one side. But until agreement you must allow the present arrangement to stand.' Jones, *Whitehall diary*, volume III, 130.

[6] Para. 79 (f).

[7] Para. 78.

[8] Paras 76–8.

[9] Exact text of a manuscript note in Lynch's handwriting, a copy of which is in my possession.

[10] Hansard, House of Commons Debates (hereafter cited as HC Deb), 24 March 1972, vol. 833 cc1859-74.

[11] Bew and Gillespie, *Northern Ireland*, 57. Keogh, *Jack Lynch*, 367, quoting Jonathan Bardon, *A history of Ulster*, 701, says 103 British soldiers, 41 members of the RUC and the UDR and 323 civilians. This would give the total as 467.

[12] Philip's brother Bobby was elected president of the Union a few years later. Both brothers later joined the Department of Foreign Affairs and each, like their father, served with distinction as ambassadors in various important posts abroad.

[13] Drawn from a personal note dated '4 a.m. Saturday morning 25 November 1972', which I made on return to Dublin.

[14] NAI DFA 2003/13/11. Lynch himself subsequently made minor corrections to the report. See also Keogh, *Jack Lynch*, 364–6.

[15] Abbreviation for unilateral declaration of independence.

[16] The government had probably been determined to take a tough attitude since an earlier episode, in September, when they had issued a 'directive' to RTÉ. Gerard Collins, as minister for posts and telegraphs, was responsible for RTÉ. I think it probable that he told the taoiseach on the phone to London what he proposed to do and got final approval to go ahead.

[17] My private note of 25 November 1972.

[18] Summary note on NAI DFA 2004/15/16.

[19] Another proposal to reduce the voting age from 21 to 18 was voted on at the same time and adopted by a broadly similar margin—85 to 15 per cent.

A Council of Ireland?

Towards the end of 1972 a good deal of work was done in the Interdepartmental Unit on the North (IDU) to flesh out the concept of a Council of Ireland. This was now becoming more relevant because of the recognition in the British Green Paper of 30 October of the need to take account of the 'Irish Dimension'. Since the proposal for a Council was to loom large in the preparations for the Sunningdale conference, at the conference itself, and in the aftermath, I will look here at the background to the idea.

The concept of a Council of Ireland goes back to the Government of Ireland Act 1920, which the British government envisaged as the amendment to the Home Rule Act that had been promised when the Act was passed in 1914 and suspended during the war years. When the war ended, British government thinking on how to amend the Act turned to finding some way to accommodate, either temporarily or on a permanent basis, the vehement opposition of Ulster Unionists to Home Rule. In November 1919 a cabinet committee chaired by Walter Long proposed to the government

to follow the Peace by respecting the principle both of responsible government and of self-determination and to give to the two parts of Ireland immediately *state rights* together with a link between them, and to give them also the power to achieve Irish unity on any basis ranging from federal unity for the United Kingdom to a qualified Dominion status which they can agree upon among themselves.[1] [Emphasis in the original.]

The report of Long's committee, as Ronan Fanning puts it, 'signalled the most decisive shift in Britain's Irish policy since Gladstone drafted his first home rule bill in 1886'.[2] The 1920 Act was substantially shaped by the committee's recommendations.

The Act provided for the division of Ireland into two parts—'Northern Ireland' and 'Southern Ireland'. Ireland as a whole was to remain within the overall sovereignty of the United Kingdom but each of the two parts would have its own subordinate parliament of the Home Rule type with devolved powers over certain matters.[3] The two were to be linked by a Council of Ireland, which would promote mutual cooperation and which might eventually be replaced by a single parliament for the whole island if the two parliaments so decided.[4] The Council was to have forty members—twenty elected by each of the two parliaments. Its president would be nominated by the king's representative, the lord lieutenant.

Section 2 (1) of the Act set out the role of the proposed Council as follows:

> With a view to the eventual establishment of a Parliament for the whole of Ireland, and to bringing about harmonious action between the parliaments and governments of Southern Ireland and Northern Ireland, and to the promotion of mutual co-operation and uniformity in relation to matters affecting the whole of Ireland, and to providing for the administration of services which the two parliaments mutually agree should be administered uniformly throughout the whole of Ireland, or which by virtue of this Act are to be so administered, there shall be constituted, as soon as may be after the appointed day, a Council to be called the Council of Ireland.[5]

The new entity of 'Northern Ireland' duly came into being a year later but 'Southern Ireland', as we know, did not. Instead, the Anglo-Irish Treaty of 1921 established the 'Irish Free State' as a dominion with a much greater degree of independence. The Treaty gave the new parliament of Northern Ireland a right to opt out of the Free State; and it envisaged that if that happened—which it did—there would still be a Council of Ireland as a link between north and south. However, nothing was done to establish such a Council over the following years—the executive council, which is to say the government, of the Free State, was, to say the least, not enthusiastic about it. This seems to have been largely because of what Kevin O'Shiel of the Boundary Commission, writing in 1924, referred to as 'its tendency to treat the Six or Four Counties, or whatever it may be, as the equal of the Free State'.[6] Already, as early as 21 March 1922, Michael Collins, in a minute directed to other members of what was at that stage still the Provisional Government, had spoken of 'keeping the Belfast Government well within its powers'. He also thought it important to make clear that 'there is no question of the Council of Ireland arising under the Treaty'. His six colleagues annotated his minute and recorded their agreement (though one pointed out that in fact there was provision for the Council in the Treaty).[7]

The focus, instead, in those early years of the state, was on the Boundary Commission, which was to determine the definitive border between north and south.

In 1925 the Commission collapsed in disagreement, and it never published any formal report. Instead, a new agreement, 'amending and supplementing' the 1921 Treaty, was reached between 'the British Government and the Government of the Irish Free State being united in amity in this undertaking with the Government of Northern Ireland', as it was put in the preamble.[8] In effect it abolished the Boundary Commission, left the border as it stood and assigned to the parliament and government of Northern Ireland the powers which the proposed Council of Ireland was to have in relation to Northern Ireland. It also provided that the governments of the Irish Free State and of Northern Ireland were to meet together as and when necessary to consider 'matters of common interest arising out of or connected with the exercise and administration of the said powers'. This never happened, and the proposal for some kind of structured link between north and south took its place among the many other ghostly 'might have beens' of Irish history.

Over the years a degree of economic cooperation developed, by agreement, between north and south in specific areas such as railways, the control of fisheries on the River Foyle and the Erne hydroelectric scheme. A study by Michael Kennedy has shown that, notwithstanding the cold and often antagonistic public rhetoric, a good deal of mutually beneficial cooperation also took place over the years from 1925 to 1968 at a practical, sub-political level.[9] However, faint memories of the original idea of a structured link still lingered and the idea of some kind of Council was touched on in public on a few occasions.

It was mentioned by Eamon de Valera, for example, though only in passing, in a debate in the Senate (Seanad Éireann) on 29 January 1958 on a motion by Senator Professor Stanford that requested the government 'to set up a commission or to take other decisive and energetic steps to consider and report on the best means of promoting social, economic and cultural cooperation between the Twenty-Six Counties and the Six Counties.' In a far-sighted speech for that era Senator Stanford, having explicitly ruled out 'political matters...matters of loyalty and allegiance', listed many areas where practical cooperation would benefit both parts of the island. In his response, the taoiseach Eamon de Valera was not unsympathetic but at his suggestion the Seanad did not proceed with the motion. He said he favoured cooperation but he believed government action would be 'suspect from the start' and he thought it better to begin with 'ad hoc arrangements between cultural, social and economic groups'. Stanford had cited the Council of Europe in Strasbourg as a possible model. De Valera had a positive view of that body but he pointed out that, since there was an agreed framework in Strasbourg, the situation there differed significantly from that in the island of Ireland. Somewhat surprisingly perhaps, when he was explaining this point he referred in quite positive terms to the Council of Ireland envisaged in 1920.

> You had at Strasbourg, at any rate, representatives from the various countries of Europe, including

France and Germany, and you had present individuals from these countries and people could meet there, and in that you had the first step taken—the representatives had met together. We have not real representatives of the various shades of opinion in the Six Counties and shades of opinions here meeting together. In the 1920 Act, an attempt was made to have a Council of Ireland in which you would have representatives from the different parts coming together. The existence of that, even though at the start it might not have very great power, would ensure that these people came together and would supply what Strasbourg supplied, a coming-together of authoritative representatives of the two parts. Even though it was not on a fair proportional system, the mere fact that they were coming together would give a centre on which to work. If such a body existed, we would not have to speak of one side setting up a commission, and I would not have to appeal for another half to come from somewhere else. It would be there already. That body would naturally seek to bring about, between the two parts, that co-operation which has been suggested here.[10]

There was another brief flurry of interest in the idea of a Council in the early months of 1965. There had been a historic first meeting between the taoiseach Seán Lemass and the Northern Ireland prime minister Terence O'Neill in Belfast on 14 January 1965 and this raised hopes of a new era in north-south relations. A Mr J.J. Quigley of Carrickmacross, in a letter to the editor published in the *Irish Press* of 29 January 1965, outlined the Council of Ireland provisions in the 1920 Act, and recalled that, three years previously, he had suggested in a local paper that, with membership of the EEC in prospect, the concept of such a Council might become relevant again. On 18 February 1965, during an interview on Telefís Éireann (as it then was), Terence O'Neill was asked about the idea of a Council. According to the *Irish Independent* the next day 'he did not think the climate of opinion was right for setting up an Irish Council as originally envisaged in the Treaty'.[11]

The idea of a Council of Ireland was raised again at a meeting in Dublin on the evening of 19 February 1965. According to a report in the *Irish Times* the following day the meeting was held 'under the auspices of National Unity'. The main speaker was Ernest Blythe, who was at the time director of the Abbey Theatre and had been a minister in the Cumann na nGaedheal government in the 1920s. His theme was that Irish unity could not be rushed; and it could not be achieved by transferring powers from Westminster to Dublin. A new treaty of union would be needed. Britain would not oppose it but it would be difficult to negotiate. More interesting now, however, is what was said by another speaker—E.G. Quigley, who was described as 'chairman of the Belfast group of the National Party, and Northern secretary of the I.N.T.O'.[12] His theme was 'things can never be the same again'. He spoke about the Lemass-O'Neill meeting the month before and went on to outline a wide range of areas where north and south could cooperate. At civil service level 'it might be possible to establish joint authorities' for such areas as tourism, transport, fisheries, agriculture and the fire prevention and ambulance services. There could also be cooperation in such matters as industrial, agricultural, educational and medical research and joint conferences of municipal authorities and county councils on areas such as town planning, urban renewal and house-building techniques. Some consideration might also be given to the establishment of 'an Irish Parliamentary Union'; and a stage was being reached 'where the Parliaments of Northern and Southern Ireland might agree that there were areas where they could, and should, operate united services throughout the country'. If this stage were reached 'it might be desirable to put this exercise on a formal basis with a body such as the Council of Ireland.'[13]

The Department of External Affairs took an interest in Mr Quigley's speech. At the request of the secretary a note was prepared internally on his ideas, along with a background note on the Council of Ireland as envisaged in the 1920 Act. The note suggested that 'it would be going too far too fast to give serious consideration to…promoting the idea of a Council of Ireland at this stage', since there would have to be 'a re-definition of the constitutional positions' north and south. However, after considering two international bodies—the Inter-Parliamentary Union and the Inter-Parliamentary

Consultative Council of Benelux—as possible models, the note said that an Irish Parliamentary Union could serve a useful function; and it concluded that the advantages of such a body would outweigh the possible disadvantages.[14]

Over the years 1965–8 there were further meetings, alternately in Dublin and Belfast, between the prime ministers—first O'Neill and Lemass and then O'Neill and Lynch. Cooperation between north and south increased and became more open. It was still kept to specific issues at the practical level, however, and the idea that it should be formalised under an institutional structure such as a Council was not raised.

The skies darkened in Northern Ireland in 1968 as civil rights protests and marches were harshly dealt with by the police. O'Neill's efforts at reform faltered in face of strong opposition and he resigned in April 1969. By then the cross-border cooperation process, which had reached a high point in 1967, had ground to a halt. The belief that north-south relations would steadily improve through what Michael Kennedy describes as 'occasional meetings between the two prime ministers, frequent meetings of ministers and ongoing meetings of civil servants' was no longer tenable.[15] As he put it

> Dublin's Northern policy since the early 1960s had been to build links with the Unionist Party and to move the Nationalist Party into Stormont so as to create the conditions under which reform could take place. In short, it was to try to reform Northern Ireland from within, rather than from without by ending partition, as had been the strategy in the 1950s.[16]

Summit meetings from time to time, cooperation on a widening series of practical matters, and occasional thoughts of reverting to the 1920 concept of a Council of Ireland, were all fully compatible with such a policy—indeed these were precisely the ways in which it could best be given effect. Now, however, the climate had changed sharply. The sustained demands of a newly resurgent minority for full civil rights, the manifest inadequacy of the reforms offered and the often harsh policing response, showed that Northern Ireland was beginning to fracture along a fault-line which, arguably, had been built into it from the outset. In such an atmosphere, and in face of the reactions it evoked in the south, a policy of developing quiet north-south cooperation on practical issues, and perhaps establishing a Council of some kind to promote it, was no longer tenable.

This remained the case as the conflict in Northern Ireland grew increasingly serious in the early 1970s. As the taoiseach, Jack Lynch, began to work his way slowly towards a more coherent response to the deteriorating situation, his concerns were to re-assert the moderate nationalist aspiration to Irish unity, while also rejecting those who sought to realise it by violent means; and to press for change and reform of the system which had proved to result in permanent one-party government in the north. It was not a time when much thought was being given to establishing a Council of Ireland to link north and south; and neither of his two main advisers over this period was emphasising the idea.

Ken Whitaker's advice continued to look towards a long-term policy of 'seeking unity through agreement in Ireland between Irishmen', the approach set out in Lynch's Tralee speech of September 1969 (which he had drafted). The very lengthy paper drafted with the help of colleagues in the Department of Finance, which I referred to in Chapter 4, talked about a variety of ways of drawing north and south together but it made no explicit mention of a Council of Ireland. Indeed, it would seem from Anne Chambers' biography, that Whitaker's first explicit proposal for such a body may have been in a letter of 14 March 1972 to his opposite number, Sir Leslie O'Brien, the Governor of the Bank of England, in which he proposed a Council of Ireland, 'to which specific functions could gradually be transferred' and through which 'we could all creep up on a new and united Ireland.' O'Brien, in turn, passed the proposal to the prime minister, Ted Heath, who, as we now know, was preparing to prorogue Stormont, and did so a week later.[17]

As I explained in earlier chapters, the advice Lynch was receiving from his other adviser, Eamonn Gallagher, focused mainly on two points: asserting a role for the Irish government in relation to the north; and the complete unsuitability of the Westminster system as a model for devolved government at Stormont. The idea of a Council of Ireland linking north and south did not fit well with this approach. It is true that in the brief for the second Chequers meeting at the end of September 1971, which I referred to in Chapter 6, Gallagher suggested that the taoiseach might look for the creation of an 'Economic and Social Council of Ireland' at 'sub-parliamentary level'—mainly, I think, so that Lynch would have something to show after the meeting; and Lynch himself had indeed touched on that idea in the Dáil on 6 August 1971, in a comment on a suggestion by Jim Callaghan.[18] Although there was a reference to such a body in the draft communiqué proposed by the British side towards the close of the Chequers meeting, Lynch pressed successfully to have it dropped because he considered it premature to set up any such body until there had been progress on other matters 'including the re-structuring of Stormont'.[19] He judged, correctly, that it did not make much sense at that stage to seek to set up a new structure linking the Irish government and the Northern Ireland government at Stormont while at the same time pressing, as he did, to have the latter re-structured radically.

Things had changed by mid-1972, however. The Stormont parliament had been prorogued—in effect abolished—some months earlier and it was clear now that the British government was seeking a new approach. In June 1972 Brian Faulkner was reported as saying that, at the Chequers meeting, Lynch had rejected Faulkner's own proposal for 'an All-Ireland Council'. Lynch issued a clarifying statement in which he was able to be much more open to the idea of a Council than he could have been a year earlier. It said that, at the Chequers meeting in 1971,

> Mr. Faulkner saw such a body operating only in the context of Unionist rule in the North being maintained. Naturally an inter-governmental body in such a context was not acceptable to me.

> There has for many years been co-operation in economic and other spheres between South and North and I am anxious to see this expand as I am sure it will

be in the interests of all the people of Ireland, especially when the communities in the North come to live together in peace and justice. Only last month I said at a press conference that a council representative of South and North would be to our mutual advantage now that both parts of the country were about to join the European Economic Communities.[20]

The situation developed further by late 1972 because the British Green Paper published at the end of October envisaged new political structures and a sharing of power in a new devolved government in Northern Ireland. This meant that a Council of Ireland established now would be part of the more comprehensive package involving 'the re-structuring of Stormont' that Lynch had argued for at Chequers the year before.[21] There was also the prospect now of a Council with a remit much wider than purely cross-border economic issues.

So now, more than half a century after the 1920 Act, the idea of a north-south Council had once again become relevant. The Irish government wanted such a structured link, and in Northern Ireland even parties committed to the Union were open to considering something of the kind—as is clear from the summary of proposals by the various parties contained in Part II of the Green Paper. Indeed, in his memoirs published six years later, Brian Faulkner, who had been the leader of the Ulster Unionist Party at the time, went so far as to argue that his was the first party in modern times to propose a Council of Ireland, albeit one that would have a particular role in relation to security issues:

> The detailed proposals for an inter-governmental Council of Ireland put to Ted Heath before direct rule had been reiterated in our blueprint for the Darlington. The idea of a Council of Ireland, in the recent history of Northern Ireland at least, was therefore Unionist originated. This is not really surprising, as it was Northern Ireland which was suffering and had suffered from political aggression and terrorist incursions, and it was in our interests to secure the co-operation of the

Dublin government against the IRA if we were to succeed in defeating them.

He noted, however, that

> some of the loyalists had been becoming increasingly unenthusiastic about the whole idea in recent months. Bill Craig, in appending his signature to our Darlington proposals, had in fact approved the Council of Ireland idea, and the Unionist Council had supported it too. But 'loyalist' candidates during the Assembly elections had attacked any Council of Ireland, arguing that it would only lead to a united Ireland, and an Orange Order statement had urged support only for those candidates opposed to it.

He put the blame for this growing opposition on the over-ambitious approach of Irish nationalism:

> These pronouncements were a reaction to the fact that the SDLP and the Dublin government had been increasingly taking over the Council of Ireland idea and building it up into a grand design for the whole of Ireland on the European model in order to express Nationalist aspirations. We saw it as the only vehicle through which we could secure progress on the important matters of recognition and security, but we would obviously have to approach the idea cautiously if the loyalists were not to capitalize on the fears which statements emanating from Dublin were creating among Unionists.[22]

The actual proposals of the Ulster Unionist Party at the time the Green Paper was published envisaged a joint 'Irish Inter-Government Council'—but on certain conditions. There would be 'acceptance by the South of the right of the people of Northern Ireland to self-determination'. This would mean 'asking Southern Politicians to translate their verbal commitments to the idea that force will not be allowed to bring about a United Ireland into political and constitutional action'. This declaration would be 'in the form of a solemn and binding agreement between the three governments concerned as in 1925.' There would be inter-government discussions about security matters leading either to the re-negotiation of the extradition treaty or, preferably, 'the British Isles [would be] made a Common Law enforcement area. A warrant issued in Belfast would be executed in Dublin in the same way as it would be in Sheffield.'

> Such action would enable a joint Irish intergovernmental council to be formed with equal membership from the governments of the Northern Ireland and the Irish Republic. Such a Council could discuss matters of mutual interest, particularly in the economic and social field.[23]

Like the Ulster Unionists, the other main parties that favoured maintenance of the Union were also prepared to accept some kind of structure to give expression to the 'Irish Dimension'.

The Alliance Party, for example, favoured 'the creation of machinery to achieve not only better understanding between Northern Ireland and the Irish republic but also joint planning for common economic, social and agricultural problems'. But rather than a Council of Ireland it wanted an Anglo-Irish Council with representatives drawn from Westminster, the Dáil and the proposed new Northern Ireland assembly.[24]

The Northern Ireland Labour Party thought that '[s]erious (and realistic) consideration must be given to the relations between the two parts of Ireland.' The republic's 'claim of jurisdiction over the whole of Ireland' was 'a major irritant'. However, if the republic were 'prepared to recognise its role in the matter', there should be negotiations 'to establish a new Council of Ireland as a consultative and deliberative body' to explore 'areas of mutual cooperation for the benefit of all who live in Ireland.'[25]

The Ulster Liberal Party favoured the setting up of 'a new type of Legislative Assembly' in Northern Ireland with a minimum of 75 members elected by proportional representation and 'a built-in system for the sharing of power as widely as possible'. Instead of a Cabinet and prime minister, there should be a system of 'Departmental Committees' elected by the assembly on a proportional basis. There should be '[p]ermanent consultative machinery' between north and south to deal with matters of common interest. This would take the form of a Joint Council 'appointed in equal numbers by the Northern Ireland Finance Committee and the Government in Dublin'. It would have no executive powers 'but one of its functions would be to investigate the necessity for joint Commissions upon which powers could be conferred by the Dáil and the Assembly for specific purposes.'[26]

The New Ulster Movement saw it as a prerequisite that there should be 'recognition by the Republic of the political status in international law of Northern Ireland as a region of the United Kingdom and its right to remain such until a majority of its citizens decide otherwise'. It wanted nationalists and republicans to be assured that there was 'absolutely no impediment' preventing 'social, economic, cultural and political exchanges—even if these might ultimately lead to agreed changes in political relationships.' It proposed a series of 'devices or structures' conducive to 'a permanent policy of good neighbourliness', cooperation and joint action between north and south. These included a Human Rights Act with an ultimate appeal to a Tribunal of Judges drawn equally from north and south; 'the creation of an all-Ireland Standing Committee to keep the laws of Northern Ireland and the Irish Republic under constant review and to keep divergences to a minimum'. This 'might well include Great Britain'. There would be 'a sharing of power through a system of Parliamentary Committees in the Dail', which would allow meetings on matters of common interest between Northern Ireland assembly committees and committees of the Dail. There would also be 'meetings on matters of common interest between the committees of the Northern assembly and committees of the Dáil', a standing committee on educational matters, 'administration of matters of joint interest by joint statutory bodies' and a joint development commission between north and south.[27]

The SDLP, in contrast, wanted the new structures to be directed towards the long-term aim of Irish unity. They proposed that

188

Britain should make an immediate declaration 'that she believes that it would be in the best interests of all sections of the Communities in both Islands, if Ireland were to become united on terms which would be acceptable to all the people of Ireland.' The declaration 'should contain no hint of coercion'. In the meantime, 'an interim system of government for Northern Ireland' should be established. Britain and the republic, by treaty, would agree to accept joint responsibility for this interim system 'to be known as the Joint Sovereignty of Northern Ireland', while 'reserving to themselves all powers relating to foreign affairs, defence, security, police and financial subventions'. There would be an 84-member assembly, a 15-member executive elected by the assembly by proportional representation, a chief executive and a constitutional court. There would also be 'a National Senate of Ireland', with equal representation, elected by proportional representation, 'from both the Dublin Parliament and the New Northern Assembly'. Its basic function would be 'to plan the integration of the whole island by preparing the harmonisation of structures, laws and services of both parts of Ireland and to agree on an acceptable Constitution for a New Ireland and its relationships with Great Britain'. '[N]o preconceived concept should be placed before the Senate' but 'a new concept of a new Ireland' should evolve from discussions, although [the SDLP] would envisage the emergence of a Parliament for the whole Ireland directly elected.'[28]

These were all publicly stated positions. In Dublin, behind the scenes and without any publicity, a great deal of preliminary work was being done at official level in the IDU. As early as May 1971 it prepared an eighteen-page summary note that included a comprehensive survey of cross-border cooperation between government departments and subsidiary bodies. In late 1972 a series of individual papers by Foreign Affairs members of the IDU, and more formal papers by the IDU as such, examined a whole range of issues that would need to be considered in relation to the structure and function of a Council of Ireland.

One such paper was prepared in November 1972 by Joe Small, a first secretary in the Anglo-Irish division in the Department of Foreign Affairs, who was secretary to the IDU. It summarised the main features of the Council envisaged in the Government of

Ireland Act 1920 and outlined the various ideas put forward by Northern Ireland parties and others. It then noted points of difference from the situation in 1920; and it made suggestions as to guiding principles, composition, powers and functions for a proposed new Council with both an executive and a consultative tier, equal representation from north and south and a permanent secretariat. Another paper, prepared jointly with Small's colleague, Michael Lillis, in December 1972, looked at constitutional aspects, including the possibility of 'an Anglo-Irish Treaty or Agreement' resulting from 'negotiations with the British…on all aspects of an all-Ireland Council'. It then considered ways in which the EEC might provide a useful model for 'a strong, meaningful body with real powers of its own'.[29]

As head of the Press and Information section, which was closely linked to the Anglo-Irish division, I attended IDU meetings regularly at this stage. On 6 December 1972 I followed my other two colleagues by also contributing a paper on the possibilities for a Council of Ireland. It started by noting that 'our hope would be to establish now an institution which will have within itself the potential for growth towards unity in Ireland.' This was difficult since we had as yet no idea of what kind of new administration might be established on 'the other bank' in the north, or how far British thinking might go 'to meet us on a Council with real functions…[and] real growth potential'. The paper then suggested that, while our maximum wish might be for 'a strong Council with real functions', if all that could be achieved at present was a weaker Council we should not flatly rule that out. The most basic reason for what was sometimes referred to as the 'failure' of the Council idea in the early 1920s was that such a Council never came into existence.

> If—conceivably—the North were to settle down now gradually under a new, reformed administration with full redress of grievances, if we continue in the South with our own process of change, and if even a mere talking shop North-South institution were now to come into existence and begin to function, there are real possibilities over the next 15 to 20 years that movement

could come from this. We could realistically expect that, over that period, under the harmonising influence of EEC membership for both parts of Ireland, without the aggravation of minority grievances and majority reaction, and with the experience of 'talking'—even though only in a 'talking shop'—there would be a gradual abatement of present apparently implacable Unionist attitudes so that movement towards unity in Ireland on their part could then seem tolerable.

My paper, like others at the time, reflected an interest in the structures of the EEC as a possible model: it suggested an executive Council of Ministers with six from the proposed new Northern executive and six from the government in Dublin, a parliamentary assembly of twenty members each from the assembly and the Dáil, and a small permanent secretariat. It should deal at first with matters which were 'fairly mundane, pragmatic and unlikely to cause confrontation', and which, at the outset, met some unionist concerns. It also outlined a range of possible functions for the Council, and touched on the possibility that some functions might be devolved direct to it by Westminster rather than via the Northern Ireland assembly. Three of the many possible functions it suggested seem to me now in retrospect to be still worth mentioning because of later developments.

1. There might be a reciprocal arrangement between north and south which would allow an offence committed in either part of the island to be tried in the other jurisdiction. This would, in effect, be a substitute for extradition, which had been one of the specific conditions set by the Unionist Party for acceptance of a Council of Ireland but which would always be difficult for us. It could be an area where the Council would have some kind of supervisory role; and perhaps, eventually, some kind of responsibility for judicial appointments and even for security and police forces.

2. Another was that, under the aegis of the Council and with the aim of increasing understanding, each part of the island

would be opened completely to the TV and radio stations of the other.

3. A third suggestion was that, with the assistance of Euratom, the Council might plan for a single nuclear generator to serve the whole island.

The first two of these suggestions were followed through to an extent in later years—though I doubt if I can attribute this directly to my paper. Granted later attitudes to atomic power, including my own very different attitude today, the third of my 1972 ideas—and the fact that I even mentioned it—are perhaps best left in the obscurity of the archive files.

On 20 December 1972 the IDU, drawing to an extent on these documents by individuals, submitted a series of papers in response to a request from the taoiseach, relayed to us by Dan O'Sullivan, Secretary to the Government, a gentle Kerryman, who chaired the Unit at the time. These were accompanied by a summary paper headed 'Possibilities for a settlement in regard to the North (Taoiseach's request of 14 December 1972)'.

Perhaps I might add two personal memories from that time. One is of Dan's slightly unorthodox way of telling us about a request that the taoiseach had made for options papers—'lads, we have to prepare three wearable blueprints'—a droll way of putting it which became a source of mild hilarity for some time afterwards to those of us involved. Another memory is that, after I had asked at a particular IDU meeting if there might possibly be a file in the Taoiseach's Department on the concept of a Council of Ireland, which after all had been envisaged as a possibility half a century before, Dan turned up to the next meeting with a very, very slim file on the subject. I seem to remember that there were some brief exchanges on that file, in good civil service style, between some of those prominent in the early years of the state. No doubt the years since then have coloured my memory. It occurs to me now, how-ever, as I write this, that perhaps what I saw may have been the minute from Michael Collins, with comments by six other minis-ters, which I referred to earlier in this chapter? Whatever it was, what I found intriguing was that the file from which it came, and which Dan produced that day, seemed to be still a current file in his department and not something he had dug out of the archives— even though there seemed to be no entry on it since the 1920s.

I should perhaps include here an extract from the summary IDU paper I mentioned above, which may help to provide an overview of the thinking of the time, in what would prove to be the closing months of that government's term in office.

> The attached papers...are concerned with proposals for new institutions rather than with the immediate political situation on the ground. The approach taken throughout is based on the following premises:

(a) No new approach to the Northern problem in purely Northern Ireland terms will work.

(b) Immediate unity in Ireland, however, is not feasible; and it is not our aim.

(c) Nevertheless, there is at least a possibility now of working out a settlement which could bring peace.

(d) Such a settlement would provide for new institutions in the north and an institutional link between north and south with the potential for organic growth.

(e) Our hope in accepting such institutions would be to start a process of convergence between north and south, because we believe this to be the only way to bring long-term and lasting stability to the whole island.

(f) It is preferable to concentrate on getting the process going now rather than try to work out now the detailed shape of the new Ireland which we hope may result. If a new Ireland does come about, it will emerge organically from the process of change and convergence.

The following additional points are basic to the approach suggested in these papers:

(i) There are indications in the Green Paper in particular, that the British government may be willing to come some way towards a settlement on these lines. How far is not yet clear. They certainly do not wish to return to the *status quo ante*.

(ii) It is not possible now to bring everyone in the north along in any settlement. Hope must rest, therefore, on achieving a settlement which will, at a minimum, be acquiesced in by a sufficiently large majority in both communities to work; and which will allow the intransigents to be isolated and out faced.

(iii) Any settlement would also have consequences for the south, and, if satisfactory, would call for a response from it.

In the interest of complete disclosure, perhaps I should add that it was I who drafted that particular document. However, I believe that, in drafting it, I reflected reasonably well the kind of ideas we were discussing at the time and recommending to the taoiseach and which indeed he was probably quite ready to accept.[30]

I have dwelt so far on the many positive aspects of the British government Green Paper of 30 October 1972. But, as I mentioned in the preceding chapter, the Green Paper also repeated the commitment which Heath had made in March 1972, when Stormont was prorogued, to hold a plebiscite 'early in the New Year' to ascertain 'the wishes of the people of Northern Ireland on their relationship to the United Kingdom and to the Republic'.[31] Now, a year later, the British government moved to implement this commitment: the first 'border poll' was to be held on 8 March 1973.

The Irish government thought this decision regrettable. I see from notes prepared in the IDU in November 1972, which I had some hand in drafting, that our view at the time was that where there was division between communities which must learn to live together it could be harmful and not helpful to invite each community, in a yes or no poll, to affirm its position. Admittedly John Hume, in a submission to the Crowther (later, Kilbrandon) Commission in February 1970, had proposed a periodic referendum in order to 'take the border out of Irish politics'.[32] But, as our IDU paper put it, 'border' in this context meant not just a line on a map but rather

the whole issue of relations between communities, how power will be shared between them and whether one will dominate the other. It is an issue compounded of dissensions and bitterness going back many generations, and fears and hopes for the future. Whether or not a plebiscite is to be held, it is naïve to expect that to hold it will 'remove the border from politics'.

What was needed rather was 'to encourage both communities to accept their situation and begin to work with political institutions which would help to bring reconciliation'. Furthermore, these papers argued that if a plebiscite were to be held, it would be unwise, as the British government proposed, to limit the choice to two stark options—remaining part of the UK or joining with the republic of Ireland outside the UK. The Green Paper of 30 October had provided a context for an answer to the first question by setting certain requirements and opening up certain options. But no such work had been done, through consultation or negotiation with the Irish government, to set a framework for a meaningful response to the second question about a possible united Ireland. [33]

We were also asked in the IDU to make suggestions for redrafting the questions which the government might possibly press the British government to adopt. The idea behind the request seemed to be that some clever redrafting of Question 2 might induce the Alliance Party to support it, or that rewording the questions in some other way might help to split the unionist (small 'u') vote. But this, we thought, would be unwise.

> If, as we believe, the plebiscite is retrogressive in itself, then our interest is served, not by improving the questions, but by having them as stark as possible. This makes it easier to reject its results, leaving our policy to stand as the only sensible alternative which others may come to accept when the plebiscite fails to solve the problem.

In the event the plebiscite went ahead as planned on 8 March 1973 and the questions remained unchanged. The SDLP, the main nationalist party, called for a boycott of the vote and a majority of nationalists did not vote. The result was a foregone conclusion.

The turnout was 604,256 (58.7 per cent of the electorate): of those who voted, 591,820 voted to retain the Union; only 6,463 voted in favour of unity with the republic; and there were almost 6,000 spoiled votes.[34]

On 1 January 1973 Ireland and the UK, together with Denmark, were admitted to membership of the EEC. Dr Hillery, the minister for foreign affairs, left for Brussels to become a member of the Commission. He was replaced as minister by Brian Lenihan. By then, however, even though it might have seemed that it still had more than a year to run, the political life of Jack Lynch's government was drawing to a close. Lynch called an election on 5 February 1973. In the poll held on 28 February Fianna Fáil lost power for the first time in sixteen years and Fine Gael, led by Liam Cosgrave and Labour, led by Brendan Corish, came together to form a new government—the national coalition.

Perhaps I may finish this account of the Lynch years with another personal anecdote. Some weeks before the election was called, I received a request from the taoiseach through his political adviser for a draft speech on Northern Ireland. As I explained in Chapter 9 this kind of request seldom if ever came with an indication of what line to take. More often than not drafting a text called for some measure of what I could call careful creativity— finding a judicious blend of what one believed policy actually was and what one thought it ought to be, and might perhaps become: in brief, what the speaker would be glad to have said once he—or she—had said it. I duly drafted a text and sent it across to Merrion Street as requested. Weeks passed with no sign of 'my' speech. I forgot all about it. An election was called and lost; the new Dáil met in mid-March; a new government took office; and Jack Lynch, the previous taoiseach, took his place across the floor as leader of the opposition. In one of his first speeches, he devoted some time to the issue of Northern Ireland. As I read about it in the papers next day I thought that some of the wording was familiar. Then I realised that he was using my draft—at last—or some of it at least. I didn't tell anyone at the time but, privately, as a civil servant, I was mildly pleased to have helped in a small way to promote bi-partisanship across the aisle of the Dáil on a most difficult and complex question for the state.

[1] Quoted in John Kendle, *Walter Long, Ireland, and the Union, 1905–1920* (Dublin, 1992), 183. The excerpt cites 'First Report of Cabinet Committee on the Irish Question', 4 November 1919, C.P. 56, Cab 27/68. Long was a Conservative and Unionist MP from 1880 to 1921 and a Cabinet minister for sixteen of those years.

[2] Fanning, *Fatal path*, 206.

[3] Government of Ireland Act (10 & 11 Geo. 5. Ch. 67), Section 75.

[4] Government of Ireland Act, Section 3.

[5] Government of Ireland Act, Section 2 (1).

[6] Memorandum of 28 January 1924 by Kevin O'Shiel in *Documents on Irish foreign policy,* volume II, *1923–1926* (Dublin, 2000), 257. See also the reference in a memorandum of 25 September 1924 by Kevin O'Higgins, Minister for Justice, in same volume, 345–6.

[7] The document is reproduced (as an illustration) on page 235 of Michael Laffan, *Judging W.T. Cosgrave: the foundation of the Irish state* (Dublin, 2014).

[8] The text was appended as a Schedule to the Treaty (Confirmation of Amending Agreement) Act 1925 [No. 40]. The full text is also in *Documents on Irish foreign policy,* volume II, *1923–1926,* 533–4. See also Arthur Mitchell and Pádraig Ó Snodaigh (eds), *Irish political documents, 1916–1949* (Dublin, 1985), 164–9.

[9] Michael Kennedy, *Division and consensus: the politics of cross-border relations in Ireland, 1925–1969* (Dublin, 2000).

[10] Seanad Éireann Debates, vol. 48, no. 15, Wednesday, 29 February 1958, available at: http://oireachtasdebates.oireachtas.ie/debates%20authoring/debateswebpack. nsf/takes/seanad1958012900006 (13 June 2017).

[11] Newspaper clippings of both of these items are on NAI DFA 2000/14/444.

[12] This was Gerry Quigley, who grew up in Belfast, and was later general secretary of the INTO (the Irish National Teachers' Association) and president of the ICTU (Irish Congress of Trade Unions). I don't know whether or not he was related to J.J. Quigley, the author of the letter to the *Irish Press* who must have been a prominent figure in his home town. There is today a J.J. Quigley Memorial Park in Carrickmacross, Co. Monaghan.

[13] *Irish Times,* 20 February 1965, available at: https://www.irishtimes.com/newspaper/archive/1965/0220/Pg004.html#Ar00400 (12 October 2016).

[14] NAI DFA 2000/14/444. I recognise the initials on the paper dated 11 March 1965 as those of Brendan T. Nolan, who was then a first secretary in the Political section. It was submitted to Dr Ned Brennan, the counsellor in charge of the section and presumably passed to the secretary, Con Cremin, who had asked for a note on the issue. I am grateful to Professor John Coakley who brought this file and a number of others to my attention.

[15] Kennedy, *Division and consensus,* 301.

[16] Kennedy, *Division and consensus,* 308.

[17] Chambers, *T.K. Whitaker,* 307. This is the first explicit reference to a Council of Ireland in Chambers' biography. She does not give details of the proposal and Lynch's biographer, Dermot Keogh, does not mention the matter. We must assume that Whitaker would have kept Lynch informed, although Chambers does not say this explicitly. I am not aware whether or not Foreign Affairs was advised of the proposal.

[18] See Chapter 6.

[19] See Chapter 6. Irish note on the meeting NAI DFA 2003/13/7, 32.

[20] Government Information Bureau statement, 9 June 1972. NAI DFA 2000/14/444.

[21] Green Paper, para. 79 (f).

[22] Faulkner, *Memoirs of a statesman*, 208.

[23] Ulster Unionist Party, *Towards the future*. For full text see Annex 4 to the Green Paper, 45–57.

[24] Green Paper, Annex 5, 59–60.

[25] Green Paper, Annex 6, 71.

[26] Green Paper, Annex 8, 85–6.

[27] Green Paper, Annex 9, 97–8.

[28] Green Paper, Annex 7, 72–82.

[29] Much later, on 16 November 1973, some weeks before the Sunningdale conference, Michael Lillis, in a further paper, elaborated on the advantages of the EEC model.

[30] Copies of the various papers on the Council mentioned in the possession of the author.

[31] Green Paper, para. 82, 37.

[32] The Royal Commission on the Constitution set up by Harold Wilson's government in 1969 to examine and make recommendations on the structure and functions of 'the present legislature and government in relation to the several countries, nations and regions of the United Kingdom'. It reported in 1973 but some members dissented and others supported different options. *Royal Commission on the Constitution 1969–1973, volume I: Report*, October 1973, Cmnd. 5460.

[33] Copy of the paper in the possession of the author.

[34] Bew and Gillespie, *Northern Ireland*, 60.

CHAPTER 12

The White Paper

By the time Jack Lynch lost office in March 1973 he had been taoiseach for a little over six years. When the Troubles erupted in Northern Ireland in 1968–9 he had had to face some of the most turbulent years in the history of the state. Tied to an extent into an 'anti-partitionist' tradition, and under severe pressure on security issues, including pressures from the British government on cross-border security cooperation, he was uncertain at first in his response to the escalating conflict. In May 1970 he had to sack several of his more strong-minded and impetuous ministers who were accused of seeking to import arms for the beleaguered minority in the north. Despite these difficulties, he remained a moderate nationalist who maintained a strong commitment to democratic values at a time when others favoured an approach that would have put the state on a very dangerous path. Drawing on advice from several sources, he gradually developed a coherent policy response to the conflict in the north and continued to press the British government to rethink their approach.

In this chapter I want to consider the task that the new coalition government under Liam Cosgrave faced in preparing for the Sunningdale conference of December 1973. Before I do so however

I want to consider whether there was a substantial change in policy on Northern Ireland—or was it rather that the new government shaped and developed ideas and concepts which Jack Lynch as taoiseach had been working towards and seeking to persuade the British government to accept?

I must start by acknowledging the tendency of a civil servant like myself to see a continuity of policy where political leaders will want to stress differences between their approach and that of their predecessors in office. While making due allowance for that, it still seems to me that there was a relatively smooth policy transition between the outgoing and the incoming governments in 1973. Certainly Garret FitzGerald, the new minister for foreign affairs, was ready to acknowledge that Lynch had moved the policy of his party and government on considerably from the simplistic anti-partitionism of an earlier era; and I think he would probably also agree that Lynch had done much to convince the British prime minister, Ted Heath, of the need for a radical new approach to Northern Ireland. Garret had a personal regard for Jack Lynch—rather more so perhaps than had his leader, Liam Cosgrave—and there was between them none of the asperity that sometimes characterises relations between political opponents. In his autobiography, speaking of a slightly later period, Garret says of Lynch:

> While there were, inevitably, some differences in emphasis between our approaches, we were much closer in our views than he was to the 'rhetorical republicans' in his own party.[1]

In the final two years of his term in office, as I explained in earlier chapters, Lynch's approach had been to try to get across to Heath that the old Stormont system was most unsuited to a divided community; that in any new arrangement for devolution power must be shared between elected representatives of both communities; and that Dublin must have a role in a settlement. It may be indeed that Heath's own thinking would have begun to turn towards ideas of this kind once he made Northern Ireland a top personal priority and began to examine the options, as he did in the days following Bloody Sunday.[2] But, in my view, there can be little doubt but that the arguments that Lynch had been pressing on him over the years 1971 and 1972 influenced his decision in favour of a radical new approach.

One measure of how far Lynch had succeeded in gaining at least broad acceptance in London for these ideas is that some of the more important of them were reflected in the British 'Green Paper' of October 1972. They appear again in the lengthy presentation of his thinking on the forthcoming White Paper which the secretary of state for Northern Ireland, Willie Whitelaw, made to the British Cabinet on 1 March 1973—which, as it happened, was the day of the election in Ireland.[3]

Whitelaw's approach in briefing the Cabinet was realistic: he said he had 'some hope' of achieving a settlement but he thought that some extremists on both sides would reject his proposals and he expected IRA violence to continue. He was also clear that his proposals would have to be 'reasonably acceptable' to the Irish government. In developing them, he said, he had regard to five basic requirements.

> First, it was essential that the White Paper and the subsequent Constitutional Bill should command bipartisan support in the Parliament at Westminster.
>
> Second, the proposals must be reasonably acceptable to the government of the Republic since, even though they might not be prepared to give us positive support, they would be able to hinder our efforts if they could not at least acquiesce in our proposals.
>
> Third, the minority in Northern Ireland must feel that they were being given a genuine chance to share in the government and administration of the Province.
>
> Fourth, the settlement must be such as to give encouragement to moderate opinion.
>
> But fifth, our proposals must not be of a kind to lead the Unionists to refuse all cooperation.

If it were possible to devise arrangements that satisfied these criteria, there was some hope that a settlement might be achieved, even though the proposals would probably be rejected by Protestant extremists and would be unlikely to suffice to cause the Irish Republican Army to cease their violence.

He then looked at alternative courses of action and explained why none was acceptable:

Complete integration of Northern Ireland with the rest of the United Kingdom would be opposed not only by the minority and many others in the Province but also by the Irish Republic and by the opposition in the Parliament at Westminster. It would also impose an intolerable strain upon the Westminster Parliament if all Northern Irish business had to be conducted there; and even those elements in Northern Ireland who claimed to favour integration would come to resent having their affairs controlled entirely from London.

A reversion to the old Stormont system was 'equally out of the question; it was no more likely to prove acceptable to the minority in the future than it had in the past'; and a genuinely independent Northern Ireland was 'a wholly unrealistic concept.'

Whitelaw then moved on to relations with the republic:

Finally, it was important, not least because of the attitude of the Government of the Republic, that the White Paper should contain a constructive passage on the 'Irish Dimension'; and it was therefore envisaged that it should indicate that, following the elections to the new Northern Ireland Assembly, the Government of the Republic and representatives of the Parties in the Assembly would be invited by the United Kingdom Government to take part in a conference to discuss how a Council of Ireland might be developed.

A substantial part of Whitelaw's presentation to the Cabinet was taken up with reflections on how an executive in Northern Ireland should be formed; how it would relate to the proposed assembly; and the role of the secretary of state. Following his presentation, the Cabinet discussed whether it would be preferable to lay down some of these matters explicitly in the White Paper or to adopt an 'evolutionary approach' that would leave much to be decided by the assembly itself. In summing up, the prime minister fudged the issue by proposing that Whitelaw should hold further discussion on these 'critical issues'. He said that, when it was completed, the draft for the White Paper would be discussed by the ministers involved and then by the Cabinet itself. In the meantime, he would himself 'discuss the government's proposals, particularly the "Irish Dimension" with the Prime Minister of the Republic in the light of the General Election in the Republic which was taking place that day'.

It was prudent of Heath to refer to 'the Prime Minister of the Republic' and not simply to 'Mr Lynch'. It became clear within days that, as a result of the election in Ireland, a new coalition government was about to take office with Liam Cosgrave as taoiseach and Brendan Corish as tánaiste.

In Britain, after a government is defeated in an election, the transition to the new government can be immediate: the outgoing prime minister leaves Downing Street and his successor, appointed by the queen, moves in the next day. In Ireland, the constitutional position is different: the formal transition must await the election of a taoiseach by the Dáil, which usually holds its first meeting a week or two after the General Election. The person who gains a majority in the Dáil is then formally appointed taoiseach by the president. He or she then nominates the ministers who are to form the new government and they, in turn, are approved by the Dáil and receive their seals of office from the president. In 1973, however, while this constitutional procedure had to be observed, there was an urgency about ensuring that those who were to lead the incoming government would be involved as quickly as possible in the issue of Northern Ireland: the British government was to publish its White Paper on Northern Ireland shortly and the incoming Irish government would want to ensure that their views were taken fully into account. For that reason, in a break with precedent, Cosgrave and Corish, the two party leaders who were to form the new coalition government, travelled to London for discussions with the prime minister on 8 March, a week after the election, and a week before they formally took up office.

As it happened, the day of their visit to London was eventful in two other respects. One was that that happened to be day of the border poll in Northern Ireland. Notwithstanding the concerns expressed by the previous Irish government, the British government had chosen to go ahead with the poll in order to fulfil the commitment Heath had made a year earlier when the old Stormont parliament was prorogued. As I mentioned at the end of the previous chapter, the result of the count was predictable. Since most nationalist voters boycotted it, the poll simply established what was already very well known—that a clear majority of the population in Northern Ireland wanted to maintain the Union. Another more tragic event that day showed clearly that, poll or no poll, those who were engaged in violence were likely to continue. Two IRA car bombs in London killed one person and injured close to 250 other people; two other car bombs were defused before they exploded.

It is an indication of the importance Heath now attached to the issue of Northern Ireland that, notwithstanding the death and destruction on the streets of London, he devoted a great deal of time over two days to discussion with his two visitors from Dublin, who were accompanied by Hugh McCann, secretary of the Department of Foreign Affairs and the Irish ambassador, Donal O'Sullivan. Heath had with him the foreign secretary, Sir Alec Douglas-Home and, for part of the time, the defence secretary, Lord Carrington. The meetings, which included a dinner at Downing Street, stretched to seven hours over that afternoon and the next morning. As a result, Cosgrave and Corish, who can hardly have expected to be plunged into these issues so quickly, had every opportunity to make their views known on what the forthcoming White Paper should contain. The two also had discussions with the leader of the opposition, Harold Wilson.

At the start Heath told his visitors that he hoped to continue with them the same kind of frank and confidential talks that he had been able to hold with Jack Lynch. The forthcoming White

Paper would probably come before Cabinet for approval in about two weeks. It had not been discussed with anybody in Northern Ireland. The decision to impose direct rule had been very difficult. It had been followed by a reform programme imposed by the British government by way of Orders in Council. Next, he said, was the question of 'constitutional reform and the border'. He hoped the border poll would take the border out of politics. It would be necessary then (a) to develop an acceptable form of internal administration in Northern Ireland; and (b) to give appropriate expression to the 'Irish Dimension' which had been recognised 50 years previously but not given expression.

As he saw it, there were three main possibilities for Northern Ireland.

(1) Full integration into the UK. This would be simplest but it would impose a heavy legislative burden on Westminster, deprive Northern Ireland of a local parliamentary structure and be regarded as a retrograde step by the republic. However, it should not be ruled out if no other solution would work.

(2) An independent Northern Ireland (UDI). This would not be viable without the British subsidy of £300 million.

(3) A unicameral assembly elected by proportional representation, and exercising devolved legislative powers in certain areas, subject to the consent of the Northern Ireland secretary of state; and an executive where power was shared on a basis to be worked out in discussions between the party leaders and the secretary of state after the election of the assembly. Overall responsibility for security would, however, have to remain with Westminster for as long as the present situation continued—though certain powers would be devolved as and when the Northern Ireland administration proved itself capable of handling them. This third option was what would be proposed in the forthcoming White Paper.

Turning to the 'Irish Dimension', Heath said that it would be a mistake to define it in detail in advance. He had concluded that the best approach was to call a tripartite conference when the Northern Ireland institutions had been established, in order to consider the structure and functions of a Council of Ireland. He wondered if the Council should be tripartite—in view of Westminster's many continuing responsibilities and EEC issues—or should it be purely north-south?

Liam Cosgrave, replying, welcomed what had been said about the White Paper—and proportional representation—but he was disturbed that it would not define power-sharing more clearly and also that the Council of Ireland would be left to be settled after the establishment of the Northern assembly. Brendan Corish said the Council should have specific functions—it should not be a façade. Other issues raised by the two Irish leaders included a Bill of Rights and the right of the Northern secretary to veto any discriminatory legislation. They undertook to think over what the prime minister had said, while also noting that, as yet, they had no government at home to consult on these issues.

During discussion at the dinner that followed, Liam Cosgrave and Brendan Corish argued that the new executive should broadly reflect, on a proportional basis, the make-up of the assembly, a view to which Heath gave 'general agreement'.

When the talks resumed for another two hours the next morning, both Irish leaders argued again that the shape of the power-sharing executive should be clearly spelled out in the White Paper but Heath favoured leaving the details to talks between the Northern Ireland secretary and the party leaders when the assembly had been elected. Corish said they would reflect further on their return to Dublin and then give Heath a clear view of what they would wish him to do. In a discussion of border security Heath spoke of IRA 'Active Service Units' operating across the border and he urged the fullest possible exchange of information between north and south. In response, Cosgrave repeated his strong opposition to violence. It would be a help to Dublin, he said, if there were confidence in the police in the north. Lord Carrington agreed, saying there was 'a distrust of the uniform'. Corish spoke of the large number of guns, licensed and unlicensed, in the north. When discussion returned to the Council of Ireland, the Irish side again said that it was too vague and they argued for more detail in the White

Paper in relation to form and functions. Liam Cosgrave also gave a firm view that the Council should be bi-partite—that is, confined to north and south, without direct British government involvement. Heath took up this point and promised to put it to his Cabinet. (In my view this exchange was to prove highly significant in achieving Dublin's strong preference for a north-south Council with no direct role for the British government.)

In the closing stages of the discussion, Sir Alec Douglas-Home raised the case taken to Strasbourg by the Irish government under the European Convention on Human Rights. Could Dublin reconsider its position if the overall situation improved? Heath said that the complaint was that atrocities were an administrative practice of the British government—a most serious allegation which the government would defend vigorously. It would argue also that IRA activity is organised from the south. Mud-slinging would not help either country. Liam Cosgrave replied that he was not yet in government: he would look into the matter after he took office. Heath also wondered who best to deal with on the minority side in Northern Ireland and how best to influence minority opinion. The two Irish leaders said that their respective parties had kept in close touch with the minority leaders. This exchange concluded the discussions.[4]

The pace the two leaders of the new Irish government set by this first visit to London continued when they took office. At its very first meeting a week later the new Irish government approved a message to the British government which was delivered to Downing Street while the British Cabinet was meeting there. The government also decided to send Garret FitzGerald, the newly appointed minister for foreign affairs, to London where he, too, met the prime minister and the foreign secretary, Sir Alec Douglas-Home. In his autobiography Garret recalls that he tried, without success, to convince them of the value of providing for a judicial review of human rights. He also told them that he would be visiting Northern Ireland regularly in his new capacity as Irish foreign minister.[5]

Five days later, on 20 March 1973, the British government issued the long-awaited White Paper. It was entitled *Northern Ireland: Constitutional Proposals*.[6] In many respects it followed the approach of the Green Paper of October 1972, with the difference that what had earlier been presented as issues for discussion had now crystallised into specific policy proposals. In view of its importance at the time as a basis for the Sunningdale conference and the new Northern Ireland institutions, I feel I ought to describe its provisions here in some detail.

The White Paper began by recalling eight 'fundamental criteria' already set out in the Green Paper. I can summarise these as follows:

- Northern Ireland would remain part of the United Kingdom for as long as that was the wish of a majority of the people—'but that status does not preclude the necessary taking into account of...the "Irish Dimension"';
- 'As long as Northern Ireland remains part of the United Kingdom the sovereignty of the UK Parliament must be acknowledged and due provision made for an effective voice for the UK government in Northern Ireland's affairs, commensurate with the commitment of financial, economic and military resources in the Province';
- Any division of powers between the national and regional authorities would have to be logical, open and clearly understood;
- The two primary purposes of any new institutions would have to be—first, to seek a much wider consensus than has hitherto existed; and second, to work efficiently and provide the concrete results of good government: peace and order, physical development, social and economic progress. 'This is fundamental because Northern Ireland's problems flow not just from a clash of national aspirations or from friction between the communities, but also from social and economic conditions such as inadequate housing and unemployment.'
- Any new institutions would have to be of a simple and business-like character, appropriate to the powers and functions of a regional authority;
- A Northern Ireland assembly or authority would have to be 'capable of involving all its members constructively in ways which satisfy them and those they represent that the whole

community has a part to play in the government of the Province'. At a minimum this would involve 'assuring minority groups of an effective voice and a real influence' but 'there are strong arguments for giving minority groups a share in the exercise of executive power if this can be achieved by means which are not unduly complex or artificial and which do not represent an obstacle to effective government';

- There would have to be a built-in assurance of absolute fairness and equality of opportunity for all. The future administration would have to be 'seen to be completely even-handed both in law and in fact';
- Future arrangements for security and public order would have to command public confidence both in Northern Ireland and in the UK as a whole. They 'must be seen in practice to be as impartial and effective as possible'; and since the army and the civilian police were both involved, it was essential that there should be a single source of authority—which must mean Westminster control, since it alone could control the Armed Forces of the Crown. Any future arrangements must ensure the UK government 'an effective and a determining voice' in any circumstances that involve 'the commitment of the Armed Forces, the use of emergency powers, or repercussions at international level.'[7]

The White Paper said that consultations since the publication of the Green Paper had not produced any single set of agreed proposals for a constitutional settlement. However, there were significant areas of agreement, including devolved government of some kind; a single-chamber elected legislative assembly of 80 to 100 members; powerful assembly committees; and provision 'in some way or other' for protection of human rights. Furthermore:

Almost all the parties are prepared to accept new institutional arrangements for consultation and co-operation on an all-Ireland basis, although some make their agreement conditional or limited.

In a section that still seems relevant today, part 2 of the document pointed out that the situation in Northern Ireland was complex: it extended beyond the question of constitutional proposals into education, housing and employment.

> It would be impossible to devise a prescription for all the problems of Northern Ireland during a twelve-month period of direct rule. Many of the steps which remain to be taken will be for new Northern Ireland institutions, and many more will be outside the field of government altogether. 'There cannot be a "governmental settlement", only a "community settlement"; and its full achievement will be a matter of years. What can be done is to make a good start; to set off in the right direction'.[8]

The recreation of communal confidence was bound to be a long and slow affair that could not be accomplished by any single means. The paper outlined serious economic and social problems that needed to be dealt with. One obvious factor, it said, was the high degree of educational segregation arising from the fact that certain of the churches, in the UK and many other countries, had a deep conviction about the need for an underlying religious basis to all teaching. This was not peculiar to Northern Ireland. Although it was the Roman Catholic church that maintained a separate system in Northern Ireland, it could not be assumed that all Protestant parents would be happy to see a completely integrated school system. To make the educational system the scapegoat for all the ills of Northern Ireland would obscure other more complex problems. However, the paper went on, it was difficult to see how mutual mistrust could be broken down unless, in the future, a greater sense of community could be fostered among young people.

Part 3 of the White Paper contained proposals for new constitutional legislation to replace the previous arrangements which had been based largely on the Government of Ireland Act 1920 and which had been set aside under direct rule. The commitment in the Ireland Act 1949 that Northern Ireland would not cease to be part of the UK 'without the consent of the Parliament of

Northern Ireland' would be replaced by a statutory declaration that 'Northern Ireland remains part of the United Kingdom, and will not cease to be part of the United Kingdom without the consent of the people of Northern Ireland.'[9] Northern Ireland would retain its twelve seats in the House of Commons at Westminster.

There would be a Northern Ireland assembly of about 80 members elected, in principle for a four-year term, by the single transferable vote system of proportional representation which would be applied to the twelve Westminster constituencies.[10] There would also be an executive comprising the heads of government departments, each of whom would also chair a 'functional committee' with a membership reflecting the balance of the parties in the assembly.[11] Collectively, these heads of departments would constitute the executive.[12] The White Paper accepted, in effect, that that executive would have to be based on a cross-community sharing of power. Hitherto a party which over half a century had never returned to parliament a member of the minority community had been the majority party after every election. Under the proposed new arrangements, however, the executive could 'no longer be solely based upon any single party, if that party draws its support and its elected representation virtually entirely from only one section of a divided community'.[13]

Extensive law-making powers in certain areas would be devolved to the assembly and there would be a broadly corresponding devolution of executive powers to the executive but this would not diminish in any way the right of the United Kingdom parliament to legislate for Northern Ireland...in relation to any matter whatever.[14] There would also continue to be a secretary of state for Northern Ireland, who would be a member of the United Kingdom Cabinet.

The scheme for devolution of powers from Westminster would follow a pattern similar to that in earlier Home Rule Bills. There would be three categories: 'Excepted matters' such as the armed forces and foreign affairs would not be devolved; 'Reserved matters', including aspects of the courts and the criminal law, would not be devolved for the present but might be devolved at some point in the future; the third category, 'Transferred matters', would be areas where the assembly would be given power to legislate. On such matters Westminster would legislate only in exceptional circumstances, or at the request of the executive, but there could be 'no room for ambiguity' about its right to do so.[15] The authority of the new assembly in relation to taxation would be quite limited. There would also be no further appointments to the Privy Council of Northern Ireland, which, in effect, would cease to function as such. The new constitutional Bill would also rule out any discriminatory legislation by the assembly or any discriminatory action by departments.

The legislation dealing with terrorism and violence would be revised and, 'so long as intimidation continued, some form of detention would be necessary'.[16] 'Law and order' powers would be reserved 'for the time being' to Westminster but there would be a series of measures to promote public cooperation and goodwill. These would include reconstitution of the police authority 'so as to introduce an element drawn from elected representatives'; and a capacity for new District Councils to form local committees with an advisory role in relation to the policing of their districts.

Part 4 of the White Paper outlined a series of proposals which, it said, would constitute a charter of human rights for Northern Ireland. These included additional restraints against the abuse of legislative and executive powers, 'machinery to deal with job discrimination' and the establishment of a Standing Advisory Committee on Human Rights.

Part 5, the final section, apart from the summary and conclusion, dealt with 'Relations with the Republic of Ireland'. The 'Irish Dimension' referred to in the Green Paper, it said, had not been a political judgment but an acknowledgment of an evident fact. It went on to recall what the Green Paper had said about this.

Since this was to become the basis for the Sunningdale conference, and for the months of negotiation with the Irish government on a Council of Ireland which led up to it, I will quote the text of this section here in full.

> Whatever arrangements are made for the future administration of Northern Ireland must take account of the Province's relationship with the

Republic of Ireland: and to the extent that this is done, there is an obligation upon the Republic to reciprocate. Both the economy and the security of the two areas are to some considerable extent interdependent, and the same is true of both in their relationship with Great Britain. It is, therefore, clearly desirable that any new arrangements for Northern Ireland should, whilst meeting the wishes of Northern Ireland and Great Britain, be so far as possible acceptable to and accepted by the Republic of Ireland, which from 1 January 1973 will share the rights and obligations of membership of the European Communities. It remains the view of the United Kingdom Government that it is for the people of Northern Ireland to decide what should be their relationship to the United Kingdom and to the Republic of Ireland; and that it should not be impossible to devise measures which will meet the best interests of all three. Such measures would seek to secure the acceptance, in both Northern Ireland and in the Republic, of the present status of Northern Ireland, and of the possibility—which would have to be compatible with the principle of consent—of subsequent change in that status; to make possible effective consultation and co-operation in Ireland for the benefit of North and South alike; and to provide a firm basis for concerted governmental and community action against those terrorist organisations which represent a threat to free democratic institutions in Ireland as a whole.[17]

These conclusions, it said, had received a general welcome in the republic; and virtually all the Northern Ireland parties had envisaged some sort of institutional arrangements between north and south which many described as a 'Council of Ireland', although there were different concepts of such a Council, and in some cases an emphasis upon conditions that would have to be met. The UK favoured, and would facilitate, the formation of such a body which might operate at different levels, including the inter-governmental and the inter-parliamentary. However, if it was to be a useful mechanism in north-south relations it had to operate with consent. So both majority and minority opinion in Northern Ireland had a right to be involved in deciding its form, functions and procedures. Accordingly, after elections to the new assembly, the UK government would invite the Irish government and 'the leaders of the elected representatives of Northern Ireland opinion' to participate with them in a conference to discuss how best to pursue the three objectives in the Green Paper:

(a) the acceptance of the present status of Northern Ireland, and of the possibility—which would have to be compatible with the principle of consent—of subsequent change in that status;
(b) effective consultation and cooperation in Ireland for the benefit of north and south alike; and
(c) the provision of a firm basis for concerted governmental and community action against terrorist organisations.

These objectives were interrelated. If and when firm agreements were reached, consideration could be given to 'the means by which they should be formally adopted as between sovereign states'. Since some important functions would be reserved to the UK government and not devolved it would also be necessary to consider 'how the United Kingdom authorities can best be associated with discussion of these subjects either within a Council of Ireland or otherwise.'

The White Paper concluded by saying the proposals were designed to benefit

> the law-abiding majority in both communities, who may have conflicting views on the ultimate constitutional destiny of Northern Ireland, but who seek to advance those views by democratic means alone, and have strong mutual interests in making social and economic progress.[18]

The proposals offered firm assurances to those who supported the union that it would endure and be defended for as long as that was the wish of a majority of the people of Northern Ireland. They sought to strengthen the democratic institutions of Northern Ireland 'by winning for them that wide-ranging consent upon which the government of a free country must rest.' To those who sought the unification of Ireland by consent, but were genuinely prepared to work for the welfare of Northern Ireland, they offered the opportunity 'to play no less a part in the life and public affairs of Northern Ireland than is open to their fellow citizens'. To all, whatever their religion or their political beliefs, they would ensure protection against any arbitrary or discriminatory use of power. The proposals could be frustrated 'if interests in Northern Ireland refuse to allow them to be tried or if any section of the community is determined to impose its will on another.' That would be a prescription for disaster. However, the government believed the majority had 'an overwhelming desire for peace' and that they would accept the opportunity the proposals offered.[19]

NOTES

[1] FitzGerald, *All in a life*, 331.
[2] See Chapter 8.
[3] TNA CAB 128/51/13. Confidential Annex to the minutes of a Cabinet meeting on 1 March 1973 [CM (73) 12th conclusions, Minute 7].
[4] I have based this summary of the discussions on the very detailed reports by Ambassador O'Sullivan, which are on NAI DFA 2004/15/16.
[5] FitzGerald, *All in a life*, 114.
[6] *Northern Ireland Constitutional Proposals* (HMSO, London) March 1973, Cmnd. 5259.
[7] White Paper, para. 2, 1–2.
[8] White Paper, para. 16, 6.
[9] White Paper, para. 32, 9.
[10] White Paper, para. 39, 11.
[11] White Paper, para. 44, 11.
[12] White Paper, para. 73, 19.
[13] White Paper, para. 52, 103.
[14] White Paper, paras 53–4, 14.

[15] White Paper, paras 56–7, 14–15.
[16] White Paper, paras 58–62.
[17] White Paper, para. 107, 29.
[18] White Paper, para. 118, 34.
[19] White Paper, paras 118–22, 34.

CHAPTER 13

The new Irish government responds

The Irish government responded positively for the most part to the publication of the White Paper, while expressing some disappointment at the absence of detail in regard to proposals for a Council of Ireland. An initial statement issued on 21 March said that the government were giving 'earnest consideration to the matters covered by the White Paper'. They accepted that there was no quick or easy solution to the many problems of Northern Ireland but they saw in the White Paper proposals 'which could help towards a solution'. They were glad to note the proposed system of power-sharing in an elected assembly and executive and 'constructive elements' such as proposals on human rights and ending discrimination. They noted 'with some regret' that the proposals for a Council of Ireland had not been outlined in greater detail but since they believed the White Paper left open the negotiation of 'an effective bipartite Council of Ireland' they were ready to enter into discussion with all the parties concerned.

In expressing 'regret' in this initial statement at the absence of detail the government were echoing an argument that had been touched on, but ruled out, in the White Paper. That was that, in consultation with the Irish government, 'a complete scheme for such a Council' should have been written into the constitutional

Bill for Northern Ireland. To do that, the White Paper said, would be 'unrealistic': majority and minority opinion in Northern Ireland had 'a right to prior consultation and involvement in the process of determining its form, functions and procedures.' So this, with other issues, was something to be negotiated at the conference to which 'the government of the Republic of Ireland and the leaders of the elected representatives of Northern Ireland opinion' were to be invited.[1]

The Dáil debated the White Paper on 8 May, some seven weeks after its initial responses. In opening the debate the taoiseach, Liam Cosgrave, offered a considered, and more positive, response on behalf of the government. The overall aim of the paper, he said, was 'to establish in Northern Ireland a broader consensus than has hitherto existed so that its people may enjoy the benefits of good government and social and economic justice'; and the proposals it contained 'could help towards a solution'. He welcomed the idea of an assembly elected by proportional representation, the intention to ensure power-sharing in the new executive, and the promise of 'strong and positive safeguards against discrimination'. He also stressed that an 'acceptable police force or forces' would be crucial in establishing stability. In similar vein the leader of the opposition, Jack Lynch, in his response to the taoiseach, said that while the White Paper did not of itself produce a solution to the Northern problem it held out 'a prospect of progress towards a solution'; and he recalled that in a statement issued just after it was published his party had given it 'cautious approval'.

In addition to welcoming many of the specific proposals, the taoiseach also set out in broader terms his view of the Northern Ireland problem and the principles that should guide the establishment of new political institutions. What he said helps to explain, in particular, why Dublin insisted that an effective Council of Ireland had to be part of any settlement.[2]

The underlying problem, the taoiseach said, was that each of the communities in Northern Ireland feared that any definitive settlement would leave it a permanently disadvantaged minority—in the one case, as part of a united Ireland: in the other as part of a new and permanent settlement in Northern Ireland. It was difficult to see how any definitive settlement could be arrived at without meeting the hopes of one community at the cost of alienating the other. What the situation called for was not a static, one-dimensional settlement, but one flexible enough to meet all of the dimensions of the problem—a settlement that would positively encourage movement and growth towards reconciliation. This did not mean that there should be uncertainty or indecision—definite political structures and institutions were called for. But they should, as far as possible, be of a kind that would encourage reconciliation between the communities and provide scope for the aspirations of both.

However, reconciliation within Northern Ireland could not be brought about successfully in isolation from the larger issue of reconciliation within the island as a whole, since hope for a coming together of north and south was an essential part of the aspiration of one of the two communities in the area. That was the real meaning of the 'Irish Dimension'—it was a dimension, an essential and not a secondary aspect of the problem. It was primarily as an institution that could respond to this need, and not simply as a means of smoothing out minor overlapping problems deriving from a common border, that a Council of Ireland was called for. It should be seen as an important element in a settlement in the north, and not simply a later and possibly superfluous addition to it. The Council should contain within itself the seeds of evolution and it should not be constituted in such a way that any one interest or party could stifle or dominate its development. The Council could be a means for reconciliation if it had substantial functions that engaged the common interests of north and south and encouraged them to work together to common advantage. For that reason we would be ready to entrust important interests of our own to an effective Council.

> But this does not mean that we see a council as a Trojan horse to deceive the North, or as a device to lure it towards eventual unity which it does not accept. We do not deny our aspirations but I believe I speak for a wide range of opinion here when I say that we are more anxious to see a process of co-operation, of growth towards reconciliation, get under way than to set a timetable or try to determine in advance what exactly the end result would be. To speak of growth, is indeed

to envisage a process which would not be exclusively within the control of either party and which would have no fixed or predetermined outcome.[3]

By May 1973 the new coalition government had settled into office. Following the Dáil debate on the White Paper, it began to turn its attention in earnest to preparing for the proposed conference which seemed likely to take place towards the end of that year. First, of course, it would be necessary for the parties in Northern Ireland under the chairmanship of the Northern Ireland secretary to reach agreement on the setting up of a power-sharing executive. The Irish government was to have no direct role in this but it would want to follow the talks closely since the conference envisaged in the White Paper at which the setting up of a Council of Ireland was to be discussed would be held only after agreement had been reached on an executive. In any case, apart from its direct interest in the establishment of a Council, an Irish government could not but feel a broader concern about all aspects of the conflict in Northern Ireland and a responsibility to do all it could to contribute to a solution.

Preparation for the proposed conference called for a very considerable mobilisation of effort on the part of the Irish government over the Summer and Autumn of 1973. It was clear that the conference would be important and that the government would have to be well prepared, with major issues of policy agreed well in advance. In order to ensure that this would be done the minister for foreign affairs, Garret FitzGerald, who was well aware of the potential historic importance of what lay ahead, submitted a series of formal memoranda to government on behalf his department over the following months.

In the discussions in the Cabinet on these issues there was an interplay between several strong and assertive ministers—in contrast to the previous eighteen months when Lynch had more or less single-handedly set Irish government policy on Northern Ireland. Liam Cosgrave as taoiseach of course had a central role. His pragmatic and somewhat undemonstrative approach came to be respected by Heath; and, later, at Sunningdale, he developed a good relationship with Brian Faulkner, the Unionist leader, with whom he shared some characteristics and, incidentally, also a love of horses. In government discussions his down-to-earth political shrewdness could at times be a useful, if not always welcomed, counter-balance to the more activist instincts of some of his ministers; and he worked well with his partner in government, the tánaiste, Brendan Corish.

As might be expected, Garret FitzGerald as minister for foreign affairs was one of the most active. He had a lead role in relation to Northern Ireland issues as well as on EEC matters, and his energy, enthusiasm and creative thinking were evident in the proposals he brought regularly to Cabinet through the Summer and Autumn of 1973. He had a strong family background in Irish nationalism but, through his mother, he also had Northern unionist family links, and he consciously tried to reflect this mixed heritage by showing a measure of sympathy and understanding for the unionist position.

Conor Cruise O'Brien was minister for posts and telegraphs but in forming his government Liam Cosgrave had given him an additional role as government spokesman and, in effect, minister for information, particularly in relation to Northern Ireland. Though he and Garret FitzGerald were personally friendly, and remained so, Conor's role did not always make for a very comfortable relationship where Northern Ireland was concerned, and there were sometimes tensions between them on that issue. More than twenty years before, as an official in the Department of External Affairs, and then as head of the Irish News Agency, Conor had been, as Garret put it later in his autobiography, 'an exponent of the prevailing sterile anti-partition propaganda line'.[4] However, his views had changed greatly in the intervening period. In 1972, the year before he became minister, he published *States of Ireland*,[5] an influential book that attracted a great deal of attention at the time and can indeed be considered as a work of some historic importance. It was an elegantly written challenge to the myths of Irish nationalism and a warning of the disaster to which, if acted upon, they might lead. Now, as a government minister, he frequently expressed serious concerns about pressing the unionists too far. His doubts were salutary as a corrective to some of the more ambitious proposals for a Council of Ireland that came before Cabinet at the time—even if, as Garret put it years later, his views were sometimes expressed 'with the fervour of a convert'.[6] But while unionist fears were important, and rightly needed to be taken into account, they were still only one aspect of the complex problem of Northern Ireland. If the role of the prophet as one who warns the people of impending disaster is vital, as indeed it is, then so too is that of the person who takes on the role of leader and tries to steer them past other dangers and out of the wilderness. I greatly admired Conor for what he did in the first role, where his was sometimes a solitary but necessary voice. But I always felt that in opting to play this role, he had either overlooked—or had chosen to leave it to others—to offer leadership on how to balance nationalist fears and grievances with the fears and concerns of unionists. Perhaps he felt there were too many others who believed they knew how to do this.

Another relationship that had some potential for tension in that government was that between Garret FitzGerald, who believed that if there were to be a Council of Ireland, the south should be prepared to transfer substantial functions to it, and the minister for justice, Patrick Cooney, who was inherently more conservative than Garret, and concerned too about protecting the interests of his own department.

Over these months the principal focus for discussion in the government in Dublin was naturally on north-south aspects—in particular on the development of proposals for a Council of Ireland. The British government and the parties in Northern Ireland had come to accept the concept in principle but there was still a great deal to be done to ensure that it would be a body of substance and not, as the phrase used at the time had it, merely 'a talking shop'. Like its predecessor, the government also continued to press for reform in the north, including reform of policing, and a sharing of power within any new devolved institutions, as essential elements in any settlement.

It was also evident that unionists would need assurance that proposals for new political institutions in Northern Ireland and a Council of Ireland of some substance were not simply designed to 'slide them against their wishes into a united Ireland'. So they would expect some kind of guarantee or assurance from Dublin on what came to be called 'the consent issue'. In effect this would be seen as an assurance to the unionist population as such that there would be no unity in Ireland without their consent. However, it could not be put in precisely those terms. It would have to be stated in more generally acceptable terms: that there would be no change in the constitutional status of Northern Ireland without the consent of a majority of the population there. Since the unionist population were in fact a majority this distinction would make no difference for the foreseeable future, though it might become important at some future date.

This promised to be a difficult issue for the Irish government. From a unionist viewpoint the requirement for majority consent was a self-evident democratic principle. For Irish nationalism however, it meant moving away from the historic argument that the unit for 'self-determination' should rightfully have been the whole island and not what it saw as the artificially established entity of Northern Ireland. Apart from this ideological/historic point, there was the serious legal problem of the Irish Constitution adopted by referendum in 1937. Article 2 declared the 'national territory' to be 'the whole island of Ireland, its islands and the territorial seas', though Article 3 had the effect of restricting the exercise of that jurisdiction in practice to the 26 counties of the republic. To hold a referendum to change these Articles would mean risking a defeat that would further entrench them. It was a risk the government was not prepared to run.

So it would be necessary to keep whatever was to be done within the existing constitutional limits. The attorney general, Declan Costello, had the difficult task of devising a formula on the 'consent' issue which would reassure unionists without falling foul of the constitutional provisions. Jack Lynch, had he continued in office, would I think have been even more constrained—not only by the Constitution but by the more activist anti-partitionist policy of his party—although, like others later, he might have found it possible to rely on a distinction between accepting *de facto*, but not *de jure*, that Northern Ireland was part of the United Kingdom. I don't doubt that Lynch accepted personally that a united Ireland could not be achieved without the consent of a majority in the north. But how far could he have gone in spelling this out in an agreement? Some of his speeches had indeed spoken of his hope for 'unity by agreement' but this term, at least as his policy adviser Eamonn Gallagher understood it, concealed a measure of deliberate ambiguity in that it did not specify whose agreement would be necessary—would that of the two sovereign governments be sufficient or would it be essential that a majority of the population of Northern Ireland should also agree?

A further issue that would undoubtedly continue to arise was the pressure from the British side, as well as from unionists in Northern Ireland, for more whole-hearted cross-border security cooperation. There was cooperation by Dublin but it could be patchy at times; and seamless interaction between police forces would continue to present difficulties for the south until there was a major reform of policing and in the behaviour of the security forces in the north. There were also difficulties in regard to direct liaison between the military forces on either side of the border. The British wanted the army units on the northern side to maintain direct contact with Irish troops on border duty in the south. The Irish government, however, wanted it to be clear that the role of the Irish army was always that of 'aid to the civil power' and for that reason they insisted that cross-border security liaison was a matter for the respective police forces on each side. Extradition too was an issue. Unionist leaders and the British government believed that there were training camps in the south and that, after attacks in the north, IRA members could find a 'safe haven' here, while the Irish government believed that it was barred by the Constitution from agreeing to extradite persons accused of 'political offences'. Neither could it agree to hand over persons simply 'for questioning'.

I have referred to some of the more prominent ministers in the government who were involved in preparing for the proposed conference. Perhaps I should also say something here about some of the officials who had a role in dealing with Northern Ireland issues, though I will not try to list all of those who were involved.

In the Department of the Taoiseach, Dermot Nally, who was assistant secretary to the government at the time, had a central role. Then, and for many years later as secretary to the government, he was a close and wise adviser to taoisigh of both main parties. He accompanied each successive taoiseach over some twenty years to meetings with British prime ministers and other foreign leaders; and the small, flexible, tan-coloured notebooks carried in his hip pocket in which he took detailed notes of what transpired, but which only he could read, were legendary among his colleagues. Of course he wrote up more formal reports later from these first scribbled drafts of history as it was being made but those small notebooks, too—if they can be deciphered—could well be a treasure trove for historians.[7]

Muiris MacConghail, a distinguished producer with RTÉ at the time, had been appointed government press secretary with the rank of assistant secretary in the Taoiseach's Department. He was active and highly effective in that role; he transformed the Government Information Service and made it much more effective; and, where he thought it necessary, as well as greatly improving the public communication of policy by the government, he did not hesitate to offer trenchant advice to a minister if he thought the occasion required it. He worked closely with Conor Cruise O'Brien and reported to him as well as to the taoiseach. Since I was responsible for Press and Information work in Foreign Affairs at the time, he and I developed a very good working relationship, which continued at the personal level, and we shared a deep sense of concern about the conflict in Northern Ireland. I think that, between us, we were able to ensure that the potential for tension between our respective roles in two separate departments was kept to an absolute minimum.

In Foreign Affairs, Hugh McCann, who had been the secretary of the department for many years, was a steadying influence when Jack Lynch as taoiseach faced difficult and uncertain times in 1969 and 1970; and he and the British ambassador John Peck between them had kept communication channels open between the two governments. Though much of the earlier planning for a Council of Ireland was done at a lower level, he became more deeply involved as the proposed conference drew closer and he led for the Irish side at several official-level negotiations with the British in the weeks before Sunningdale.

Bob McDonagh was the first head of the new Anglo-Irish division in Foreign Affairs, which was established in early 1972. He had a major role in relation to Northern Ireland issues from then until early 1973. However, he moved to a new assignment in the department before the Sunningdale conference and he was succeeded as head of the division by Charles Whelan.

Of the officials at my own level of counsellor, I will mention two in particular here—Mahon Hayes, the department's legal adviser—a quiet, shrewd expert on international law; and Sean Donlon, who in later years was head of the Anglo-Irish division and later still, after a number of years as ambassador in Washington, became secretary general of the department. As I explained in an earlier chapter, Sean travelled regularly to the north and maintained invaluable contacts on behalf of the government with politicians and community leaders there—a role that had earlier been performed by Eamonn Gallagher. This was particularly important in the lead-up to Sunningdale. Initially, and understandably perhaps, his contacts were closest with members of the SDLP—particularly with John Hume, but also with others such as Seamus Mallon, Austin Currie, Paddy Devlin, and the party's leader, Gerry Fitt. When he became minister in the Spring of 1973 Garret FitzGerald ensured that as far as possible these contacts would extend also to unionist politicians and the unionist community. Sean also had a very active role in assembling detailed information for the case taken in 1971 and 1972 by the Irish government against the British government in Strasbourg under the European Human Rights Convention. The case was not to be a subject for discussion at the proposed conference, but it was continuing in the background so perhaps I should explain briefly here what it was about.

The complaint, lodged by the Irish government in 1971 and 1972 after the introduction of internment in Northern Ireland, related to allegations of torture by the security forces of some of those detained. Subsequently, aspects of the Bloody Sunday events of January 1972 were added to the complaint. The Irish government pursued the complaint in Strasbourg over a number of years. At the period in question here the responsibility lay with the attorney general, Declan Costello, who took a very active interest in the case. In 1976 the European Commission of Human Rights ruled that, cumulatively, the five interrogation techniques in question in the case constituted torture. The British government appealed that ruling of the

Commission to the European Court of Human Rights, as it was entitled to do under the Convention. In 1978 the Court decided that the 'five techniques', as they came to be called, did not amount to 'torture' but did constitute 'inhuman and degrading' treatment in breach of the European Convention on Human Rights.

The case was an important one internationally and the precedents it set were cited later elsewhere—for example when allegations of torture or inhuman and degrading treatment were made against US and British forces in Iraq. During the 1970s, while the case was under way, it was raised frequently in Anglo-Irish ministerial meetings. But, while it was pressed strongly on the Irish side, and it was undoubtedly a continuing point of considerable difficulty in Anglo-Irish relations, it did not seem to damage that relationship on other matters in any serious way. Nor do I think that it had any adverse effect on the negotiations with the British government on a Council of Ireland over the months leading up to the Sunningdale conference. In saying this, I do not of course wish to minimise the seriousness of the issue for those who were subjected to these wholly unacceptable techniques during interrogation or, more generally, to overlook its importance in establishing principles in relation to the observance and enforcement of human rights.

Other 'travellers' who, like Sean Donlon, visited Northern Ireland regularly at that time to help keep the government informed of opinion there included John Swift, who worked later with the Law Commission set up after the Sunningdale conference, John McColgan, and Jim Flavin. I should emphasise that while, understandably, they had to be careful about personal security on their travels, their activities related to political contact work and extending dialogue as widely as possible with community leaders in Northern Ireland. It was not covert and it had nothing to do with what might be called 'secret service activities'. I have already mentioned Michael Lillis—who subsequently played a major part in the Anglo-Irish Agreement of 1985—and Joe Small, as colleagues actively involved in Dublin in the preparatory work for the forthcoming conference.

Having spoken about several of my colleagues, I should perhaps add a word about my own position during this period. As head of the Press and Information section I continued to be responsible for relations with the media as well as for the general information work of the Department of Foreign Affairs. The section was closely integrated into the Anglo-Irish division at the time and, largely because of this, I became involved on occasion in drafting speeches on Northern Ireland—more often for the taoiseach than for our own minister, Garret FitzGerald, who was indefatigable in banging out most of his own speeches on his typewriter, often late at night.

As an example, I should perhaps mention two particular speeches on Northern Ireland the taoiseach made during that Summer of 1973.[8] The theme of both was broadly similar to that of his earlier speech in the Dáil on 8 May in that they spoke of the need to get a process under way that would promote reconciliation, within Northern Ireland and between north and south, rather than looking at that point for a definitive solution.

In the first of these two speeches, to a meeting in his own constituency in Blackrock, Co. Dublin on 21 June, the taoiseach again referred to the two apparently incompatible aspirations in Northern Ireland.

> To satisfy either aspiration definitively now would be to finally frustrate the other. Both communities know this. Each sees that a definitive settlement would finally confirm one or other community as a permanent minority—in the one case in a united Ireland; in the other, in a Northern Ireland permanently accepted as part of the United Kingdom. The experience of 50 years in one case, and the insecurity of the past four or five years in the other, have sharpened the issues for both sides and aggravated the fear of each that it will be thrust permanently into a minority position. The result is a chronically unstable society where some persons on either side in varying numbers are committed to opposing or threatening to wreck any settlement.
>
> Is there any way out?
>
> If a broad and genuine consensus transcending community differences could now emerge as a basis for a definitive settlement, I for one would welcome it. But

such a broad consensus seems unlikely at present. So it is necessary to work towards it by seeking to promote reconciliation as the essential preliminary basis for a settlement. This is more likely to be a gradual process rather than a single event...[It] is not a process that can be confined to the North nor can be undertaken successfully within that area alone.[9]

The second speech delivered at Westminster in London on 2 July to the 1900 Club, a backbench committee of Conservative MPs founded by Arthur Balfour, was longer and more comprehensive. It drew on phrases from Balfour about 'the tragic goings-on on the other side of St. George's Channel', and it sought to address the 'incomprehensibility of the [Northern Ireland] problem as seen from London'. The speech, before explaining the approach of the Irish government, looked first at various other proposals advanced in relation to Northern Ireland to show that none of them would work. Since this speech reflected reasonably well the thinking of the government at the time it may be worth giving a fairly full account of it here.

Whatever the legalities of the situation, the taoiseach said, each of the two communities in Northern Ireland felt under threat. The crucial question was which was definitively to be the minority when and if a settlement was reached?

> This is not a matter of logic or legality—but one of emotions and fears...Any definitive settlement, it seems, must satisfy one aspiration and frustrate the other...This is the Irish Question of 50 years ago in distilled form...The majority in each community seek peace. But they are also fearful and insecure. An extreme minority on either side stands ready to play on these fears and threatens to wreck by violence any settlement which might adversely affect the position of their community. This fear...has generated an atmosphere of instability which has exploded into violence in almost every decade since the original settlement.

Many of you will say, no doubt, that this question is not open; that Northern Ireland is part of the United Kingdom; that the majority of the people of the area wish it to remain so; that majority rule should determine these issues; and that the only question remaining is that of suppressing terrorism. Grant that those are the facts, as they have been for 50 years. What does this solve? You have simply restated the problem—not proposed a way of dealing with it.

He then considered in sequence, and rejected, a series of possible approaches that might have been followed.

- Irish unity, an aim he shared, could still be seen in the all-island structures of the churches, sports organisations, trade unions and the banks. But to press the aim of unity at that point would exacerbate tensions; and to carry it through, even if it were possible, would make the Northern majority an alienated minority in a new Ireland and double the problem at a stroke.
- It was hard to see how independence for Northern Ireland could bring a solution. Would consensus suddenly emerge with independence? and would a minority, which had been alienated and disadvantaged under a limited, local administration with a permanent majority, now accept definitive minority status in an independent state without hope of recourse to any higher authority than that majority?
- Re-partition would involve either voluntary or enforced population movements which would perpetuate violence. The mere belief that it was to happen would lead each community to try consolidate its position with a real danger of inter-communal conflict.
- Precipitate British withdrawal without a settlement—or even an announcement of a set date for withdrawal—would have similar consequences. Attempts by communities to consolidate their positions and clear out so-called opponents could be a prescription for civil war.

Since none of these proposals offered any hope of peace or stability, he said; he saw only one possibility:

> That would be a settlement—I will not yet say a solution—which could offer scope to the aspirations of both communities while they remain opposed, and encourage them to work together to common benefit without resolving the issue definitively in favour of either...Northern Ireland's greatest need now is [for] political structures and institutions which will promote reconciliation.

Such an approach entailed requirements for Northern Ireland and for the people of both islands, which he summarised as follows:

- Britain should see the issue in context—not as some incomprehensible and peculiarly Irish manifestation but as a legacy of a complex past relationship to the peoples of both islands for which each carried responsibilities. We respected the British genius for the pragmatic—an approach which first made institutions work and only then sought to define them. This was evident in the British government's decision to legislate for a Council of Ireland without raising abstract logical or constitutional obstacles.
- In Northern Ireland new structures would now be needed to develop consensus and be a focus with which people of both communities could identify. This implied a sharing of power and also provision for the aspiration of the minority through a Council of Ireland which could engage common interests in joint projects of common benefit.
- The Irish government and the majority in Ireland as a whole had to accept that the past attitude of Irish nationalism, which saw 'the Irish Question' as one to be settled by a majority, was too simplistic. It was necessary now to accept that no one tradition or community could determine the political future of the island. An abstract approach or rigid concepts should not deter us from getting the necessary

process of reconciliation under way. We had to trust the process itself to determine the outcome.

It will be clear from the accounts I have given that Liam Cosgrave's speeches around this time were directed more to the idea of encouraging an open-ended process of reconciliation than trying at that point to achieve a final settlement of the Northern Ireland problem. Looking back now I ask myself if the emphasis I put on this approach in drafting these and other speeches for the taoiseach was really a fair reflection of Irish government policy in the lead-up to Sunningdale and at the conference itself? I would like to think that it was. Both the taoiseach and Garret FitzGerald were moderate nationalists. Each had a strong family connection to the 1916 Rising, the War of Independence and the early years of the Irish Free State. Neither had given up on the nationalist aspiration for eventual Irish unity. Had they done so indeed, their approach would no longer have reflected the complexity of the unresolved legacy of the old 'Irish Question' that underlay 'the Troubles' in the north; nor would it have been acceptable to the minority there or to the SDLP, the elected leaders of the minority at the time. So it is hardly surprising that in their planning over this period they and their colleagues should have aimed at establishing a Council that would have a capacity to evolve, by consent, towards Irish unity; or that they had some hope that it might eventually become the embryo of a government for a future united Ireland. This was not a concealed objective, nor was the approach in any way deceptive. I would argue, however, that the two ideas— an open-ended approach that emphasises reconciliation, and a hope that such a process might ultimately help to bring about Irish unity—are not fundamentally incompatible. It is a matter of how genuinely open is the approach. And I believe that, without denying the aspiration of Irish nationalism to unity, the Irish government really did want an open-ended engagement with northern unionists that would have no predetermined outcome. As the taoiseach's Blackrock speech put it, what was needed was

a conscious effort by all of us to cease trying to impose on each other our particular concepts of the kind of

Ireland that will eventually emerge from this turmoil. We are all struggling to break free from the shackles of the past; let us not impose new rigidities on our present hopes.

In Dublin through the Spring of 1973 work had been continuing, in the IDU and otherwise, to develop the concept of a Council in preparation for the discussions ahead. In addition to drafting occasional speeches, I, too, was drawn, on occasion during this period, into contributing some further ideas in regard to a Council of Ireland. A lengthy paper of 16 April elaborated further on some of the ideas in an earlier paper of December 1972 which I mentioned in Chapter 11.[10]

The paper began by suggesting that there were three possible purposes for a Council of Ireland:

(a) to ensure common action in areas where the interests of north and south overlapped;
(b) to provide a symbolic north-south link sufficient to induce the Northern government to accept the new political structures and allow the Irish government to accept the new settlement;
(c) to promote reconciliation by involving north and south in projects of mutual benefit and to set both parts of the island on a converging path without necessarily specifying the ultimate shape or timetable for possible unity between them.

Unionists, in accepting, on conditions, the idea of a Council of Ireland, saw it as limited to the first of these aims while the Irish government, like its immediate predecessor, focused on the third. The paper, repeating a point made in the earlier paper, suggested that the second aim should not be ruled out completely if that was all that could be achieved at present. Such a Council, in addition to being a symbolic link, could promote practical cooperation, have wide-ranging powers of discussion, and have a provision that would allow it, over time, to assume additional functions by agreement. If there were now to be a reformed administration in the north, with full redress of grievances, if the south continued its own process of change, and if even a 'talking shop' north-south link was established and began to function, there was a real possibility of movement over the following fifteen to twenty years.

However, the paper went on to assume that it remained government policy to look for a strong Council with real—perhaps even some exclusive—functions and an inbuilt capacity for growth. If that was the case, then we would have to be ready to risk committing some of our own interests to it: it would have to be the Council of Ireland and not merely the Council of Northern Ireland. On the assumption that the aim of the government was a strong Council the paper offered a series of proposals.

> The structure could be tripartite (North, South, Westminster) or North-South only. The latter would be preferable; and Prime Minister Heath had confirmed in the House of Commons on 28 March 1973 that his government would be prepared to accept such an arrangement.[11]

The paper also suggested that we could try to get the British to agree that certain functions would be devolved direct to the Council rather than to the new institutions in Belfast to be exercised by them through the Council. It could have an executive Council of Ministers—six each from the Irish government and the new Northern executive—meeting four times a year; an assembly of twenty from the Dáil, and perhaps the Seanad, and twenty from the new Northern assembly (which, like the executive, had not yet been established at the time); and an administration drawn initially from government departments, north and south, with an early transition to a small permanent secretariat and perhaps a permanent secretary general. However, although a single all-island High Court of Appeal (which some had suggested) would be attractive from a Dublin viewpoint, it was unlikely to be accepted by unionists—though it might come to seem desirable later.[12]

The paper, developing ideas put forward in the previous paper, also considered a wide range of possible functions that might be assigned to the Council. These could include aspects of EEC membership; reciprocal arrangements for the administration of justice with trial in one jurisdiction of offences committed in the other; joint approach on atomic energy (which was then being considered but, happily, I can say now, never came about); joint tourism and industrial development promotion abroad; possibly mineral and oil exploration rights; a joint Arts Council and Museum and Art Gallery Councils; a schools text book board; opening each part of the island to the radio and TV of the other part; and perhaps even acting, formally at least, as a channel for transmission of customs duties collected at the border. Ideally the Council should have its 'own resources' but since it would be difficult to get agreement on that, it could be funded at the outset jointly by north and south. There might also be a possibility of economic/financial support from the EEC. The Council could meet eventually in a new venue such as Armagh or elsewhere but for the moment it should meet alternately in Belfast and Dublin.

The Council would be brought into being on the British side by an Act of Parliament. On the Irish side it would be necessary to consider whether the Constitution would have to be amended or whether, if the possibilities in some of its existing provisions were used creatively, an Act of the Oireachtas would suffice.[13] Unionists seemed to envisage a formal intergovernmental agreement like that of 1925, in which the south would effectively 'recognise' Northern Ireland. However, what they appeared to want was not formal recognition in international law but rather that we should cease to claim jurisdiction over the area in our Constitution. To do this by amending the text of Articles 2 and 3 would be difficult but by negotiating, legislating for, and working the proposed Council, Dublin would show that we had decided to rest our hopes on acceptance of the present status of the north, with a Council as a vehicle for greater 'convergence'. We would, in other words, have recognised the new settlement.

A final paragraph in the paper suggested that if we hoped for 'a process of convergence between North and South', we should seek to give that process momentum by changes in our laws and practice. Political leaders could also do much to encourage change in areas outside direct government responsibility that had community repercussions—such as education and the Catholic Church's *ne temere* decree. We should also consider adopting a Bill of Rights that would parallel exactly whatever was to be done in the north.

Ministers and officials did a great deal of work over that Summer and Autumn to prepare for the Sunningdale conference and particularly to shape the proposals for a Council of Ireland which the government would put forward. Others, too, put forward ideas. Did the particular ideas I outlined above have some influence? Perhaps. But, looking back now many years later, the most I can say is that I think they may have contributed, with many others, to the 'mix'.

NOTES

[1] White Paper, paras 111–12.

[2] I should acknowledge that it was I who drafted this section of his speech.

[3] Dáil Debates, vol. 265, no. 5, 8 May 1973.

[4] FitzGerald, *All in a life*, 197.

[5] Cruise O'Brien, *States of Ireland*.

[6] FitzGerald, *All in a life*.

[7] Dermot Nally's papers have been donated by his family to the UCD Archives.

[8] The text of both speeches was published in pamphlet form by the Government Information Service (GIS) and later, along with other documents such as the Sunningdale Communiqué, in book format under the title *Northern Ireland 1973/74: official documentation* (copy in the possession of the author). A copy of the Blackrock speech of 21 June 1973 is on NAI TSCH 2004/21/624 (folder 2).

[9] In his autobiography *All in a life* (202–3), Garret FitzGerald seems to imply that he drafted most of this speech. My recollection is somewhat different. He is correct, however, in saying that the taoiseach dropped certain passages that referred to 'our willingness to re-examine our Constitution and laws'. There is a copy of his letter transmitting the speech to the taoiseach on NAI TSCH 2004/21/624 (folder 2).

[10] Copy on NAI TSCH 2004/21/2.

[11] Hansard, HC Deb, 28 March 1973 vol. 853, 1330.

[12] Donal Barrington, later a distinguished judge of the Supreme Court, in a lecture to the Irish Association talked of a possible single High Court of Appeal for the whole island. A provision on these lines in the Government of Ireland Act 1920 was never implemented. For the Barrington proposal see *Administration* (Institute of Public Administration, Dublin) 20 (4), Winter 1972.

[13] Article 15.2.2 of the Constitution, for example, allows provision to be made by law for the creation or recognition of 'subordinate legislatures'.

CHAPTER 14

Deciding on proposals

In the course of the Summer and Autumn of 1973, the Irish government engaged in detailed planning for the conference to be held later in the year. The nature and functions of the proposed Council of Ireland were particular concerns but other issues, too, had to be addressed. In this chapter I will focus particularly on proposals put before the government in a series of memoranda—mainly from the minister for foreign affairs, and, on occasion, the ministers for justice and finance—and on the decisions they took on the main points that were to arise at the conference.[1] In the next chapter I will deal with the other developments, meetings and contacts that took place over this same period.

In mid-April 1973 the minister for foreign affairs, Garret FitzGerald, summoned all Irish ambassadors home for a 'think-in' on Irish foreign policy which lasted three days. Discussion on Northern Ireland at the conference focused on the British White Paper, which he saw as a significant shift in British policy.[2] He subsequently submitted a detailed memorandum to the government on foreign policy and made a major speech to the Dáil. One of five foreign policy themes he identified was

> to resolve 'even on a provisional and open-ended basis' the Northern Ireland problem and to pursue

relations with the UK government to achieve this purpose.[3]

Another memorandum, dated 24 May, which the government discussed on 12 June, provides a good summary of his thinking, and the general view in Dublin at that point.[4]

The memorandum began by recalling the three objectives for the proposed conference set out in the White Paper.[5] While that British agenda did not provide explicitly for a Council of Ireland, it was clear from other terms of the White Paper that the question of a Council would be considered at the conference. The government was 'of course, in no way committed to the agenda set out in the White Paper or to any other British conditions' for the proposed conference.

> The government's stated policy is that it wishes to see a strong Council of Ireland with real functions to perform, one which would be open-ended and which could evolve with the consent of both sides, and one which commands the resources necessary to develop its own distinctive power and personality—i.e. a Council of Ireland which should be as comprehensive and authoritative as possible.

Unionists, it suggested, were unlikely to be receptive; the British might be generally favourable but they would probably leave it to north and south to agree. Representatives of the Northern minority would favour a strong Council but they might be unable to contribute much to thinking about how to achieve it. So the onus for producing 'workable proposals' would rest on the Irish government. Indeed, the memorandum added,

> it seems very desirable that the government should be in a position to produce proposals of this nature at the conference even if these proposals do not succeed in winning general acceptance from the other participants.

All existing, and any new, areas of north-south cooperation should be brought under the Council. A series of other areas where the Council could have a role were mentioned. These included a joint approach to the EEC on matters such as regional policy; reciprocal reception of radio and TV programmes; tourism; industrial promotion; electric power (atomic energy); mineral and oil exploration; and cultural exchanges. The structures of a Council would depend largely on the functions assigned to it. However, a model based on the EEC was worth considering. This could have an executive body comprising an equal number of ministers from north and south; a parliamentary level discussion forum with, say, twenty members from the Dáil and Seanad and twenty from the Northern assembly; and 'a full-time secretariat, which would, desirably, be more than a mere servicing and recording body'.

The memorandum concluded by asking the government to decide that the IDU should begin discussions with other departments on the structure and functions of a Council of Ireland; that the minister should report back to government by mid-July at the latest; and that the attorney general should set up a committee to examine the legal and constitutional implications. On 12 June the government agreed to those steps.

Over the following months, in discussing a series of further memoranda, the government refined their proposals on such issues as: the role, structure and functions of the Council, how it was to be financed, and how it might evolve; the issue of human rights; law enforcement and security; the possibility of north-south courts; how far to go on the acceptance/recognition of the status of Northern Ireland; and the practical arrangements for the proposed conference, including the venue and the chairmanship. I will recall below, in broad outline, and under the relevant headings rather than chronologically, what they decided on the main issues.

What kind of Council?

The Foreign Affairs memorandum of 24 May had envisaged 'a strong Council...which should be as comprehensive and authoritative as possible.' A later memorandum of 2 November from the minister for foreign affairs dealing with the financing of the Council was more direct. It raised a fundamental issue:

> The most important political question in relation to a Council is whether it should be a body subordinate to the two governments to which certain functions will be devolved or an embryonic all-Ireland government to which functions at present undertaken by the public authorities in the Republic and Northern Ireland will be ceded.

A week later, on 9 November, the minister, in a more general memorandum on the Council, posed the same question again and also offered a clear answer:

> The structures of the Council must derive from its purpose, functions and role. The political factor has precedence and the Minister therefore believes that the Government should seek to establish a Council of Ireland with such powers, responsibilities and financial resources as will enable it to evolve, by consent, towards the long-term objective of reintegration.[6]

'Reintegration' in this context can be read as a euphemism for future Irish unity in some form. The government decision of 13 November included the first of these paragraphs, which had posed the question, but it replaced the second paragraph above with the following modified version:

> That a positive response to this question and to the associated political demand for a Council capable of evolution with no restrictions on its development will imply that the Council possesses maximum authority and flexibility at the earliest possible date.[7]

It is interesting that the government's response to the question posed by the minister, though it included the ideas of 'authority' and '[future] development', made no explicit reference to the 'long-term objective of reintegration'.

Structures and functions

In a memorandum of 31 July Garret FitzGerald suggested structures for a Council of Ireland and proposed that it should have a range of executive functions as well as a 'harmonising' role in other areas.[8] The memorandum criticised the reluctance of other departments in discussions in the IDU to agree that parts of their departmental responsibilities could be assigned to a Council of Ireland. (As he put it later in his autobiography, '[a]s I always suspected, partition had struck deep roots in the South!'[9])

On 24 August Dermot Nally, Assistant Secretary to the Government, sent a lengthy note to the taoiseach offering his views on this FitzGerald memorandum of 31 July and also on a related issue—the future of the IDU.[10] He pointed out differences between the minister's recommendations in the memorandum and those in an earlier report of the IDU (of which he was chairman). Policing, he told the taoiseach, as distinct from matters relating to the courts, should not come under a council as the minister for foreign affairs had recommended (see below); the idea of having an economic and social council associated with the Council of Ireland ought to be considered; the Council should have direct control over finance for its operations—at a minimum through block grants with no controls on the details of expenditure by Dublin or London; and it would be preferable to have a core of permanent ministerial representatives from north and south attend the Council rather than representation that changed according to the issues to be discussed. He also added that the working methods of the IDU, where the Taoiseach's Department provided the chair, and Foreign Affairs much of the staff, were unsatisfactory.

These comments on the Foreign Affairs document, which Garret FitzGerald may not have seen at the time, and which are not mentioned in either of his two autobiographies, were surprisingly critical. This would suggest a certain impatience on Dermot's part with some of the ideas Garret FitzGerald was proposing—or perhaps some tension at that stage between Dermot and Foreign Affairs officials—though I don't recall anything like that at the time. On the contrary, my memory, extending over many years, is that we always had very good personal and working relationships with Dermot and with the Taoiseach's Department—something I always thought particularly important and which I and others did our best to achieve.

Some of Dermot's suggestions to the taoiseach, including the idea of proposing an economic and social committee and a permanent core of ministers on the Council, were taken up and approved in later government decisions. However, notwithstanding his recommendation to the contrary, the government in late October decided that 'a combination of a common form of policing and a common law arrangement for the whole of Ireland under the Council of Ireland is desirable'.[11] As to Dermot's concerns about the working of the IDU, the taoiseach, in a laconic manuscript note on the submission, said that '[i]t may be as well to await developments' before taking a decision.

On 11 September the government decided that the Council should have three possible roles: executive authority on an all-Ireland basis for certain functions; a harmonising role in respect of functions retained by the two administrations; and 'a general consultative role'. It would be structured in two 'tiers': a ministerial executive comprising an equal number of ministers from north and south would be the highest decision-making institution; and a consultative assembly, which would be a parliamentary-type body with a membership of 60 drawn, in proportion to the respective populations, from the Dáil and the Northern Ireland assembly. There would also be a secretariat with a permanent, full-time staff, headed by a secretary general with powers of initiative.[12]

Initially the government wanted the precise composition of the executive—that is the ministerial-level tier—to vary according to the agenda. However, in discussions the British suggested that this would be inefficient. The Irish side came to accept this view—which indeed was what Dermot Nally had advocated in his submission of 24 August to the taoiseach. So a memorandum of 9 November proposed that there should be a core of permanent members, including the respective finance ministers.[13] Other ministers outside the core group would also attend whenever the agenda made this desirable. It would operate, 'initially at least', on a basis of unanimity. The executive would have an equal number of ministers from north and south, but the membership of the assembly tier should come from north and south in proportion to their respective populations. This would mean that seats in an assembly of 60, for example, would be divided something like 40-20 between south and north. However, the memorandum described this as a proposal 'made with a view to the negotiation'.[14] This was a recognition that it would probably not be possible to maintain this position at the conference itself since the SDLP and other Northern parties were committed to equal north-south representation. This indeed proved to be the case.

Brian Faulkner, leader of the Ulster Unionist Party, was prepared to agree to a north-south Council at ministerial level but at this stage he was opposed to the inclusion of a parliamentary tier because he saw 'a grave danger that wreckers on both sides would make it totally unworkable'.[15] He had already voiced his opposition to a parliamentary tier for any north-south body two years earlier at the meeting with Ted Heath that preceded the talks with Jack Lynch at Chequers at the end of September 1971;[16] and again to Dermot Nally and Sean Donlon in discussions on 26 October which I will describe in the next chapter. The memorandum for government of 9 November was rather more sanguine than he was about the likely attitude of those opposed to the Council. It spoke of

> a change in policy of many of the so-called wreckers in regard to the Northern Assembly which gives hope that they will nominate representatives for the Consultative Assembly [of the Council of Ireland] who would play a role that would not necessarily be totally negative. In the Minister's view it is desirable to provide scope for the presence of representatives such as Mr. Paisley and others who regard themselves as 'Loyalists', who would otherwise stay aloof and represent a focus of opposition to the Council.

It also recommended that if 'Northern parties outside the executive'— that is so-called 'unpledged unionists' and loyalists—refused to nominate representatives to the Council assembly, their seats, which might amount to seven or eight in a 60-member assembly, should be left vacant in hope that they might eventually agree to take part.

Future evolution of the Council

On 11 September the government decided that it should be for the consultative assembly, 'on the basis of an agreed majority, to make decisions about the future evolution of the Council'.[17] A crucial point that it did not address was what the 'agreed majority' should be. However, since the Northern side of the Council would include both nationalist and unionist representatives, it would probably have to be set at a level high enough to ensure, in practice, that the Council would not evolve further without unionist consent. Even with such a safeguard in place, it was likely that unionists would be wary of the whole idea of a Council that could evolve in an open-ended way, and possibly even towards 'the long-term objective of reintegration' referred to in the Foreign Affairs memorandum of 9 November mentioned above.

Was there an inconsistency between this objective and the taoiseach's speeches in which he spoke of beginning a process that would promote reconciliation, while leaving it to future generations to decide how far they wanted to go? There was certainly a difference of emphasis. But, as I have already suggested, it does not seem to me unreasonable for the taoiseach, Garret FitzGerald, and other Irish ministers, as moderate nationalists, to have retained their hope of eventual Irish unity, while committing themselves sincerely to an open-ended process with no predetermined outcome.

Law enforcement

Policing was considered by a legal committee chaired by the attorney general. At this stage the SDLP wanted control over the gardaí and the RUC to be exercised through either one or two police authorities operating under the Council of Ireland. The view of the attorney general's committee, however, was that giving control of the gardaí to anyone other than the Oireachtas would contravene Article 6 of the Constitution which deals with the exercise of powers of government in the state. So a document given to the British in September put the idea in more general terms: it proposed that if the policing function were to be devolved to Northern Ireland, then the Council should 'have a role in the area of policing.' The British took the view that policing was so divisive that 'devolving policing to a Council was not feasible at present'. However, they did not completely exclude some connection between policing and the Council, provided it extended also to the gardaí.[18] In a statement on 19 October, the Northern secretary, Willie Whitelaw, recalled that 'law and order and police matters would be reserved to Westminster for the time being'; a Northern Ireland executive would act as an advisory committee on reserved matters; and the RUC would remain the police service for Northern Ireland.[19]

Taking these exchanges into consideration the memorandum of 23 October from Foreign Affairs suggested a more limited kind of accountability than the SDLP had proposed. The Council would be able to ask for reports from both the gardaí and the RUC and investigate complaints; it could arrange institutional cooperation between the two police forces in non-sensitive areas such as training, communications and, possibly, secondments; and it would also be able to promote formal cooperation, for example on conditions of service, between the respective police representational bodies.

Courts and human rights

The government took a rather more ambitious approach in the matter of courts. It proposed that common courts to try terrorist offences, with judges appointed by the Council of Ireland, would be established in both jurisdictions in Ireland; the European Convention on Human Rights would be incorporated into domestic law in both jurisdictions; 'a Council of Ireland Court' would deal with issues in the area of human rights; and the Council would have a 'harmonising role' in relation to legislation, especially emergency-powers type legislation, relevant to both courts.[20]

Financing the Council

The financing of the proposed Council would also be important—especially if it were to be given, or to develop, the substantial role envisaged by the government. Would it depend on annual grants from the two administrations on the island? Or, to use a term much in vogue at the time in the EEC context, would it be financed by 'own resources'—that is, would it have its own sources of income, whether through power to raise some money from taxation or otherwise? Following discussion at a meeting on 14 November, the government decided on 28 November to propose that 'own resources' financing should be introduced within three years, subject to adoption of a constitutional amendment in the south to permit it. In the meantime, the Council would be financed by grants from the two administrations: administrative expenditure would be shared equally between north and south, while other costs would be shared broadly in proportion to where the expenditure arose or the expected benefit was likely to accrue. British subsidies to Northern Ireland should continue but this should not involve British control of the Council's activities.[21]

The 'status' of Northern Ireland

The so-called 'status' issue would require particularly careful handling. This term came to be used as shorthand for what the Irish government would say by way of acceptance of the position of Northern Ireland. Clearly it had to be a sensitive issue for any Irish government, since, at the time, Article 2 in the Constitution defined 'the national territory' as 'the whole island of Ireland, its islands and the territorial seas'. The Foreign Affairs memorandum of 9 November said that it was 'of the highest importance' to settle in advance how far the government would go to meet British and unionist positions on this issue.[22] It also saw significance in the fact that in October Brian Faulkner had spoken of 'acceptance' rather than 'recognition'.[23] However, it did not advert to the fact that what

Faulkner was calling for was 'the acceptance by the South of the right of the people of the North to self-determination'. In normal usage self-determination would include the possibility of independence for Northern Ireland, which was something neither the British nor the Irish government would be prepared to accept.

In a look back at history the memorandum also made a point in regard to the provisions of the Anglo-Irish Treaty of 1921, which came into effect in 1922. This was a point which I had heard Garret FitzGerald argue for on several occasions and which, I have no doubt, it was his personal decision to include in the memorandum. But, although the argument appeared ingenious, I could never see it as valid. It went as follows.

The formal title of what we now call 'the Treaty' was 'Articles of Agreement for a Treaty between Great Britain and Ireland.' So, initially, the Irish Free State which it established would extend to the whole island. However, as I explained in Chapter 1, Article 11 of the Treaty provided that, for one month, the powers of the parliament and government of the Free State would not extend to Northern Ireland. This was followed by Article 12, which read as follows:

> If before the expiration of the said month, an address is presented to His Majesty by both Houses of the Parliament of Northern Ireland to that effect, the powers of the Parliament and the Government of the Irish Free State shall no longer extend to Northern Ireland, and the provisions of the Government of Ireland Act, 1920 (including those relating to the Council of Ireland) shall so far as they relate to Northern Ireland, continue to be of full force and effect, and this instrument shall have effect subject to the necessary modifications.

The effect of these provisions, in brief, was that the Northern Ireland parliament had the right, within one month, to opt out of what was to become 'the Irish Free State'. If it did so, then Northern Ireland would remain part of the United Kingdom with its own local parliament in Belfast. The Foreign Affairs memorandum for the government, however, summarised the effect of these two Articles as follows:

> These provisions make it clear that in 1922 Northern Ireland was given power to opt out of the Irish State *for a period of undefined duration*, in recognition of the prevailing views of a majority of its population. It is arguable that the Treaty of 1922 thus constituted a 'national territory' of Ireland (subsequently referred to in the 1937 Constitution as such) with, however, power for Northern Ireland to withdraw from the jurisdiction of this State *until such time as its people decided to agree to participate in the State.*[24]

The contention here, in effect, was that the opt-out allowed under the Treaty to Northern Ireland was not to be definitive but rather 'for a period of undefined duration'; and it would last only 'until such time as its people decided to agree to participate in the [Irish] State.' To interpret the Treaty phrase 'no longer' as meaning 'for a period of undefined duration' seemed to me to be dubious to say the least: I thought then and since that that was carrying optimism and creativity a bit too far.

In considering what was to be said about 'the status' of Northern Ireland at the forthcoming conference, the memorandum of 9 November recommended, rather optimistically, that 'an oral declaration by the Taoiseach at an appropriate time might meet the needs of the situation', and it proposed a text. The key paragraph, which was somewhat convoluted, would read:

> (iii) That for so long as a majority of the people of Northern Ireland wishes to maintain its present status, the Irish Government *accepts this position and* will work in friendship and cooperation with the legitimate institutions that have been established in Northern Ireland with the full consent and participation of a majority of the Northern Ireland Assembly, this majority comprising representatives elected by the votes of both communities in Northern Ireland. [Emphasis added.]

The government decision on 13 November agreed to the text of the proposed declaration but with the omission of the phrase I have put in italics.

It also decided that:

> the formulation of our position on the status of Northern Ireland be enunciated through an oral declaration by the Taoiseach on the occasion of the final agreement covering such matters as the Council of Ireland, formation of the Northern Ireland executive, policing and common law enforcement etc.[25]

On 5 December, the day the delegation left for Sunningdale, the government agreed to accept a revised version of the above text, which had been proposed to them by the SDLP. This version added a preambular 'whereas' paragraph, which had the effect of linking the declaration to the establishment of a Council of Ireland. It also substituted 'Government of the Republic' for 'Irish Government'. This was the text proposed by the taoiseach at the conference, next day.[26]

I turn now, in the next chapter, to the other events and meetings that took place over that Summer and Autumn preceding the conference.

NOTES

[1] The brief for the Sunningdale conference, which is in NAI TSCH 2004/21/626 (folder 2), gives in section II the text of all the decisions the government took in relation to the Council and the conference. I will refer to it here simply as 'Sunningdale brief, section II'.

[2] FitzGerald, *All in a life*, 120–1.

[3] FitzGerald, *All in a life*, 121.

[4] NAI TSCH 2004/21/624.

[5] Listed in Chapter 13.

[6] NAI TSCH 2004/21/625 (folder 1).

[7] Sunningdale brief, section II, government decision S.18966 B of 13 November 1973.

[8] NAI TSCH 2004/21/624.

[9] FitzGerald, *All in a life*, 203.

[10] NAI TSCH 2004/21/3; also 2004/21/624.

[11] Government decision S.1834 of 26 October 1973, Sunningdale brief, section II.

[12] Government decision S.18966 of 11 September 1973, Sunningdale brief, section II.

[13] NAI TSCH 2004/21/625 (folder 1). See also Sunningdale brief, section II on file 2004/21/626 (folder 2). It would seem from the list of decisions on the latter file that some of these details had already been agreed in government decision S. 18966 of 11 September 1973.

[14] Para. 17.

[15] Memoranda of 23 October, para. 11, and 9 November, para. 16. NAI TSCH 2004/21/625 (folder 1). For Ulster Unionist Party proposals see Chapter 11 and also Green Paper, 57.

[16] See Chapter 6.

[17] Government decision S. 18966. See Sunningdale brief, section II.

[18] Memoranda, 23 October, para. 17.

[19] NAI TSCH 2004/21/626 (folder 2) Sunningdale brief, Appendix 3.

[20] Government brief for the conference, section V, NAI TSCH 2004/21/626 (folder 2).

[21] Government decision S. 18966 B of 28 November 1973. See Sunningdale brief, section II.

[22] NAI TSCH 2004/21/625 (folder 1).

[23] Para. 18.

[24] Para. 20. (My emphasis.)

[25] Government decision S 18966 B of 13 November 1973. See Sunningdale brief, section II. (My emphasis.)

[26] See Chapter 17.

CHAPTER 15

Summer and Autumn 1973

The British White Paper had a mixed reception in Northern Ireland in the Spring and early Summer of 1973. On 27 March the Unionist leader, Brian Faulkner, won an important vote when the Ulster Unionist Council, the governing body of the Unionist Party, defeated a motion to reject the White Paper by 381 votes to 231. However, a few days later some of the defeated minority withdrew to form the 'Vanguard Unionist Progressive Party'. Their leader, William Craig, said they wanted to maintain the Union but he also spoke of the possibility of an independent status for Northern Ireland. At Westminster the British government followed through on the commitments in the White Paper: a 'Northern Ireland assembly' Bill became law on 3 May and a 'Northern Ireland Constitution' Bill on 18 July. On 30 May new district councils in Northern Ireland were elected by proportional representation and elections to the new assembly were held on 28 June. The turnout was high—72 per cent. Parties favouring the White Paper—'official' Unionists, SDLP, Alliance and Northern Ireland Labour Party (one member)—between them won 63.2 per cent of the first preference votes and 52 seats, while those who opposed it—DUP, Vanguard, West Belfast Loyalists and eight dissident Unionists—won 32.1 per cent and 26 seats. However, although Faulkner carried his own party, there were signs that his nominal support within the party was far from solid.[1]

During his visit to London to address a Conservative backbench Committee on 2 July,[2] the taoiseach met the prime minister, Ted Heath. On his return he told the Dáil in a brief statement that they had had 'a wide-ranging and valuable exchange of views': they 'took stock' of the results of the election to the Northern Ireland assembly and of 'possible developments thereafter...in relations between the two parts of Ireland'. In his response to this very cursory account of the meeting, the opposition leader, Jack Lynch, maintained an encouraging degree of bi-partisanship. He said he appreciated the need for confidentiality in regard to such exchanges. On the assumption that there was 'no fundamental change in our policy... and that the ultimate solution of it lies in the ultimate re-unification of our country', he saw two immediate priorities: an end to violence and its replacement by 'political processes'. A 'policy of reconciliation by peaceful means and by agreement' had been 'in operation over the last three or four years'.

> If reconciliation and peace are to be achieved it is
> essential that we maintain that unified approach. We
> have the support of all our people and the support of
> the public and elected representatives of the people.[3]

This commitment to bi-partisanship seemed to be threatened briefly in August. One of the two Littlejohn brothers arrested in Dublin for a bank robbery claimed to have been working for MI6, the British Intelligence Service, to infiltrate the Official IRA. The British government declined to comment. Jack Lynch initially demanded an enquiry but to his great embarrassment it then emerged from briefings by ministers that the British ambassador had informed Dublin of the British government's connection with the case in January 1973, while Lynch was still taoiseach. He apologised for his memory lapse and the government, anxious not to damage him, let the affair die.

Garret FitzGerald spoke often of his connections with Northern Ireland through his mother, whose family background was unionist. On 15 August he visited Belfast to meet with community leaders on both sides. At a briefing beforehand for Irish political correspondents he explained that he wanted such visits to be seen as a normal and regular matter. He believed the fears of the Protestant community could be overcome only through direct personal contact of this kind. He also wanted to reassure the Catholic community, since there were misunderstandings in regard to the attitude and policy of the Irish government. His comment to the journalists on this shows a degree of caution about appearing to allow too close an identification. The situation of the Catholic community was, he said, difficult.

> They identify with us. But they expect reciprocal identification—though this would be disastrous in terms of winning over the majority. Of course we can't say this publicly. But the minority do need assurance.[4]

Three weeks later, as he was about to begin a tour of capitals to lobby on regional policy, he convened a conference in Dublin of Irish ambassadors to EEC member states. In the course of a session devoted to Northern Ireland he explained that the government's tactics since it came to office six months previously had been to establish the best possible relations with the British government 'so that when we begin to get tough we are in a strong position'. The government had begun 'to seek the pay-off' three weeks previously when he told the British ambassador what Dublin had done in comparison to how little London had done. The British side were now starting to show some signs of responding: there had been serious discussion of police reform and signs that civil service reform, including correction of existing imbalances, was being taken seriously. They were even beginning, for the first time, to admit to some problems with individual units or commanders in the army.[5]

In mid-August FitzGerald sent a letter in similar terms to the taoiseach. He told the taoiseach that 'we had seen virtually no quid pro quo for the uniformly constructive and friendly approach to Britain which, since our Government had been formed in March, we had undertaken at considerable political risk to ourselves.' He proposed that the government should take the opportunity to demand what the British had hitherto failed to concede: reform of the Northern Ireland civil service and police...release of some forty or fifty detainees who had severed their connection with the IRA...and a 'substantial and perceptible change in the manner in which the British Army is carrying out its duties in Northern Ireland'.

While his proposal was not adopted in that form, a note 'in somewhat less aggressive terms' was sent to the British government.[6]

On Monday 17 September the British prime minister Ted Heath travelled to Dublin to meet the taoiseach. This was the first official visit to Dublin by a British prime minister in office in the history of the state. For security reasons, the meeting was held at Baldonnel military aerodrome where Heath's plane landed. Security fears were taken so seriously at the time that journalists covering the historic visit were assembled at a press centre in the Shelbourne Hotel in central Dublin but were not told where the meeting was to take place. When it ended they were taken to Baldonnel in a special bus for the press conferences. But, as we learned later, even the bus driver had not been told where to go so he drove around Dublin in some confusion until he found out. The story may even be true.

The meeting between the two leaders was a long one. It began about 10.45 a.m., broke for lunch, resumed in the afternoon and finished eventually about 8 p.m. with separate press conferences. When I got home at midnight I recorded my impressions in a brief note that described it as 'a long tiring day'. In the week before the meeting, the Government Information Service and Foreign Affairs had brought over a group of those earlier mentioned select lobby correspondents from Westminster for a briefing visit. Muiris MacConghail and I had rather 'talked up' to them the fact that Dublin had detailed proposals for a Council of Ireland to put forward. Now I had to admit to myself in the note that '[the] results frankly, were not too good from our point of view'.

The main issue discussed in the talks between Heath and Cosgrave was the proposed Council of Ireland. Heath accepted the concept but we were disappointed at his unwillingness to use words like 'strong' or 'effective'. There was also a brief discussion of the human rights case taken by the Irish government in Strasbourg, where a hearing was due on 2 October. My note goes on:

> The points at issue on the Council were its functions and role and the timing of the push for its establishment in relation to the Executive. The SDLP and our own position has been to insist on simultaneous movement on all fronts ('the Council is a pillar of the structure not an optional addition'). The British would not go with this, wanting to push for the Executive [to be set up] first.

> A statement was issued at the end of the conference but it is not great from our viewpoint. The reality is that we got little of what we wanted—only Heath's coming, which is…positive [as]…a symbolic recognition of the 'Irish Dimension', and a reaffirmation of the commitment of both governments to the concept of a Council.[7]

At his request the leader of the opposition, Jack Lynch, also met the British prime minister while he was in Dublin. The statement Lynch issued afterwards maintained an encouraging, if conditional, bi-partisanship between the opposition and the government so far as Northern Ireland was concerned. Lynch said he had told Heath that he and his party would expect the functions of the proposed Council to include security, economic matters, tourism and a role in relation to EEC regional policy. Any devolution of power from the government of Ireland to the Council would, he said, require a constitutional referendum, so the full support of the opposition of the day would be necessary. 'As long as the government are continuing the policy on Northern Ireland pursued by the Fianna Fáil government they will have our support.' However, he had also repeated to Heath his 'belief that the lasting peaceful solution can only be found in the context of a united Ireland'.

In early October the three Northern Ireland parties willing to negotiate within the framework of the British White Paper—the

Ulster Unionists, Alliance and the SDLP—met for talks chaired by the Northern secretary, Willie Whitelaw. The central issue was whether they would be willing to form an executive in which they would share power. After several meetings they reached a broad measure of agreement on an economic and social programme, and limited agreement on some aspects of law and order issues—though not on policing, internment or a Council of Ireland.[8] Separately, there was also some progress in talks between British and Irish officials. It appeared that the British side was willing to accept a Council of Ireland with some executive functions, subject to the agreement of Brian Faulkner's Ulster Unionist Party.

In mid-October 1973, the government in Dublin had an indication through John Hume that Brian Faulkner would like to meet Irish officials in order to get an outline of what Dublin was proposing on a Council of Ireland. On 26 October 1973 at the request of the taoiseach, Dermot Nally, assistant secretary to the government, and Sean Donlon of Foreign Affairs, travelled to meet Faulkner at his home in County Down, where they had a working lunch and an extensive discussion in a very friendly atmosphere. The two officials gave Faulkner the text of the Irish government's proposals on a Council, which, up to then, had been given only to the British government—although an outline of the content had been conveyed verbally to the SDLP and Alliance parties. Faulkner glanced at the document and promised to study it in detail. In discussion he then outlined his own views on the proposed Council:

- The Council should be inter-governmental—between Dublin and Belfast.
- It should have executive functions from the outset. That is to say ministers would decide on a course of action at the Council and then go back to their respective governments for approval. If that were forthcoming, then the decisions would be implemented by the Council secretariat.
- One of the Council's main initial functions should be to institutionalise security cooperation. The gárda and RUC Special Branches had cooperated well before 1971 and perhaps now, in the context of a Council, an all-Ireland Special Branch could be set up. The two officials explained that,

while Dublin's proposals were not yet fully developed, they envisaged that the Council could have a role in relation to policing if that function were to be devolved by the British government. There could also be a common court system under the Council for certain violent offences.

- It would be 'totally unworkable' to have a parliamentary body as part of the Council because of the danger of 'wreckers' on both sides and because backbenchers of some of the parties in the executive might use it to impede progress. However, a north-south inter-parliamentary union could be considered. [The difference, he seemed to think, was that an 'inter-parliamentary union' would be largely what at the time we called a 'talking shop'.]
- The Council secretariat should not become a massive bureaucracy.
- He saw no need for a Council role on human rights. There were now good safeguards in the north and it was up to the republic to do what it saw fit on its own territory, including, if the people wanted it, a code providing for a particular approach to moral questions.

As to the immediate future, Mr Faulkner said that he hoped the Northern Ireland executive would be formed by the end of November. The SDLP were behaving well in the talks but he was concerned about visits to the north by Irish ministers at a moment when the talks were at a delicate stage and while he was trying to sell the idea of a Council to his party. When it joined the executive his party would give a definite commitment to move rapidly towards setting up a Council of Ireland; the proposed tripartite conference, at which a formal agreement would be signed, could be held over about two days at the end of December or in January; and the first formal meeting of the Council could take place shortly thereafter. He said that he and his supporters had not had enough time to 'sell' power-sharing to the party but he was now remedying this. His position as party leader had been confirmed, by a small margin, at the Unionist Standing Committee on 23 October and he hoped for a decisive victory at a special meeting of the Unionist Council, probably within a month.

Mr Faulkner emphasised the need for absolute secrecy about their meeting: he would not tell any other member of his party about it; and he wanted no other channel of communication with the Unionist Party other than that which they had now established (through him). He also commented that the use of the words 'reconciliation' and 'Council of Ireland' did not make it easy to sell the proposals to his supporters: 'reconciliation' was seen as meaning 're-unification'; and 'a Council' was reminiscent of the concept in the 1920 Act.

As the two Dublin officials were leaving, he spoke of having met the minister for foreign affairs, Garret FitzGerald, once in Belfast. He then recalled various meetings with the taoiseach, Liam Cosgrave, and asked to be warmly remembered to him. He was sorry it had not been possible to respond more favourably to the taoiseach's invitation to talks before the latter met Prime Minister Heath at Baldonnel. However, without wishing to anticipate the appointment of a chief minister in the proposed executive, he hoped that, if it were he, then one of his first acts would be to welcome the taoiseach on a visit to Northern Ireland.[9]

Dublin took some encouragement from the progress in talks with the British side and the attitude shown by Brian Faulkner at this meeting. However, an incident at the end of October brought home to some of us that the reasonably positive approach of the British in discussions with the Irish side did not always go very deep in the case of certain British officials. Six Irish political correspondents had been invited to Belfast for briefing on 29 October. They were entertained to lunch by the Northern secretary, Willie Whitelaw, and some of his officials. I learned shortly afterwards from Muiris MacConghail, our government press secretary, that on their return the journalists had told him privately that in the course of the lunch, Frank Cooper, the permanent secretary of the Northern Ireland office, had made insulting comments about two ministers in the Irish government—Garret FitzGerald and Conor Cruise O'Brien. The journalists were quite put out at this—so much so, indeed, that they had decided on their return that they would not write about their visit. Whitelaw, they thought, had heard Cooper's comments and did not demur, though some of the other officials seemed embarrassed. They also noted a very negative reaction on the British side to ideas then current in Dublin about a joint approach to the EEC on possible regional policy spending in Northern Ireland. More ominously still, Cooper had asked 'do you think seriously that the British government is going to put money into this [expletive] Council of Ireland?'[10]

Perhaps this disagreeable undercurrent is best understood as evidence of a 'good cop, bad cop' approach by some British officials at the time: Cooper may simply have wanted to lower Irish expectations. In any event the report of what he had said had no great effect on the preparations for the proposed conference.

Exchanges between the Irish and the British governments continued through the month of November. On 8 November, in the course of a visit to London, Garret FitzGerald had a full discussion of the issues with the Northern secretary, Willie Whitelaw.[11] He discussed the situation again with the foreign secretary, Sir Alec Douglas-Home, on 20 November when both were in Copenhagen for an EEC foreign ministers meeting. Late that evening, after his return via Brussels, he wrote to Paddy Devlin of the SDLP in order to keep that party informed about his discussion with the foreign secretary. The letter refers to 'several points I want to make to you and your colleagues before your meeting tomorrow, Wednesday.' It goes on, '[I] told him [Sir Alec] that we were dissatisfied with many features of their proposals as communicated to you [by the British side] yesterday'. It also notes five points in particular that were not agreed: the concept of a preliminary conference (this had been suggested as a way of allowing a hearing to some Unionist leaders such as Ian Paisley who were not willing to attend the main conference); the relationship between the formation of an executive in the north and the tripartite conference; issues in regard to the inclusion of policing, common law enforcement and human rights on the agenda; the question of a joint invitation from both governments; and the chairmanship of the forthcoming conference.[12]

This letter refers to the intensive negotiations on the formation of an executive which the Northern secretary, Willie Whitelaw, had been conducting for weeks with three of the Northern Ireland parties—Unionists, SDLP and Alliance. It was already clear that the Unionist leader, Brian Faulkner, would have difficulty holding his party together. At a meeting of the Ulster Unionist Council on

20 November a proposal to reject power-sharing was defeated by 379 to 369—a narrow margin indeed.[13] Nevertheless, he continued to take part in the talks. As late as the morning of 21 November Whitelaw was pessimistic about the outcome. The negotiations continued all that day, however, and after another ten hours they ended in success when the three parties agreed to set up an eleven-member executive in which power would be shared between them.[14]

Irish government ministers had been anxiously following these talks between the parties in the north on which so much depended. Sean Donlon had stayed in Belfast to keep in close touch with the SDLP while the talks were under way. Late on the night of 21 November he rushed back to Dublin to report on the successful conclusion to our minister, Garret FitzGerald, who had been waiting anxiously at his home for news of what had happened, along with Charles Whelan, head of the Anglo-Irish division in Foreign Affairs and myself. The minister was understandably pleased at the outcome and our discussion with him continued until 3.15 a.m. as I see from a brief note made on my return home in the early hours.

The agreement between the three Northern Ireland parties on the formation of a power-sharing executive was a very important step in clearing the way for the proposed conference. This, however, was agreement in principle only. The SDLP, speaking for the minority community, were not prepared to accept a purely 'internal' settlement in Northern Ireland and the Irish government supported them fully in this. For both it was essential that, as well as a power-sharing executive in Northern Ireland, the new institutions should also include a Council of Ireland to give effect to the 'Irish Dimension'. That, of course, was an issue that would have to be negotiated at the forthcoming conference. Up to a late stage Dublin and London had differed over whether the formation of the executive or agreement to set up a Council should come first. This potential problem had by now been finessed, however, by way of a compromise that first emerged at the Baldonnel meeting of 17 September. First there would be agreement in principle on the formation of an executive so that the three Northern parties attending the conference would do so with some sense of common commitment, but the executive would formally take office only after the proposed structures, and in particular the north-south arrangements, had been agreed at the forthcoming conference.[15]

In a statement to the Dáil on 22 November 1973, the day after the agreement on the formation of an executive, the taoiseach, Liam Cosgrave, congratulated the three parties involved, and the Northern secretary Willie Whitelaw who had chaired the talks, on what they had achieved. He explained what had been agreed in regard to the proposed Northern Ireland executive and gave an account of what had been agreed so far with the British government in regard to the proposed Council of Ireland. In retrospect it serves as a reasonable summary of the Irish government's expectations at that point, and it shows the extent to which there had already been agreement in principle on much of the structure of the proposed institutions in the weeks immediately before the Sunningdale conference.

The Council, Cosgrave said, would be confined to Northern Ireland and the republic (subject to suitable arrangements to safeguard continuing British government interests); it would have 'some executive functions as well as a consultative role' and, subject to agreement between the two governments and the Northern executive, it should be able to play 'a useful role' in relation to matters still reserved to the British government in the areas of law and order and human rights. At governmental level the Council would comprise representatives from the Northern executive and the Irish government and it would operate on the basis of unanimity. On 'a separate advisory and consultative level' there would be representatives drawn from the parties in the Dáil and in the Northern Ireland assembly. The Council would have its own secretariat.

In response, the leader of the opposition, Jack Lynch, also welcomed the agreement to form an executive. He recalled the efforts he had made as taoiseach in his own consultations with successive British prime ministers and British governments to bring about peace with justice in the north:

> The partnership now proposed between the different
> faiths and the different political traditions offers great
> hope for the people of Northern Ireland. We also hope
> that this partnership within Northern Ireland will be

followed by a new partnership North and South based
on mutual respect and tolerance which will allow all
Irishmen to co-operate in maintaining peace on this
island and to work for the economic prosperity of all
its people.[16]

That evening the taoiseach spoke to the Irish people on radio and
television in terms very similar to his statement to the Dáil. He
concluded by 'asking for your support and the support of all those
of goodwill in this island.'

On 25 November, in a 'personal message', he responded to a
letter from the British prime minister, Ted Heath. He assured
Heath of 'our determination…to press on to a solution of outstanding issues at the forthcoming Conference'; and, he said, he had
authorised Irish officials 'to enter into preliminary discussions with
yours on the financing and functions of the Council and policing
and common law enforcement.' It is clear from this message that
the Irish government was still sensitive about having its status
recognised at the forthcoming conference: Cosgrave noted the
agreement to hold the conference in Great Britain, 'preferably near
to London'; and he went on to say that 'our two governments will,
of course, participate in it on an equal footing, as the two sovereign
governments involved' (my emphasis). He proposed that 'the form
of joint sponsorship be settled at the outset' of the discussions
between officials; and he suggested that several options were open
as to the chairmanship. 'We had hoped that a Northern Ireland
chairman acceptable to all three parties there might have been
found, to whose nomination we could have readily consented' but
this was now improbable. The government's preferred alternative
would be 'an EEC statesman' but another possibility would be an
alternating joint chairmanship between nominees of the British
and Irish governments respectively.[17] (The 'EEC statesman' suggestion originated with Garret FitzGerald. He had in mind Gaston
Thorn, the Luxembourg foreign minister, who was later to be, successively, prime minister of Luxembourg, president of the UN
General Assembly and president of the EEC Commission).

The discussions with British officials to deal with outstanding
issues to which Cosgrave had referred in his message duly took place

in Dublin on 28 and 29 November. The secretary of the Department of Foreign Affairs, Hugh McCann, led for the Irish side.[18]

At this stage there was broad agreement between the two governments on the substance of the agenda for the conference, though not on the order in which the three items were to be considered. For the Irish side the order ought to be (1) The Council of Ireland; (2) policing, common law enforcement and human rights; and (3) the status of Northern Ireland. The British, on the other hand, wanted to maintain the order set out in the White Paper, which put 'acceptance of the present status of Northern Ireland' (together with the possibility of change by consent) first, north-south consultation second, and concerted action against terrorist organisations third. They argued that if something positive on 'status' could be said at the outset by the Irish government it would encourage the unionists to be more cooperative on other issues. The underlying view on the Irish side was the converse—agreement on an effective Council of Ireland might make it easier for them to say something substantial on 'status'. At this preparatory stage, however, McCann and his colleagues, knowing that 'the status issue' was particularly sensitive, took the prudent course of saying that it should be left to ministers to deal with at political level.

These talks were to be the final exchanges at official level before the conference itself. The overall atmosphere was positive and, allowing for a more cautious approach on the British side on some matters, it was evident that there was already a considerable measure of agreement between the two governments on the proposed Council of Ireland. The British side made it clear, of course, that they could not speak on behalf of the parties from Northern Ireland, who all had their own positions. However, they warned about certain points where the Unionists might have difficulties. One was talk of a 'harmonising role' for the Council in legislative and related areas—the Unionists, they said, were allergic to the word 'harmonising'. Unionists, they also said, were not yet fully committed to the idea of having a 'consultative assembly' as part of the structure of a Council, though they would probably acquiesce in this in due course. And Unionists were very wary indeed about the suggestion that the assembly, by an agreed majority, should have power to decide on the future evolution of the Council.

The British side also had sensitivities of their own in certain areas. Although they accepted that the Council would be essentially a north-south body, they also wanted to ensure appropriate arrangements for British government representation when matters where they had either a reserved function or a substantial financial interest came before the Council. They reacted with great caution to the Irish idea that the Council should be able to develop a system of 'own resources' to finance itself—they saw this as meaning that it would have power to impose taxation. They were dubious too about some aspects of the Irish proposals in the areas of policing and human rights. Nevertheless, they saw some attraction in principle in the idea of an arrangement, common to north and south, in regard to some aspects of law enforcement. This might, for example, allow for trial in ordinary courts of a person arrested in one jurisdiction and accused of an offence committed in the other, or even, possibly, trial of such a person by an all-Ireland court. However, they saw no possibility of committing themselves, in any way or at any time, to some form of common policing for the whole of Ireland.

By now, in the last days of November 1973, a good part of the programme outlined in the Green and White papers had been achieved. The three parties willing to participate in devolved government in Northern Ireland had agreed in principle to form a power-sharing executive; and agreement had also been reached between them on the allocation of posts. The new Northern Ireland assembly was in being: it had been elected on 28 June and had held its first meeting on 31 July. And, now that these two days of talks between senior officials had concluded, the two governments believed that, bilaterally, they had done as much as was feasible to clear the ground for further negotiation on the concept of a Council of Ireland. So the way was now clear for both governments, and the three Northern Ireland parties who were willing to participate, to move to the negotiating table at the conference where they would 'discuss how best to pursue three inter-related objectives' as the British government White Paper of March 1973 had proposed.[19]

It was agreed that the conference would begin on Thursday, 6 December; and it was expected that it would last for perhaps two and a half days. It would take place at a civil service training college in Sunningdale in Berkshire, within easy reach of London. Heath had demurred at the Irish proposal for 'an EEC statesman', Gaston Thorn, as neutral chairman. So, on 30 November the government approved a further message from the taoiseach to Heath reverting to an earlier proposal that the chairmanship should alternate between Heath and himself, and, on occasions when Heath could not attend, between the tánaiste, Brendan Corish, and the foreign secretary, Sir Alec Douglas-Home. This approach, too, did not appeal to Heath. In his response he said he felt they were both anxious to keep discussion as informal as possible.

> If we were to nominate chairmen, we would run the risk that the Conference would get out of control, and I have no doubt that you and I must work closely together if we are to bring it to a successful conclusion.
>
> I have always had it in mind that you ought to take the lead at some of the sessions, and we can make arrangements about how this should work which would be more helpful and more flexible than a formal alternating chairmanship. I am sure we can settle this along these lines the first morning.[20]

The Irish government let the matter rest at this for the moment.

In late November I was asked to draft an opening statement for the taoiseach to use at the conference; and told to clear it, when written, with the minister for posts and telegraphs, Conor Cruise O'Brien. This somewhat unusual arrangement—which, in effect, seemed to bypass my own minister, Garret FitzGerald—was an indication of the particular role in relation to Northern Ireland issues that the taoiseach, Liam Cosgrave, had assigned to Conor. I had worked under Conor when I first joined the department thirteen years earlier, when he was a counsellor in charge of the Political section of the Department of External Affairs, and I admired him greatly. I still do—though I would not agree with all of his views, particularly some positions he took in his later years. Since his days in External Affairs he had gone on to a most distinguished, if sometimes controversial, career—he was successively the centre of global attention for a time as representative of the UN secretary general in Katanga in 1961, vice-chancellor of the University of Ghana and a distinguished professor at New York University. He was now, however, a government minister to be treated with a certain deference—it would not do, I thought, to presume too much on our earlier acquaintance.

I duly sat down to draft an opening statement for the taoiseach that would set the tone and the terms for the Irish government's participation in the conference. Conscious of what I believed to be the importance of the occasion, I started with a rhetorical flourish—something about meeting 'in the long shadow of history'—not quite as elevated a flight of rhetoric perhaps as Tony Blair's feeling 'the hand of history' on his shoulder after the Good Friday Agreement of 1998, but roughly similar in its intent. I presented the draft to Conor in due course. He thought it acceptable, subject to one substantial comment: I should remove my fine first paragraph. Why? Perhaps in reality because it was a bit overblown. But what he actually said to me was that it evoked for him an image of Eamon de Valera in his long black overcoat casting his shadow over much of recent Irish history! I removed the offending paragraph, and, with de Valera's shadow gone to appease Conor, the draft was I think the better for it. After a few further amendments suggested by Dermot Nally, the text was approved by the taoiseach.[21]

In one of its final preparatory discussions, on Wednesday, 28 November, the government agreed on the ministerial-level delegation to attend the talks. It would be led by the taoiseach, Liam Cosgrave. Since this was a coalition government, the tánaiste, Brendan Corish, would also attend; and the delegation would include five other ministers as well as the attorney general. A historian today might wonder why not only the taoiseach and the tánaiste, but almost half the Irish government, should travel to attend such a conference. The answer lay in their memories of certain momentous events of more than half a century before.

As I remember it there was a general belief among many of us in government and official circles in Dublin in late November and early December of that year that the forthcoming conference could well prove to be the most important Anglo-Irish negotiation since the Treaty of 1921. I recall for example that both Muiris MacConghail, with whom I worked closely and well over this whole period, and I, had each been reading our respective well-thumbed copies of Tom Jones's *Whitehall diary*, vol. III, which had been published two years previously. Jones, Assistant Secretary of the Cabinet in Whitehall, and a fellow Welshman, worked closely with Lloyd George over many years and he had a generally sympathetic attitude to Ireland. He had been present by Lloyd George's side throughout the Treaty negotiations and the diary he kept from 1918 to 1925 is an invaluable source for historians today.[22]

I do not suggest that our ministers, or the taoiseach, were reading Jones as avidly as Muiris and I, but they were certainly very well aware of the controversy, and the disastrous civil war, that followed the signature of the Anglo-Irish Treaty in London on 6 December 1921. The questions raised by those events had continued to resonate through subsequent Irish history; and indeed, for some in that government, were family memories. Had Collins and Griffith and the rest of the negotiating team succumbed too easily to threats, pressure and bluff from Lloyd George? Why had they not referred back to the Cabinet in Dublin before they signed? Did their initial designation as 'plenipotentiaries' mean that they had full authority to sign or was that merely conventional diplomatic usage? And why had Eamon de Valera, the president, who was to reject the Treaty, not led the delegation himself? Liam Cosgrave, as taoiseach, would have been particularly aware of the resonance of these events of half a century before. It was the vote of his own father, William T. Cosgrave, that had tipped the scale in the seven-member Cabinet in favour of acceptance of the Treaty in December 1921; and it was his father who, as president of the executive council, had subsequently steered the government of the new Irish Free State through the difficult first decade of its existence.

Against this background, it is perhaps not so surprising that there was a belief at the time in Dublin that we were about to enter a negotiation of historic importance for Anglo-Irish relations. There was a good deal of evidence for this. After 50 years of devolved government the British government had resumed direct rule over the area; they had drawn unionists and nationalists into the negotiation of a radically new form of devolved government based on a sharing of power; they had recognised that there was an 'Irish Dimension' intrinsic to Northern Ireland that would have to be taken into account and given institutional expression; and they were now prepared to work with the Irish government to devise a structure of a wholly novel kind in the island—a Council with potentially substantial powers linking north and south in which the UK government itself would have no direct role. All in all, it appeared that the British government had, in effect, come to accept that, insofar as Northern Ireland was concerned, the settlement of 1920–21 had to be re-visited; and it was reasonable to hope that the issues which had been left unresolved by that settlement and which had come to a head in Northern Ireland were now about to be addressed.

The government took a formal decision on 5 December 1973, the day the delegation was to leave for Sunningdale, 'that the Ministerial delegation to the Sunningdale talks should have plenipotentiary powers'.[23] This was an interesting indication that the arguments of that earlier era had not been forgotten—although, if things had not gone well, there could still have been controversy about the precise meaning of 'plenipotentiary', just as there had been in 1921.

On Monday, 3 December, the start of the week when the conference was to take place, came the unwelcome news that William Whitelaw was to be replaced as secretary of state for Northern Ireland. Whitelaw, the first person to hold that office, had achieved a great deal since his appointment in March 1972. He came across as a larger than life personality, whose apparently jovial character, masking a shrewd political brain, appeared to produce an emollient effect in difficult negotiations. I think a paragraph in a note assessing his approach, which I wrote the day after he gave an exclusive interview to RTÉ in July 1972, captures something of this.

> Mr. Whitelaw's general style in interviews seems to be one of blandly parrying difficult questions with rather platitudinous answers expressing goodwill and determination and a willingness to listen reasonably to all sides. In dealing with the North in particular he seems to have decided to be soothing to each of the

parties involved in what he sees as a complex and tangled situation of long standing (though in the extreme case, where a party does not respond to this approach, he may give up on them and try to isolate them, as he is now doing with the IRA Provisionals). In interviews and speeches he tends to say nothing too abrasive; he either allows each of the contending parties to take away from what is said what it most wishes to hear—or at least he ensures that they will not hear a blunt rejection of their viewpoint. We must accept that the taoiseach and the government here are seen by him, to some extent at least, as one of the parties to be soothed and placated.[24]

In twenty months as the first secretary of state for Northern Ireland he had played a large part in bringing the three Northern Ireland parties to the conference in Sunningdale. Now, however, Prime Minister Heath, who was having serious difficulties with the National Union of Mineworkers, felt that he badly needed Whitelaw back in London as secretary of state for employment. He appointed Francis Pym, the chief whip, to replace him in the Northern Ireland post. Pym, who in later governments was to be successively secretary of state for defence and foreign secretary, held his new post only for some twelve weeks, as Heath's government was to lose office in the election of 28 February 1974. Pym was described in his obituary, many years later, as 'a courteous, sensible, socially conscious Tory traditionalist', but he knew nothing of Northern Ireland, and had no hope of learning anything useful about it in the three days between his appointment and the opening of what promised at the time to be the most important negotiation about its future since it was created more than half a century before.

Perhaps I can conclude this chapter by relating another, lighter, memory from the week immediately before the conference. In those years, long before emails and the internet were ever heard of, the Irish embassy in London and the Department of Foreign Affairs in Dublin were connected by a teleprinter. This was a permanent tele-communication link on which messages could be typed and sent in either direction over a telephone line which, I presume, was rented on a standing basis through the respective Posts and Telegraphs authorities on either side of the Irish Sea. Shortly before the conference began, Foreign Affairs decided to add an improved facility to the teleprinter line for the encryption of messages so that coded messages could be exchanged with Dublin at crucial stages during the negotiations that lay ahead. This was duly done. Shortly thereafter, the British postal authorities contacted the Irish embassy in London to ask if we were having difficulties with the teleprinter connection between London and Dublin: if so, they would be glad to help. We thanked them for their kind offer of assistance and declined politely. We also quietly took it as an indication that, as well as terminals in the embassy and in Dublin, our rented line had a third terminal that we had not known about, with others looking at our messages, somewhere on the English mainland, and probably much closer to GCHQ in Cheltenham, and thus, to Whitehall, than to the Irish embassy in Grosvenor Place where it was supposed to terminate.

NOTES

[1] Bew and Gillespie, *Northern Ireland*, 65–6.
[2] See Chapter 13.
[3] Dáil Debates, vol. 267, no. 2, 4 July 1973.
[4] My personal note of the briefing.
[5] My note of what Garret FitzGerald said to the ambassadors. It is consistent with what, in *All in a life* (204–5), he refers to as his 'frame of mind at that time'.
[6] FitzGerald, *All in a life*, 204–5.
[7] My personal note of 17 September 1973. There is a full report of the meeting on NAI TSCH 2004/21/673.
[8] Bew and Gillespie, *Northern Ireland*, 67.
[9] Report on NAI TSCH 2004/21/625.
[10] From a personal note I made at the time. See also FitzGerald, *All in a life*, 207–8. I told Garret about the incident but at the time I thought it kinder not to tell him the precise details of what Cooper had said, though I did so much later. Cooper referred to the two ministers as 'third-rate academics', one of whom 'was involved previously in some kind of second-class colonial area' (a reference to Conor Cruise O'Brien's stint as UN representative in Katanga in 1961.) Some of the Dublin journalists thought that he was inebriated. Others disagreed—they felt he had come to the lunch to make these disparaging remarks and then left early.

[11] FitzGerald, *All in a life*, 208–9.

[12] Copy on NAI TSCH 2004/21/625 (folder 1). Copy also in the possession of the author. The letter, from his home address, was obviously typed by Garret FitzGerald himself. It is dated 'Tuesday night 20th November' and is addressed 'Dear Paddy'. According to a note on the file by Sean Donlon, the letter that the minister had wished to have sent by hand was duly delivered by Sean to Paddy Devlin in time for the meeting the next day, Wednesday.

[13] Bew and Gillespie, *Northern Ireland*, 68–9.

[14] Bew and Gillespie, *Northern Ireland*, 68–9. There were to be six members of the (Faulkner) Unionists, four from the SDLP and one from Alliance and also four non-voting members—two SDLP, and one each from the Unionist and the Alliance parties.

[15] FitzGerald, *All in a life*, 206, attributes the idea to the secretary of foreign affairs, Hugh McCann.

[16] Both statements in Dáil Debates, vol. 269, no. 3, 23 November 1973. (I should acknowledge that I prepared the first draft of the taoiseach's statement, which was amended further by the minister, Garret FitzGerald and by the taoiseach himself.)

[17] NAI DFA 2004/15/25.

[18] I was at the talks but I draw for my account of the discussions on the note of 29 November by Hugh McCann. NAI TSCH 2004/21/625 (folder 2).

[19] White Paper, para. 116 (xxxi), p. 33.

[20] NAI TSCH 2004/21/626.

[21] For successive drafts see NAI TSCH 2004/21/625.

[22] I quoted from it in Chapter 1.

[23] NAI TSCH 2004/21/626.

[24] From a note of 29 July 1972. This was three weeks after the collapse of his talks in London with the IRA and the end of their ceasefire, a week after 'Bloody Friday' when twenty-six bombs killed eleven in Belfast, and two days before he authorised 'Operation Motorman' which ended 'no-go' areas in Belfast and Derry.

CHAPTER 16

Arrangements for the conference

Sunningdale, which describes itself as 'a large village', is situated in the Royal Borough of Windsor and Maidenhead in Berkshire, some 24 miles west of London. It is probably best known today for its fine golf course. In 1973, at the time I write about, it was also home to a large civil service staff training college, which has now been turned into a privately managed resort hotel. This was to be the venue for the conference on Northern Ireland.

The college, as it then was, was situated in Sunningdale Park, an estate of 65 acres with a private lake and fine gardens laid out, so we were told, 'in the style of' Capability Brown, the great eighteenth-century landscape gardener. The central building is a neo-Georgian mansion, Northcote House, which was built in the 1930s. There were also various other buildings scattered around the grounds which, between them, offered a total accommodation of several hundred bedrooms. This was fortunate, since something like 120 people were to attend the conference. One particular building in the estate was designated for use as a press centre. It was well away from the main buildings, however, so as to ensure that the press would be kept well away from the delegates—and the delegates from the press—until the end of the conference.

Our meetings took place in Northcote House and we also had our meals there. We stayed in nearby residences on the estate. As I remember it there was a very large 'baronial' hall in the centre of the main house. A fine staircase led up to balconies that ran all around the hall at first-floor level. Along the balconies were large arches supported on stone pillars from which one could look over the ornate stone balustrade and see down into the central hall. Off the balconies were doors leading to other smaller rooms that served as offices for the delegations—the two governments and the three Northern Ireland parties that had agreed to form an executive.[1]

The taoiseach, ministers and officials who made up the Irish delegation travelled to London on Wednesday, 5 December, the evening before the conference opened. Prime Minister Heath had invited the taoiseach, his six ministers, the Northern Ireland politicians, some of his own ministers and a number of the more senior officials to dinner in Downing Street that evening. No doubt he hoped to break the ice before the first session began on the following morning.[2] In the early evening, before they left for Downing Street, we had a short briefing session with the taoiseach in the embassy. Some of our ministers—particularly Garret FitzGerald and Conor Cruise O'Brien—still seemed to have some concern about the 'declaration' the Irish government would make in regard to the status of Northern Ireland: would it be enough for Brian Faulkner, whose support within his own party was far from assured? After a brief discussion, four of us officials—Mahon Hayes, Sean Donlon, John Swift and myself—were asked to stay behind and try our hands at a somewhat more supportive version of the draft. We weren't altogether happy about this. It meant missing the prime minister's dinner in Downing Street—though thinking back now I am not altogether sure that we had been invited. To add to our sense of grievance there was no sign that we were to get even a sandwich in the embassy—though, having served later there myself I now realise that an ambassador handling a visit by the taoiseach and half the Irish government was unlikely to have given much thought to providing unexpectedly for four middle-level officials left behind at the last moment. However, we dutifully sat down together in the ambassador's office and began to draft. As I remember it, as a first step, Sean Donlon took a blank sheet of paper and wrote 'Draft no. 42'—or some such number—on top to show our ministers how diligently we had worked in their absence.

The dinner at No. 10, as we heard later, was convivial to say the least: the wine was good and Ted Heath heard some Irish songs that he had not previously known.[3] So it was well after midnight when our leaders returned to the embassy and they were still quite talkative. We four hapless officials duly produced the results of our sandwich-less night's work. The reaction was far from what we expected. Why had we tinkered with a text that had been carefully drafted and approved by the government before the delegation left Dublin? Who did we think we were? We tried in vain to explain— we had been told to stay behind and asked to soften the draft. No one seemed to remember what had happened before they all left for dinner or why we had not been with them for what seemed to have been a memorable evening. Crestfallen, and more than a little resentful, we gave up trying to explain. The discussion began to turn to some other aspects of the forthcoming conference but Conor Cruise O'Brien, rightly gauging that the convivial mood that had carried over from the dinner was not well suited to taking serious decisions, was wise enough to suggest to the taoiseach and his fellow-ministers that they should defer any further discussion until the morning.

The conference opened in Northcote House, Sunningdale, shortly after ten o'clock the next morning, Thursday, 6 December.

The parties represented at the conference were the British government, the Irish government, the Ulster Unionist Party, the SDLP and the Alliance Party. As I explained in Chapter 14, the three Northern Ireland parties that attended the conference had agreed in principle on 21 November to set up an eleven-member power-sharing executive in Northern Ireland. The executive was to be formally appointed, and take office, only if and when agreement was reached at the conference on a structure for north-south cooperation; that is to say a Council of Ireland. For this reason the three parties took part in the Sunningdale conference, and argued for their respective positions as individual parties and not yet as a joint executive. The Ulster Unionist Party and the SDLP delegations, each of six members, were led by Brian Faulkner and Gerry Fitt respectively; the Alliance by Oliver Napier, who was accompanied by two other members of his party. There were some women secretaries among the support staff and Helen Gavigan, a first secretary in the Department of Foreign Affairs, was a member of our delegation.[4] But, as I remember it now, all of those, apart from her, who participated in the conference as such were men—a gender imbalance which would today be noteworthy and a matter for serious criticism but which went wholly unremarked on in that era.

Two other Northern Ireland Unionist parties—Ian Paisley's Democratic Unionist Party and William Craig's Vanguard Party—were not invited to take part in the conference. Nor, of course, was Provisional Sinn Féin, which was associated with the Provisional IRA in the republican movement: it had not participated in the elections to the Northern Ireland assembly and it was still banned in Northern Ireland at that time.[5]

Whitelaw, the Northern Ireland secretary, explained to Garret FitzGerald when they met on 30 November 1973 that Paisley had not been invited because he had refused to attend the separate consultations offered to parties in the north who were unwilling to participate in the executive. Whitelaw said he intended to stand firm and he had solid support in parliament for this position. He was also worried about the danger of violence breaking out in Northern Ireland. He said that there had been an idea of allowing Paisley to attend, speak and then depart. In response FitzGerald said that if it were felt necessary to have him there the Irish government would not stand in the way. In fact we had been quietly encouraging the idea of participation by anti-Faulkner Unionists with a view to mitigating their hostility to the proposed agreement.[6]

The authorised biography of Ted Heath recounts what happened when Ian Paisley did appear outside Sunningdale.

> Ian Paisley, a corpulent would-be skeleton at the feast, turned up at Sunningdale and demanded admission. His intention could only be to bluster and condemn; Heath refused him entry to the hall.[7]

I have no personal recollection of this. I suspect he must have been stopped at the outer perimeter of the estate. Had he got to the door of the building where the conference took place, we inside could hardly have failed to hear the protest which, no doubt, would have been made in his usual loud and vigorous tones.

A British summary note on the conference elaborates further on the decision not to invite the DUP or Vanguard, notwithstanding their membership in the assembly.

> The most difficult question was whether Dr. Paisley and Mr. Craig, who led parties opposed to the Executive in the Northern Ireland Assembly, should be invited. On the one hand, they were publicly opposed to the three objectives in paragraph 112 of the White Paper and the conference was being held to discuss how (not whether) to pursue these objectives. On the other hand, they were 'leaders of the elected representatives of Northern Ireland opinion'. It was decided to invite them to state their views to the Conference on the opening (Thursday) morning but not to participate thereafter: it was recognised that Dr. Paisley might well wish to fillibuster [*sic*] the Conference and it might be necessary to remove him by force. In the event, the invitation reached Dr. Paisley while he was speaking in the Assembly and he rejected it with contumely: several members of the Northern Ireland Executive at the Conference were showing the scars of violence which had occurred in the Assembly.[8]

The account by the Unionist leader, Brian Faulkner, of the meeting of the Northern assembly on 5 December, the day before the Sunningdale conference opened, throws a little more light on the issue of the invitation and it explains in somewhat more graphic detail how those 'scars of violence' came to be inflicted.

> Paisley made a long verbose speech expounding various fantasies about the Council of Ireland and the Tripartite Conference, where, he alleged, we were about to commit the heinous sin of sitting under the chairmanship of Liam Cosgrave, the Prime Minister

of the Republic (which was in any case untrue). He went on to claim that the loyalists had not been invited, but in the middle of his speech an invitation from the Secretary of State to attend the first session was handed to him. He then proceeded to explain why he could not accept the invitation. When business moved on…Paisley rose on a spurious point of order, which was clearly a pre-arranged signal for what followed. There was a concerted physical assault on the members of my party by the loyalists. Peter McLachlan was rugger-tackled by Professor Kennedy Lindsay, fell over the bar of the House, and was then kicked in the groin as he lay half-stunned on the floor. Herbie Kirk received a wound on the head which drew blood, and all around the benches members were trading punches and struggling. Basil McIvor was seized by the tie and half-strangled before he hit his attacker so hard he almost knocked him down. Once again the Assembly was adjourned by the Speaker in 'grave disorder'.[9]

By comparison, the start of the conference at Sunningdale next day was rather more orderly, not to say sedate.

When the conference opened, Prime Minister Heath, as host, took the chair and he continued in that role at subsequent sessions. The Irish government accepted this: their concern in the weeks before the conference to find a neutral chairman no longer seemed particularly relevant at this stage. Throughout the conference Heath acted admirably as a neutral, facilitating chairman, concerned to establish, and willing for his own part to accept, virtually anything on which the Irish government and the leaders of the Northern Ireland parties could agree.

The British government had expected the conference to last for about two and a half days—Thursday, Friday and perhaps Saturday morning. On that Saturday, 8 December, the Italian prime minister, Mariano Rumor, was to make an official visit to the United Kingdom. Heath had invited him to stay at Chequers and he had arranged to entertain him to lunch and to dinner there that evening. In the event the conference extended over four days—and nights—from Thursday morning, 6 December to 9.30 p.m. on Sunday evening, 9 December 1973. It would perhaps have been understandable if, after the first two days, Heath had left what was happening at Sunningdale to his ministers while he attended to his other commitments. In fact he showed a deep personal commitment to the work of the conference over the whole four days and nights, notwithstanding his obligations as host to the Italian prime minister. On the Saturday afternoon the defence secretary, Lord Carrington, stood in for him at the lunch for Rumor at Chequers while Heath stayed on at Sunningdale until the very last moment at which the helicopter pilot, who was to ferry him to Chequers to dine with Rumor, could take off in the fading light of a winter evening. By 10.45 p.m. Heath was back in Sunningdale, involved again in discussions that continued through the night until after 7 a.m. on Sunday morning. After breakfast, he left again for Chequers, had a little more than an hour's sleep, and then held talks, and had lunch, with Rumor. At 3.30 p.m. on Sunday afternoon he was on his way back by helicopter to Sunningdale where he continued his work at the conference until it concluded with a press conference about 10 p.m. on Sunday night.[10]

On Thursday, 6 December, the opening day of the conference, the discussions took place in plenary session, which is to say they were attended by all participants. From the morning of Friday, the second day, onwards, there were occasional short plenary meetings to hear of progress, or the lack of it, but a great deal of the most significant negotiation took place either in smaller working groups attended for the most part by ministers and politicians only, or in bilateral meetings. From Saturday afternoon onwards these were mostly directed to trying to resolve the deadlock on policing in Northern Ireland between the British government and the Northern Ireland parties—though there was some limited input from our minister for justice and attorney general.

The British government, as hosts of the conference, had arranged for a verbatim record to be kept of the proceedings: the list of members of the British delegation includes four persons described as 'verbatim writers'. However, when the conference opened it was decided, following an Irish suggestion, that there would be no verbatim record: each delegation could keep such notes as it wished.

Though we did not know it at the time, the archives show that the British compiled their own detailed, 50-page plus, record, supplemented by shorter notes on each of the working groups. A few months later, when we asked, through the Irish embassy, whether they had any record of the conference, they decided, with the prime minister's approval, not to circulate this detailed text for fear 'people at the next conference' might be tempted to quote selectively from it.[11] Instead they sent us a shorter summary version written in the style used for records of British Cabinet discussions where the points made in each discussion, for and against, are summarised briefly without naming those who spoke. A few weeks later, at the prime minister's request, Robin Butler, one of his private secretaries, prepared the shorter, less formal, note on the conference to which I referred earlier in this chapter. So, to my knowledge, there are at least three separate records on the British side.

So far as I am aware, no particular arrangements in regard to note-taking were made on the Irish side. Dermot Nally prepared a fairly full summary note later for the taoiseach but it does not appear to have been circulated further at the time.[12] However, I kept my own notes of the discussions in plenary sessions, at all of which I was present. As the conference went on, most of the discussion shifted into smaller groups, confined for the most part to ministers and politicians only; and it began to focus in particular on policing in Northern Ireland, with only occasional re-convening of a plenary session to report progress—or the lack of it. During these days—and nights—I made occasional more personal diary-type notes from time to time, as I waited with other officials for some positive outcome to the closed group discussions. My notes for the most part are detailed, though they are not verbatim.

I think the best way to give my personal account of the conference in the present text is to offer, in the next chapter, a summary account, organised by theme rather than chronologically, and to include in an Appendix a full transcript of my own notes from the time. In doing so, I recognise that the most complete account of the proceedings, done by designated note-takers, is that British record of more than 50 pages—supplemented by further summary notes on the working groups at which I was not present—which is to be found today in the British National Archives in Kew.[13]

[1] Garret FitzGerald described the venue in very similar terms in *All in a life* (211). and also in his 'second autobiography' *Just Garret*, 244–5.

[2] TNA PREM 15/1685 and other files in the British National Archives indicate that the dinner had been planned for Thursday evening, 5 December, the first day of the conference. My clear memory, confirmed by Sean Donlon, is that it happened on Wednesday, the previous evening. Once delegations reached Sunningdale they did not leave until the conference ended on Sunday evening.

[3] A summary account of Sunningdale by Robin Butler requested by Heath and dated 1 March 1974 implies that it was an arranged music programme and not spontaneous. He said it 'started with "If you're Irish, come into the parlour", which made the guests laugh; continued with a hummed version of the Londonderry air, which made them thoughtful; and concluded with "When Irish eyes are smiling", which made them sentimental'. TNA PREM 15/1685.

[4] Helen Gavigan, who was a highly regarded first secretary in Foreign Affairs, sadly died a few years later.

[5] The Ulster Volunteer Force (UVF) and Sinn Féin were legalised on 14 May 1974 when the Northern Ireland (Emergency Provisions) Act (1973) (Amendment) Order was adopted in London without debate (Bew and Gillespie, *Northern Ireland*, 84).

[6] NAI TSCH 2004/21/626. Also FitzGerald, *All in a life*, 210.

[7] Zeigler, *Edward Heath*, 316.

[8] Butler note.

[9] Faulkner, *Memoirs of a statesman*, 227.

[10] Details from my own notes and from the Butler note.

[11] TNA PREM 15/1685, Letter, 29 January 1974 from Trevelyan of Northern Ireland Office to Butler, initialled 'Agreed' by Heath.

[12] An undated manuscript note by Dermot Nally on the cover page of the brief for the Sunningdale conference on NAI TSCH 2004/21/628 reads: 'Note: There is a separate 20-page note which I did summarising the proceedings at the Conference—copy given to the Taoiseach in December 1973'. The report itself is not on file and was not circulated at the time. However, Sean Donlon, who helped Dermot with some material, has kindly lent me his copy.

[13] TNA PREM 15/1685.

CHAPTER 17

The Sunningdale conference

The Sunningdale conference began at 10 a.m. on the morning of Thursday, 6 December 1973 with opening statements by the leaders of each of the five delegations. Prime Minister Ted Heath spoke for the British government, the taoiseach for the Irish government, Brian Faulkner for the Ulster Unionist Party, Gerry Fitt for the SDLP and Oliver Napier for the Alliance Party.

Prime Minister Heath, speaking first, described the occasion as historic and recalled the terms of the Green and the White papers. He outlined four points that the British government were ready to accept in regard to the proposed Council of Ireland:

- the Council should be confined to north and south, with proper safeguards for British government interests;
- at the executive level it would comprise representatives of the Irish government and of the Northern executive and it would act by unanimity;
- there could also be a separate advisory and consultative tier with a membership drawn from the Dáil and the Northern assembly;
- the Council should have its own secretariat.

The taoiseach spoke of the absence of a broad political consensus in Northern Ireland: two apparently incompatible aspirations kept the passions of history alive. There was no simple one-dimensional solution. The problem, however, was not limited to Northern Ireland since the aspiration of the minority there was also an aspiration of the majority in Ireland as whole. What was needed was a settlement that would foster the growth of trust and gradually ease community fears. They should let each stage evolve from the preceding one and should cease trying to determine for future generations the exact kind of institutions they would wish to live under in their day.

Brian Faulkner said that, in the past, the parties in Northern Ireland had not been willing to sit down together but they had now agreed to join in government. The path to sharing power had been difficult but an all-Ireland Council would be a hundred times more difficult since many would see it as half-way to a united Ireland. If the republic were seen to recognise the right of the people of Northern Ireland to order their own affairs they could achieve more in north-south cooperation than anyone would have thought possible. Nine hundred people to date had been killed in Northern Ireland. There should be mechanisms for cooperation between the police forces through the Council of Ireland but the Council should not control their activities. The majority in the north felt that it is they who made all the sacrifices so far. In north-south relations they should all be content at first with small beginnings.

Gerry Fitt spoke of hope: the talks on a Northern Ireland executive had succeeded, though they had opened with less hope. He listed five points: there should be a Council of Ireland; confined to north and south; with a consultative role for parliamentarians in addition to a governmental executive tier; with a secretariat; and having both an executive and a harmonising role. It was for the conference to work out the details. It was important too that everyone be able to identify with the police. The Council could have a role in this. However, the Council should not be static or rigid—it should be able to evolve.

Oliver Napier said they had all come to the conference with hope; they wanted to bury the past by recognising and accepting each other's aspirations. However, he had to say to the republic's representatives that there were things the majority in the north resented: Articles 2 and 3 of the Irish Constitution; and the difficulties about extradition of fugitives to the north. His party wanted to see a Council of Ireland but it was essential that it be part of a package.

Agenda

Following the set-piece opening statements, **Heath**, in the chair, proposed that, since all the individual items for the conference were interrelated, the exact order in which they were discussed did not matter greatly. He suggested that the main points could be grouped under three headings:

- The complex of questions relating to a Council of Ireland—its structure, functions and role;
- Law and order, the proposal for a Common Law Enforcement Area;[1] extradition; and human rights, which is closely connected with law and order issues;
- The issue of the status of Northern Ireland.

This outline agenda was generally accepted. The conference then turned to the first substantive issue, the Council of Ireland.

Gerry Fitt asked if the prime minister, who was due to be in the House of Commons that afternoon, could stay on at the conference even for a short time. **Heath** said he could.

The Council of Ireland

John Hume, in a very slight variant of Fitt's listing, set out six points about the proposed Council which he said had already been accepted by the three Northern parties on 21 November, the day they agreed in principle to form a power-sharing executive. **Brian Faulkner**, the Unionist Party leader, found the outline lists 'pretty well acceptable' but he had grave reservations about executive powers for the Council: this, he said, was something the Council itself might discuss, once it was set up and functioning.

He agreed, though with some reluctance, that the Council could have a parliamentary tier or assembly; and also that there should be a permanent secretariat, though with the proviso that it should not be too large. **Oliver Napier**, the Alliance leader, also accepted the points on Fitt's and Hume's lists.

At the afternoon session on Thursday, the first day of the conference, there was an extensive and detailed discussion of various aspects of the structure and functioning of the proposed Council of Ireland.

Council of Ministers

Agreement was reached without too much difficulty on how the ministerial level of the Council should be structured. It was already common ground that there should be equal representation from north and south, that the members would be nominated to the Council by the Northern Ireland executive and the Irish government respectively, and that the Council at this level would act by unanimity.

The Irish government position, as late as September 1973, had been that there should be 'a varying membership and no specific assigned portfolios.' However, the government subsequently revised that decision and decided instead to propose that the Council should have a core of permanent members, with other members added on both sides at particular meetings according to the agenda.[2] In the lead-up to the conference neither the Irish government nor the Ulster Unionist Party had made specific proposals on the size of the Council.

The SDLP proposed that there be five members each from north and south, that is a total membership of ten. The Alliance Party proposed seven each from north and south, which would make a total of fourteen. At one stage in the conference there appeared to be agreement on five each from north and south but when this figure leaked to the news media, it was decided to change it. The figure settled on eventually in a discussion in a sub-group was seven from each jurisdiction.

This agreement reached on the ministerial level of the Council was duly reflected in the final communiqué. It envisaged that the Council of Ministers would have a core membership of seven ministers each from the Irish government and the Northern Ireland executive respectively. Other ministers from north and south could take part when matters relating to their departments were under discussion. The Council would act by unanimity and the chairmanship would rotate 'on an agreed basis' between north and south.[3]

Consultative assembly

In its planning for a Council of Ireland, the Irish government envisaged that, in addition to the Council of Ministers, there would also be a parliamentary tier with a membership drawn from the Dáil and the Northern Ireland assembly. The SDLP and the Alliance Party had a similar position. The Unionist Party leader, **Brian Faulkner**, however, was opposed: he feared that 'wreckers on both sides' would make the Council totally unworkable; and that backbenchers from the parties in the Northern Ireland executive might use it to impede progress in the Council at ministerial level.

At the conference, **Faulkner** modified his position: in his opening statement, he agreed 'with some reluctance', to the proposal for a parliamentary tier. The debate at the conference then turned on the number of members from north and south respectively, how they were to be selected, and the role and functions of the proposed assembly. The Irish government, largely as a negotiating tactic, had decided to propose an assembly with a membership of about 60 drawn from the Dáil and the Northern Ireland assembly respectively 'in proportion to respective populations'.[4] When the **taoiseach** put forward this proposal, **Brian Faulkner** quickly pointed out that all of the Northern parties had agreed that there should be parity of representation for north and south. Faced, unusually, with a united view from the Northern Ireland parties, the Irish government accepted the point.

Garret FitzGerald for the Irish government, and **Gerry Fitt** and **John Hume** for the SDLP, argued for a consultative and advisory role for the consultative assembly: it should be able to debate and to question ministers. **FitzGerald** also proposed that the assembly should have power to decide on the future evolution of the Council. **Fitt** agreed that it should—subject to the consent of a majority of the Northern representatives.

The discussion resulted in agreement that a consultative assembly should be one of the institutions of the council of Ireland. It would consist of 60 members, 30 each from the Dáil and the Northern Ireland assembly. Each of the two bodies would chose its representatives by proportional representation using the single transferable vote. It was also agreed that members of the consultative assembly would be paid allowances.[5] There was no explicit reference in the communiqué to the 'future evolution' of the Council. That issue was, to an extent, subsumed under a provision in the 'Agreed Communiqué' which said that 'it would be for the Oireachtas (the Irish parliament) and the Northern Ireland assembly to legislate from time to time, as to the extent of the functions to be devolved'[6] (I will deal further with the issue of functions below).

The Council secretariat

The Irish government proposals envisaged that the Council should have permanent, full-time staff, appointed by, and directly responsible to, the Council. It would be headed by a secretary general with powers of initiative. The brief for the conference prepared by the Department of the Taoiseach noted that the method of staffing the secretariat would largely depend on how the Council was to operate. If it gave policy directives that were to be implemented by existing departments, north and south, then the secretariat need not necessarily be very large. However, if all of the possible functions identified in earlier memoranda were to be transferred to the Council, then the staff could be close to 6,000 and the cost close to £17 million.[7]

In discussion at the conference, **Gerry Fitt** argued for new, specially recruited, permanent, full-time, staff supplemented by staff seconded from the civil services of north and south. **Prime Minister Heath** suggested a distinction between staff to service the Council institutions and staff to carry out its functions. **Brian Faulkner** agreed. He said that while there should be a secretary general to service the Council institutions, there should not be a large new bureaucracy. Staff from the respective civil services could carry out and implement the Council decisions, under the direction of the secretary general.

The question of the secretariat was not debated at any great length. It was agreed that there would be a secretary general, appointed by the Council of Ministers, and a secretariat 'which would be kept as small as might be commensurate with efficiency in the operation of the Council'. It would service the institutions of the Council and, under the Council of Ministers, would 'supervise the carrying out of the executive and harmonising functions and the consultative role of the Council'. The staff of the secretariat were to be recruited in a way, and on terms, consistent with those applying to public servants, north and south.[8]

Functions of the Council

The Irish government proposals envisaged three possible roles for the Council:

- executive authority on an all-Ireland basis for certain defined functions;
- a harmonising role in relation to functions retained by the northern and southern administrations;
- a general consultative role.

Legislation arising from decisions of the Council would remain the responsibility of ministers, north and south. The terms 'executive' and 'harmonising' were not defined in detail.

In September 1973 a detailed list of possible functions was drawn up and passed to British officials. The British side had reservations on a number of points but they raised no substantive objection at a final round of talks between officials on 28–29 November. However, they wanted each of the proposed functions examined separately and preferred to leave it to the Council itself to study all the possibilities after it was formed.[9]

At the conference discussion centred on the issues of executive functions and the harmonising role of the Council.

Hume suggested that the harmonisation of laws already under way as a result of EEC membership could be done more efficiently under the aegis of the Council. This could also extend to laws dealing with violence. **Faulkner** said that, since the north was part of the UK, there could not be complete harmonisation of laws between north and south. **Heath** agreed, and **Hume**, too, agreed that there should be harmonisation only where it was useful.

The **taoiseach**, reflecting earlier decisions by the Irish government, said that the Council should have certain specified executive functions from the outset. **Fitt** for the SDLP also wanted a small number of executive functions defined from the outset. His colleagues, **Currie** and **Hume** also argued that the Council should have executive authority in specific areas. **Napier**, for Alliance, said that the Council should be capable of handling executive powers given to it by the Northern assembly and the Dáil, but they should not try to define at that point what they should be. **Faulkner** was not opposed to some executive functions for the Council but it should not be able to impose its views on the Dáil or the Northern assembly or to do something of which either body disapproved. **FitzGerald**, for the Irish government, said there was no question of imposition. The Council, he said, should have both harmonising and executive functions but what precisely the executive functions would be was something that could be examined. **Hume** was concerned to ensure that, where executive functions were given to the Council, the British government would not be free to block action by using provisions of the 1973 Constitution Act. **Heath** agreed to examine this issue.

After this discussion in plenary session on Thursday afternoon, and further and more detailed discussions in sub-groups, it was agreed that the Council would have a harmonisation and a consultative role. This could relate to the impact of EEC membership for example. The issue of executive functions was seen as more complex. For this reason, studies would be set in hand to report on areas where the Council would take executive decisions and, where appropriate, carry them into effect. The 'Agreed Communiqué' listed a number of broad fields within which aspects suitable for executive action could be identified. It would be for the second, formal, stage of the conference to decide what functions were to be vested initially in the Council; and the Oireachtas and the Northern Ireland assembly would legislate from time to time as to the extent of [the other] functions to be devolved to the Council.[10]

Financing the Council

The question of financing the Council was discussed for the most part in a sub-group and resolved without great difficulty. It was agreed that, initially, it would be financed by grants towards agreed projects from the two administrations in Ireland; studies would be undertaken on how to finance the Council after that initial period; the cost of the secretariat would be shared equally; and other services would be financed broadly in proportion to where the expenditure or benefit accrued. The British government would maintain its subsidy to Northern Ireland. Britain would not participate in the Council but it would be entitled to safeguard its financial involvement in Northern Ireland 'in an appropriate way'.[11]

Location of the Council

There were some brief exchanges on where the Council should be located. One suggestion was Armagh; another, that meetings of the Council of Ministers should be held alternately in the north and in the south. It was recognised, however, that a permanent location would be needed for the secretariat. Beyond that, the issue was left open. The Communiqué provided that 'arrangements would be made' for the location of the first meeting and the location of subsequent meetings would be determined by the Council of Ministers.[12]

The 'status' of Northern Ireland

The first of the three objectives for the conference proposed by the British government in March 1973 had been

> the acceptance of the present status of Northern Ireland, and of the possibility—which would have to be compatible with the principle of consent—of subsequent change in that status.[13]

The Irish government accepted in practice that, in addition to power-sharing institutions in Northern Ireland, and an institutional link by way of a Council between north and south, the deal to be negotiated would also have to include some form of reassurance to unionists against their fears of being forced, or drawn against their will, into a united Ireland. However, the relevant government decision taken in the weeks before the conference was very cautiously—even grudgingly—phrased. It provided

> [t]hat in determining our position on the status of Northern Ireland, we should seek to meet the minimal requirements of responsible Northern Protestant opinion; that we should have regard to opinion in the Republic which attaches importance to the claim inherent in Articles 2 and 3 of the Constitution; and that we should not commit ourselves to legal action which would be invalidated by an appeal to these Articles unless we intend to repeal them.[14]

The truth was that, even had they wished to, it would almost certainly not have been politically possible at that time to win a referendum to change Articles 2 and 3 of the Constitution. So the government decided instead

> [t]hat the formulation of our position on the status of Northern Ireland be enunciated through an oral declaration by the Taoiseach on the occasion of the final agreement covering such matters as the Council of Ireland, formation of the Northern Ireland Executive, policing and common law enforcement etc.[15]

At the request of the SDLP the government modified the initial draft of the proposed declaration on 5 December (see Chapter 15). The text proposed by the taoiseach at the conference was as follows:

> Whereas agreement has been reached as to the establishment and constitution of a Council of Ireland with functions in relation to policing, a common law enforcement area and human rights as well as other

executive functions, the government of the republic declares:

(i) that those who live on this island comprise different elements all of which contribute to the life and culture of Ireland, and that each has the right to pursue its legitimate ends by peaceful means;

(ii) that, accordingly, the aspirations of a majority of the people of this island to its political unity shall be pursued through reconciliation alone;

(iii) that for so long as by a majority the people of Northern Ireland maintain its present status, the government of the republic will work in friendship and cooperation with the institutions that are being established in Northern Ireland, with the full consent and participation of a majority comprising representatives elected by the votes of both sections of the Northern Ireland community; and

(iv) that accordingly, the government of the republic have agreed to join in establishing a Council of Ireland within which representatives of that government and the Dáil will participate with the Northern Ireland executive.

The convoluted prose of the third sub-paragraph of the proposed declaration was evidence of the difficulty of picking a way through the thicket of obstacles which acceptance of the 'status' of Northern Ireland while Articles 2 and 3 remained in place was likely to pose.

When discussion on the 'status' question opened at the conference on Thursday afternoon, the **taoiseach** read out the text of the proposed declaration. He also supported a request made earlier by **John Hume**, that there should be a reciprocal declaration on the part of the British government about the possibility of future change. **Faulkner**, for the Unionists, thought the declaration could be more succinct. But he wondered how it would be possible to get credibility for the Irish government's approach while Articles 2 and 3 remained in the Constitution. Could Dublin not at least make a declaration of a will to change the Constitution? His colleague **Roy Bradford** stressed that the declaration had to be a substantial one. He said that, while people in the north acqui-esced in power-sharing—though not with great enthusiasm—the Council of Ireland was deep and dangerous water. **Hume** and **Currie** for the SDLP made a point of their party's accept-ance of the Constitution Act 1973, and the willingness of the minority in the north to identify with the new institutions. This, they argued, created a new situation. **Napier**, for Alliance, said that although it was not necessary to change the Irish Constitution at that point, there must be a clear declaration by the Irish government.

Responding for the Irish government, four ministers—**FitzGerald**, **Cruise O'Brien**, **Corish** and **Tully**—all emphasised that it would not be politically feasible to change the Constitution. **Cruise O'Brien** expressed serious doubts about the outcome of any referendum on the issue. A negative answer could entrench the two Articles. In subsequent discussion he said that, because they could not make any legal commitment that would be contrary to the Constitution, a certain vagueness was required: vagueness was sometimes useful in negotiations.

Since the Irish government had made it clear in the discussion that there was no possibility of changing Articles 2 and 3 of the Constitution, the idea of dealing with the 'status' issue by way of reciprocal declarations by each of the two governments gained gen-eral acceptance. The issue was remitted to a smaller sub-group for further study. Discussion, mainly at political level, and principally between **the taoiseach** and **Brian Faulkner**, continued into Friday night.

The eventual outcome was the separate declarations by the two governments set out in parallel in paragraph 5 of the Communiqué. (I will discuss these two declarations in more detail in the next chapter.)

Common law enforcement area

The term 'common law enforcement area' was commonly used at the time of Sunningdale to cover measures to deal with security issues and crimes of violence in both jurisdictions in Ireland.

Discussion at the conference turned largely at the start on proposals by the Irish government to this end which were linked to a Council of Ireland. In the later stages of the conference, the main point at issue was the continuing disagreement between the British government and the Northern parties about whether responsibility for policing in Northern Ireland should be devolved to the new Northern Ireland institutions.

In the period before the conference, the **Unionist** position had been to demand that either 'the extradition treaty should be re-negotiated' (so as to make it possible for the republic to extradite persons accused of crimes of violence, even those claimed to be 'political offences', to Northern Ireland); or, alternatively, and preferably, that 'the British Isles [should be] made a Common Law enforcement area'. This would mean that a 'warrant issued in Belfast would be executed in Dublin in the same way as it would in Sheffield'.[16]

The **Irish government**, on the other hand, insisted that it could not agree to extradite persons accused of so-called 'political offences' because of the commitment in the Constitution to accept 'the generally recognised principles of international law', which, it argued, included an obligation not to extradite in such cases. Nor could it extradite suspects merely 'for questioning'. Instead, as an effective means of dealing with crimes of violence, the government proposed 'the achievement at the earliest possible date of a combination of a common form of policing and a common law arrangement for the whole of Ireland under the Council of Ireland.'[17]

Specifically, the government's proposals were that 'in the initial stages of a Council of Ireland' there would be interim arrangements for policing.

- a police authority would be established in the republic;
- the police authorities, north and south, would each be responsible for their own forces but both would be responsible to the Council of Ireland, which would arrange for institutional cooperation between the two forces;
- a complaints procedure or ombudsman for policing would be established by the Council.[18]

If the principle were accepted and these interim proposals agreed, then 'with a view to the provision of common law enforcement arrangements' the government would agree that

- a court or courts would be established in the two jurisdictions to try specified offences;
- the judges would be nominated by the Council of Ireland;
- there would be an equal number of judges from each jurisdiction with a presiding judge appointed in a manner to be agreed;
- the Council would have a role in harmonising legislation relevant to the proposed court(s).

These arrangements for policing and common law enforcement would be linked in turn with human rights provisions:

- the European Convention on Human Rights and its protocols, along with other human rights provisions in relation to discrimination in employment and housing for example, would be incorporated in domestic law in both jurisdictions;
- there would be a Council of Ireland Court of Human Rights.[19]

Opening debate on the afternoon of the Thursday, the first day of the conference, the Irish attorney general, **Declan Costello**, explained the difficulties about extradition and then outlined the government's proposals for new courts under the Council of Ireland. He acknowledged that there were differences between the two jurisdictions in respect of the 'scheduled offences', but said that if there were agreement in principle these differences could be ironed out. **Basil McIvor**, responding for the Ulster Unionist Party, saw this, and other major differences between the two legal systems, as posing enormous problems. The British attorney general, **Sir Peter Rawlinson**, who had ultimate responsibility in the British system, also saw these as complex matters. Both countries, he said, were parties to the Council of Europe Convention on Extradition. He was not clear as to the objective of the Irish proposals: the number of cases was limited; and it would be easier to provide in Irish law that the 'political offences' plea in extradition cases would not apply to offences involving explosives or firearms. He agreed that the proposals should be studied, but by a commission rather than in such a large conference. **Oliver Napier**, the Alliance leader, also foresaw many problems about the Irish proposals. He agreed with Rawlinson that the numbers would be limited and he thought there were much simpler ways of dealing with the matter.

When discussion turned to the Irish proposals on policing, the Irish minister for justice, **Patrick Cooney**, explained that, in the interest of effective action against terrorism, the government was prepared to cede some of its authority to a new police authority, which, in conjunction with the police authority in Northern Ireland, would have a degree of responsibility to the Council of Ireland. This led on to quite forceful arguments by the SDLP representatives—**Hume**, **Currie** and **Devlin**—about the effect on the communities they represented of the absence of a reformed and acceptable police force in Northern Ireland. Local people had to be able to identify with the police as *their* police force. If that could not be achieved, then the executive in which their party was about to take seats would be put under severe strain.

After extensive discussion, the questions that had arisen were referred to sub-groups. It was agreed eventually that, because of the legal complexities, the issues involved in the Common Law Enforcement Area proposals—including extradition and the possibility of a system of all-Ireland courts—would be considered by a commission to be set up by the two governments. The Irish government undertook to take immediate legal steps in one specific area—the trial in its jurisdiction of persons accused of murder, however motivated, in Northern Ireland. The attorney general, Declan Costello, established that this was possible—a procedure under an Act of 1861 (when Ireland was still part of the UK) could still be validly invoked in our jurisdiction. As part of this arrangement it was agreed that 'any similar reciprocal action' that might be needed in Northern Ireland would be taken 'by the appropriate authorities'.[20]

The proposals in relation to human rights were referred to the future Council of Ireland. It was agreed that it 'would be invited to consider in what way the principles of the European Convention on Human Rights would be expressed in domestic legislation in each part of Ireland'. The Council would also recommend whether further legislation or new institutions, including an ombudsman, were required to provide additional human rights protection.[21]

The issues of how to ensure that policing in Northern Ireland would be acceptable throughout the community, and whether responsibility for policing should be devolved to the new Northern Ireland executive, proved much more intractable. The problem at this stage was summarised very well years later in Garret FitzGerald's autobiography:

> The issue of policing seemed irretrievably stuck, however, with the SDLP requiring a major role for the Council, the Unionists resisting it and demanding transfer of policing to the power-sharing Executive, and the British refusing to contemplate transfer of control either to the Executive or to the Council.[22]

Discussion in a sub-group and in a series of late-night meetings and exchanges between the British government and the Northern Ireland parties prolonged the conference by two days but agreement could not be reached on the substance of the points at issue. As a result, the provisions in regard to policing in the 'Agreed Communiqué' had, for the most part, to be rather general in character: they speak of 'improving policing throughout the island and developing community identification with and support for the police services'; and acceptance by the participants 'that the two parts of Ireland are to a considerable extent inter-dependent in the whole field of law and order'. The Communiqué does record, however, that the Irish government would establish a police authority. Appointments to this body, and to the police authority in Northern Ireland, would be made after consultations with the Council of Ireland. The Communiqué also states that an independent complaints procedure was to be set up to deal with complaints against the police (in Northern Ireland). However, the thorny issue of devolution of responsibility for policing in Northern Ireland was, in effect, deferred indefinitely: it was addressed in the Communiqué only to the extent that the British government said it would wish to discuss the issue with the executive 'as soon as the security problems were resolved and the new institutions were seen to be working effectively'.[23]

Other outstanding issues

A number of outstanding issues that had been touched on earlier in discussions were dealt with in exchanges during the final days of the conference, when the draft communiqué was being prepared.

Formal conference

It was agreed that there would be a formal conference 'early in the New Year' at which the two governments and the Northern Ireland executive would consider the studies that had been commissioned, and sign a formal agreement incorporating the declarations made by each of the two governments.[24]

Registration at the United Nations

It was also agreed that the formal agreement would be registered at the United Nations. The effect of this would be to ensure that the agreement had the status of an international treaty. (Article 102 of the UN charter requires all treaties and international agreements concluded between member states to be registered at the UN).[25]

Internment in Northern Ireland

Notwithstanding the good relationship that had been established between the British and Irish governments, two important issues, which did not surface directly at the conference, remained in the background as a continuing source of tension. One was internment without trial, introduced in Northern Ireland on 9 August 1971: it was still in operation at the time of the Sunningdale conference, notwithstanding widespread acceptance that it had been implemented in a ham-fisted and one-sided way.[26] The other, related, issue, was 'the Strasbourg case'—that is, the complaint alleging torture of some of those detained, which had been taken by the Irish government against the British government under the European Convention on Human Rights.[27]

The internment issue, though not specifically a subject of discussion at the conference, was adverted to in a single brief paragraph in the Communiqué in which the conference 'took note of a reaffirmation by the British government of their firm commitment to bring detention to an end in Northern Ireland for all sections of the community as soon as the security situation permits.' The text also noted that the Northern Ireland secretary hoped to use his statutory powers to release a number of those detained before Christmas (which was then a little more than two weeks away).[28] There was no reference in the Communiqué to the Strasbourg case.

Conclusion of the conference

As I explained earlier, disagreement between the British government and the Northern Ireland parties in regard to policing in Northern Ireland prolonged the conference into Saturday and Sunday. Most of the discussion on that issue took place either in small groups or, more often, in bilateral exchanges. Meanwhile, drafting of the Communiqué was under way.

Agreement on a final text was reached eventually at 7.45 p.m. on Sunday evening, 9 December. After some hasty work in printing copies, the conference met for a final plenary session about 8.30 p.m. to approve the Communiqué and hear concluding statements by delegation leaders. Each leader thanked the others; and each, in turn, spoke warmly of what had been achieved and of his hopes for the future. For us in the Irish delegation it was of particular interest that **Brian Faulkner** expressed his appreciation to the taoiseach and to Irish ministers for the way in which 'they had always been at personal pains to help us in discussion', while **Prime Minister Heath** thanked the taoiseach for 'the very full co-operation which he has given us'. **The taoiseach** was equally warm in his thanks to the prime minister and to Brian Faulkner, as well as to Gerry Fitt and Oliver Napier.

The conference concluded with a press conference at about 9.30 p.m. on Sunday evening. The text of the 'Agreed Communiqué' was distributed to the waiting media and each of the five leaders spoke to the press on behalf of his delegation. Earlier, at the final plenary session, Brian Faulkner had spoken of the need to 'sell' the agreement—'The prime minister, the taoiseach and I must now be salesmen—we have to be super salesmen'. In what he said at the press conference the taoiseach struck a similar note. The proposals they had agreed would work only if all concerned committed themselves wholeheartedly to them as a way of easing fears and resolving conflict in the island of Ireland.

Later—much later—that night, the government delegation returned home to Dublin on a special Aer Lingus flight. The mood among ministers and officials, and then at Dublin airport, was, as Garret FitzGerald recalled years later in his autobiography, 'euphoric'.[29] Rightly so, we all thought then—the four long days and nights of negotiation had brought a settlement which, if it were accepted, could, we believed, bring peace to Ireland, north and south. But how would it be received in Ireland, north and south?

NOTES

[1] This term, in general use at the time, meant some kind of common arrangements for law enforcement in the island of Ireland and not, as it might seem, 'enforcement of the common law'.

[2] See Chapter 14.

[3] Sunningdale Communiqué, para. 7.

[4] NAI TSCH 2004/21/626 (folder 2), Government decision S. 18966 of 11 September 1973. See Sunningdale brief, section II. In the rest of this chapter I will refer simply to the 'Sunningdale brief'.

[5] Sunningdale Communiqué, para. 7.

[6] Sunningdale Communiqué, para 8.

[7] Sunningdale brief, section IV (2) and (4).

[8] Sunningdale Communiqué, para. 7.

[9] Sunningdale brief, sections III and IV (1).

[10] Sunningdale Communiqué, para. 8.

[11] Sunningdale Communiqué, para. 8.

[12] Sunningdale Communiqué, para. 7.

[13] White Paper, para. 112. See also Green Paper, para. 78.

[14] Government decision S.18966 B of 13 November 1973 on Sunningdale brief, section II. See also section VI.

[15] Sunningdale brief, section II.

[16] UUP proposals, Annex 4 to the Green Paper 1972, 57.

[17] Sunningdale brief, section II (IV), government decision S.1834, 26 October 1973.

[18] Sunningdale brief, section II (IV) (2), government decisions S. 1934 of 26 October and 2 November 1973.

[19] Sunningdale brief, section II, government decisions S. 1834 of 26 October and 28 November. See also section V.

[20] Sunningdale Communiqué, para. 10.

[21] Sunningdale Communiqué, para. 11.

[22] FitzGerald, *All in a life*, 216.

[23] Sunningdale Communiqué, paras 12–17.

[24] Sunningdale Communiqué, paras 6 and 20.

[25] Sunnindale Communiqué, para. 6.

[26] See Chapter 5.

[27] See Chapter 13.

[28] Sunnindale Communiqué, para. 18.

[29] FitzGerald, *All in a life*, 222.

CHAPTER 18

The Sunningdale Communiqué

In the previous chapter I described how agreement was reached at Sunningdale. In this chapter I want to consider just what it was that was agreed and how far it was significant.

First, I should make a point that has often been overlooked in subsequent assessments of the conference. The final document that emerged was described as an 'Agreed Communiqué' rather than an 'agreement'. This was because all the participants accepted that the four day-and-night meeting was no more than the first stage in a two-stage process. The second, formal stage of the conference was to be held 'early in the New Year', when studies in regard to the operation and functions of the Council of Ireland had been completed. At that stage a formal agreement was to be signed which both governments would register at the United Nations. In the event this never happened—the newly formed power-sharing executive in Northern Ireland collapsed in May 1974 for a variety of reasons which I will consider in a later chapter. So, when we consider the outcome of the Sunningdale conference today, the only formal document we have to go on is the 'Agreed Communiqué' of twenty paragraphs which emerged at the end of the first stage on 9 December 1973.

I turn now to consider some of the main points of this document, to explain why they were significant. The full text of the Communiqué can be found in Appendix I.

Basic aspirations

At the start of the document the taoiseach and Brian Faulkner, in separate paragraphs, clarified their respective positions. The taoiseach said that the participants had reached an 'accommodation with one another on practical arrangements. But none had compromised, and none had asked others to compromise, in relation to basic aspirations'. Brian Faulkner, in similar terms, said that

> [the] delegates from Northern Ireland came to the Conference as representatives of apparently incompatible sets of political aspirations who had found it possible to reach agreement to join together in government because each accepted that in doing so they were not sacrificing principles or aspirations.

The 'status' of Northern Ireland

Paragraph 5 of the document was devoted to separate declarations by the Irish government and the British government respectively in regard to the 'status' of Northern Ireland. These were set out in the text as printed, not in sequence but in parallel columns. Why was it done this way?

In both of his autobiographies Garret FitzGerald explains that the idea for this odd expedient came to him as 'a brainwave' in the early hours of Saturday morning, in the course of a conversation with British officials: and he saw putting the Irish government's declaration on the left-hand side as a way to 'avoid any suggestion of the British interpretation of "status" governing its meaning in the Irish declaration.'[1] In his memoirs, however, Brian Faulkner says that it was he who proposed that the declarations be set out in parallel; and he offers what was, in effect, the opposite reason for doing so: he was told 'by the lawyers', that that layout would reinforce 'the relationship between the Dublin Declaration and the British commitment to self-determination for Northern Ireland.'[2] A third claim to have originated the idea—made privately and, to my mind, more likely to be justified than that made publicly by either of the two political leaders I have mentioned—is that of Philip Woodfield, who was then deputy secretary of the Northern Ireland Office. In an internal summary note of 18 February 1974 on the discussion in the 'status' sub-group, which is now in the British archives, he says

> [i]n the early hours of Saturday morning after a brief discussion with Mr. Cooper [Permanent Secretary of NIO] I drafted two separate formulae—one for the Republic and one for HMG—and suggested to Dr. O'Brien at about break-fast time on Saturday that these two formulae might appear in parallel in the communique. He excepted [*sic*] this provided the Declaration by the Republic appeared on the left-hand side of the page: I then got Mr. Faulkner to accept the idea of parallel formulations and brought him together with Dr. O'Brien when they agreed to recommend this solution to the Plenary Conference.[3]

The credit for the idea has to remain a matter of contention between the three. In any event, whatever its origin, the proposed layout was accepted on all sides; and, happily, it seems to have reassured north and south in equal, albeit opposite, measure. I doubt, however, if many of the subsequent accounts of the conference were so meticulous as to retain the parallel layout of the two texts, which seemed so important at the time; and I think it acceptable that I consider them in sequence here.

The Irish declaration, on the left-hand side of the page, read as follows:

> The Irish Government fully accepted and solemnly declared that there could be no change in the status of Northern Ireland until a majority of the people of Northern Ireland desired a change in that status.

The British declaration, on the right-hand side, was rather longer:

> The British Government solemnly declared that it was, and would remain, their policy to support the wishes of the majority of the people of Northern Ireland. The present status of Northern Ireland is that it is part of the United Kingdom. If in the future the majority of the people of Northern Ireland should indicate a wish to become part of a united Ireland, the British Government would support that wish.

To the casual reader the two declarations might appear to be broadly similar—at least as regards their substance if not their exact wording: after all, both governments were in agreement in saying that majority consent was a necessary condition for any future change in the status of Northern Ireland. But this apparent agreement about future change concealed a fundamental disagreement about the existing status of the area. For the British government, Northern Ireland was part of the United Kingdom and they said so unequivocally. The Irish government could not say this. So long as Articles 2 and 3 of the 1937 Constitution, as they then were, remained in the Constitution, they had to be wary of a constitutional challenge in the Irish courts; and, as I explained in an earlier chapter, they were unwilling to risk a referendum to change those Articles since they knew they might lose. That would entrench the two Articles even further. So the Irish declaration focuses on the possibility of future change in the status of Northern Ireland while remaining silent about its present status.

There is also another, somewhat more subtle distinction between the two texts. The British government text speaks of '**the** majority of the people of Northern Ireland'. The Irish declaration refers to '**a** majority of the people of Northern Ireland', which implies a purely arithmetical majority. The Irish side feared that, granted the common usage at the time, the phrase with the definite article which was used in the British text might conceivably be construed as meaning that the consent of the unionist community, as such, rather than the consent of a simple majority of the total population of the area, would be required before there could be a united Ireland.[4]

Notwithstanding these ambiguities, both declarations are, nevertheless, of interest in that they marked limited, but significant, changes in the respective positions of each of the two governments.

The British declaration went beyond previous British government positions in three respects: it made the possibility of change in the position of Northern Ireland as part of the United Kingdom dependent on the wishes of a majority of the population there rather than on a decision of a parliament or assembly in Northern Ireland; it spoke more explicitly of the possibility of a united Ireland than any British legislation or formal statement had done in over half a century; and it committed the British government not just to 'accept', but to 'support', the wish of the majority of the people of Northern Ireland if in future they should indicate a wish to become part of a united Ireland. A glance back at the situation from the 1920s onwards will help to show the significance of this evolution in British policy.

Both the Government of Ireland Act 1920, which first divided the island, and the 1921 Treaty which followed, at least mentioned Irish unity as something that could be restored, or maintained, in certain circumstances. Later enactments, however, ceased to refer to it explicitly even as a possibility.

The 1920 Act, as I explained earlier, provided that if a majority in each of the (proposed) parliaments of 'Northern Ireland' and 'Southern Ireland' so agreed, then the island could be reunited under a single government and parliament exercising devolved 'Home Rule' powers within the larger framework of the United Kingdom. In practice, this made the restoration of Irish unity dependent on the agreement of the Northern Ireland parliament. This, of course, was a remote prospect at the time since Northern Ireland was being created precisely because unionists, who were now to be a majority in the area, had objected for more than a generation to the very idea of a united, Home Rule Ireland within the United Kingdom.

The Anglo-Irish Treaty a year later, notionally at least, took Irish unity as its starting point. The Irish Free State, which it established as a dominion within the Commonwealth, was to extend initially to the whole island. However, it also allowed the newly created parliament of Northern Ireland to opt out within a month—an option it promptly exercised. The effect in practice was to consolidate the division of Ireland and to limit the Free State to the 26-county area.

Some three decades later, new British legislation reaffirmed that Northern Ireland would not cease to be part of the United Kingdom without the consent of its parliament, but there was no longer any explicit reference to the possibility of Irish unity. The Ireland Act 1949 (passed in response to the passage in Dublin of the Republic of Ireland Act 1948, which described the state as a republic), contained a provision that appeared, rather, to be a further consolidation of partition:

> It is hereby declared that Northern Ireland remains part of His Majesty's dominions and of the United Kingdom and it is hereby affirmed that in no event will Northern Ireland or any part thereof cease to be part of His Majesty's dominions without the consent of the Parliament of Northern Ireland.[5]

When the Heath government decided to prorogue Stormont in March 1972, it took the precaution of including the following provision in the legislation:

> Nothing in this Act shall derogate or authorise anything to be done in derogation from the status of Northern Ireland as part of the United Kingdom.[6]

Here, too, there was no mention of Irish unity, even as a possibility, though because it was essentially a 'holding' position, pending a decision on what was to replace Stormont, that was hardly surprising.

In contrast to these earlier enactments, the declaration by the British government at Sunningdale was quite different in tone—and, indeed, to an extent, in content. It did not of course endorse Irish unity, or in itself bring it any closer. But its significance was two-fold: it was the first explicit reference in a formal British government statement to the possibility of Irish unity since the largely notional references in both the 1920 Act and the 1921 Treaty; and it went beyond both in committing the British government not just to 'accept', but to 'support' Irish unity, if that should be the wish of the majority in Northern Ireland. It is true of course that it was a 'solemn declaration' and as such it did not have legislative force. But the British side also agreed that, following the second stage of the conference, the declaration would be incorporated in an international agreement to be registered at the United Nations—a step that would have given it force in international law. Further Westminster legislation to take account of the commitment would probably also have been required.

It is true that the British declaration involved a condition that was quite unlikely to be met in any near or middle-term future. So I should not exaggerate its immediate importance. But, taken together with British willingness to agree to a Council of Ireland between north and south with no direct British government involvement it does, I think, point towards a historic change in British government attitudes to Ireland. It seemed no longer to be taken for granted that the 1920–21 settlement was definitive. The British government now appeared to be accepting that there were still issues to be dealt with; and accepting, in effect too, that the Irish government would have to be involved in some way in resolving them. Nationalists in Northern Ireland too could now believe that the legitimacy of their aspiration to Irish unity had been recognised, even if in practice its realisation remained no more than a distant—even perhaps a remote—possibility. True, Margaret Thatcher was to say later that 'Northern Ireland was as British as Finchley' but that sentiment did not match her later action in signing the Anglo-Irish Agreement, which admitted the Irish government to a role that came to be described as 'more than consultative but less than executive', in the governance of Northern Ireland while direct rule continued there. Later still, in a highly significant speech on 9 November 1990, the Northern Ireland secretary of state, Peter Brooke, said

> [th]e British government has no selfish strategic or economic interest in Northern Ireland: our role is to help, enable and encourage…Partition is an acknowledgment of reality, not an assertion of national self-interest.[7]

This was an expression of openness, not to say neutrality, in the British government's approach; and it is rightly seen as having been important in furthering the peace process that led eventually to the Good Friday Agreement of 1998. I don't think it too much to suggest, however, that, taking a longer perspective, the remote origins of Brooke's statement could be traced back to the Heath government's agreement at Sunningdale to include in an international agreement a commitment to 'support' Irish unity if that were to be the wish of the majority in Northern Ireland.

The Irish government's declaration at Sunningdale too, for all its caution and ambivalence, was something of an advance on the previous position of Irish governments. Irish nationalists had never accepted that it was legitimate to partition Ireland contrary to the will of the majority of its population; and, prior to Sunningdale, no Irish government would have been willing to make a solemn declaration that the status of Northern Ireland could not change without the consent of a majority of the population in that area. Still less would an Irish government have agreed to include such a declaration in an international agreement to be registered at the United Nations. It is true that, by accepting the 1921 Treaty which allowed an 'opt out' to Northern Ireland, and the subsequent Boundary Agreement of 1925 which left the border unchanged, the Free State government could be said to have also accepted, albeit reluctantly and, as it might have argued later, under a degree of constraint, that Northern Ireland would remain part of the United Kingdom. However, this reluctant acquiescence in the division that took place in the early years of the 1920s did not mean that the members of that government had abandoned the belief that in principle the unit for 'self-determination' should have been the island as a whole. In later decades successive Irish governments contended strongly that the partition of the island by Britain was a wrong that ought to be righted—indeed for a time they conducted an essentially futile international campaign on that issue. This view, tempered by pragmatism, was given subtle expression by de Valera in the drafting of the 1937 Constitution. By asserting in principle a jurisdiction over the whole island while limiting it in practice to the existing state, Articles 2 and 3, implicitly at least, denied legitimacy to the position of Northern Ireland as part of the United Kingdom.

Notwithstanding this, however, there was substantial north-south cooperation on a range of practical issues over the years.[8]

In December 1967 one of the recommendations of a cross-party Committee of the Oireachtas was that the so-called 'claim' to jurisdiction over the whole island in Article 3 of the Constitution should be replaced by a sentence reading 'The Irish Nation hereby proclaims its firm will that its territory be re-united in harmony and brotherly affection between all Irishmen'. (The Committee had no women members, which may in part, perhaps, account for the failure, no doubt through inadvertence, to offer to extend the bonds of harmony and affection to Irish women.) The report was an indication of greater openness, but its recommendation, which would have made it necessary to hold a referendum, was not implemented.[9]

When the Troubles broke out in the late 1960s some politicians in Dublin—including some who had been ministers in Lynch's government until they were dismissed during the Arms Crisis of 1970—reverted to the outdated and simplistic view that the fundamental cause of the problem was 'partition'. However, though still unwilling to give any kind of legal recognition to Northern Ireland, the main parties in the south were gradually coming to accept, at least as a practical matter, that there could not be unity in Ireland without the consent of a majority of the population in that area.

Garret FitzGerald, as I recall, always asserted that Fine Gael, under his influence, was the first to move to make its acceptance of this fully explicit. I feel that perhaps he does not give enough credit to Jack Lynch who, as taoiseach, personally went quite far in his ground-breaking Tralee speech of 20 September 1969 where he spoke of a policy 'of seeking unity through agreement in Ireland between Irishmen' and 'a free and genuine union of those living in Ireland based on mutual respect and tolerance'. The speech, drafted by Ken Whitaker, was clear enough about the 'consent principle':

> It will remain our most earnest aim and hope *to win the consent of the majority of the people in the Six Counties* to means by which North and South can

come together in a re-united and sovereign Ireland earning international respect both for the fairness and efficiency with which it is administered and for its contribution to world peace and progress.

We are not seeking to overthrow by violence the Stormont Parliament or government but rather *to win the agreement of a sufficient number of people in the North to an acceptable form of reunification.* [My emphasis.]

That said, I think that Garret FitzGerald may be correct in saying that he was the first to bring his party to adopt the 'consent principle' as a formal party policy. In his autobiography, he recounts how it happened. In the Autumn of 1969, while still in opposition, he drafted a paper for the party on Northern Ireland in which he stressed the 'consent principle' as 'the only way in which the present divided state of the island can or should be modified'. (It also, he says in his autobiography, urged the then government to press Britain to provide for minority representatives in the government of Northern Ireland and sought the creation of a body similar to the Council of Ireland envisaged in the 1921 Treaty.)

> For me the crucial issue was to get acceptance by the party of the principle that, whatever we might think of partition and however much we might feel that the division of the island had been damaging to its peace and prosperity, given that this division had become an established fact it could and should be ended only with the consent of a majority in Northern Ireland. This had never been accepted, overtly at any rate, by Fianna Fáil as a party, to some extent perhaps because of a feeling that to do so would have been to weaken their hold on a segment of republican opinion that might then have drifted towards support for the IRA. I had always believed, however, that Fine Gael had the duty to take an unambiguous stand on the issue. In fact, the party had participated in—and from its vantage point in government in 1949 had even led—an

anti-partition campaign that echoed the traditional republican slogans 'The North has no right to opt out', 'Ireland has a right to its six north-eastern counties', and so on. I did not believe that this approach would ever bring about Irish unity.

He knew that if he were to submit a policy document on this issue it 'might receive less than a warm reception from some members of the front bench'. So he asked his colleague Paddy Harte, who represented a Donegal constituency, to submit it under his own name. Harte prudently sought the opinions of two leading SDLP members, John Hume and Austin Currie. He then submitted the paper to the front bench of the party. Two of its four 'more traditionally anti-partitionist members' were absent abroad; and the party leader, Liam Cosgrave, and another senior colleague, Gerard Sweetman, had to leave the meeting early. The policy went through without difficulty and Liam Cosgrave approved it subsequently with a minor deletion.

By Garret's account other political parties—first Labour and later Fianna Fáil—followed the lead of Fine Gael:

> The principle of 'no reunification without consent' was soon adopted by the Labour Party. And after the 1970 Arms Crisis had changed fairly radically the composition of the Fianna Fáil Government, Jack Lynch edged Fianna Fáil gradually towards the same stance, so that when the Sunningdale agreement, incorporating this principle, was signed in December 1973 he was able to get his party to accept it.

> This did not mean, however, that traditional anti-partition rhetoric vanished overnight from Fine Gael or Labour, let alone from Fianna Fáil.[10]

Measured against the cautious approach Garret FitzGerald felt it necessary to take, even within his own party, in 1969, the 'solemn declaration' by the Fine Gael-Labour coalition government at Sunningdale in 1973, for all its ambivalence, has to be seen as a considerable advance on the position of previous Irish governments.

Its significance was all the greater because the government also agreed that after the second stage of the conference this 'solemn declaration' would be incorporated in an international agreement to be registered with the United Nations. It is a matter of speculation whether or not this further step giving it international legal status would ultimately have been ruled by the Supreme Court to contravene Articles 2 and 3 of the Constitution. At least one of the judgments subsequently issued when the Supreme Court considered the constitutionality of the Sunningdale Communiqué could be read as implying that this might possibly have been the case.[11]

The two parallel declarations, important as they were, took up no more than a single short paragraph in the Communiqué. Much of the remainder of the text dealt with the agreement to set up a Council of Ireland, and issues of law and order and security.

Council of Ireland

The provisions in regard to a Council of Ireland in general corresponded quite closely to the proposals the Irish government had brought to the conference, although there were some points of difference. As the government had proposed, the Council would be confined to representatives of the two parts of Ireland, with appropriate safeguards for the British government's financial and other interests. It would comprise a Council of Ministers with 'executive and harmonising functions and a consultative role', as well as a consultative assembly 'with advisory and review functions'. The Council of Ministers was to have a core membership of seven members each drawn from the Irish government and the Northern Ireland executive—though other non-voting members from each side would attend when matters for which their departments were responsible were to be dealt with. The chairmanship would rotate between north and south; and the Council would act by unanimity. There was also to be a consultative assembly of 60 members. The Irish government had proposed that the membership should come from north and south in proportion to their respective populations. This would give the south twice as many members as the north. This proposal, however, was 'made with a view to the negotiations' and, at the conference, the government agreed, readily enough, to parity of membership: there were to be 30 from the Dáil and 30 from the northern assembly, chosen in each case by proportional representation. A secretariat, headed by a secretary general, would service the Council institutions and 'would, under the Council of Ministers, supervise the carrying out of the executive and harmonising functions and the consultative role of the Council.' The Council of Ministers would decide on a location for the headquarters of the Council and the secretary general would draw up the necessary plans.

A further paragraph dealt with the functions of the Council. In its harmonising and consultative role it would 'undertake important work relating, for instance, to the impact of EEC membership'. The executive functions of the Council, however, would need to be defined and agreed in detail. So, as the Communiqué put it,

> in view of the administrative complexities involved, studies would at once be set in hand to identify and, prior to the formal stage of the conference, report on areas of common interest in relation to which a Council of Ireland would take executive decisions, and, in appropriate cases, be responsible for carrying those decisions into effect.[12]

The studies were to consider eight broad fields in order to identify aspects suitable for executive action by the Council. These were: natural resources and the environment; agricultural matters; cooperative ventures in trade and industry; electricity generation; tourism; roads and transport; public health advisory services; and sports, culture and the arts. The initial functions to be vested in the Council would be decided at the formal stage of the conference, on the basis of the studies. Thereafter, it would be for the Oireachtas and the Northern assembly 'to legislate from time to time as to the extent of functions to be devolved to the Council'. The British government would cooperate where necessary in this devolution of functions.

During an initial period the Council was to be financed by grants from the two administrations in Ireland towards agreed projects and budgets. Further studies of possible methods of financing the Council after this initial period would be completed as soon as possible. The cost of the secretariat would be shared equally while other services would generally be financed in proportion to where the expenditure or the benefit arose. Britain would continue to pay subsidies to Northern Ireland although it would not participate in the Council. However, 'it would be legitimate for Britain to safeguard in an appropriate way her financial involvement in Northern Ireland'.[13]

Most of the rest of the Communiqué dealt with issues which had caused difficulties at the conference and which it had been decided to leave over for further study or future decision. These included the question of how persons accused of crimes of violence in either part of Ireland were to be brought to trial; issues of security and policing; and the application of the principles of the European Convention on Human Rights.

Prosecution for crimes of violence—Commission to examine

On the issue of prosecutions, the Communiqué set out a general principle:

> It was agreed by all parties that persons committing crimes of violence, however motivated, in any part of Ireland, should be brought to trial irrespective of the part of Ireland in which they are located.

The difficulty was how this was to be done. Unionist leaders frequently complained that IRA members who carried out attacks in Northern Ireland could find safe haven across the border. The British government, too, were critical from time to time of what they saw as less than wholehearted cooperation by the Irish government on cross-border security cooperation. Successive governments in Dublin, on the other hand, strongly rejected these criticisms and argued that violence for the most part was indigenous to Northern Ireland and particularly found support in what were virtually 'no-go' areas for the RUC and the British army in places close to the border.

A particular point of contention, then and later, was whether the republic would allow persons accused of crimes of violence in Northern Ireland to be extradited there for trial. This was a complex issue. Each of the two jurisdictions in Ireland already had legislation that would permit extradition to the other jurisdiction of a person accused or convicted of what might be called 'ordinary crimes'.[14] However, in each of the two jurisdictions the relevant Act provided for an exception in relation to political offences. The legislation in Northern Ireland barred extradition where the offence was 'an offence of a political character'. This provision was mandatory. The legislation in the republic gave the minister for justice or the High Court power to direct the release of a person accused of a 'political offence or an offence connected with a political offence.' This provision appears discretionary in form but the Supreme Court had held in 1972 that in effect it was mandatory.[15]

The British view, shared later by Lord Chief Justice Lowry of Northern Ireland, was that the best way to give effect to the principle set out in the Communiqué I have quoted above would be to amend the relevant legislation in each of the two jurisdictions so as to permit extradition for crimes of violence—either by way of a general principle or by listing certain specific offences. This could be done for Northern Ireland by an Act of the Westminster parliament. The Irish government, however, argued that it would have a constitutional difficulty about enacting similar legislation in the republic. Article 29.3 of the Constitution reads as follows:

> Ireland accepts the generally recognised principles of international law as its rule of conduct in its relations with other States.

The contention of the Irish government was that it was a 'generally recognised principle of international law' that a person accused of a political offence should not be extradited to another jurisdiction to face trial there; and, since that was the case, Article 29.3 would not permit it to legislate to permit extradition in such cases. The attorney general, Declan Costello, in particular, held strongly to this view. As Garret FitzGerald pointed out later, it also reflected a judgment of the High Court in a case that the government had felt to be so conclusive that it had decided not to appeal to the Supreme Court.[16] The British on the other hand argued that, while there was indeed such a principle in international law, its exercise was discretionary and not mandatory: that is to say, the principle 'recognise[d] the right, without imposing the duty, to refuse extradition of such offenders'.[17]

While I don't doubt Declan Costello's integrity or his legal acumen, I recall that at the time some of my colleagues and I were inclined to think that the government's argument on this issue was rather thin—not to say specious. Legal issues apart, I think there was also another, and perhaps even a stronger, reason at the time for our reluctance to agree to legislate to permit the extradition of persons accused of crimes of violence. This was the lack of full confidence in the legal and security system in Northern Ireland on the part of the government and a belief that handing over accused persons to be dealt with under that system would evoke a great deal of public and political criticism in our jurisdiction. At that time, not only was internment still in force but the Irish government was still actively pursuing the case it had taken in Strasbourg under the European Convention on Human Rights, alleging the torture and mistreatment of detainees in Northern Ireland. Indeed, according to an internal British report on the conference sub-group that discussed extradition, Declan Costello acknowledged that the real problem was political.

> This meeting was notable for the fact that towards the end of it the Irish Attorney General admitted that the difficulties about the extradition solution were neither legal or constitutional; they were political in the sense that the Government could not command a majority in the Dail or the support of public opinion for an amendment of the extradition laws.[18]

This did not mean of course that the government in any way condoned the violence in Northern Ireland or wanted the south to provide some kind of refuge for those engaged in it. In the lead-up to Sunningdale various alternative ideas for dealing with offenders, other than extradition, had been discussed on our side. One such proposal that the attorney general and the minister for justice argued for at the conference was that a special, temporary court to try specified offences would be established for the whole island. There would be either three or five judges nominated by the Council of Ireland; and the trial would be held, and any sentence imposed served, in the place where the accused had been arrested. However, the points at issue, and the various solutions proposed, were thought to be too difficult to be settled at the conference itself. So, as the Communiqué says,

> [i]t was agreed that problems of considerable legal complexity were involved, and that the British and Irish governments would jointly set up a commission to consider all the proposals put forward at the Conference and to recommend as a matter of extreme urgency the most effective means of dealing with those who commit these crimes.

The commission, comprising judges and other legal experts—four from the British and four from the Irish side—was duly set up after the conference.[19] Its report submitted on 25 April 1974 examined various proposals. Some it disposed of briefly: it did not recommend the so-called 'all-Ireland court method' because it did not believe it would offer 'a practicable immediate solution'; it saw no legal objection to 'the extra-territorial method exercised by domestic courts'; and it did not recommend 'the mixed court method' since, it said, it offered no advantage over the extra-territorial method. On the contentious issue of extradition it could not agree: 'We can make no agreed recommendation about extradition. We are evenly divided on this method.'

All eight members of the commission were, no doubt, appropriately dispassionate in their approach. However, strangely—or perhaps not so strangely—the four British appointed experts thought that amending the legislation on extradition was a feasible approach; the four Irish experts thought that it was not.

Since the Sunningdale settlement collapsed a month after the report was submitted the issues it raised were not pursued further.

However, something in relation to this particular issue was achieved at Sunningdale. The Communiqué put it as follows:

> The Irish government undertook to take immediate and effective legal steps so that persons coming within their jurisdiction and accused of murder, however motivated, committed in Northern Ireland will be brought to trial, and it was agreed that any similar reciprocal action that may be needed in Northern Ireland will be taken by the appropriate authorities.[20]

This was possible because Declan Costello found a basis in older legislation of 1861 (when Ireland was part of the United Kingdom), which would permit introduction by order of a measure to allow our courts to exercise extraterritorial jurisdiction in cases of murder. There was a similar legislative provision in Northern Ireland. Together, these provisions would allow the relevant authority in either one of the two jurisdictions in Ireland to bring to trial in its domestic courts a person accused of murder in the other jurisdiction.[21]

Human rights issues

For the Irish government it was important that, in parallel with whatever was done in regard to the trial of offenders, there should also be effective action in Northern Ireland in relation to human rights. Our proposal was that the rights specified in the European Convention of Human Rights should be incorporated into domestic law in both jurisdictions; and that a five-judge all-Ireland Human Rights Court (with at least two judges each from north and south) be set up to deal with breaches of human rights legislation in either part of the island. The Communiqué (paragraph 11) left these matters to the Council:

> It was agreed that the Council [of Ireland] would be invited to consider in what way the principles of the European Convention on Human Rights would be expressed in domestic legislation in each part of

Ireland. It would recommend whether further legislation or the creation of other institutions, administrative or judicial, is required in either part or embracing the whole island to provide additional protection in the field of human rights. Such recommendations could include the functions of an Ombudsman or Commissioner for Complaints, or other arrangements of a similar nature which the Council of Ireland might think appropriate.

Policing

A third area where decisions had to be deferred was the vexed issue of policing and what the Communiqué called 'the need to ensure support for and identification with the police service throughout the whole community'. It was this issue, and in particular the sharp differences of position between each of the two main Northern Ireland parties and the British government on the possible devolution of responsibility for policing in Northern Ireland, that had caused the conference to run on for some two days longer than expected. As I explained earlier the SDLP wanted the Council of Ireland to have an important role; the Unionists wanted policing to be devolved to the new Northern Ireland executive; and the British government were not at that stage prepared to devolve responsibility to either body. The most that could be achieved in the Communiqué was a statement that deferred—not to say fudged—the issue:

> Accordingly, the British government stated that, as soon as the security problems were resolved and the new institutions were seen to be working effectively, they would wish to discuss the devolution of responsibility for normal policing and how this might be achieved with the Northern Ireland Executive and the Police.[22]

In the event it was more than three decades before this responsibility could be devolved.

The Communiqué did, however, record progress on one point. In order to improve policing throughout the island and develop community identification with the police, it was agreed that the governments concerned would cooperate through their respective police authorities under the auspices of a Council of Ireland. The Northern Ireland secretary was also to set up an all-party committee from the Northern assembly to examine how best to introduce effective policing and achieve greater public identification with the police throughout Northern Ireland; and there was a commitment in the Communiqué that an independent complaints procedure would be set up to deal with complaints against the police. There was already a police authority in the north, but not in the south, so the Irish government agreed to set up such a body. It would appoint its members after consulting the Council of Ireland. Similarly, appointments to the Northern Ireland police authority would be made after consulting the Council. My memory is that the Department of Justice were none too happy about our government's agreeing to set up a police authority. For whatever reason nothing was done about it and it is only now, some 43 years later, that a police authority has been established in our jurisdiction.[23]

Internment in Northern Ireland

Internment, introduced by the Stormont government in 1971, and badly mishandled, was still in operation in Northern Ireland at the time of the Sunningdale conference. Notwithstanding the many criticisms levelled against it, the British government did not yet feel it could agree to bring it to an end. So the most that could be recorded in the Communiqué was a rather vague commitment.

> The Conference took note of a reaffirmation by the British government of their firm commitment to bring detention to an end in Northern Ireland for all sections of the community as soon as the security situation permits, and noted also that the Secretary of State for Northern Ireland hopes to be able to bring

into use his statutory powers of selective release in time for a number of detainees to be released before Christmas.[24]

Next steps: devolution of powers to Northern institutions; formal conference

In the penultimate paragraph the British government stated that they would now seek parliamentary approval in Westminster to devolve full powers to the Northern executive and assembly. The formal appointment of the Northern executive would then be made.

The Communiqué concluded with a single-sentence final paragraph:

> The Conference agreed that a formal conference would be held early in the New Year at which the British and Irish governments and the Northern Ireland Executive would meet together to consider reports on the studies which have been commissioned and to sign the agreement reached.

None of us knew it then but 'early in the New Year' was to be a long time coming.

NOTES

[1] FitzGerald, *All in a life*, 216; also FitzGerald, *Just Garret*, 249–50.

[2] Faulkner, *Memoirs of a statesman*, 230.

[3] TNA PREM 15/1685.

[4] Irish governments have not, I think, always been so concerned about the niceties of terminology on this point. In his Tralee speech of 20 September 1969, the then taoiseach, Jack Lynch, spoke of 'our earnest aim and hope to win the consent of the majority of the people in the Six Counties to means by which North and South can come together in a re-united and sovereign Ireland.'

[5] Ireland Act 1949 (1949 c. 41), Section 1 (2). Another, more positive, provision giving Irish citizens a special status in UK law, attracted little attention. Section 2.1

provided that while the republic had ceased 'to be part of His Majesty's dominions' it was 'not a foreign country' for the purposes of UK law.

[6] Northern Ireland (Temporary Provisions) Act 1972 (1972 c. 22), Section 2.

[7] See, for example, extract in Eamonn O'Kane, 'Anglo-Irish relations and the Northern Ireland peace process: from exclusion to inclusion', in *Contemporary British History* 18 (1) (Spring 2004), 78–99: 78–79. O'Kane is here quoting Peter Taylor, *Provos: the IRA and Sinn Féin* (London, 1998), 318.

[8] See Chapter 11.

[9] *Report of the Committee on the Constitution* (Dublin, December 1967, PR 9817). The committee, established largely at the instigation of Seán Lemass, shortly before he left office as taoiseach, was chaired by George Colley, who was at the time minister for industry and commerce.

[10] FitzGerald, *All in a life*, 88–91.

[11] See Chapter 20. In his judgment, Mr Justice O'Keefe did not say this directly but he did appear to be warning the government against acknowledging that the state does not claim to be entitled as of right to jurisdiction over Northern Ireland.

[12] Sunningdale Communiqué, para. 8.

[13] Sunningdale Communiqué, para. 9.

[14] For details see the *Law Enforcement Commission Report (Prl.3832)* (Dublin, 1974), chapters III, VI and VII. The relevant legislation in the republic was the Extradition Act 1965, Sections 44 (2) and 50 (2); in Northern Ireland it was the Backing of Warrants (Republic of Ireland) Act 1965, Section 41.

[15] *Law Enforcement Commission Report*, para. 11. The case was *Bourke v. Attorney General* [1972].

[16] FitzGerald, *All in a life*, 213.

[17] *Law Enforcement Commission Report*, para. 75 (a).

[18] TNA PREM 15/1685. Note of 15 February 1974 by G.W. Watson.

[19] The members appointed by the Irish government were Justices Walsh and Henchy, Tom Doyle S.C. and Declan Quigley, head of the attorney general's office; the British government appointed Lord Justice Scarman, the Lord Chief Justice Lowry of Northern Ireland, Sir Kenneth Jones and J.B.E. Hutton Q.C.

[20] Sunningdale Communiqué, para. 10.

[21] FitzGerald, *All in a life*, 216.

[22] Sunningdale Communiqué, para. 14.

[23] Writing years later, Garret FitzGerald depicts the minister for justice and his department as having viewed this aspect of the 'package' with 'less than enthusiasm'. At the time, they seemed to see a police authority as 'an intrusive body coming between them and the Garda Síochána', FitzGerald, *All in a life*, 232.

[24] Sunningdale Communiqué, para. 18.

CHAPTER 19

How Sunningdale was received

In his opening statement to the conference, the taoiseach, Liam Cosgrave, said that he was under no illusion that the outcome would end violence now. That indeed would have been too much to expect. But the hope of those involved had been that the agreement would have such wide support across all communities, north and south, that violence would be reduced to a minimum level where it could be dealt with by what the Communiqué called 'improving policing throughout the island' and developing greater 'identification with, and support, for the police services'.[1] In the event the violence did not stop. In his history of the IRA, Ed Moloney describes how that organisation reacted:

> There was widespread agreement within the republican movement that the IRA had better move to kill off Sunningdale before Sunningdale killed it, as a key strategist of the time recalled: 'Our objective was to ensure that the Sunningdale Agreement would not succeed. [Dáithí] Ó Conaill was pushing us to blow up [the] Stormont [parliament] with a massive bomb and the Belfast leadership was trying to devise a method of getting a bomb onto a ship and blow it up

in order to block the main channel in Belfast harbour. We wanted to make our presence felt as a force without which there could be no solution that was not to our liking.'[2]

Fortunately, the security forces were able to thwart these plans by pre-emptive action.

Loyalist paramilitaries, too, reacted strongly against the Sunningdale settlement. On 10 December they formed the Ulster Army Council, an umbrella body for the most important loyalist paramilitary groups (including the UDA and UVF).[3] As I will explain later, however, it was primarily the actions of two other bodies formed, with strong loyalist support, to oppose Sunningdale—the United Ulster Unionist Council (UUUC) and the Ulster Workers' Council (UWC)—which were to bring the whole Sunningdale edifice crashing down eventually.

In the south, the Communiqué was well received: as Garret FitzGerald noted years later: 'Sunningdale—like the Anglo-Irish Agreement twelve years later—proved much more popular with public opinion in the republic than those of us in government had foreseen.[4]

There were of course some, very much a minority, who saw it as a betrayal of Irish nationalist principles and aspirations. Kevin Boland, a member of a staunch Fianna Fáil family, who had resigned from Jack Lynch's government at the time of the Arms Crisis in May 1970, began proceedings in the High Court to have the Communiqué declared contrary to the Constitution.

Speaking in the Dáil on 12 December 1973, the taoiseach gave a summary of what had been agreed at Sunningdale. He said that it opened out a new prospect of hope for peace and reconciliation and cooperation in the island. This would require patience. The agreement was a unit: no one part could be taken in isolation.

> Those who say that they do not want the statements on the status of Northern Ireland must also say that they do not want a Council of Ireland. The policing, human rights and law reform proposals are equally part of the totality of the agreement. In particular anyone who contemplates rejecting the agreement

should remember that without that agreement—and I mean the whole of that agreement—the power-sharing Executive in the North could not come into being.

He paid a warm tribute to Prime Minister Heath, who had shown 'his sense of the importance of these proceedings by the assiduity with which he took part in the conference, and the notable personal contribution which he made to them.' The three parties in the Northern Ireland executive, too, had shown 'the same resource and the same combination of firmness and flexibility that had enabled the Executive to come into being.'[5]

In his response, Jack Lynch took quite a positive view of what the government had achieved—although he was rather unfairly criticised by one government minister, in the subsequent debate, for having stopped short of using the word 'welcome'.[6] Lynch said that he and his party would facilitate the implementation of the 'practical proposals' agreed at Sunningdale. He had appreciated the approach of the then opposition parties (now in government) in maintaining the issue of Northern Ireland above party politics. His party, now in opposition, would do the same.

His positive reaction was hardly surprising—he had done a great deal while he was in office as taoiseach, to prepare the ground for what had been agreed at the conference.

> We advocated long before the Northern Assembly elections that there should be an administration in the North to replace Stormont which would have in it representatives of the minority tradition in Northern Ireland, with power-sharing as an important ingredient of it. In my talks with Mr. Heath, and they were many, I consistently advocated the establishment of a Council of Ireland, a Council that would have executive functions, a Council that would be capable of evolution. These two things are the positive proposals coming from the Sunningdale talks.

He said he had not been impatient that the talks took so long—'it is very difficult in four days to solve the problems built up over many hundreds of years before'. However, he had some reservations. He had been concerned at first that in press coverage the Irish government declaration was shown as following that of the British government but he had been reassured to see the official text, which showed the two in parallel columns.

> To what extent one binds the other is a matter for clarification but taking the Irish government's acceptance and declaration that there could be no change in the status of Northern Ireland, one could accept this as stating the position, the factual position, that has obtained over many years. It has been the common policy in this country of all political parties represented here that the reunification of the country can come about only by peaceful means and that implies procuring the consent of all those who would subscribe to that objective.

He said he expected that when the agreement was finalised it would be brought before the Dáil for approval.

Lynch also took a quite a positive approach on other aspects of the Communiqué. He recalled that he had argued that the Council of Ireland should have an executive and a consultative assembly and executive and harmonising functions—'that is what we advocated and that is what we support'. On extradition he mentioned the constitutional issue and the international convention on extradition to which Ireland is a party and he accepted that the government 'had no room to manoeuvre in this matter'. However, he saw practical difficulties about the proposal to charge persons arrested in one jurisdiction for crimes committed in the other. Because of this he agreed with the government that the most practical suggestion was to establish an all-island court that would also have 'civil rights and human rights functions'.

As to policing, he knew that it was a very difficult area. He made a suggestion for a single all-island police force which was more far-reaching than anything the government had envisaged and which, I think, went well beyond what his party had previously envisaged, or, indeed, would have been willing to contemplate in later years:

> I suggest it would be much simpler if the police North and South are a single police force responsible to the one court in respect of scheduled areas of criminality and certain areas of human rights. That court need not be confined to one or other part of the country. It would be far better that that court would be mobile, mobile to the extent that its jurisdiction would extend North and South.[7]

In London, storm clouds were gathering over the Heath government as the mine-workers prepared for another strike which, within two short months, would reduce British industry to working a three-day week. For the moment however, Heath himself enjoyed something of a triumph. Lord Hailsham, who had strong family connections to Northern Ireland, had told him in early December not to be depressed if he did not solve a 400-year old problem by the end of the weekend. Undeterred by this pessimistic advice, Heath had devoted himself wholeheartedly for four days and nights to the Sunningdale conference, except for those few hours when he had to break off to meet the Italian prime minister in Downing Street; and he was entitled to considerable credit for what appeared initially to be a very successful outcome.

I can add a brief personal anecdote as to Heath's mood at the time. Within days of the end of Sunningdale, EEC heads of state and government, faced with the first 'oil crisis', gathered for a Summit meeting in Copenhagen. Muiris MacConghail and I, among others, accompanied the taoiseach and Garret FitzGerald, the minister for foreign affairs, to the meeting. On our way into a formal function for visiting delegations, Muiris and I found ourselves immediately behind Heath, who recognised Muiris from Sunningdale and made a jovial reference to a controversial 'leak' to the press at the conference in which Muiris was involved.[8] It was plain, even from this brief chance encounter, that he had a good memory of those four intensive days of negotiation. Nor had he forgotten it when I met him on occasion when I was in London a decade later, as he lived out a long and brooding retirement during the Thatcher era.[9]

Heath's authorised biographer has a tart comment about what happened in the months after Sunningdale.

> It had taken four hundred years, as Hailsham had pointed out, but the Irish problem was finally solved. It stayed finally solved for about two months.

But his overall assessment of Sunningdale and of Heath's own role was generous.

> It was back to square one. And yet it was not. The principles that had been thrashed out before and at Sunningdale were not to be forgotten...It would be an over-simplification to say that without Sunningdale there would have been no Good Friday Agreement, but the link between the two is palpable...He [Heath] had his vision and he fought for it with courage and tenacity.[10]

In Northern Ireland, however, the hope that followed the agreement was short-lived: whatever support there was for it within the unionist community began to unravel almost immediately. It was not surprising of course that Ian Paisley, who had rejected an invitation to address the opening session of the conference, and whose will and capacity to pull down each successive effort to achieve a settlement were then at their height, should be strongly opposed to Sunningdale. At a rally attended by 600 delegates in the Ulster Hall on 6 December 1973 just after the start of the Sunningdale conference, he had joined with William Craig, leader of Vanguard, his rival for loyalist support, other dissident unionists led by Harry West, and members of the Orange Order to form 'the United Ulster Unionist Council', which opposed power-sharing and shortly afterwards launched a 'Save Ulster' campaign. At the first meeting of the assembly on 22 January 1974 he and his followers disrupted the proceedings and he was forcibly removed from the chamber—it took eight RUC officers to carry him out.[11] According to

Brian Faulkner, Professor Kennedy Lindsay (then a member of Vanguard) danced on the speaker's table and chained himself to one of the benches, the mace was passed around among loyalist members and five policemen were injured.[12]

Opposition by Paisley and Craig was more or less to be expected. Much more serious, however, was the very considerable drop in support for Brian Faulkner over the weeks following the conference. As Unionist leader, with a settlement involving power-sharing and a Council of Ireland to sell to his party, his position was never wholly assured. It was further weakened by a series of events in late December and early January that could be seen as casting doubt on the significance of the Irish government's declaration on 'the status' of Northern Ireland.

On 16 December the taoiseach, Liam Cosgrave, responding to a question in a *Sunday Press* interview, said that there was no question of a change in our Constitution on the 'sovereignty' issue: unexceptionable in itself, and perhaps seen in Dublin as a necessary clarification, but hardly helpful to Faulkner's need to convince his party that attitudes in the south had changed.

On 17 December 1973 Kevin Boland took an action in the High Court in Dublin asking to have certain paragraphs of the Sunningdale Communiqué declared 'an infringement of the territorial sovereignty of Ireland and repugnant to the Constitution.'[13] Two weeks later, on 2 January 1974, the government submitted its defence. For good legal reasons, government lawyers, led by the attorney general, Declan Costello, felt it necessary to rebut every point in Boland's case except one, since the court was likely to regard any point that was not rebutted as having been conceded. One point the government side stood firmly by in its defence, however, was the declaration by the Irish government in paragraph 5 that 'there could be no change in the status of Northern Ireland until a majority of the people of Northern Ireland desired a change in that status'. The overall approach taken by the government in its defence of the action was to show that the Sunningdale Communiqué had not involved any new departure. No doubt the arguments for this were legally sound; and to lose the case would certainly have been disastrous. But, legally sound or not, the effect was to diminish the political importance of the Communiqué and drain it of the political impact the government had hoped to achieve. That was damaging for Faulkner and his supporters. Writing nearly twenty years later Garret FitzGerald was clear about this:

> Politically, in its impact on unionist opinion, it was totally disastrous. The subtle legal arguments used to defend the agreement were not merely lost on unionists: they totally destroyed the value of the declaration.[14]

A third development was meant to have a reassuring effect on unionists but turned out to have an effect opposite to that which was intended. Some fifteen people suspected of involvement in the IRA were arrested on the southern side of the border but most had to be released without charge shortly afterwards.[15]

In Northern Ireland shortly after Sunningdale, some members of the Unionist Party called a meeting of the 820-member Ulster Unionist Council, the governing body of the party. It included among its members a bloc nominated by the Orange Order.[16] At the meeting, held on 4 January 1974, the Council voted by 427 votes to 374 to reject the 'proposed all-Ireland Council settlement'.[17] The defeat, albeit by a majority of only 53 out of some 700, was a catastrophe for Faulkner. He resigned as leader of the Unionist Party on 7 January but retained his position as leader of the party in the assembly and head of the newly established executive. In his memoirs published four years later he is bitter about the Unionist Council, which he describes as 'an archaic body, designed for a situation which no longer existed'. As he explains:

> I noticed once again that a well-known member of the Vanguard Party, Rev. R. Bradford, who was later to become one of its MPs at Westminster, was on his feet in the hall, shouting. He was present as an Orange delegate, as were many of his party colleagues. It was so ludicrous that a major political party should have on its most powerful body members of hostile and competing parties that I was convinced the

Unionist Council had ceased to be a suitable organization for the propagation of Unionist policies in Ulster.[18]

Faulkner maintained a good face in public, however, but in contacts with the Irish and British governments he appealed for greater support and tried to slow the pace of developments. In the course of a phone call to Dermot Nally, Assistant Secretary to the government, he said he had to ask that no north-south meetings of ministers take place for the time-being.

Prime Minister Heath, too, was becoming worried. In a concerned but carefully phrased personal message to the taoiseach on 10 January he said that Faulkner's difficulties in the Unionist party could

> lead to a position in which the majority of the people of Northern Ireland no longer supported the Executive. [This] would threaten all that has been achieved so far and everything contained in the Sunningdale Agreement.

He said he had thought of suggesting a meeting with the taoiseach to discuss the situation but feared that this would encourage opponents of the Agreement. They should, however, 'keep in the closest touch'. While Faulkner and his colleagues were doing what they could 'to establish support for their policies in the constituencies', Heath said he had 'no doubt that, as Faulkner has himself said publicly, the help which will really make the difference must come from you.' Speaking frankly, he said that some of the remarks attributed to the taoiseach and some of his colleagues had been interpreted as maintaining the republic's claim on Northern Ireland and saying that there was no prospect of a change in the law on extradition. Heath said he understood the government's difficulties in going further on the 'status' issue as the High Court action was about to begin.

> But if you can find a way of making it clear publicly within the next few days that your Declaration in that Agreement can give the majority in Northern Ireland real confidence that the government of the Republic will not seek to realise the aspiration for a united

Ireland until the majority of the people of Northern desire it, that will be of enormous value.

As to security matters:

> What would really help in the immediate future would be if you could mount a major and really effective campaign which resulted in the arrest of some well-known Provisional IRA figures.[19]

Cosgrave replied within days. He said he was anxious to do everything possible to help in winning the widest possible public acceptance for the settlement while bearing in mind that it was necessary also to ensure confidence and trust in it by a majority in the republic. Both he and the minister for foreign affairs had reiterated several times the assurances in regard to the maintenance of the present status of Northern Ireland 'until such time as a majority of its people may decide in favour of a united Ireland.' He would try to find another opportunity to speak along these lines. On his side he was concerned about some 'distinctly unhelpful' speeches by politicians in Northern Ireland

> suggesting that we have failed to take some unspecified action with respect to status and that there are certain pre-conditions to the next formal stage of the Conference which never arose at Sunningdale; ignoring the existence and role of the Commission on Common Law Enforcement; demanding action of a kind in this matter which it was clearly understood and accepted at Sunningdale could not be taken; and imputing bad faith to us in the matter of dealing with the IRA.

Public reaction in the republic, he went on, showed that these statements were damaging to the whole Sunningdale concept and especially to the public reception of our security operations. Public opinion here was 'still in great majority favourable to Sunningdale' and it was important that that should not be jeopardised.

He believed they should now act firmly and quickly to carry through the agreement and get the Council of Ireland established as soon as possible

> so that within months it will become clear that it does not contain the dangers that many members of the majority in Northern Ireland have seen in it. This could clear the way for a possible test of public opinion in the early Summer, as suggested by Mr. Faulkner.

He proposed to Heath that the formal stage of the conference be held at a location in Ireland on 8 February. In the meantime more preparatory work would have to be done. So he would take up with Faulkner the possibility of a meeting between them. He also thought it would be desirable that he and Heath should meet to ensure 'against misunderstandings that could hold up progress.'

On 16 January the High Court gave judgment against Kevin Boland in the constitutional action he had taken against a number of paragraphs in the Sunningdale Agreement. Judge Murnaghan held, in particular, that, contrary to what had been alleged, paragraph 5 containing the parallel declarations did not acknowledge that Northern Ireland was part of the United Kingdom; that paragraph was no more than a statement of policy; and the court should not usurp the functions of the Dáil in seeking to control the government in the exercise of its functions. On that same day the taoiseach met Brian Faulkner at Baldonnel.[20] The tone of the personal relationship between the two was quite cordial—as indeed it had been at Sunningdale. Faulkner, however, was clearly under pressure; he felt that such support as there had been for the Agreement among unionists had begun to fray badly; and he pressed the taoiseach repeatedly to offer some further public 'clarification' on the status issue and also for greater evidence of action by Dublin on security. He warned, presciently as it turned out, that if an early election were called, more than half the Westminster seats—seven out of twelve—could go to hard-line unionists.

At the start of the discussion Faulkner stressed that the Sunningdale Agreement could be of great benefit 'if we could take the people along with it.' He was happy that the new executive was working well as a team. He attributed the negative vote in the Unionist Council largely to the fact that it was taken before there had been time to 'sell' the ideas of Sunningdale and also to the bloc vote of the 120 Orange Order delegates. If the meeting had been held a month later the result would have been different. The Unionist Council, he said, did not control policy within the Unionist Party—he could have taken the issue to the smaller policy committee of some 300 but as chief executive he had felt that could be humiliating. However, five out of ten leading party members, all except one of the office staff at party HQ, and about half of the constituency associations were with him. The Assembly Party too was solidly behind him—as to eighteen of its members; and so long as this was the case, working with the SDLP and Alliance, they would have a majority of twenty in the assembly.

Perhaps feeling that this half-and-half account hardly sounded reassuring, he went on to give a much more positive overall assessment of the initial response to the Agreement.

> Immediately after Sunningdale things were going well. This had really been the most important political event in Ireland over the last 50 years. He had never seen such support. He thought that some 80% of the Catholic community would stand absolutely by him and about 60% of the Unionist community—perhaps more.

However, there had been an erosion of this position over the previous three weeks—in relation to the 'status' question and because of the release of a large number of those arrested in the republic in the previous week.

On 'status' he said that the joint declarations in the Agreement had been accepted as a recognition of the position of Northern Ireland within the United Kingdom. However, certain comments and newspaper articles in December (an obvious reference to the taoiseach's *Sunday Press* interview), and the Boland case, had really robbed the Sunningdale supporters of credibility. In fact, he said, 'we do not have any credibility at all'. All pro-union people would accept a Council of Ireland if it is needed to enable 'your people' to identify with the institutions of government but it was more difficult to sell than power-sharing since they saw it as a half-way house towards a united Ireland. (At a later stage he said he had the feeling that there were differences in regard to the Council within the SDLP: John Hume was strongly in favour while Gerry Fitt and Paddy Devlin were less enthusiastic.) The only way of selling the Council (to unionists) was by saying that the 'status' position was guaranteed. What was needed above all was clarification of the position of the Irish government on 'status'. There was no hope of his attending the second stage of Sunningdale until that was cleared up and there was some firm action on terrorism. The future of the power-sharing executive depended on those two things. The announcement that morning that the government was recruiting another 500 gardaí was helpful, he said, and he respected the determination of the taoiseach and government to achieve results on security.

In response to Faulkner's veiled criticism of what he had said about the Constitution in a press interview in December the taoiseach said that what had been emphasised, then and since, was the declaration that there could be no change in the status of Northern Ireland unless a majority there desired it. He explained the legal reasons for the defence submitted to the Boland case. The *sub judice* rule made it impossible for either him or for the government to comment on the issue. This would remain the case if the judgment were to be appealed. However, the attorney general had told him that there would be no objection to going ahead with the second stage of the Sunningdale conference while the case, or a possible future appeal, was still pending. The taoiseach argued that a great deal was being done by the security forces in the south to combat violence, which was largely a spill-over from the north; and he mentioned some actions by Northern politicians that had caused embarrassment in the south, such as a letter to the *Irish Times* by Oliver Napier[21] and a proposal for some alternative to Sunningdale by Desmond Boal.[22] He recalled that in his message of congratulation to the new executive he had emphasised the government's acceptance of the institutions established in Northern Ireland and their intention of defending them against violence. Articles 2 and 3 were part of a Constitution that could be changed only by referendum. We could not go to the people on these two Articles alone—that would be extremely risky. What was needed was a new Constitution. This could be discussed further at a suitable opportunity. In a later exchange he added that the Constitution was 30 years old and obviously in need of revision. That was being looked at by an all-party committee [sic].[23]

Faulkner said he saw no reason why inter-ministerial meetings between the Northern executive and the Irish government should not take place but he could not go into the formal conference until the status issue was cleared up. If that were to arise (that is, convening the formal stage without clarity on 'status') he would resign from the executive and there would be no Unionists at the conference. In later exchanges he warned that if an election were called soon and the present ambiguities were to remain, the whole position could well be hopeless.

Dermot Nally pointed out that registration of the (future formal) agreement at the UN would give the Irish government's declaration international status. The taoiseach added that if the government were to change the law on extradition it would have to derogate from an international agreement. The solution was an all-Ireland court.

Faulkner said that they now understood the position on 'status' a lot more clearly than when they arrived. It was full of difficulties—none or not many of which could be remedied by the government. He returned to the issues of security and extradition. He also said he agreed that a Council of Ireland was a good thing for both north and south but 'we cannot rush it or we will smash up the whole thing.' He said again that it was particularly important for them in the north to have some clarification on 'status' and some evidence of sufficient action against terrorism. He emphasised strongly the need to hasten slowly on (the formal stage of) the conference.

As the meeting concluded with an informal discussion word was received of the High Court judgment in the Boland case and the welcome vindication of the position of the government.

It seems that Faulkner felt afterwards that the discussion had been useful, even though he had not got much further in the exchanges on the status issue, or on extradition. At a meeting with Garret FitzGerald in London on the following day the Northern secretary, Francis Pym, said that Faulkner had told him that he had been 'very pleased' with the previous day's meeting with Cosgrave. FitzGerald urged on Pym

> the importance of not delaying unduly the formal second-stage Sunningdale conference, because it was vital that the people of Northern Ireland should see the agreement working before a referendum that it was proposed to hold in the North that summer.[24]

In Dublin in the immediate aftermath of Sunningdale the task of planning and co-ordinating the practical details of the Council of Ireland was passed to the Department of the Public Service. Towards the end of January that department circulated to other departments a substantial report that considered the functions and the staff numbers from various state bodies that could be transferred to the Council. Its approach, as later events were to show, was wildly over-ambitious (as indeed the government brief for Sunningdale had also been):

> If our recommendations for the transfer of functions to the Council were to be effected in full, some 6,000 civil servants and 3,000 industrial employees at present employed under Ministers, together with up to 4,000 public servants employed in State bodies, would be employed under the Council of Ireland. This is not to say they would all form the Secretariat of the Council.[25]

This, apparently, refers to the numbers to be transferred by Dublin; if say, half as many again came from the north, the total could amount to close to 20,000. It is, I think, unfair to blame the civil servants who drew up the report for its unrealistic assessment. No doubt they were given to understand that the government wanted a 'strong and effective' Council and they worked assiduously, to the limit of what they thought feasible, to find functions to transfer. But their report, a compilation of what was mathematically and economically possible, showed little or no understanding of political realities or of the need to overcome unionist distrust. Fortunately it did not become public at the time. Had it done so it would undoubtedly have ended all hope that Faulkner, already faint-hearted by then, would be able to 'sell' the concept of the Council to moderate unionists—or even be willing to try.

As head of the Press and Information section of the department I was not involved in these meetings though I did read the internal reports on the discussions. By then I was beginning to believe privately that the idea of Sunningdale as a single coherent package which all would stand by and implement, was being eroded—by various speeches, by demands for 'further steps' by the south, by criticism from various sources and by the silence imposed on the Irish government by the Boland case. I found a conversation I had around this time with Robin Baillie—a liberal-minded unionist who had been minister for commerce in Stormont in the two years before it was abolished—particularly worrying. In May 1973 he had advocated a referendum in the north on the British government's White Paper: he believed that it would have been approved at that time by a very substantial majority. A referendum now on Sunningdale, he said, would be badly defeated. He gave the Irish government credit for its approach at Sunningdale and for its forbearance in supporting Faulkner. But he thought now that Dublin had over-estimated what Faulkner could sell, while Faulkner himself had badly mis-judged the situation—he simply could not deliver moderate uni-onist support for the Agreement.

It was certainly clear that Faulkner's position had weakened but our view in Dublin still was that this was no time to falter—it would be better for all concerned to consolidate what had been done at Sunningdale by fixing an early date for the second, formal, stage of the conference. My position in dealing with the media at the time was somewhat out of the direct line of policy formation; and I knew that perhaps I did not see the full picture. Nevertheless, I thought I should put my concerns into a paper that suggested—not a change to what had been agreed at Sunningdale but what I called an 'in-flight course correction' to the path mapped out six months before.

The paper argued that the Sunningdale settlement was now beginning to 'fray'. In the south, the government had had to maintain an enforced silence and it had not replied to criticism of what some described as 'a British settlement'—although almost every aspect of it derived from ideas put forward by Dublin over the previous few years. Also, it did not seem to have dealt too well with the Fianna Fáil opposition, or taken adequate account of Jack Lynch's difficulties with some of his own party: perhaps through an oversight, he had not even been given an official text of the Communiqué until some days after Sunningdale. More serious, however, was the situation in the north. There was now serious doubt about Faulkner's position and his ability to deliver middle-of-the-road unionist support for, or even acquiescence in, the Sunningdale Agreement.

The paper then put forward four ideas. One was a definitive speech by the taoiseach re-stating the thinking underlying our whole approach to Sunningdale. Another was that we accept that a 'strong and effective' Council of Ireland would not necessarily require a large secretariat to carry out 'executive functions' (as the report by Public Service Department had assumed)—Council decisions could be implemented by the respective administrations, north and south. A third was that we consider not insisting on our full proposal for a new all-island court with links to the Council of Ireland: we could settle for an arrangement under which offences in one jurisdiction could be tried by the ordinary courts in the other.

The fourth suggestion was the most substantial. This was that the government, at a suitable time, could consider a referendum—not to *delete*, but to *add* new phrasing to, Article 3 of the Constitution. The aim would be to give the government's Sunningdale declaration in relation to Northern Ireland constitutional status in our jurisdiction—and, indirectly, to secure public endorsement of the whole Agreement. This could be done by proposing, by referendum, to insert a new sub-paragraph in Article 3 that would ask the electorate to insert into the Constitution the principle of 'consent' which the government had already accepted solemnly in the Sunningdale declaration. The suggested amendment to the Constitution could read as follows:

> 3.2 The re-integration of the national territory referred to in this Article shall not take place until a majority of the population of Northern Ireland so desire.

Or, alternatively:

> 3.2 The re-integration of the national territory referred to in this Article shall be subject to the consent [as expressed by a poll] of the population of Northern Ireland.

I passed this informally to some colleagues but was hesitant about doing anything more with it at the time; and I don't think I mentioned it in discussions with our minister, Garret FitzGerald. As the situation in the north deteriorated further, however, I turned some of these ideas into a longer paper on very similar lines in late March. That second paper did receive wider circulation and consideration internally.[26] I will discuss that further in the next chapter.

The Sunningdale Communiqué provided that, prior to the formal stage of the conference, studies would be set in hand to identify areas of common interest where a Council of Ireland could be given executive functions. Civil servants from north and south began this process in January 1974.

On 1 February 1974 the taoiseach, Liam Cosgrave, accompanied by the tánaiste, Brendan Corish, five other ministers and the attorney general, as well as a team of eight officials, met with the chief minister of the Northern Ireland executive, Brian Faulkner, the deputy chief minister, Gerry Fitt, five other ministers from the executive and ten officials from the Northern Ireland administration at Hillsborough, Co. Down. An official from the Northern Ireland Office attended as an observer on behalf of the British government.[27]

The account of the overall situation Faulkner gave at the meeting was very similar to his presentation at the Baldonnel meeting two weeks before. Unionist reaction to Sunningdale, he said, was more hostile than expected—there were deep suspicions about the Council of Ireland even among unionists who supported the power-sharing executive. He realised that the Council was important to the Irish government and to the SDLP and for that reason he himself was ready to proceed to ratification but that could be done only with the support of the majority in all parties. Furthermore, before it could be ratified it was essential that it have the support of a majority of the Protestant community—if not it would not last. The Boland case and the government's defence had undermined the value of the declaration made at Sunningdale. There could be no signature of a formal agreement until first, there was no longer the possibility of the courts overturning the declaration and second, there was a public statement completely clarifying the definition of the status of Northern Ireland. The right of Northern Ireland to self-determination must be made clear.[28] 'Do you [the Irish government] recognise Northern Ireland as part of the U.K.? If this is not accepted, there can be no progress.'[29]

Cosgrave replied that he thought that question had been disposed of at their Baldonnel meeting. He was still bound by the *sub judice* rule and Boland had until 7 February to appeal to the Supreme Court. The attorney general, Declan Costello, then went on to explain again the legal reasons why it had been necessary for the defence to rebut all but one of the points made in the Boland claim: at no stage, however, had the government resiled from the Sunningdale declaration that there could be no change in the status of Northern Ireland until and unless a majority there consented.

During further discussion John Hume suggested that in a clarifying statement the taoiseach could use some of the language of the High Court judgment. Garret FitzGerald said he could refer to the *de facto* position and not to whatever the *de jure* position might be. Faulkner said again that it must be firmly understood that he could not move further in ratifying Sunningdale without an assurance that Dublin accepted the status of Northern Ireland within the UK and that that status would not be changed without the consent of a majority.

Discussion moved on to the Law Enforcement Commission. Faulkner said that while law and order were matters for the UK government the executive had to 'carry the can'. At present terrorists could flee to a safe refuge in the south. He was disturbed to learn that the Irish government was ruling out the possibility of extradition. Before any formal agreement could be signed they in the north had to know what decisions would be implemented after the Commission had reported. The Council of Ireland could be sold to unionists only with the practical benefits which it would produce on law and order. In further exchanges Garret FitzGerald argued that the Commission had been set up to examine the Irish government's proposals (such as an all-Ireland court) and not extradition. It had not been intended that the formal stage of the agreement would have to await the report of the Commission. Faulkner responded that the Communiqué had said the Commission's work was to be done 'with extreme urgency'. If there were action on extradition, and dealing effectively with terrorists, then the package could be sold. If not, they had not 'a snowball's chance in hell' of selling it. John Hume suggested fixing a date for signature of the formal agreement and telling the Commission so that it could submit its report.

Conor Cruise O'Brien said that there was a link between the issues of status, common law enforcement and the functions of a Council of Ireland. If there was no sign of the Council coming into being when the Irish government prepared to give concessions on status (that is a clarifying statement by the taoiseach) then our end of the package would crumble. 'We will have to take some fire on status. This we accept but we cannot do it if the formal signing is left open.'[30]

In the course of lengthy discussions on security issues, Faulkner continued to argue that persons engaged in violence sought refuge in the south. Irish ministers on their side disputed the figures, cited the steps being taken in the south, including the recruitment of an extra 500 gardaí, and argued that the problem was essentially internal to the north.

Discussion then turned to the functions of a Council of Ireland. Faulkner entered a note of caution: if handled with prudence and discretion, the Council could play an increasingly useful part in future political arrangements. However, it was immensely more difficult to get the Council set up than it had been to get the executive established. Too much haste, too grandiose a scheme, could ruin the possibilities. There were two patterns for the transfer of functions—those for 'executive decision' by the Council which would then be implemented by the two administrations; and those for 'executive action' which the Council itself would implement. They would have to proceed with extreme caution on the latter: the functions transferred should be practical and uncontroversial and there should be no question of establishing an all-Ireland government in embryo. The meeting then discussed a series of functions for possible transfer in areas that included cultural institutions, energy resources, tourism, aspects of agriculture, health and social welfare, national parks, transport, water supply and anti-pollution measures. It was agreed that there should be further discussion of functions by joint working parties and a Steering Group of officials would co-ordinate and report back to ministers within 21 days.

Following a suggestion made by Conor Cruise O'Brien a sub-committee of seven ministers withdrew towards the close of the meeting to work out a possible formula the taoiseach might use in due course in a clarifying statement on the 'status' issue, Those involved were: Richie Ryan (Minister for Finance), Garret FitzGerald (Minister for Foreign Affairs), Conor Cruise O'Brien (Minister for Posts and Telegraphs) and Declan Costello (Attorney General), from the Irish government; and John Hume, Roy Bradford and Oliver Napier from the Northern executive. The group agreed on outline points that might be included in a government statement or a speech by the taoiseach but only once the Boland case had concluded.

> There would be a reference to the declaration made at Sunningdale; a recognition that misunderstandings had arisen; that the matter had been legally clarified in the High Court on 16 January; that the Irish declaration was contained in paragraph 5 of the Sunningdale Communiqué; that the High Court pointed out that this paragraph related to the de facto status of NI; this had been the intention of the Irish government; as everybody knows the de facto position is that Northern Ireland is within the United Kingdom; there would be a reference to the fact that the Communiqué

contemplated that a change in status could come about and how that change could be affected [sic].[31]

Shortly after the Hillsborough meeting, Brian Faulkner wrote to the taoiseach. After touching again on security cooperation issues he said he had intended to ask at the Hillsborough meeting that the establishment of the consultative assembly—that is the parliamentary tier of the Council—which he saw as posing difficulties for him, should be postponed.[32] On 13 February Cosgrave replied in friendly terms but he said that the concept of an assembly preceded Sunningdale and that to postpone it now would cause 'a dangerous and perhaps fatal loss of credibility in the Sunningdale package'.

Officials from north and south duly met for further studies and reported back within 21 days, as agreed at the ministerial meeting on 1 February. Their report, 'Transfer of Functions to the Council of Ireland', divided possible functions into four groups:

(1) Functions which north and south agreed could be transferred to the Council for executive action (including aspects of tourism, infrastructure, transport and horse racing);
(2) Functions where executive decisions could be taken by the Council, with implementation being left to separate agencies north and south;
(3) Functions where it was agreed there should be further studies and consultation;
(4) Functions where there was disagreement between officials from north and south.[33]

In preparation for the formal stage of the conference, some other preparatory work was also being done in Dublin. A draft of the statute to provide for the setting up of the Council of Ireland which would eventually be part of the formal agreement was sent to Faulkner on 6 February and also sent to the British side; a draft for the formal agreement itself was sent to the British on 11 March and to Faulkner on 21 March.[34] The permanent secretary to the executive, Ken Bloomfield, replied with a number of detailed comments on 26 March. By then, however, a momentous change had taken place in London: following a General Election a new Labour government had taken over from Ted Heath's Conservatives. In the next chapter I will consider the consequences that followed the change.

NOTES

[1] Sunningdale Communiqué, para. 15.

[2] Ed Moloney, *A secret history of the IRA* (London; 2nd edn, 2007), 139. In a footnote, the author attributes the quotation from 'a key strategist' to an interview with 'former Belfast IRA (B), Dr. Anthony McIntyre, Linen Hall Library (embargoed collection)'.

[3] Bew and Gillespie, *Northern Ireland*, 75.

[4] FitzGerald, *All in a life*, 223.

[5] Dáil Debates, vol. 269, no. 11, Wednesday, 12 December 1973.

[6] The criticism came from the minister for justice, Patrick Cooney.

[7] Dáil Debates, vol. 269, no. 11, Wednesday, 12 December 1973.

[8] See my account in Appendix 2.

[9] He came to lunch in the embassy and later entertained my wife, Caitríona, and myself to lunch in his house in Salisbury.

[10] Ziegler, *Edward Heath*, 317.

[11] Bew and Gillespie, *Northern Ireland*, 73. See also Ed Moloney and Andy Pollak, *Paisley* (Dublin, 1986), 354–5; and W.D. Flackes, *Northern Ireland: a political directory* (London, 1983), 173.

[12] Faulkner, *Memoirs of a statesman*, 248.

[13] Sunningdale Communiqué, specifically paras 5, 6 and 20.

[14] FitzGerald, *All in a life*, 226.

[15] At a meeting with Brian Faulkner on 16 January 1974 the taoiseach implied that the fifteen arrests were made at the behest of SDLP members, 'acting on Mr. Faulkner's behalf': the gardaí had been most reluctant to do it. NAI DFA 2007/111/1863.

[16] The Orange Order group included members of Vanguard and the DUP—two rival parties to Faulkner's Unionist Party (Craig, *Crisis of confidence*, 175).

[17] Bew and Gillespie, *Northern Ireland*, 77.

[18] Faulkner, *Memoirs of a statesman*, 245.

[19] NAI DFA 2007/111/1863. Copy of text in the possession of the author.

[20] Baldonnel is a military aerodrome just outside Dublin. The taoiseach was accompanied by Dermot Nally and Muiris MacConghail; Faulkner had with him Ken Bloomfield, who was, in effect, Cabinet secretary to the new power-sharing executive, and Tommy Roberts, its chief press officer.

[21] In an open letter to the people of the republic published in the *Irish Times* on 28 December, Napier asked 'Do you really want a Council of Ireland?…The Council of Ireland hangs by a thread…if you do nothing in the next few weeks, history will judge you and its judgement will be harsh and unforgiving.' That would be 'the second time in history that you have wrecked a Council of Ireland'. He called for 'a

new Constitution which is consistent with your government's solemn declaration of recognition'; amendment of the law on extradition; and 'even stronger efforts to prevent border raids on this province'. *Irish Times*, 28 December 1973. See also Bew and Gillespie, *Northern Ireland*, 76.

[22] Desmond Boal was a former Unionist MP and a former chairman of the Democratic Unionist Party. In a Belfast paper, the *Sunday News*, on 6 January 1974, he said he had been driven to the conclusion that the only viable conclusion was 'an Amalgamated Ireland', with a federal Irish parliament and a provincial parliament at Stormont. His views were dismissed by other Unionists, including Ian Paisley of the DUP, William Craig of Vanguard and Harry West, who, shortly afterwards, on 22 January 1974, succeeded Brian Faulkner as leader of the Ulster Unionist Party. See report by David McKittrick in the *Irish Times*, 7 January 1974.

[23] Presumably Liam Cosgrave had in mind the Committee on the Constitution chaired by George Colley, which submitted its report in December 1967. If so, what he said was not correct—the Committee had completed its work and was no longer in existence.

[24] FitzGerald, *All in a life*, 228.

[25] NAI TSCH 2004/7/665. *Transfer of functions to the proposed Council of Ireland* (Department of the Public Service, Dublin, 1974), para. 7.6. The Sunningdale brief had suggested a possible staff level of 6,000. See Chapter 17.

[26] There is a copy of that second paper, dated 23 March 1974, in NAI DFA 2007/111/1863.

[27] Draft report and also the final version are in NAI DFA 2007/111/1863.

[28] A right to 'self-determination', properly understood, should include a right to independence and not simply a right to choose between Irish unity and remaining part of the UK. I doubt if Faulkner was thinking of this here. No one on the Irish government side seems to have taken him up on this point however.

[29] NAI DFA 2007/111/1863.

[30] NAI DFA 2007/111/1863.

[31] See NAI DFA 2007/111/1863, letter and memorandum of 4 February 1974 from the attorney general to the taoiseach.

[32] NAI DFA 2007/111/1863; also Cosgrave response.

[33] See general summary note included as item 2 in brief for the taoiseach's meeting with Prime Minister Wilson on 5 April 1974 (7–8). NAI TSCH 2005/7/607.

[34] Brief for 5 April meeting, 7.

CHAPTER 20

The end of the Agreement

In Britain, in those first months of 1974, the prime minister Ted Heath was in serious political difficulty. In an effort to face down striking coal miners, he decided, after weeks of indecision, to call an election and on 4 February he asked the queen to dissolve parliament. In the General Election that took place on 28 February, his campaign slogan was framed as a question—'Who governs Britain?' The outcome of the election was not conclusive in the sense that no party gained a clear overall majority: the Labour Party had more seats even though the Conservatives had a majority of the votes. After an unsuccessful effort to agree on a coalition with the Liberal Party, Heath resigned as prime minister on 4 March and was replaced by Harold Wilson as leader of a minority Labour government. In a second election that took place in October, some seven months later, Wilson was returned to office with a very small majority. Heath, who had presided at the Sunningdale conference and whose meetings since 1972 with two successive Irish taoisigh, Lynch and Cosgrave, had prepared the way for the agreement, was never to see office again. He was replaced by a new prime minister who, understandably perhaps, did not have the same sense of commitment to what had been achieved. A new secretary of state, Merlyn Rees, took charge of the Northern Ireland Office.

To say that the outcome of the election in Northern Ireland was not good would be a serious under-statement: it was disastrous. Candidates of the UUUC (the United Ulster Unionist Council), formed on 6 December 1973, campaigned on the slogan 'Dublin is only a Sunningdale away'.[1] They won eleven of the twelve Westminster seats with just over 51 per cent of the vote; the SDLP won 22.4 per cent and its leader, Gerry Fitt, who was now the deputy chief minister, retained his seat; pro-assembly 'Faulknerite' Unionists received 13.1 per cent and Alliance 3.2 per cent. Fitt commented, correctly, that the election had 'come too soon for the people of Northern Ireland to really begin to understand what Sunningdale really means'. The result did not bring down the executive immediately but it allowed opponents of the Agreement to claim a mandate to do so; and it made it impossible thereafter for Faulkner to claim that he had majority support in the unionist community.[2]

In Dublin, on 22 February, the Supreme Court delivered its verdict on the Boland case. The five judges upheld the decision of the High Court rejecting the claim that the government had acted unconstitutionally in agreeing to the Sunningdale Communiqué. In his judgment Chief Justice FitzGerald said that the action had been misconceived: the courts have no power to interfere with the exercise by the government of its executive functions unless there is 'a clear disregard' of its powers and duties under the Constitution. Unlike other paragraphs in the document, paragraph 5, where the separate declarations of the two governments were set out in parallel, was 'not capable of being construed as an agreement.' The 'status of Northern Ireland' was a reference to the *de facto* position 'and nothing else'; and the respective declarations were 'no more than assertions of the policies of the respective governments, matters clearly within their respective executive functions'. Judge Budd agreed that the government's declaration in paragraph 5 of the Communiqué was a statement of policy. This was a matter for the executive—that is to say the government—which is responsible to the Dáil: it was not a matter for the courts. Judge Griffin too, agreed to dismiss the appeal. He noted that the Communiqué provided for a further conference at which a formal agreement would be reached. The government had the power under Article 29 of the Constitution to enter into international agreements and any attempt to restrain it from entering into that agreement would be unwarranted. However, it was very likely that legislation would have to be enacted to approve that formal agreement. At that stage it might come before the Court either by way of a reference of the Bill by the president or by way of a constitutional action challenging the legislation. But the stage at which the courts should intervene, if they should at all, had not been reached and was unlikely to be reached in the near future. So the plaintiff had no cause of action. Judge Pringle agreed in dismissing the appeal for the reasons given by his colleagues. In a very brief judgment he said, 'I am satisfied that the courts have no power to interfere with the exercise by the government of its executive functions in the circumstances relied upon by the plaintiff.'

Judge O'Keefe agreed with the chief justice and his other colleagues. However, his judgment also included what could be seen as a veiled warning to the government that it could not go too much further without running into constitutional difficulties (an implication that could also be read into certain aspects of the judgments of some of his colleagues).

> An acknowledgment by the government that the State does not claim to be entitled *as of right* to jurisdiction over Northern Ireland would in my opinion be clearly not within the competence of the government, having regard to the terms of the Constitution. I cannot presume that the government would consciously make an acknowledgment of that kind and accordingly I accept the view of the Chief Justice that clause 5 represents no more than a reference to the *de facto* position of NI coupled with a statement of policy in regard thereto.[3]

In early March, within days of the new Labour government's taking up office, the minister for foreign affairs, Garret FitzGerald, met Merlyn Rees, the new Northern Ireland secretary in London. They had already met in mid-January while Rees was still opposition spokesman. Rees assured him the Labour government's commitment to the Sunningdale Agreement was absolute: they would not move at all from the basic position of the previous government. He said that the Faulkner Unionists were 'deeply gloomy' and inclined to defer ratification 'miles into the future'. FitzGerald told him the Irish government wanted it ratified by Easter. Rees offered some suggestions which he thought might help Faulkner, including an early declaration from Dublin on 'status'.[4]

With the Boland case finally disposed of, the taoiseach was now free at last to make the promised 'clarifying statement' on status. An advance copy was sent to Brian Faulkner. Garret FitzGerald also sent an advance text to Rees under cover of a personal letter of 11 March, in which he complained about adverse briefings, by 'a Whitehall official' and 'British government sources', after their meeting the week before.[5]

The taoiseach duly made the clarifying statement in the course of a short speech in the Dáil on 13 March. The government, he said, considered that peace and progress could best be achieved by allaying fears.

> Their object therefore in making their solemn declaration to the Conference was to reassure those in the majority community of Northern Ireland who were apprehensive of the new institutions which were being created—the power sharing executive and the Council of Ireland. The government, therefore, declared that there could be no change in the status of Northern Ireland until a majority of the people of Northern Ireland desired a change in that status. The declaration was, of course, referring to the *de facto* status of Northern Ireland, that is to say the factual position, to which reference is made in recent judgments in the High Court and the Supreme Court. The factual position of Northern Ireland is that it is within the United Kingdom and my government accept this as a fact.
>
> I now therefore solemnly reaffirm that the factual position of Northern Ireland within the United Kingdom cannot be changed except by a decision of a majority of the people of Northern Ireland. This declaration,

I believe, is in accordance with, and follows from, the resolve of all the democratic parties in the Republic that the unity of Ireland is to be achieved only by peaceful means and by consent.[6]

The Irish government's declaration in the Sunningdale Communiqué had studiously avoided any reference to the current status of Northern Ireland—it focused entirely on possible future change. Now however, influenced perhaps by the judgments in the Supreme Court, the taoiseach rested his position on an explicit distinction between accepting its *de facto* and its *de jure* status. (A pedant might perhaps suggest that it should have been the acceptance rather than the status that was described as *de facto*).

Garret FitzGerald noted that both Oliver Napier, leader of the Alliance Party, and Frank Cooper, Permanent Secretary of the Northern Ireland Office

> told us that this declaration had achieved its objective and that 'status' was no longer an issue although Rees had some difficulty in persuading Faulkner to accept it gracefully and not to raise fresh issues.[7]

However, Faulkner's acceptance was something less than whole-hearted. In a letter of 31 March, in response to a letter he had received from the taoiseach, his first comment was somewhat ambiguous, not to say Delphic: 'I am glad you feel that my response was as positive as it was intended to be'. He went on:

> We must hope that this particular issue will now decline in prominence. I fully recognise that in the context of your own political realities, such a statement of *de facto* recognition is a major and courageous step. It is however open to doubt whether our Protestant community at large will ever be satisfied with anything less than an amendment to your Constitution, and this attitude is of course reinforced every time a member on the Fianna Fail side goes out

of his way to say that the constitutional claim remains in full force and effect. In the longer term, therefore, I hope very much that it will be possible for you to move in this direction.

His letter recalled that, on the basis of what had been agreed between them on 1 February, the next step should be a further inter-ministerial meeting. However, he said, this would not be possible until the Law Enforcement Commission report was available; and, even though he recognised the benefits of early ratification, it would be quite premature to envisage an early date for this. As to the Council of Ireland:

> I personally remain convinced that a structure on the general lines contemplated at Sunningdale could make a most worthwhile and practical contribution to relations between North and South. I fully recognise, too, the importance of such a concept as a means of 'Identification' for the Catholic community here. I have personally done my very best to advocate its benefits.
>
> The fact of the matter, however, is that the concept in the precise terms envisaged at Sunningdale does not at present enjoy sufficient support in Northern Ireland.
>
> I know full well that this is also a very important issue for my SDLP colleagues—that indeed they have been taking the line that full ratification of Sunningdale is a *sine qua non* of their continuance in the Executive. But I must tell you that if we cannot now find the means to secure for the Council of Ireland concept a broader basis of acceptability, then the power-sharing experiment is doomed. That would be a tragic situation the consequences of which cannot be calculated.[8]

Towards the end of his letter Faulkner proposed sending Ken Bloomfield, 'my Permanent Secretary who is fully in my confidence in the matter', to Dublin towards the end of the following week. In a further letter to the taoiseach on 3 April, he outlined the alternatives as he saw them:

(1) early ratification of Sunningdale: this was no longer in the realm of practical politics;
(2) delay the Council of Ireland for a substantial period: this was 'unattractive';
(3) drop the idea of executive powers for the Council and also the second tier, that is the parliamentary assembly;
(4) make progress towards the structure envisaged at Sunningdale, by stages, and phased in a way to win public confidence.[9]

Perhaps here I may revert again to a more personal note. In my role of dealing with the news media I was closely linked with the Anglo-Irish division of the department, but, as I explained in the previous chapter, I was not part of the direct line of policy formation on Northern Ireland at the time. Nevertheless, towards the end of March, I came to feel that the situation was so worrying that I should draw my thoughts together in another lengthy personal paper, headed 'Sunningdale?' and do a bit more to gain attention for it this time.

This second paper developed some of the ideas in the paper of late January 1974 which I referred to in the previous chapter. It suggested that, while the particulars of Sunningdale might be questioned, there was no alternative to the broader principles underlying it. However, the rejection of the agreement by a majority of the unionist interest meant that it no longer commanded moral authority as a point of equilibrium between all the major political forces in the island. So there were now five possible options. The first four, none of which offered much hope, were:

1. look for another, quite different, solution (federal, confederal, 'independent British Ulster', etc.);

2. try to re-negotiate the whole package, or parts of it;
3. accept that accommodation was impossible and prepare for further deterioration of the situation;
4. ratify and implement Sunningdale and hope that when the Council had got under way it would be seen as less alarming by unionists.

The fifth option, which, the paper suggested, was worth considering, was

> to ratify Sunningdale now, but only on the explicit and public condition that the agreement would not come into effect until it had been approved electorally—say six months hence (by referendum in the North, or in both parts of Ireland; or by new PR elections to the Northern Assembly); clearly tie every aspect of the settlement together as a single package in practice as well as in theory; and have all those involved make a concentrated and concerted effort in the intervening six months to 'sell' that package throughout the island.

The paper further suggested that

> the necessary electoral ratification could be either confined to Northern Ireland (either a referendum or a new PR Assembly election); or sought simultaneously in both parts of the island. If the latter option were chosen we might think of providing ratification here by way of a constitutional amendment.

That could be done by way of a proposal to add the 'consent' principle, which the government had already accepted at Sunningdale, to Article 3 of the Constitution (as suggested in the earlier paper). This second paper offered three possible variants of suitable wording, one of which was:

> The re-integration of the national territory referred to in this Article shall be subject to the consent of the

people of Northern Ireland [*or* the consent of the
people of both parts of Ireland] [as expressed in a poll
held for that purpose].

This paper received wider circulation. I passed a copy informally
to the minister, Garret FitzGerald, and a copy went to Dermot
Nally in the Department of the Taoiseach.[10] The paper was also
incorporated, more or less in full, though with some additions and
amendments, in a long paper prepared in the IDU towards the end
of April in response to a request from the government that 'a study
of all possible alternative courses of action should be undertaken'.[11]
While the IDU paper did include the fifth option mentioned
above, it was rather more cautious about it than I had been: it
stopped short of including the specific wording for a possible addition to Article 3 of the Constitution; and it added a sentence suggesting that a constitutional amendment at that point might be a
step too far.

> If this approach were adopted, the necessary elect-
> oral ratification could be either confined to
> Northern Ireland (either a referendum or a new PR
> Assembly election) or sought simultaneously in
> both parts of the island. If the latter option were
> chosen we might think of providing for ratification
> here by way of a Constitutional amendment. This
> solution at this stage may appear too radical and
> would certainly raise issues which the Unionists at
> least would wish to keep buried. At the same time it
> has advantages in that it could demonstrate the
> degree of public support for Sunningdale, through-
> out the island.

The overall conclusion of the IDU paper was that 'the best course
of action is to press ahead with early ratification and implementation of the Sunningdale package'. There could, however, be some
flexibility on matters such as the range of executive functions of the
Council, the initial size of the secretariat and, possibly, deferral for
a year of the consultative assembly. However, there should be no

departure from what had been agreed 'in respect of matters explicitly set out, with particularity' in the Communiqué.

What would have happened if the Irish government had decided to try for a constitutional amendment at that stage? would it have succeeded? and would it have made a difference?

In his autobiography, nearly two decades later, Garret FitzGerald considered these questions.

> [A]t the time we ruled out, with no serious discussion that I recall, the possibility of amending the Constitution along these lines in the aftermath of Sunningdale. Should we have given such a move more serious consideration? There is a case to answer.[12]

He goes on to consider both sides of the argument. A referendum would have been a gamble 'to consolidate the achievement of a power-sharing arrangement in Northern Ireland that we then felt was likely to succeed without any further intervention on our part'. There would have been a risk of not alone destroying the agreement but of damaging the position of Jack Lynch, the opposition leader, and 'undermining the consensus within our democratic system upon which…the peace of our own state arguably depended.' Nevertheless, he believed, with hindsight, that it might have been worth attempting the gamble. In his second autobiography, nearly twenty years later, he takes up the same arguments again, in almost the same terms. Again, he says, there is a case to answer:

> Sunningdale, like the Anglo-Irish Agreement twelve years later, proved much more popular with public opinion than those of us in government had foreseen. But Fine Gael and Labour in government tended for historical reasons to feel more vulnerable on the 'national issue' than they need be, and thus too underestimated the potential public groundswell in favour of 'moderate' stances on the Northern Ireland issue… And I should, perhaps, add that a moderate nationalist supporter of Fianna Fáil who was deeply concerned

about Northern Ireland, and who was quite close to Jack Lynch, reminded me years later that before Sunningdale he had told me that we should 'go for' a constitutional referendum immediately after the conference and had given it as his view then that Fianna Fáil would not have opposed such a move.

As against that, he again notes how high the stakes were: to try for a referendum and fail would destroy the Sunningdale settlement. Still, very fairly, he does not try to reach a definitive conclusion.

> I recite the two sides of the argument on this issue in order to place these events in their historical perspective, lest the hindsight view that it might have been worth attempting the gamble of a constitutional referendum on Articles 2 and 3 be given undue weight.[13]

Perhaps now I should offer my own view. If there had been a referendum to remove or rewrite Articles 2 and 3 substantially, I think it would not have succeeded at that time; and if it had been tried and failed, the Sunningdale settlement would have collapsed even earlier than it did. But what I had suggested was more modest than what Garret discussed in either of these two books—it was not that Articles 2 and 3 should be amended or rewritten but that a single-sentence sub-paragraph reflecting more or less exactly the text of the government's Sunningdale declaration should be added to Article 3. I can't help thinking now that, granted the generally favourable view of the agreement in the south in early 1974, the electorate might well have approved of this; and the principle of 'consent' would then have been imbedded in the Constitution. But then, of course, even that might not have saved the agreement: unionists might well have continued to object that what they saw as a 'territorial claim' in Article 2 had been left untouched. And there is a further point to consider. We could not have known this at the time but perhaps, in retrospect, and taking the very long view, we might now ask if it was not better after all that a complete reformulation of the two Articles remained available as a major step to be taken by the south as part of the Good Friday Agreement a quarter of a century later.

In a personal message on 21 March to the new British prime minister, Harold Wilson, the taoiseach suggested that a meeting between them would be helpful. The meeting took place in London on 5 April. The taoiseach was accompanied by the tánaiste, Brendan Corish, and the minister for foreign affairs, Garret FitzGerald. Wilson had with him the foreign secretary, Jim Callaghan, and the Northern secretary, Merlyn Rees.

The brief prepared for the taoiseach before the meeting gives a good indication of how the deteriorating situation was seen from Dublin at that point. It advised Cosgrave that

> it is vital to consider with the British whether they wish to go ahead with the implementation of Sunningdale, and what sort of pressure they can exert on Mr. Faulkner to carry out his obligations.

The brief recognised that Faulkner's position was 'one of extreme difficulty'. However, it went on,

> he has compounded his own difficulties by apparently failing to sell the Sunningdale agreement and by concentrating on issues which are extraneous to the agreement, like that of status, or of security or the Law Enforcement Commission, etc. He has not attempted, so far as can be seen, to put across the idea behind the concept of a Council, which is that it should provide a mechanism through which the public in the North can identify with the institutions of government. In this failure, he is falling in with the 'Loyalist' attack on the Council as an instrument of Irish unification.

The brief also predicted the consequences for if Sunningdale were not implemented:

(1) the power-sharing executive would collapse;
(2) direct rule would be resumed;

(3) there would probably be a constitutional conference; and
(4) it would be a tacit understanding at this conference that the British would withdraw from their commitments in Northern Ireland.

It went on to recall Harold Wilson's fifteen-point plan of a few years earlier 'in which a British withdrawal from the North after fifteen years was mooted.' This would have some advantages from a British viewpoint. But it would do Ireland as a whole irreparable damage and hurt the British economy.

Garret FitzGerald in his memoirs gives a very critical account of the 5 April meeting of the two prime ministers:

> We went round and round various issues in a thoroughly disorganised way. The three British participants had clearly not got their act together, and much of the discussion was in reality a debate between them, in which Rees, who had clearly lost confidence in his capacity to carry Sunningdale through to a successful conclusion, argued for delay and dilution against a tough and determined Callaghan and a Wilson who was trying, not with complete success, to appear decisive and in command.[14]

The Irish side pressed again for an early date for the formal ratification stage of the conference. While no specific date was fixed there seemed to be some willingness, notwithstanding Rees's misgivings, to focus on some date in early May. Discussion on security issues took the usual form—the British side pressed for more cross-border cooperation while the Irish pointed to what was being done and argued that the main source of the problem was indigenous to Northern Ireland. FitzGerald was concerned about critical remarks by Wilson about his predecessor, Ted Heath. However, Wilson assured the Irish side that 'Labour... remained firm on the bipartisan approach'. More disturbing was his speculation on what, in the worst case, might lie ahead:

> If because of a breakdown of the Executive they had to return to direct rule, all hope would then be destroyed;

the issue of British soldiers serving in the North could then bring about an 'agonising reappraisal'.

An echo, perhaps, of Wilson's fifteen-point plan. In the background too, must have been the memory on the Irish side that Wilson had had a covert meeting with the Provisional IRA when he visited Dublin as leader of the opposition in 1971.

All in all, FitzGerald concludes, 'it was an unimpressive occasion'. He goes on:

> In retrospect both ourselves and Harold Wilson and Jim Callaghan were probably unrealistic, having failed to appreciate the scale of the growing crisis inside unionism in Northern Ireland. Rees was clearly much more aware of this crisis; but he had failed to devise an appropriate approach to the problem, and his suggestions, which were not supported by his colleagues, bore little relation to Faulkner's actual concerns as expressed to us around this time.[15]

The taoiseach's brief for his meeting with Harold Wilson on 5 April also includes a draft document headed 'Outline of Statute or Annex Supplemental to a Formal Sunningdale Agreement'.[16] The document, which is annotated in manuscript as 'addition to the Sunningdale Communiqué (suggested by Mr. Faulkner?)', seems to be Faulkner's suggested revision of the draft statute that had been sent to him by the Irish side on 6 February.[17] It envisages that, after ratification of the formal agreement, the Irish government and the Northern executive would each nominate seven ministers to 'an Irish Council of Ministers.' The purpose would be closer cooperation in social and economic affairs in specified areas to be agreed in joint studies. The Council would review progress in the implementation of the agreements; have a role to be specified on policing and human rights; and discuss any other matters of mutual interest and concern. The most significant part of the document is a provision that would make the further development of the Council subject to 'a Test of Opinion' by a secret postal ballot held on the same day in the republic and in Northern Ireland at a time when the benefits of this Agreement as a whole have had an opportunity to manifest themselves, and in conditions permitting a free expression of voting intentions, not unduly influenced by violence or intimidation.

If a majority in both north and south voted in favour, then legislation in the Oireachtas and the Northern assembly would provide that the areas already agreed as matters for cooperation would become executive functions of the Council. A consultative assembly might also be set up at that stage.[18]

The main idea in this proposal, if accepted, would have meant a modest beginning for a Council of Ireland, at ministerial level only. Initially at least, it would simply promote north-south cooperation and have no executive functions. This was consistent with Faulkner's position over this whole period as expressed direct to the taoiseach, and conveyed to Irish officials by Ken Bloomfield at the meeting in Dublin on 8 April, which I will refer to below. Bloomfield himself, writing many years later, argued that the attempt to begin with a strong Council meant that

a great opportunity had been missed. Nationalist Ireland, as represented by the Irish government, would have done well to recognise that it would be better to feed and nurture a tiny plant than to establish an outsize bush on barren soil.[19]

Maybe so. But 'a tiny plant' would have been too weak an expression of the 'Irish Dimension' for the SDLP and the Irish government to settle for at Sunningdale; and, by April 1974, after four months of steady erosion of Faulkner's position, it would probably still be more than his opponents on the Unionist side could accept. Ken Bloomfield also recalls that some of Faulkner's supporters, who believed that he had exceeded his electoral mandate, argued for a referendum on the outcome of Sunningdale.[20] This may perhaps be a reference to the proposal in the Faulkner document for a 'Test of Opinion' by postal ballot. It is hard to know how seriously to take that particular proposal: it was strange, to say the least, to envisage a postal vote; and it is hard to imagine that such a procedure, as a less formal alternative to a referendum, would have been acceptable in the south.

Rees, himself, summarised the difficulties of the time very succinctly in his memoir eleven years later:

> Without the Council of Ireland, the Irish government and the SDLP would find it impossible to continue with Sunningdale; with it, Brian Faulkner would be totally rejected.[21]

On 8 April 1974 Ken Bloomfield came to Dublin, as Brian Faulkner had suggested in his letter of 31 March to the taoiseach, and he spent the day in discussion with Irish officials, led by Dermot Nally.[22] The message he conveyed from Brian Faulkner was sombre. The implementation of what was agreed at Sunningdale 'just was not on at present so far as the Protestant community in the North were concerned'. This was due to the deteriorating security situation, the effects of the Westminster election, the disruption of the Unionist Party and 'the general atmosphere of distrust and harassment'. The community were in a worrying mood; they felt 'unheeded'; and their pent-up feelings were becoming stronger by the day. There was a great danger that, if the eleven MPs they had sent to Westminster were unable to achieve anything for the community, the community as a whole 'would lose whatever remaining faith they had in the democratic process and turn to violence'. At the very least there could be widespread Protestant civil disturbances. Power-sharing had been accepted only with reluctance and it was still viewed with scepticism, if not open hostility. If a new point of balance was not found within the Sunningdale concept, the executive was going to break down. Faulkner, Bloomfield said, had been in a weak position at Sunningdale, where he had to negotiate with two sovereign governments. He had been pushed beyond his election manifesto and this left him in a weak position on his return. It was 'only by the skin of his teeth' that he had prevented 'the door being slammed on the whole concept' during a number of meetings of the Assembly Unionist Party.

Nevertheless, Bloomfield said, Faulkner was 'extremely anxious to have the Sunningdale Agreement ratified and had done everything in his power to sell it'. What could be sold, he believed, was establishing the Council with the policing and human rights functions envisaged in the Sunningdale Communiqué. It could also have the task of reviewing progress in relation to a list of functions which would be the subject of discussion and cooperation between the Northern Ireland executive and the Irish government, but which, for the present, would not be executive functions of the Council. The concept of a consultative assembly (the parliamentary tier) could not be pushed for the present—loyalists (by which he surely meant unionists) felt that, in the institutions of the Council—ministerial, parliamentary assembly, and all-island court—they were being compelled to accept embryo institutions for a united Ireland.

When asked what Faulkner's position would be if his proposals were rejected, Bloomfield said that Faulkner would resign and 'take up farming'. He had 'the best will in the world for implementation but it was just not practicable at present'. When asked whether the consequences of non-ratification of Sunningdale had been considered, Bloomfield replied that he himself was well aware of them but that the majority of people in Northern Ireland would not accept those consequences until things such as the closure of the Harland and Wolff shipyard actually happened. In such a situation he thought what the majority would go for would be a Protestant hegemony with a much reduced standard of living—possibly after a great deal of civil disturbance.

In reporting to the taoiseach on the meeting, Dermot Nally made three points:

1. The choice might be between keeping the Northern executive in office and having a Council with executive powers. That was a choice to be made in the first instance by the parties in the executive. So the first step should be to consult them and see whether they thought there was anything the Irish government could do to help.
2. Since there was a strong possibility of a total breakdown in the Sunningdale Agreement, the Irish government should

ensure they would not be put in the position of being responsible.

3. If the Northern executive were to fall, the likely next step would be the re-imposition of direct rule—which Prime Minister Wilson had said would not be 'of the same sort' as previously. The implication of this was not clear but it could mean that there would, at the same time, be an indication of an intention (by the British government) to withdraw (from Northern Ireland). If that were to happen, 'it would be necessary that our security forces should be in a position to meet the situation likely to emerge in the North. The implication of this is that we should go ahead with the strengthening of these forces as approved as quickly as possible.'[23]

Prime Minister Wilson himself visited Northern Ireland on 18 April. In a press conference he said: 'We stand by the Sunningdale Agreement. We want to see it become a reality.' However, not long afterwards, the secretary of state for defence, Roy Mason, warned in a speech that pressure was mounting in Great Britain to pull out the troops and to set a date for withdrawal so that 'the leaders of the "warring factions" could get together and hammer out a solution'.[24]

The Ministry of Defence then issued a statement saying that there was no change in policy. However, the Irish government was worried. Merlyn Rees recalled in his autobiography that he reassured Garret FitzGerald at a meeting in London that there would be no withdrawal of troops: 'The Irish government was not, however, entirely convinced: it was not sure of a Labour government and there was always a lingering historical feeling in Dublin about perfidious Albion.'[25]

On 1 May a large-scale meeting of British and Irish officials took place in Dublin. Leading figures on the seven-strong British side, in addition to the ambassador, Sir Arthur Galsworthy, were Philip Woodfield, the deputy secretary, and D.J. Trevelyan, under secretary at the Northern Ireland Office, and a senior official each from the Home Office and the attorney general's office. The lead on the Irish side was taken by Paul Keating, who had recently been appointed secretary of the Department of Foreign Affairs in succession to Hugh McCann.[26] Others included Andy Ward, Secretary of the Department of Justice, Dermot Nally of the Taoiseach's Department, and Declan Quigley, the most senior official in the attorney general's office. While there were some differences, both sides were in broad agreement about the need to move as quickly as possible on what Keating called 'the Sunningdale timetable'. Woodfield noted that the Council as agreed at Sunningdale was to be north-south, not tripartite; and he said that, although they had kept a close eye on what was happening, 'the British government had been careful not to move in to try to mastermind developments'. They believed, however, that, provided there was some basis for agreement within the executive, the sooner there was some move, the better. Further delay would mean even more disillusionment. Dermot Nally was somewhat less sanguine—he saw indications that the executive parties 'might be on a collision course'.[27]

In these early days of May, however, the truth was that the agreement launched in hope in Sunningdale on 9 December was beginning to founder. As May went on, there was talk of the possibility of jettisoning some of its content—temporally at least—in an effort to save it from sinking irretrievably. For example, the Irish government on 3 May approved a further letter to Faulkner asking him to establish what kind of consensus he could achieve within the executive on the proposals he had been making, and also stressing their concern to be as helpful as possible. In a brief reply on 7 May Faulkner said he was 'most grateful for the positive and sympathetic way in which you have responded to my explanation of our current difficulties and I am heartened to think we are now in general agreement on the way to proceed'. He was very anxious to make progress as rapidly as possible. He agreed with the taoiseach that the first stage must be 'to find a consensus' among the parties in the executive, something they were pursuing 'most actively'. If that could be done, then the next stage would be another meeting between the executive and the Irish government—but that would have to be well prepared.[28]

In Dublin on 8 May, the taoiseach had a meeting with those 'Sunningdale ministers' who were available. Three officials—Dermot Nally, Charles Whelan and Sean Donlon—were also present.

The ministers had before them a report from Sean Donlon on his meetings with contacts in the north, particularly the SDLP; and they considered what he should convey to the SDLP in regard to the government's position when he returned to the north that evening. After discussion it was agreed that it was preferable not to give the SDLP too 'restrictive' an indication of the government's position on issues such as the functions, or the second tier (the consultative assembly), of the Council of Ireland: the SDLP would want to get 'the best bargain possible without bringing down the Executive.' Donlon could tell the SDLP that the government 'would be prepared to countenance postponement of the convening of the consultative assembly'; and, 'if necessary, but with greater reluctance, it would be prepared to accept that the Council might not have any executive action functions in the initial stages.' However, it continued to favour early publication of the Law Enforcement Commission report. In further discussion the attorney general, Declan Costello, was hopeful it would be agreed that 'extradition was definitely out', but he was worried that the SDLP might concede on that point; and the minister for justice, Patrick Cooney, showed reluctance about moving on legislation to set up a police authority in the south, as agreed at Sunningdale.[29]

On 13 May the minister for foreign affairs, Garret FitzGerald, told the Northern Ireland secretary, Merlyn Rees, at talks in Dublin, that the government could accept a phasing in of the Council of Ireland.[30]

None of this did—or at that stage could do—anything to change the situation on the ground in Northern Ireland. Already on 23 March a new loyalist group, the Ulster Workers' Council (UWC), had issued a statement threatening widespread civil disobedience unless fresh assembly elections were held. On 10 May they again demanded elections.[31] However, the Sunningdale settlement still commanded support in the Northern Ireland assembly: on 14 May the assembly, by 44 votes to 28, rejected a motion condemning power-sharing and the Council of Ireland. But by then that was of little avail—the action had moved elsewhere. That evening, in reaction to the assembly vote, the UWC announced a strike and the next day they called for a general work stoppage. The strike began on 15 May with power cuts to the electricity system and factory closures; road blocks were erected; paramilitaries began to appear on the streets; and there was widespread intimidation. That same day, Stan Orme, one of Rees's ministers of state at the Northern Ireland Office, met a delegation from the UWC: with them were Ian Paisley, leader of the DUP; Bill Craig, leader of Vanguard; John Laird (an Ulster Unionist Assembly member, later to be a member of the House of Lords); and UDA and UVF leaders; as well as three armed individuals described as 'observers'.[32] In the House of Commons, Merlyn Rees said that it was

> a matter of regret that certain Members of this House should attempt to set up a provisional government in Northern Ireland by issuing their own ration books and so on.[33]

Larne was cut off by armed paramilitaries and workers in Harland and Wolff and elsewhere were intimidated.

In central Dublin on 17 May three car bombs exploded during rush hour. Twenty-two people were killed and more than one hundred were injured. Five others were killed and twenty injured that same day by a car bomb in Monaghan. Eventually the death toll rose to thirty-three persons in all. This was the largest number of people killed—in the north, the south or in Britain—on any one day over the whole period of the Troubles.[34]

In Northern Ireland the grip of the strikers on the economic and business life of the area was tightening; and even British ministers found it difficult to get about by road.[35] The UWC had decided to go for an all-out strike. When Rees considered using technicians from the military to man the power stations he was advised that they would not have the expertise to man the system without the help of middle management in the electricity industry—but middle management refused to help.

At this point the prime minister, Harold Wilson, had a bright idea.

> A message from Harold Wilson asked me to investigate the possibility of anchoring a submarine in Belfast Lough to supply power, but I was advised by the army at Lisburn that for technical and security reasons any power generated could not be put ashore.

Rees goes on:

> We were in fact beaten technically on all aspects of the
> strike, and the army also advised me that even if this
> were not the case, it could not guarantee to protect the
> power stations or the pylons.[36]

On 22 May the executive agreed that the Council of Ireland would
be implemented in phases: the second phase would come only after
a test of opinion at the next assembly election some time in 1977–8.
An SDLP party meeting had difficulties about this but they eventually agreed to accept it. On 24 May Wilson invited the leaders of
the three executive parties—Faulkner, Fitt and Napier—to
Chequers. Mason, the defence secretary, Rees himself, and the
attorney general, Sam Silkin, were also present. At the meeting,
Rees recalls:

> Brian Faulkner was clear that effective administration
> was in the hands of the strikers. He did not want me
> to talk with the UWC, and he was still of the view
> that if the UK government asserted its control, sup-
> port for the strike would decline. Gerry Fitt also
> believed that in the face of effective action by the gov-
> ernment, the strikers would back down.

In the House of Commons Gerry Fitt criticised the BBC and the
newspapers for 'acting for those behind the strike'. Rees took a similar view:

> I had no doubt that the UWC had been helped all
> along by the BBC's treatment of the strike as an indus-
> trial dispute and not a political stoppage. Individual
> members of the UWC had become overnight the stars
> of television and radio. Complaints had poured in
> from Brian Faulkner and the executive members in
> particular, and from the SDLP and the minority pop-
> ulation in general. Stan Orme considered that the
> BBC acted as 'quislings', and I later learned that the

Irish government had also reacted strongly to the BBC's policy, though that is perhaps understandable given its own policy of 'control' of RTE.[37]

On the evening of 25 May Prime Minister Wilson gave a television and radio address which, however well meant, seemed to have the effect of inflaming the situation. He called the strike an attempt 'to set up a sectarian and undemocratic state, from which one-third of the people would be excluded'. It was run by 'thugs and bullies' 'purporting to act as if they were an elected government [who] spend their lives sponging on Westminster and British democracy and then systematically assault democratic methods. Who do these people think they are?'[38]

Then on the evening of 27 May, at a meeting with Rees, Faulkner renewed his proposal for the appointment of a mediator (for a dialogue with the UWC): he suggested that it could be either the archbishop of Canterbury or Lord Grey.[39] Rees rejected the proposal.

On 28 May the crisis came to a head. Rees's memoir records the sequence of events that day.

> Electricity cuts were to be longer than ever before—up to eighteen hours in twenty-four. Throughout the day the front route into Stormont was blocked by a tractor demonstration by farmers, who were addressed by Glen Barr, John Taylor and Ian Paisley. 'Rees must talk with the UWC' was a favourite placard.[40]

Faulkner's account of the start of the final meeting of the executive at 11 a.m. that morning is even more graphic.

> Only one item was on the agenda—the 'Emergency Situation'. I opened by summing up the situation. The Army was operating a minimal petrol and oil supply. The Belfast gas plant was out of operation. The power stations were dangerously near total shutdown, and even if the Army had the technical capacity to restore partial functioning there would be a total blackout for

several days at least. The water supply and sewerage services were at grave risk, and the flooding of large parts of Belfast with raw sewage was a real possibility. Basic food distribution was in jeopardy. Supplies of feedstuffs to farms had stopped.[41]

Faulkner's backbench supporters said they would not continue to support him unless a dialogue was begun with the strikers. Later that morning the Unionist and Alliance members of the executive, against the wishes of the SDLP members, decided that Rees should be told that a dialogue, through a mediator, should begin between the government and the UWC. Faulkner put the case for this to Rees at a formal meeting.

> He was not prepared, he informed me, to accept responsibility for seeing his beloved Northern Ireland grind to a halt. Support from his own people had fallen away. He again put the case for a mediator and said that unless I would accept this, he was going to resign and with him the other Unionists. The others could speak for themselves. He finally advised me to initiate negotiations among the parties to see if power sharing could be preserved on some other basis.
>
> I could not accept this and I formally accepted his resignation. Brian said that he would make clear to his administration that they should take their own decisions, which was a curious way of putting it since with the Chief Executive gone the Executive was finished as far as I was concerned. I explained that I would not negotiate with the UWC because the point at issue was the whole future of the constitutional framework in Northern Ireland and particularly power sharing and Sunningdale.[42]

Rees may have been clear that 'the Executive was finished' but the two other parties in the executive did not agree that all was over.

The SDLP and Alliance 'heads of departments' decided not to resign, but they were ignoring reality— as I told them when they came to see me. Gerry Fitt was playing a game that the SDLP was still in office, but the situation was too serious for pretence. I decided that the constitutional position needed to be clarified and at 2 p.m. that day I issued a statement that I had accepted the resignation of Brian Faulkner, Chief Executive Minister, together with the resignations of Unionist members in the Northern Ireland adminis- tration; that under the terms of the Constitution Act 1973, 'there is now no statutory basis for the Northern Ireland Executive'; and that 'arrangements exist for the continued government of Northern Ireland in accordance with the Northern Ireland Constitution Act. In particular the Secretary of State remains responsible for the preservation of law and order'.[43]

So, six months after the Sunningdale conference, the agreement reached there was at an end and the hope that it had kindled was extinguished: the British government had resumed direct rule in Northern Ireland.

Coincidentally, at just this time I moved to a wholly different area of work in the Department of Foreign Affairs and I became preoccupied with preparations for Ireland's first EEC presidency, which was only eight months away. Northern Ireland issues came to seem a bit more distant, although never very far away. I was not to know then that I would be drawn back again into the question later in my career. But that is another story...

NOTES

[1] The UUUC, founded to oppose power-sharing, was established at a rally of 600 delegates from Unionist Party constituency associations, Vanguard, the DUP and the Orange Order. Bew and Gillespie, *Northern Ireland*, 73.
[2] Bew and Gillespie, *Northern Ireland*, 78–82.

³ *Kevin Boland, Plaintiff v. An Taoiseach and Others, Defendants.* [1973 No. 3289 P.] [1974] IR 338. The full text of the judgments was published by the Government Information Service in book format, along with the text of the Sunningdale Communiqué, the Law Commission Report and selected speeches by the taoiseach.
⁴ FitzGerald, *All in a life*, 230.
⁵ Copy in the possession of the author.
⁶ Dáil Debates, vol. 271, no. 2, Wednesday, 13 March 1974.
⁷ FitzGerald, *All in a life*, 231.
⁸ NAI DFA 2007/111/1863.
⁹ See Nally note of 9 April on Bloomfield's subsequent visit to Dublin NAI DFA 2007/111/1863.
¹⁰ There is a copy in NAI DFA 2007/111/1863.
¹¹ The IDU paper is in NAI TSCH 2005/7/629 (folder 1 of 3).
¹² FitzGerald, *All in a life*, 222–4. The phrase 'amending the Constitution along these lines' does not refer to my proposal for an addition to Article 3 but rather to Garret's own ideas for a reformulation of Articles 2 and 3, which he had mentioned in a previous paragraph.
¹³ FitzGerald, *Just Garret*, 256–7.
¹⁴ FitzGerald, *All in a life*, 232.
¹⁵ FitzGerald, *All in a life*, 232–4. Dermot Nally's report of the meeting is on NAI DFA 2007/111/1863.
¹⁶ NAI DFA/111/1863. There is also a copy at Appendix VII, pages 86–7 of the brief for the meeting of 5 April 1974. NAI TSCH 2005/7/607.
¹⁷ NAI TSCH 2005/7/607. Brief for the meeting of 5 April 1974, page 7. A copy was sent to the British at about the same time.
¹⁸ Merlyn Rees in his book *Northern Ireland: a personal perspective* (London, 1985), 59, refers to a letter from Faulkner to Liam Cosgrave in early April which outlines similar proposals but he makes no reference to the proposed 'Test of Opinion'.
¹⁹ Bloomfield, *A tragedy of errors*, 145.
²⁰ Bloomfield, *A tragedy of errors*, 140.
²¹ Rees, *Northern Ireland*, 59.
²² Others present were Wally Kirwan of the Department of the Taoiseach and Charles Whelan, head of the Anglo-Irish division in Foreign Affairs. Tomás Ó Cofaigh of the Department of Finance and Matt Russell of the attorney general's office were present for part of the discussions.
²³ NAI DFA 2007/111/1863. I am grateful to Professor John Coakley for bringing this document to my attention.
²⁴ Rees, *Northern Ireland*, 60–61.
²⁵ Rees, *Northern Ireland*, 61.
²⁶ McCann had been appointed ambassador to France.
²⁷ Report of the meeting is on NAI DFA 2007/111/1863.
²⁸ NAI DFA 2007/111/1863. It is evident from their various exchanges of letters that Cosgrave and Faulkner had relatively good personal relations and were on first name terms.
²⁹ NAI DFA 2007/111/1863.
³⁰ FitzGerald, *All in a life*, 237.
³¹ Bew and Gillespie, *Northern Ireland*, 83–4.

[32] Bew and Gillespie, *Northern Ireland*, 84–5; FitzGerald, *All in a life*, 238; Rees, *Northern Ireland*, 65.

[33] Rees, *Northern Ireland*, 67.

[34] Bew and Gillespie, *Northern Ireland*, 85.

[35] Rees, *Northern Ireland*, 73.

[36] Rees, *Northern Ireland*, 69.

[37] Rees, *Northern Ireland*, 74. Orme was minister of state at the Northern Ireland Office from 1974 to early 1976.

[38] Bew and Gillespie, *Northern Ireland*, 87–8.

[39] Lord Grey of Naunton, a New Zealander, the 5th and last governor of Northern Ireland. The post had been abolished when the British government resumed direct rule in March 1972.

[40] Rees, *Northern Ireland*, 86.

[41] Faulkner, *Memoirs of a statesman*, 4. Curiously, Faulkner mistakes the date—he says that this final executive meeting was on 29 May. The Chronology of Events on page 294 dates the collapse of the executive to 30 May. In fact, both events occurred on the previous day, 28 May—see Rees, *Northern Ireland*, 86.

[42] Rees, *Northern Ireland*, 86.

[43] Rees, *Northern Ireland*, 87.

CHAPTER 21

Conclusion: Slow learners?

It has to be said that Sunningdale failed in its main objective in that it did not end the conflict in Northern Ireland. Seventy-four people were killed in the first four months of 1974 and several thousand more in the next twenty-five years; the power-sharing executive in Northern Ireland collapsed after five months; and the Council of Ireland, which was to promote reconciliation and cooperation between north and south, never came into being. Nevertheless, Sunningdale was important. In this final chapter I want to draw together all that I said in earlier chapters about the background to the conference, the structure of what was agreed there and what it was designed to achieve. I will then consider various reasons for its collapse. But I will also argue that the agreement marked a historic turning point. Lessons were learned that remained relevant to subsequent settlement efforts: concepts developed at that time were available to be drawn on in the structure of the Good Friday Agreement of 1998; and it was also seen that some other things were better avoided.

First I want to recall the situation as the Irish government saw it at the time. I am, no doubt, somewhat partial, and it may well be that other participants would see it differently. I am well aware of the important role of the SDLP on the ground in Northern Ireland

and particularly the role played by its deputy leader, John Hume, although I have dealt very briefly with both here. It is also no doubt true that successive British governments had some experience of dealing, not always very successfully, with divided societies in other parts of the world. However, that said, I would argue that it was largely the ideas that two successive Irish governments pressed Ted Heath's government to accept which helped to shape what was agreed eventually at Sunningdale.

It is true that it is now possible to read in the British archives a paper submitted to Prime Minister Heath by his private secretary, Robin Butler, on 4 December 1973, which none of us outside the British system knew about at the time.[1] The paper is described as 'A draft Heads of Agreement'; and it can be seen now, in retrospect, to be a remarkably good shot at imagining the shape and content of the final communiqué, two days before the Sunningdale conference was due to open. The paper is a clear example in practice of the maxim good diplomats follow—don't go to an important meeting, particularly at Summit level, without at least a first draft of the final statement in your back pocket.

At first sight—or taken in isolation—it might seem that the existence of this document shows that the British side 'managed' the conference to such good effect that the Irish government and the Northern Ireland parties were steered gently, and unknowingly, towards an outcome that was more or less precisely what the British government had wanted to achieve from the start. I would hope that everything I have said in earlier chapters will show that this was not the case. Rather, it was the ideas and arguments that two successive Irish governments pressed on their British counterparts over several difficult years, the actions of the SDLP on the ground in Northern Ireland—and also, I should say, the openness of Ted Heath to new thinking after he had been shocked by the events of Bloody Sunday— which brought the British government to a stage where they were ready to envisage an outcome like that in Robin Butler's paper.

By the early 1970s it was becoming clear that the long-standing and deep-rooted conflict of aspirations between two traditions in the island of Ireland had not been settled in 1920–21. It had been bottled up in Northern Ireland where it erupted in aggravated form in the late 1960s when the disadvantaged minority community began to assert its rights. In earlier chapters I recounted how two successive Irish governments, that of Jack Lynch and that of Liam Cosgrave, responded to these events. I will recall that briefly again here.

When the Troubles erupted in 1968–9, Jack Lynch's Fianna Fáil government was at sixes and sevens, caught between Lynch's innate caution and the outlook of some of his ministers who saw this as an opportunity to push hard on their anti-partition agenda. From 1970 onwards, freed now of the need to accommodate the views of the ministers whom he had sacked during the Arms Crisis, Lynch began to develop a more realistic approach to the growing conflict in the north, without abandoning his own broadly nationalist views. He was advised in this, first by Ken Whitaker and for a time by Eamonn Gallagher; he was supported by his minister for foreign affairs, Patrick Hillery, and, after the Arms Crisis, his minister for justice, Des O'Malley; and Donal Barrington remained a quiet and supportive adviser. Through the regular contacts, developed first by Gallagher and then by Sean Donlon and a series of other officials who travelled regularly to the north, Lynch also kept in close touch with, and was deeply influenced by, the views of John Hume and other members of the emerging SDLP.

Lynch's relationship with the British prime minister Ted Heath was initially somewhat difficult but as time went on Heath, who had been shocked by the events of Bloody Sunday in 1972, became more responsive to his arguments. By the time Lynch left office in March 1973 he had brought home to Heath two fundamental points which Eamonn Gallagher in particular had advised him to make: one was that the Irish government had a role to play in working towards a resolution of the conflict; the other was the utter unsuitability of the 'Westminster model' for devolved government in the North. Both points found an echo in the British government's Green Paper of October 1972, which canvassed a new form of government for Northern Ireland and, for the first time in such an official document, recognised that there was an 'Irish Dimension' that would have to be accommodated in any stable settlement.

Lynch's political opponent, Liam Cosgrave, together with the ministers in the Fine Gael-Labour coalition government which he headed, picked up the baton when they came to office in March 1973. The British White Paper, published just at that time, confirmed the commitment of the British government to the new approach outlined in the earlier Green Paper. Through the rest of that year the taoiseach and the Irish government, with Garret FitzGerald in a leading role, elaborated the broad ideas that had already begun to emerge under the previous Irish government, into a series of detailed and ambitious proposals for a Council of Ireland that would give expression to the 'Irish Dimension'. In parallel the SDLP negotiated with the Faulkner Unionists and Alliance for the establishment of a new power-sharing administration in Northern Ireland.

The governments of Lynch and Cosgrave were both nationalist in outlook—Lynch and Fianna Fáil somewhat more assertively so than their Fine Gael rival. Each repudiated violence; each wanted to see Irish unity, achieved in agreement and by peaceful means; and each hoped—and believed—that the process of reconciliation that the proposed Council of Ireland was designed to encourage would bring it closer. But as the situation in the north deteriorated each in turn also had to accept that the conflict of aspirations in Northern Ireland could not be settled definitively either way at that stage since loyalties and traditions on both sides were too deep-rooted for either to agree to yield its position to the other.

The situation that faced the Irish government in the months before the Sunningdale conference could be summarised as follows:

- The minority who had lived in a position of disadvantage for fifty years under a permanent Unionist government were not prepared to do so any longer; and a campaign of violence aiming ultimately to achieve Irish unity had now gained significant support in that community.
- The SDLP, the party that spoke as the democratically elected representatives of the minority, rejected violence but it was likely that they would forfeit much of their support if they were to accept an 'internal settlement'—which is to say an arrangement confined to Northern Ireland that took no account of the 'Irish Dimension'.
- In the south the great majority repudiated violence but latent support for the minority in the north and for the

ultimate objective of Irish unity was still strong. No Irish government could ignore this or abandon unity as an ultimate objective. Nor indeed would any Irish government in those years wish to do so.

- Unionists, fearful of their position, were vehemently opposed to Irish unity—or even any modified version such as a federal or confederal Ireland; and loyalists were already engaged in serious violence. Any attempt to impose a settlement of that kind would create a serious danger of civil war in Ireland. The risk of that was unacceptable.

- Contrary to what Kevin Boland and others argued at the time, a British withdrawal was most unlikely to induce unionists to come to terms with the majority in the island and accept some such solution. Even the mere prospect of British withdrawal could lead to an immediate attempt by extremists on both sides to consolidate their positions and that could quickly degenerate into virtual civil war.

- Since that was the situation it seemed clear that the only alternative was an accommodation between elected representatives of the two main traditions which would be the basis, not for a static solution of any kind, but for a process that would promote and encourage reconciliation.

- This could best be achieved through new institutions within Northern Ireland, and at an all-Ireland level, to which those involved would commit themselves in good faith without seeking to predetermine the precise outcome.

- Such a settlement would not end violence—indeed the situation was such that no settlement at that stage would end violence immediately. But an accommodation worked out between the two governments and democratically elected representatives of the political parties in Northern Ireland that were willing to participate, would offer the best hope of reducing violence to a minimum: it could then be dealt with by some kind of new all-island court system and/or reciprocal arrangements for trial of offenders, together with improved security cooperation between north and south.

- Britain could be expected, at least to accept, and at best to encourage and support, such an approach. In an earlier era it had a direct national interest in retaining a foothold in Ireland. That, it seemed, might no longer be the case—though it had a responsibility to remain engaged there so long as it believed that withdrawal could lead to greater conflict.

The Sunningdale Communiqué, which was to be turned into a formal agreement in due course, was designed to respond to the situation I have just described. The agreement was to rest on three pillars: power-sharing in Northern Ireland would provide a role in government for elected representatives of the minority; and a link with the south through a Council of Ireland would meet the need to provide for an 'Irish Dimension'. These two institutions were closely linked, even inter-dependent: if there were no Council of Ireland the SDLP would not go into government with the Unionists in what would then be a purely 'internal settlement'. As an engineer or architect might put it, the Council, which was to promote cooperation between north and south, was also a load-bearing beam supporting other parts of the structure. The structure as a whole would also have to be based on a firm foundation. This 'third pillar' was to be provided by the parallel declarations of the two governments. On the one hand these declarations reassured the unionists that there would be no united Ireland without majority consent; equally they assured nationalists that if there were to be majority consent to Irish unity the British government would give it their support.

The Sunningdale Agreement was born in hope but it failed in its most fundamental aim of bringing peace to Northern Ireland. Why was this? In public affairs, as in our individual lives, it is not always easy to trace what happens back to single causes. There may be multiple reasons and, as was the case here, a sequence of unplanned-for events may play a part. It may be helpful to list here the reasons that contributed to the failure of Sunningdale.

1. Sunningdale was only the first, informal, part of what was to be a two-stage conference. The outcome was described as an 'Agreed Communiqué' because it was not yet a formal agreement. The second, 'ratification', stage of the conference was to take place 'early in the New Year' when studies in

regard to the functions of the Council of Ireland had been completed. But that second stage never took place. The consequence was that the Council was announced as a concept with little or no specific content and it became a ready focus for the worst fears of unionists.

2. A General Election through the whole United Kingdom took place in February 1974, just two months after Sunningdale and before the second, formal stage of the conference took place. This meant, in effect, that the Northern Ireland electorate was invited to pass judgement on the proposed new structures at the worst possible time—before they were fully in place and before they had time to bed down and prove their worth.

3. The General Election brought a new government to power in London. The new Labour prime minister, Harold Wilson, when he was in opposition, had put forward a fifteen-point plan designed to lead eventually to Irish unity, but he and his ministers had much less personal commitment to Sunningdale than Heath and his colleagues who had negotiated it;[2] and Merlyn Rees, the new Northern Ireland secretary, proved weak in face of the challenge of the Ulster Workers' strike.

4. A legal challenge to Sunningdale was brought by Kevin Boland in the High Court and the Supreme Court. As I explained earlier, with the issue still *sub judice,* the taoiseach, Liam Cosgrave, and his colleagues in government, were strongly advised not to make further public statements about what had been agreed. But this was just the time when Brian Faulkner was most in need of a lifeline. He and Cosgrave ought to have been able, in parallel, to 'sell' the outcome of Sunningdale to their separate electorates, north and south, as a historic compromise that could bring peace to the island. Instead, until the Supreme Court finally dismissed Boland's legal action in late March 1974, the government in Dublin remained largely silent, despite increasingly desperate signals from Faulkner; and he, on his side, in addressing unionists, was more apologetic than assertive in claiming credit for what he had done.

380

5. The argument that the Irish government's legal team felt they had to make in court in order to defeat Boland's challenge was politically very damaging to Faulkner. They played down what had been agreed and described it as nothing really new. This may have been the legal imperative of the moment but the political imperative was precisely the opposite. Faulkner needed to be able to show doubting unionists how much he had achieved in the negotiations. The last thing he wanted to hear from the courts in Dublin was that there was nothing whatever new in what had been agreed.

6. And crucially, the drumbeat of paramilitary violence on both sides continued in Northern Ireland, and, on occasion, in the south, where there was a very high death toll in the Dublin and Monaghan bombings that took place in May 1974. Unionists still felt under siege and, understandably, many believed that the continuing violence showed they had nothing to gain and much to lose from the agreement. The cautiously drafted solemn declaration by an Irish government unable to go further without facing constitutional difficulties, proved to be quite insufficient to allay their fears.

The confluence of these events and causes undoubtedly made for an inauspicious start to the short life of the Sunningdale Agreement. Its failure also raises three other issues that I should like to consider in more detail. Two relate to the structures as they were agreed and the third is a question as to the timing of the whole attempt at a settlement.

It is often said that the Sunningdale project collapsed because the Irish government and the SDLP demanded too much, too soon, in regard to the Council of Ireland: it would have been better to allow power-sharing to take root and defer the idea of a Council until later. This is the view, for example, of historians such as Alvin Jackson,[3] of Ken Bloomfield[4] and of many others. It is associated also with Conor Cruise O'Brien, himself a participant in the Sunningdale conference, who criticised Garret FitzGerald and John Hume on that account in some of his later writings.[5] At the time however, although he was certainly more cautious than some of his colleagues, he shared the general view that 'visible progress on the Council of Ireland' was necessary if the government was to maintain its support in the south—though it is understandable that he should take this position as a member of a government engaged in negotiation at the time.[6]

I have a certain amount of sympathy for the view that it might have been prudent to hasten more slowly. An outsider might say of course that it is a bit unfair to expect the Irish government in a negotiation to keep in mind at all times not only its own requirements but also those of the party on the other side with whom it is negotiating—but that is a responsibility that our particular history has seemed to impose.

It is certainly true that the calculation in the Department of the Public Service planning document that up to 20,000 staff might possibly be transferred to work under the Council was grossly excessive; and if it had become public at the time it might well have sunk the concept of the Council on the spot. It is also true that even though the taoiseach and Garret FitzGerald had some understanding of unionist fears and were prepared to engage in a Council of Ireland without seeking to predetermine the outcome, they also had more than a gleam in the eye at times about the possibility that the Council might set the island on a long-term path to unity. But I believe it is going too far to conclude that it would have been better to limit the agreement to power-sharing in the north, and not to include any provision at that stage for a Council of Ireland— if that was indeed Conor's view. I do not believe that there would have been an agreement at Sunningdale if there had been no provision for a Council of Ireland. The SDLP in the north were simply not prepared to leave themselves open to the charge of cooperating in a purely internal settlement that took no account of the 'Irish Dimension'. They would have been accused of accepting a 'partitionist' approach that disregarded the aspiration of the minority community—and indeed of that of much of the rest of Ireland— and their support would have bled away at a time when they were trying to establish themselves as a moderate, democratic alternative to the violence of the IRA. The Irish government too, would have left themselves open domestically to similar accusations; and the Fianna Fáil leader, Jack Lynch, notwithstanding his own more moderate views, would have been hard put to maintain any semblance of bi-partisanship with the government on the Northern Ireland issue.

For those reasons, it seems to me that provision had to be made for the Council as a necessary sustaining pillar of the whole Sunningdale edifice. On that point I am more inclined to agree with the Conor of 1974 than the Conor of 1998. It is easy, however, in retrospect to agree that the proposal for the Council might have been more prudently handled at the time; and it would have been preferable not to have pressed too strongly for the Council to assume substantial executive functions from the outset.

It is interesting that the Unionist leader, Brian Faulkner, writing several years after the fall of the executive, blamed, not the Council as such, but what he called its 'structure' and its 'appendages'. In fact, he thought a Council at ministerial level could have had a valuable practical role when it came to security and social and economic cooperation. Having claimed—incorrectly in my view—that there had been 'recognition by the Republic of our right to self-determination within our existing boundaries', and an informal commitment to remove 'the constitutional claim' at the earliest opportunity, he went on:

> The price we had paid for this progress—and one usually pays some price for progress in negotiations—lay in the structure of the Council of Ireland. The Council of Ministers had a valuable role in formalizing co-operation on security and social and economic matters. In a very real sense getting the Dublin Government to treat Northern Ireland representatives as equals on an inter-governmental body underlined their acceptance of partition...But the other appendages of the Council—the consultative assembly, the permanent secretariat, the executive functions of the Council of Ministers—fell in my mind into the 'necessary nonsense' category. They were necessary to get the co-operation of the SDLP and the Dublin Government. But nothing agreed on at Sunningdale infringed on the powers of the Northern Ireland Assembly by which everything would have to be approved and delegated.

Given the overwhelmingly unionist composition of that body and the unanimity rule in the Council of Ministers we were satisfied that the constitutional integrity of Northern Ireland was secure.[7]

I have to acknowledge that Brian Faulkner was not always consistent in the views he expressed later on Sunningdale. That said, I am tempted to leave the last word to what he said in a letter he wrote in 1976, a few months before he died, to Roy Magee, a political opponent who was later to be an active intermediary in the peace process:

Certainly I was convinced all along that the outcry against the Council of Ireland was only a useful red herring—the real opposition was to sharing of power.[8]

A second, and now very obvious, weakness in the Sunningdale structure was that the declaration of the Irish government on the issue of 'consent' fell well short of what was needed to reassure unionists against their fear that the Council of Ireland proposal was intended to trundle them into a united Ireland against their will. It is true that the Irish government believed that they had made a considerable effort in going as far as they did in declaring solemnly that 'there could be no change in the status of Northern Ireland until a majority of the people of Northern Ireland desired a change in that status'. Nationalist feeling was still quite strong; no previous Irish government had gone so far; the declaration was to be given additional weight by being incorporated in a formal international agreement registered at the United Nations; and, as I explained in earlier chapters, the Irish government were constrained by Articles 2 and 3 of the Constitution from going any further. In the circumstances of that time, they could not, even if they wished to, risk a referendum to amend or delete those Articles lest a rejection of such a proposal entrench them further. Even the declaration they did make at Sunningdale might possibly be ruled as unconstitutional, if a challenge to it were brought in the Irish courts once it had been included in a formal international agreement.

All that said, it remains that the Irish government had to limit their solemn declaration to the need for majority consent to any future change in the status of Northern Ireland: they were unwilling and unable to refer unequivocally in the Communiqué to its existing status as part of the United Kingdom. This was far from enough to reassure even the liberal-minded unionists from whom Faulkner hoped for support for what he had achieved; and this greatly weakened the foundational support that the parallel declarations of the two governments were intended to provide for power-sharing and the Council of Ireland—although the taoiseach's statement in the Dáil on 13 March accepting 'the factual position of Northern Ireland…within the United Kingdom' did something to help.

Looking back now I am tempted at first to think that the idea I put forward very tentatively in two informal discussion papers in late January and late March 1974 would have helped. That was that the government should propose a referendum—not to delete Articles 2 and 3 but to *add* the wording about 'consent' that they had accepted in their declaration at Sunningdale to the existing wording about 'reintegration of the national territory' in Article 3 of the Constitution. This might have defused the threat or 'claim' that Articles 2 and 3 seemed to imply and thereby provided the necessary reassurance that Faulkner needed for his party. However, I have to acknowledge, as I did already when I referred to this idea in earlier chapters, that in retrospect it could be seen as fortunate that the idea of constitutional change was not 'used up' at that early stage—the commitment to make more substantial and carefully negotiated change in the Irish Constitution was still available to be included as an important part of the 1998 Agreement which eventually brought the conflict in Northern Ireland to an end.

A third reason, often given and now widely accepted, for the failure of Sunningdale is that it was a settlement built on the centre ground which did nothing to bring in the extremes from both communities that were actually engaged in violence. In that it is contrasted with the Good Friday Agreement of 1998. That later agreement was the product not alone of negotiations between the two sovereign governments and the democratic parties in Northern Ireland but also of long discussions on texts with associates of extremist groups on both sides; and it was this painstaking

385

work that eventually, and with some difficulty, induced those groups to turn from violence towards negotiation. The situation in 1973 was quite different. The violent conflict had not run its full course and its futility had not yet become evident to those who were engaged in it. Republican and loyalist extremists with diametrically opposed views were locked into a violent zero-sum game with no willingness to compromise. So there was very little possibility at that time that they could be drawn into a political negotiation. Some might say it follows from this that Sunningdale was premature—'Ripeness is all' says Edgar in Shakespeare's *King Lear*;[9] and in 1973 the time was not ripe for a genuine settlement.[10] There is truth in that, but whether or not the time is ripe at any particular stage is something that becomes evident only in retrospect; and a society faced with the lived reality of an apparently endless conflict can hardly afford to await the judgement of history on whether the time is ripe for a solution to end it. In any event things happened as they did; and I think it is always well to keep in mind the words of the distinguished historian Sir Lewis Namier: 'it serves no purpose to expostulate with history'.[11]

However, if Sunningdale failed to bring peace, it still marked a turning point of great historic importance. By Sunningdale here I mean, not just the Sunningdale Communiqué of December 1973 but the complex of events in 1972–3 that led up to it. That includes the British government's decision to suspend the Stormont parliament in March 1972, the Green and White papers that followed and the agreement between the parties in Northern Ireland to form a power-sharing administration. There are a number of reasons, in my view, why Sunningdale was important:

- Over those two years, for the first time in half a century, the British government came to recognise that the settlement of 'the Irish Question' in 1920–21 had to be re-opened so far as Northern Ireland was concerned. The division of the island at that time had left a large and long-neglected nationalist minority submerged in a situation of permanent disadvantage in Northern Ireland under a never-changing one-party devolved government. That was no longer tolerable. If in future there was to be devolved government, then representatives of the minority would share in exercising the devolved powers and the aspiration of the minority to Irish unity achieved by consent would have to be recognised.

- When Stormont was prorogued—in effect abolished—little more than 50 years after it was set up, a range of possibilities opened up. The Heath government set an important precedent for the future in ruling out two possible options, either tacitly or explicitly—independence for Northern Ireland and full integration of Northern Ireland into the UK.

- It is arguable that, in declaring that it would support Irish unity if that were the wish of the majority, the British government tacitly acknowledged for the first time what the Northern Ireland secretary, Peter Brooke, was to say more explicitly 25 years later—that it had 'no selfish strategic or economic interest' in Northern Ireland.[12]

- At Sunningdale, too, the Irish government, by making a solemn declaration on the 'consent' principle which was to be incorporated into an international agreement, turned definitively from the sterile anti-partitionism of earlier decades which blamed everything on Britain, and began the slow progress towards the definitive acceptance by the electorate in the 1998 referendum of a dual requirement: that Irish unity could come about only if and when a majority in Northern Ireland, and a majority in the republic, gave their consent.

- The approach of the two governments at Sunningdale—and particularly the willingness of the British government to agree to a north-south Council of Ireland in which they would not participate directly—made it evident that the two governments now accepted a shared responsibility to deal with the legacy that a complex history of interaction had left to the peoples of both islands. This was a remarkable change from the rebuff by British ministers to Dr Hillery as 'a representative of a foreign government' following the Apprentice Boys march in Derry in 1969 to which I referred in Chapter 2. This new cooperative approach did not always run smoothly over the following decades and there were many bumps on the road. But the pattern of engagement that was developed for the first time at Sunningdale led eventually, through the Anglo-Irish Agreement of the 1980s and the Stormont talks of 1990–92, to the working relationship that framed the 'peace process' of the 1990s and was essential to the negotiation of the 1998 Good Friday Agreement. It is now a close relationship of good neighbours and it reached its high point in the welcome given in both islands to the highly successful exchange of visits by our respective heads of state visits in recent years—even though, as I write, the intention of the UK to leave the EU—Brexit—is creating new and unwelcome uncertainty about the future.

In these ways, notwithstanding its failure to end the conflict, seeds were sown at Sunningdale which were to germinate and grow into a more substantial and lasting settlement a quarter century later. Even though they had collapsed in 1974, the new political structures agreed at Sunningdale also remained available, conceptually, as a pattern that, in greatly strengthened form, could be drawn on in the building of the Good Friday Agreement of 1998, as a comparison of the two will show.

- In 1998, as at Sunningdale, it was clear that there had to be a solid foundation for the new political institutions. One community needed assurance that there would not be Irish unity without majority consent; the other, assurance that there would be unity if and when that consent was forthcoming. But at Sunningdale these assurances rested on a relatively weak base—the parallel 'solemn declarations' of the two governments. The Good Friday Agreement rests on a surer foundation: it is a formal international agreement; it has involved a change in the Irish Constitution; and it has been ratified not only by the respective parliaments in Dublin and London but by the electorates in Ireland, north and south, in simultaneous referenda.
- The requirement of an obligatory sharing of power in Northern Ireland between elected representatives of the main Northern communities as envisaged at Sunningdale is

replicated in the 1998 Agreement, with additional rules for how it is to apply, which now include specific procedures and formula for voting and for allocation of posts.[13] Once the main paramilitary groups that had been involved on both sides turned away from violence, the way was open for them, and for those associated with them, to seek to build up political support at the ballot box. As a result, for all its ups and downs, devolved government in Northern Ireland now rests on a much broader electoral base in both communities than the short-lived executive and assembly established under Sunningdale.

- The 'Irish Dimension' too, is provided for in the 1998 settlement. In contrast to the proposed Council of Ireland—a concept that was highly contentious in 1973—the north/south ministerial council is now an agreed part of the institutional framework, though with a somewhat different role. It is complemented by a broader British-Irish Council comprising representatives of the two sovereign governments, the devolved institutions in Northern Ireland, Scotland and Wales, and the Isle of Man and the Channel Islands, as well as by a standing British-Irish Intergovernmental Conference.

The outline of the institutions devised at the time of Sunningdale to meet the particular situation of Northern Ireland is, I suggest, still discernible in these ways, although of course that earlier agreement did no more than provide a partial template for the much more comprehensive Good Friday Agreement on which the present peace in Northern Ireland rests.

There were also, on the other side, lessons to be learned from the experience of Sunningdale about points that did not work well and issues which were not, and probably could not be, addressed at the time but which, so long as they remained unaddressed, continued to impede a settlement. Among them were:

- The importance of ensuring that the police force was impartial and accepted in the community. This issue was not resolved at Sunningdale; and the need for reform of the

RUC remained a point of contention for decades afterwards. It was resolved eventually through what the 1998 Agreement called 'a new beginning to policing in Northern Ireland.' The Patten Commission, set up to advise on this, said it did 'not accept that the RUC should be disbanded', but it recommended that it be reorganised, and renamed. This was done: the police service is now the PSNI, that is the Police Service of Northern Ireland.[14]

- Issues in relation to symbols and parades—matters of great importance as assertions of identity in a divided society that are not fully resolved even today.

- The need, in seeking a settlement to a deep-seated conflict, to build on the widest possible base. This may entail a long, difficult and even morally ambivalent dialogue with those who are actually engaged in violence. I have touched on this earlier in considering the argument that, since that was unlikely to be possible at Sunningdale, the time was not ripe for a genuine settlement. In many cases such a dialogue will simply not be possible, and if attempted it may not succeed. But if it does, and violence is ended, there will not only be immediate benefit for a scarred society but hope that, over time, an end to violence will grow into real peace.

- The importance in the particular circumstances of Northern Ireland of a continuing, sustaining role for the two sovereign governments. The power-sharing arrangement agreed at Sunningdale was vulnerable and it collapsed as the political support from unionists that Faulkner had hoped for drained away. When next the British and Irish governments made a joint effort to address the problem—in the Anglo-Irish Agreement of 1985—they built the settlement in the first instance on a continuing, institutionalised structure for cooperation between themselves, while allowing scope, and indeed inducements, to the Northern Ireland parties to take a fuller role—if and when they could agree to share power in new, devolved institutions. In later settlement initiatives, through the 'peace process' of the 1990s to the Good Friday Agreement of 1998, and afterwards, the close involvement of the two governments continued to provide a much-needed framework for the protracted and difficult negotiations that led eventually to Northern Ireland as it is today.

There are other aspects of what I might loosely call 'the Sunningdale approach', which were carried forward into the 1998 Agreement, and which, though not much spoken about, must still raise questions.

Acceptance of the right of the minority to pursue the aspiration to unity peacefully was a necessary element in both settlements, as was the principle that Irish unity could be achieved only if and when a majority in Northern Ireland consent. The Good Friday Agreement, and the constitutional change in the south that followed, go further: they make it explicit, in a way Sunningdale did not, that 'a united Ireland shall be brought about only by peaceful means with the consent of a majority of the people, democratically expressed, *in both jurisdictions in the island*'.[15] The hope, both at Sunningdale, and again in the current settlement, was that, once there was an agreement in place on the necessary conditions for any future change in the constitutional status of Northern Ireland, parties representing the majority and minority communities would focus in the immediate future on working wholeheartedly together for the benefit of all the people of Northern Ireland. Two questions arise from this arrangement.

One is whether a divided community, where two conflicting aspirations for the whole future of the area remain in contention, can really develop into a truly peaceful society. The present settlement has the great merit of being broadly based, since both Sinn Féin and the DUP have been centrally involved in working it. But these are two political parties whose opposition from outside brought down earlier settlement attempts; and there is reason for concern over the extent to which they still seem to conduct their underlying contention about the very future of Northern Ireland within the governmental institutions that it is their responsibility to operate. If cooperation between them is to remain essentially a zero-sum game, there will not be much room for the kind of generosity in dealing with representatives of the other community that could help to consolidate a stable peace in Northern Ireland. Still, it must be said, the present situation is immeasurably better than the decades of conflict which preceded it, and which the agreement reached at Sunningdale, for all the hopes that initially reposed in it, was unable to resolve.

The second question that emerges, seldom spoken about, relates to the agreement, both at Sunningdale and in the 1998 Agreement, that the consent of a majority of the population in Northern Ireland is a necessary condition for possible future Irish unity. As a principle this is perfectly valid, and it should not now be called into question. But there may still, in the future, be a question as to whether it would be at all feasible politically to move to Irish unity with the consent of no more than a simple—and possibly very slim—majority of the Northern Ireland population. Perhaps that issue is best left to the wisdom of future generations, north and south.

I return to the theme of this memoir for a final word. Seamus Mallon, an SDLP politician of the greatest courage and importance throughout the Troubles, encapsulated a whole history of missed opportunities in a lapidary phrase when he characterised the 1998 Agreement as 'Sunningdale for slow learners'. He did not specify to whom his implied reproach was addressed. But he must surely have had in mind that if all those who opposed Sunningdale—politicians, paramilitaries and their associates on both sides of the community— had been prepared for compromise in 1973–4, the conflict could have been ended with far less suffering and loss of life. I cannot but agree— though perhaps my own involvement as an official at that time means that I am not wholly objective. That remains a path not taken, one of the 'what ifs' of history. Still, the situation in Northern Ireland today is incomparably better than that of the early 1970s; and lessons have been learned, not only by those who opposed Sunningdale at the time but by all concerned—the two governments, the political parties and the people of Ireland north and south.

NOTES

[1] TNA PREM 15/1685 Minute on 4 December 1973 from Robin Butler to the prime minister attaching '(i) A draft Heads of Agreement; and (ii) A draft of your opening statement'. Marked in manuscript 'seen by the PM'.

[2] Hansard, HC Deb, 25 November 1971, vol. 826, col. 1586. Wilson proposed that, once violence ceased, a commission set up by the British, Irish and Northern Ireland governments would examine what would be involved in agreeing on the constitution of a united Ireland to be reached by agreement. Subject to ratification by all three parliaments, it could come into effect after fifteen years.
[3] 'With the benefit of hindsight it might have been better to bank the achievement of a power-sharing executive and postpone the adjustment of cross-border relations until the new consensual government in the North was more securely rooted.' Jackson, *Home Rule*, 270.
[4] 'My considered judgement is that the SDLP, from whom the Irish government was bound in considerable measure to take its lead, was over-ambitious in its insistence upon executive functions.' Bloomfield, *A tragedy of errors*, 197.
'At a critical moment the Irish government at Sunningdale, as ever urged by the SDLP, had pushed the Faulkner unionists into the danger zone of a Council with executive functions.' Bloomfield, *A tragedy of errors*, 252.
[5] In Conor Cruise O'Brien's book *Memoir: my life and themes*, 349, he recalls a discussion in Cabinet. 'I warmly welcomed the idea of a bipartisan government for Northern Ireland. But I thought the Council of Ireland, with the implication of progress towards a united Ireland, might be a bridge too far...Garret [FitzGerald] answered, in a tone of cold superiority such as he had never used to me before, that my information was out of date. Northern Ireland was no longer like that. The Protestant population would accept the Council of Ireland without difficulty. This I knew was a certitude he had derived from John Hume.'
[6] For example, when Cosgrave and Faulkner met at Hillsborough on 1 February 1974, Conor Cruise O'Brien is recorded as telling Faulkner that 'by giving the [proposed] statement on status which the Unionists required we were already putting our political necks on the line and unless there was visible progress on the Council of Ireland these difficulties would be increased. We had to ensure that in facilitating Mr. Faulkner's party, we did not erode our own support and it was therefore essential that the second stage of Sunningdale should not be left in the air.' NAI DFA 2007/111/1863.
[7] Faulkner, *Memoirs of a statesman*, 237.
[8] The letter is reproduced as 'Epilogue' in Faulkner, *Memoirs of a statesman*, 287–8. Reverend Roy Magee was a Presbyterian minister, who at one time was associated with the UDA and with Vanguard, but later played a very important and positive role as intermediary between loyalist paramilitaries and the British and the Irish governments.
[9] William Shakespeare, *King Lear*, Act V, Scene 2.
[10] I think of my former colleague Seán Ó hUiginn, whose contribution to the present peace settlement in Northern Ireland was immense, who often said as much to me about other, later, negotiations in which we both played some part.
[11] Quoted by Nicholas Mansergh in Diana Mansergh (ed.), *Nationalism and independence: selected Irish papers* (Cork, 1997), 12. The quotation comes from L.B. Namier, *Avenues of history* (London, 1952), 44.
[12] Brooke said this on 9 November 1990. See Chapter 18.
[13] The 1998 Good Friday Agreement specified that the first minister and the deputy first minister would be jointly elected by the assembly voting on a cross-community basis (involving either parallel consent or a weighted majority), while

ministerial posts in the executive were to be allocated on the basis of the d'Hondt system.

[14] See item 17.6 on page 99 of the Patten Report.

[15] Article 3 of the Irish Constitution as amended following the 1998 Good Friday Agreement referendum. (My emphasis.)

Appendix I

The agreed Communiqué

Agreed Communiqué issued following the conference between the Irish and British governments and the parties involved in the Northern Ireland executive (designate) on 6, 7, 8 and 9 December 1973. [Text published as Government Documentation (N.I.4) by the Government Information Service, Dublin, December 1973.]

1. The conference between the British and Irish governments and the parties involved in the Northern Ireland executive (designate) met at Sunningdale on 6, 7, 8 and 9 December 1973.

2. During the conference, each delegation stated their position on the status of Northern Ireland.

3. The taoiseach said that the basic principle of the conference was that the participants had tried to see what measure of agreement of benefit to all the people concerned could be secured. In doing so, all had reached accommodation with one another on practical arrangements. But none had compromised, and none had asked others to compromise, in relation to basic aspirations. The people of the republic, together with a minority in Northern Ireland as represented by the SDLP delegation, continued to uphold the aspiration towards a united Ireland. The only unity they wanted to see was a unity established by consent.

4. Mr Brian Faulkner said that delegates from Northern Ireland came to the conference as representatives of apparently incompatible sets of political aspirations who had found it possible to reach agreement to join together in government because each accepted that in doing so they were not sacrificing principles or aspirations. The desire of the majority of the people of Northern Ireland to remain part of the United Kingdom, as represented by the Unionist and Alliance delegations, remained firm.

5. The Irish government fully accepted and solemnly declared that there could be no change in the status of Northern Ireland until a majority of the people of Northern Ireland desired a change in that status.

The British government solemnly declared that it was, and would remain, their policy to support the wishes of the majority of the people of Northern Ireland. The present status of Northern Ireland is that it is part of the United Kingdom. If in the future the majority of the people of Northern Ireland should indicate a wish to become part of a united Ireland, the British government would support that wish.

6. The conference agreed that a formal agreement incorporating the declarations of the British and Irish governments would be signed at the formal stage of the conference and registered at the United Nations.

7. The conference agreed that a Council of Ireland would be set up. It would be confined to representatives of the two parts of Ireland, with appropriate safeguards for the British government's financial and other interests. It would comprise a Council of Ministers with executive and harmonising functions and a consultative role, and a consultative assembly with advisory and review functions. The Council of Ministers would act by unanimity, and would comprise a core of seven members of the Irish government and an equal number of members of the Northern Ireland executive with

provision for the participation of other non-voting members of the Irish government and the Northern Ireland executive or administration when matters within their departmental competence were discussed. The Council of Ministers would control the functions of the Council. The chairmanship would rotate on an agreed basis between representatives of the Irish government and of the Northern Ireland executive. Arrangements would be made for the location of the first meeting, and the location of subsequent meetings would be determined by the Council of Ministers. The consultative assembly would consist of 60 members, 30 members from Dáil Éireann chosen by the Dáil on the basis of proportional representation by the single transferable vote, and 30 members from the Northern Ireland assembly chosen by that assembly and also on that basis. The members of the consultative assembly would be paid allowances. There would be a secretariat to the Council, which would be kept as small as might be commensurate with efficiency in the operation of the Council. The secretariat would service the institutions of the Council and would, under the Council of Ministers, supervise the carrying out of the executive and harmonising functions and the consultative role of the Council. The secretariat would be headed by a secretary general. Following the appointment of a Northern Ireland executive, the Irish government and the Northern Ireland executive would nominate their representatives to a Council of Ministers. The Council of Ministers would then appoint a secretary general and decide upon the location of its permanent headquarters. The secretary general would be directed to proceed with the drawing up of plans for such headquarters. The Council of Ministers would also make arrangements for the recruitment of the staff of the secretariat in a manner and on conditions which would, as far as is practicable, be consistent with those applying to public servants in the two administrations.

8. In the context of its harmonising functions and consultative role, the Council of Ireland would undertake important work relating, for instance, to the impact of EEC membership.

As for executive functions, the first step would be to define and agree these in detail. The conference therefore decided that, in view of the administrative complexities involved, studies would at once be set in hand to identify and, prior to the formal stage of the conference, report on areas of common interest in relation to which a Council of Ireland would take executive decisions, and, in appropriate cases, be responsible for carrying those decisions into effect. In carrying out these studies, and also in determining what should be done by the Council in terms of harmonisation, the objectives to be borne in mind would include the following:

(1) to achieve the best utilisation of scarce skills, expertise and resources;
(2) to avoid, in the interests of economy and efficiency, unnecessary duplication of effort; and
(3) to ensure complementary rather than competitive effort where this is to the advantage of agriculture, commerce and industry.

In particular, these studies would be directed to identifying, for the purposes of executive action by the Council of Ireland, suitable aspects of activities in the following broad fields:

(a) exploitation, conservation and development of natural resources and the environment;
(b) agricultural matters (including agricultural research, animal health and operational aspects of the Common Agriculture Policy), forestry and fisheries;
(c) cooperative ventures in the fields of trade and industry;
(d) electricity generation;
(e) tourism;
(f) roads and transport;
(g) advisory services in the field of public health;
(h) sport, culture and the arts.

It would be for the Oireachtas and the Northern Ireland assembly to legislate from time to time as to the extent of functions to be devolved to the Council of Ireland. Where necessary, the British government will cooperate in this devolution of functions. Initially, the functions to be vested would be those identified in accordance with the procedures set out above and decided, at the formal stage of the conference, to be transferred.

9. (i) During the initial period following the establishment of the Council, the revenue of the Council would be provided by means of grants from the two administrations in Ireland towards agreed projects and budgets, according to the nature of the service involved.

   (ii) It was also agreed that further studies would be put in hand forthwith and completed as soon as possible of methods of financing the Council after the initial period which would be consonant with the responsibilities and functions assigned to it.

   (iii) It was agreed that the cost of the secretariat of the Council of Ireland would be shared equally, and other services would he financed broadly in proportion to where expenditure or benefit accrues.

   (iv) The amount of money required to finance the Council's activities will depend upon the functions assigned to it from time to time.

   (v) While Britain continues to pay subsidies to Northern Ireland, such payments would not involve Britain participating in the Council, it being accepted nevertheless that it would be legitimate for Britain to safeguard in an appropriate way her financial involvement in Northern Ireland.

10. It was agreed by all parties that persons committing crimes of violence, however motivated, in any part of Ireland should be brought to trial irrespective of the part of Ireland in which they are located. The concern which large sections of the people of Northern Ireland felt about this problem was in particular forcefully expressed by the representatives of

the Unionist and Alliance parties. The representatives of the Irish government stated that they understood and fully shared this concern. Different ways of solving this problem were discussed; among them were the amendment of legislation operating in the two jurisdictions on extradition, the creation of a common law enforcement area in which an all-Ireland court would have jurisdiction, and the extension of the jurisdiction of domestic courts so as to enable them to try offences committed outside the jurisdiction. It was agreed that problems of considerable legal complexity were involved, and that the British and Irish governments would jointly set up a commission to consider all the proposals put forward at the conference and to recommend as a matter of extreme urgency the most effective means of dealing with those who commit these crimes. The Irish government undertook to take immediate and effective legal steps so that persons coming within their jurisdiction and accused of murder, however motivated, committed in Northern Ireland will be brought to trial, and it was agreed that any similar reciprocal action that may be needed in Northern Ireland be taken by the appropriate authorities.

11. It was agreed that the Council would be invited to consider in what way the principles of the European Convention on Human Rights and Fundamental Freedoms would be expressed in domestic legislation in each part of Ireland. It would recommend whether further legislation or the creation of other institutions, administrative or judicial, are required in either part or embracing the whole island to provide additional protection in the field of human rights. Such recommendations could include the functions of an ombudsman or commissioner for complaints, or other arrangements of a similar nature which the Council of Ireland might think appropriate.

12. The conference also discussed the question of policing and the need to ensure public support for and identification with the police service throughout the whole community. It was agreed that no single set of proposals would achieve these aims overnight, and that time would be necessary. The conference

expressed the hope that the wide range of agreement that had been reached, and the consequent formation of a power-sharing executive, would make a major contribution to the creation of an atmosphere throughout the community where there would be widespread support for and identification with all the institutions of Northern Ireland.

13. It was broadly accepted that the two parts of Ireland are to a considerable extent interdependent in the whole field of law and order, and that the problems of political violence and identification with the police service cannot be solved without taking account of that fact.

14. Accordingly, the British government stated that, as soon as the security problems were resolved and the new institutions were seen to be working effectively, they would wish to discuss the devolution of responsibility for normal policing and how this might be achieved with the Northern Ireland executive and the police.

15. With a view to improving policing throughout the island and developing community identification with and support for the police services, the governments concerned will cooperate under the auspices of a Council of Ireland through their respective police authorities. To this end, the Irish government would set up a police authority, appointments to which would be made after consultation with the Council of Ministers of the Council of Ireland. In the case of the Northern Ireland police authority, appointments would be made after consultation with the Northern Ireland executive, which would consult with the Council of Ministers of the Council of Ireland. When the two police authorities are constituted, they will make their own arrangements to achieve the objectives set out above.

16. An independent complaints procedure for dealing with complaints against the police will be set up.

17. The secretary of state for Northern Ireland will set up an all-party committee from the assembly to examine how best to introduce effective policing throughout Northern Ireland with particular reference to the need to achieve public identification with the police.

18. The conference took note of a re-affirmation by the British government of their firm commitment to bring detention to an end in Northern Ireland for all sections of the community as soon as the security situation permits, and noted also that the secretary of state for Northern Ireland hopes to be able to bring into use his statutory powers of selective release in time for a number of detainees to be released before Christmas.

19. The British government stated that, in the light of the decisions reached at the conference, they would now seek the authority of parliament to devolve full powers to the Northern Ireland executive and Northern Ireland assembly as soon as possible. The formal appointment of the Northern Ireland executive would then be made.

20. The conference agreed that a formal conference would be held early in the New Year, at which the British and Irish governments and the Northern Ireland executive would meet together to consider reports on the studies which have been commissioned and to sign the agreement reached.

The Sunningdale conference
6–9 December 1973

[The following is not a verbatim account but rather a reconstruction from detailed notes that I kept of the discussions in plenary session at the conference, at all of which I was present. At later stages negotiations took place either in small sub-groups or in bilateral exchanges. These were confined for the most part to ministers and politicians.

In addition to my notes on the plenary sessions, I have also included the personal notes I made from time to time over the days and nights of this later phase of the conference while officials, and ministers too, at times, waited around for developments.]

***

Thursday, 6 December 1973

The conference opened in Northcote House in Sunningdale Civil Service College Park, shortly after 10 a.m. on Thursday, 6 December. After the photographers had come and gone, the delegation leaders, beginning with the prime minister, Ted Heath, made opening statements.

Opening statements by heads of delegations

The prime minister, **Ted Heath**, who, as host, had taken the chair, welcomed the taoiseach and the ministers of the Irish government and also the representatives of the parties from Northern Ireland who, he hoped, would soon take on the functions of the government of Northern Ireland over a wide range of subjects. This would affect the interests of the United Kingdom and of Ireland as a whole. He described the occasion as historic and recalled the terms of the Green and White papers. The conference, he said, of its nature was not one where an agenda or programme of work could have been fixed in advance. The aim was to arrive at an agreed 'package' but it was for the conference itself to decide how it should go about its business. He paid a warm tribute to the previous secretary of state for Northern Ireland, Willie Whitelaw [who had been replaced by Francis Pym some days before the conference opened].

The 1973 Act reflected a great deal of agreement within Northern Ireland on basic issues. The purpose of the present conference was to discuss a Council of Ireland among other matters. Heath welcomed the opportunity to do this. He then outlined the ideas for the proposed Council of Ireland, which the British government was willing to accept:

- it would be confined to north and south, with proper safeguards for British government interests;
- at the executive level it would comprise representatives of the Irish government and of the Northern executive and it would act by unanimity;
- there could also be a separate advisory and consultative tier with a membership drawn from the Dáil and the Northern assembly;
- the Council should have its own secretariat.

The government had affirmed its intention to bring detention without trial [internment] in Northern Ireland to an end as soon as the situation permitted.

The British government, Heath added, would also be willing to consider

- the 'imaginative and important concept' of a common law enforcement area;
- the question of extradition processes;
- what role the Council might play in the law and order field.
- policing—provided that it was understood that the RUC must continue to provide the police service for Northern Ireland.

The taoiseach, **Liam Cosgrave**, said that the fundamental problem in Northern Ireland was the absence of that broad political consensus within which political, economic and social issues are decided in other societies by normal political means. Northern Ireland was a response to the aspiration of a strong and coherent minority in Ireland devoted to the Union. But its establishment created another minority. Today, whatever the legalities of the situation, two apparently incompatible aspirations focused on religious affiliation were still in contention within that area. This kept the passions of history alive. But the problem was not limited to Northern Ireland: the aspiration of the minority there was also an aspiration of the majority in Ireland as a whole. Short of mass conversion or mass repression of one or other aspiration in Ireland, there was no simple one-dimensional solution. What was needed was

> a settlement which fosters the growth of trust, in a situation where community fears are gradually eased, a degree of political consensus can develop and support for violence on any side is reduced to that hard core who, in any society, resort to violence, not because they are driven to it by fear, uncertainty and political instability but by choice.

An important aspect of the promotion of trust within Northern Ireland had to be a corresponding effort to promote trust, friendship and understanding between north and south.

What I am saying is simply that all of us in Ireland should cease for the moment trying to determine for our children and our children's children the exact kind of political institutions they will wish to live under in their day—especially since our past efforts to do so have seemed to promise only new difficulties for them. Instead—if we can now get the right political structures established throughout the island, providing scope now for differing aspirations, and capable of development precisely to the extent to which time may reconcile those differences—then we should commit ourselves whole-heartedly and with trust to those structures. This would mean getting a process under way which will have no predetermined outcome in the sense that we need not try to decide now on the exact shape of the final result. Instead we should let each stage evolve from the preceding one.

Our conflicts in Ireland for the most part relate to the past or to the future. But the past is past and the future is an abstraction. All we have to build on, and live in, is the reality of the present.

The agenda for the conference had been set by the needs of the present situation; all its items were linked; and each made sense only in relation to every other.

We, as elected representatives of the people, are not meeting here in opposition to each other in the ordinary sense, but with a fundamental unity of interest in making the processes of democracy work in the spirit of co-operation and respect for the aspirations of the interests we represent. Let me say now, on behalf of my government, that, with goodwill all round, we can probably go a long way towards meeting the pre-occupations of those whose concern is with the attitude of the Republic towards Northern Ireland.

Brian Faulkner, leader of the Ulster Unionist Party, said that they all wanted to see Northern Ireland and the whole island of Ireland flourish in a way which they had not done hitherto. There were two incompatible political aspirations in Northern Ireland. In the past the parties there had not been willing to sit down together but now, without sacrificing their respective aspirations, they had agreed to join in government. He believed he spoke for all his Unionist colleagues in saying that they wished to put the past behind them.

The conference was not just about a Council of Ireland but about north-south relations and how they could be improved. One thing was vital—that the republic make it absolutely clear that it recognised the right of the people of Northern Ireland to order their own constitutional affairs. The path to power-sharing was difficult. It would not be widely accepted until it was seen to work. But to conceive of an all-Ireland Council was one hundred times more difficult since so many would see it as halfway towards a united Ireland. So he wanted to say with all his strength that the republic should be seen to recognise the right of the people of Northern Ireland to order their own affairs. If that one premise were accepted then they could achieve much more in north-south cooperation than anyone would have thought possible.

> We in Northern Ireland are in a quite different situation to anywhere else in these islands—over nine hundred of our people have been killed to date. Let us face it—in practical terms the men of violence must be dealt with all over the island of Ireland. In the late 1950s there was such close co-operation between the Gardaí and the RUC that one knew at all times what the other knew about subversive organisations.

There should be mechanisms through the Council of Ireland for cooperation between the two police forces. But this was very different from the Council's having control over the activities of the two forces. That was neither desirable nor practical and to try it would hinder, and not encourage, the whole-hearted cooperation that was necessary.

No one would have believed two months earlier that the parties could agree to form an executive. This had now been done. But he wanted to emphasise that the majority population in the north felt that they had made all the sacrifices.

> Violence continues, the Northern Parliament has been prorogued, a new Assembly has been elected, there is power-sharing by decree, there are 101 guarantees of civil rights and a complete re-organisation of the police. The unionist people do not have room for further changes.

Certainly, it was true that over the previous few months the minority as represented by the SDLP faced equal problems in sitting down with Unionists. As to north-south relations they should all be content with small beginnings and not try to build up a large bureaucratic organisation at this stage. He thought it important that the taoiseach had said that they should not try now to determine the exact shape of the Council once and for all.

Gerry Fitt, for the SDLP, in a brief opening statement said that the hopes of many were with them that day. The talks between the Northern Ireland parties had succeeded, though they had opened with less hope. He listed five points:

- There should be a Council of Ireland;
- it should be confined to north and south;
- in addition to government representatives [in the Council executive] there should be a consultative role for parliamentarians;
- the Council should have its own secretariat;
- it should have both executive functions and a harmonising role.

If these principles were acceptable to the government of the republic then it would be for the conference to work out the details of their application. He then touched on law and order issues and said it was important that everyone should be able to identify with the police. A Council of Ireland could have a role in this regard.

However, no institution of this nature could be static or rigid—it must be able to evolve. In general the problems they faced were no greater, or more bitter, than those which had divided the peoples of Europe after the war.

Oliver Napier, Alliance, concluding the first round of opening statements, said that they had all come to the conference with hope. They wanted to bury the past by recognising and accepting each other's mutual aspirations. He wanted to see a beginning of new relationships. But he had to say to the republic's representatives that there were certain things that the majority in Northern Ireland resented. One was Articles 2 and 3 of the Irish Constitution; another was the problem about extradition of fugitives to Northern Ireland. His party wanted to see a Council of Ireland established but it was essential that it be part of a package. Terrorism could not be dealt with in some kind of vacuum—as if the border were a barrier. It was important to forge new relations of trust between north and south and they wanted to create structures for that. But they had to face the fact that there were resentments on the part of people in Northern Ireland about the Irish Constitution and about extradition.

Agenda

After the leaders' opening statements, **Prime Minister Heath** as chairman suggested a meeting of leaders to see how to proceed. [This suggestion was not taken up.] The issues were clear. He agreed with the taoiseach's view that the outcome of the conference had to be an agreed 'package'. This meant that all the individual items were interrelated and so the exact order in which they were to be discussed would not matter greatly. He proposed that they should go through the various issues to identify the main outstanding points to be addressed. In his view these were as follows:

- The complex of questions relating to a Council of Ireland—its structure, functions and role; HMG had given their view on this.[1]

- Law and order, the proposal for a Common Law Enforcement Area;[2] extradition; and human rights, which is closely connected with law and order issues;
- The issue of the status of Northern Ireland.

The taoiseach, **Brian Faulkner** and **Gerry Fitt** agreed.

Fitt said he understood that the prime minister had to be in the House of Commons that afternoon. Could he stay on at Sunningdale even for a short time? Heath said he would be staying on—he had made other arrangements in regard to the House of Commons.

The Council of Ireland

John Hume, of the SDLP, listed six points about the proposed Council which he believed had already been agreed on 21 November by the three Northern Ireland parties.

- There should be a Council of Ireland;
- it should be confined to north and south—though with some provision for British government input on issues affecting British financial interests;
- it should not only involve the Irish government and the Northern Ireland executive [in a ministerial council]—it should also have a consultative tier [i.e. a parliamentary assembly];
- it should have a secretariat;
- at executive level [i.e. the ministerial council] decision-making should be by unanimity;
- it should have both executive and harmonising functions.

[His list, like that of his party leader, Gerry Fitt, was essentially similar to that offered by Heath, with the addition of the point about the functions of the Council.]

Brian Faulkner did not dissent from this. However, he had grave reservations about granting the proposed Council of Ireland executive powers—he thought this was something which the Council itself, once it was established, could discuss. He also mentioned some other points.

- He wanted equal membership from north and south;
- he agreed, with some reluctance, to the proposal that there should be a parliamentary tier or assembly as part of the Council; he would have liked more discussion of this issue;
- he agreed also that there should be a permanent secretariat provided it was not too large. There should not be a huge new bureaucracy to complement the existing civil services, north and south.

Subject to these points, he thought the outline was 'pretty well acceptable'.

The taoiseach agreed on the final point about the secretariat. Some [activities?] might be 'pooled' to avoid unnecessary bureaucracy.

Faulkner agreed.

Heath said that if, as appeared to be the case, there was agreement that there should be a secretariat, then the details could be discussed later on. He asked if the possibility that the Council could be given executive functions could be discussed?

Faulkner accepted that the possibility of taking on executive functions was something to be discussed.

Hume [implying that this was not enough] said that his party had come to the conference under the clear impression that the points he had just outlined had been agreed in Belfast. There was a document which said so.

Faulkner did not agree that this was the case but he was not going to get onto a hook on this issue.

Heath wondered if they should discuss these issues around the main table or in a smaller group?

Oliver Napier said Alliance accepted Hume's seven points.

Faulkner said that the question of a declaration on 'status' [of Northern Ireland] would be vital.

The taoiseach suggested that they adjourn for a short break.

Heath agreed. He suggested that after the break they continue by identifying the main points at issue in regard to law and order and 'status'.

Paddy Devlin expressed the hope that delegations might be given the bottom copy of the prime minister's speech [that is a carbon copy].

Heath noted that texts of the leaders' opening statements would be made available.

Contacts with the news media

This was followed by some exchanges about whether, and if so how, to brief the news media on the proceedings of the conference.

Heath thought it important to maintain confidentiality until the end of the conference. He suggested that participants should agree not to go on radio or TV or give press interviews for a limited period—until a press conference perhaps on Saturday. [**Haydon**, the prime minister's press secretary, interjected 'the end of the conference'.] This need not inhibit the release of the texts of the opening statements.

John Hume said it was important to maintain confidentiality. He asked for a commitment that there would be no press briefing by anyone.

Faulkner thought it would be unreal not to release the texts of the opening statements. However, they should avoid press briefings until at least the end of the session.

Conor Cruise O'Brien [whose ministerial responsibility on the Irish side extended to the press] argued that if there were no briefing, then the news media themselves would fill the gap with speculation. He believed that there could be briefing, but 'there should be no attempt by anyone to score points off anyone else'.

Bob Cooper [Alliance Party] said John Hume was right. What was released to the media should be limited to the opening statements. There should be no briefing until they had discussed the issue again later.

The discussion was inconclusive though the general view seemed to be against briefing, at least pending further discussion.

> During a coffee break that followed (12.15 p.m.), the taoiseach and Irish ministers in the delegation room discussed whether or not to give Brian Faulkner at that point the text of the proposed declaration by the Irish government on the status of Northern Ireland. The minister for local government, James Tully, and some other ministers were opposed, but two ministers— Conor Cruise O'Brien and Garret FitzGerald— argued that it would be better to show our hand now rather than hold it over to bargain with later. This would show a generosity in our approach which could improve the tone of subsequent negotiations with the Unionist Party. It was agreed eventually that the taoiseach should talk to Brian Faulkner and give him a general outline of what we were prepared to say on the 'status' issue. Conor Cruise O'Brien again repeated his view in favour of briefing the news media on the progress of the discussions. He said that on the British side there would undoubtedly be the usual daily Whitehall briefing for political correspondents, particularly since the prime minister was attending the conference.

Law and order issues—common law enforcement area

The morning session resumed about 12.30 p.m. with a discussion directed to identifying the main points at issue in regard to 'law and order' and 'status', as Heath had proposed earlier. After a brief attempt by Faulkner (which he did not persist in) to have the 'status' issue taken first, **Heath** invited the taoiseach to outline the Irish government's Common Law Enforcement Area [CLEA] proposals.

The taoiseach asked the attorney general, Declan Costello, and the minister for justice, Patrick Cooney, to speak on the topic.

Declan Costello, the Irish attorney general, opening the discussion, said that he was aware of the criticisms of the position of the Irish government on the related issue of extradition. He would explain that in a later session. We believed that there was no simple solution. Together with the minister for justice, **Patrick Cooney**, he then outlined the Irish government's proposals in regard to a 'common law enforcement area'.

[This envisaged an all-Ireland court—possibly with also a second, appellate level—to try listed terrorist offences in either part of Ireland. The judges—an equal number from each of the two jurisdictions—would be nominated by the Council of Ireland, and the court for each case would consist of either three or five members. There would also be an all-Ireland Human Rights Court with a president and four judges—two from Northern Ireland and two from the republic, as well as a 'defender of human rights' who would be available to advise potential applicants to that Court. The Irish government's approach also included proposals in regard to policing: the existing police authority in Northern Ireland, and a new police authority to be established in the south, would each be responsible within its own area, but both would also be responsible on certain matters to the Council of Ireland.]

Heath, in his chairing role, noted a number of points that would arise in discussion of the proposals:

- the role of the Council of Ireland in all of this;
- the membership of the proposed courts? The offences they would deal with? How the judges would be appointed? The harmonisation of legislation in regard to the courts' jurisdiction?
- the responsibility of the proposed Court [of Human Rights];
- policing—each jurisdiction would be responsible for its own police authority but would there be a role for the Council? What would be the procedure for complaints?

The 'status' of Northern Ireland

Discussion then turned to the 'status' issue [that is to say what steps the Irish government, and the SDLP, might be asked to take towards recognition of the position of Northern Ireland as part of the United Kingdom].

Brian Faulkner said that their real concern was the claim in the Irish Constitution to jurisdiction over Northern Ireland. While that remained in effect it was virtually impossible to conceive of the formation of a Council of Ireland, or to persuade the majority to sit down to work in cooperation with the south. He recognised of course that [a referendum to change the Constitution] could be a complex and time-consuming matter so what he hoped to see was a commitment to change the Constitution in due course, together with a declaration now in regard to the 'status' of Northern Ireland [as part of the United Kingdom]. It would not be good enough simply to 'recognise' the Northern Ireland institutions because in the new situation there would be the 'umbrella' of the Council of Ireland. It would be necessary to acknowledge the right of the people of Northern Ireland themselves to decide what their constitutional position should be. 'Otherwise we are simply wasting our time here'.

Oliver Napier, for the Alliance Party, said that the talks between the parties in Belfast on the formation of the executive had started with acceptance by all of the Constitution Act 1973. The status of Northern Ireland is clearly stated there as well as the conditions for any future change in that status. What they wanted now was recognition by the republic of Northern Ireland as part of the United Kingdom.

Hume, for the SDLP, pointed to the wording of the British White Paper of March 1973, to which the prime minister himself had referred. Paragraph 112 (a) had spoken of

> the acceptance of the present status of Northern Ireland, and of the possibility—which would have to be compatible with the principle of consent—of subsequent change in that status.

When they were discussing status now, therefore, they should also discuss the possibility of subsequent change in status.

Heath then said that, as he saw it, four points for consideration had emerged from the discussion so far:

- the question of the claim of jurisdiction in the Constitution of the republic;
- the possibility of a change in that Constitution;
- the question of a declaration by the republic;
- the means [i.e. the conditions and procedure] for any subsequent change in the status of Northern Ireland.

Hume responded that there was another aspect to point 4—this was what the position of the British government would be in the event of a wish [by a majority in Northern Ireland] for such a change.

Heath agreed that there was a need to clarify item 4 on this point.

The taoiseach added that the question of a reciprocal declaration by the British government to complement the proposed declaration by the Irish government might also arise.

The conference then adjourned for lunch (12.45–2.15 p.m.).

Thursday, 6 December, 2.15 p.m.
Council of Ireland

When the discussions resumed after lunch **Prime Minister Heath** listed three points where he believed there a measure of agreement:

- that there should be a Council of Ireland;
- that it should be confined to north and south with a suitable provision for the British government's concern about financial questions;
- that it would comprise a governmental-level executive and an assembly, that is a parliamentary tier with an advisory role.

He suggested they move on to discuss these issues, which were largely matters of concern to north and south in Ireland.

[In the discussion that followed specific proposals on various aspects of the Council put forward by the **taoiseach** and by individual ministers on the Irish side were commented on by **Brian Faulkner** and other Northern representatives. **Heath** acted throughout as a more or less neutral chairman seeking to establish points of agreement between north and south.]

Council—executive (governmental level)

It was generally accepted that on the governmental tier of the Council, there would be a core group of five ministers from each side, with provision to add an additional minister or ministers *ad hoc* when matters affecting their areas of responsibility were to be discussed. [Because of a leak to the news media it was later agreed to modify this so as to provide for seven ministers from each side.]

Consultative assembly (parliamentary tier)

Discussion then turned to the proposed parliamentary tier [consultative assembly]. Should there be parity of representation from north and south, or should representation be in proportion to population?

The taoiseach said that the Irish government envisaged a membership divided 40/20 between south and north.

Brian Faulkner responded that all the Northern parties had agreed that there should be parity of representation for both areas.

Cosgrave replied, jokingly, that this was what he had always feared— that the Northern parties would combine against the south.

It was agreed to leave the point over for discussion later.

Garret FitzGerald said that the Irish government envisaged that the parliamentary tier should have an advisory and a consultative role; it would debate and question ministers; and it should have the power to decide on the future evolution of the Council.

Faulkner thought it would be galling to Unionists to lay down a precise role. In any case ministers were subject to questioning in the Dáil and in the Northern Ireland assembly respectively.

John Hume, on the other hand, felt it necessary to give the parliamentary tier something of substance to do.

Garret FitzGerald said it would not be enough that ministers be questioned in their respective home institutions. The parliamentary tier should have an advisory and consultative role and it should be free to make recommendations. There should be a capacity for the Council to evolve further—subject to the consent of a majority of the Northern Ireland representatives in the assembly.

Faulkner said he would like to see in more detail what the proposals were. He suggested that they come back again later on this issue, as well as on the proportion in membership between north and south.

Heath asked if he would like to see the proposals on paper?

Faulkner replied, 'Yes'.

It was agreed that the Irish government side would give details of its ideas to Faulkner.

Heath asked if it was proposed that north and south should use the same procedure to choose their representatives on the parliamentary tier?

The taoiseach replied that the Dáil and the Northern assembly, respectively, should each nominate some of their members as delegates to the parliamentary tier of the Council.

Oliver Napier favoured election by each of the two bodies by proportional representation. A brief discussion followed about what would be done if some representatives refused to take their seats. Would the seats be left vacant? It was agreed that this would not arise if the delegates were chosen in both cases through a P.R. election.

Council of Ireland—secretariat

FitzGerald opened discussion on the Council secretariat. It should have new, specially recruited, permanent, full-time, staff. In addition, other staff could be seconded from the civil services of north and south. The head of the secretariat could be called 'secretary general' but the exact title did not matter. The important thing was to attract high-calibre personnel.

Heath suggested that there was a distinction to be made between a secretariat staff to service the institutions of the Council and a staff to service its functions. He asked whether the secretariat staff should be paid?

Faulkner agreed completely with Heath's distinction. There should be a secretary general whose role would be to service the Council institutions. Staff of the respective civil services acting under the direction of the secretary general could be used to carry out the functions of the Council. It was important to get away from the idea of a large new bureaucracy.

FitzGerald replied that the aim should be to rationalise and reduce, rather than build up, a bureaucracy.

Heath nodded in agreement.

Faulkner commented that they might be getting into an area of fundamental disagreement. He envisaged, for example, that there would be, not one, but two separate tourist boards, north and south.

Austin Currie (SDLP) said that if the Council was to have any independence it must have a secretariat of its own. Without that it would be stultified.

Heath, summarising, listed points where he thought there was agreement. There should be

- a secretariat to service the Council institutions;
- a governmental and an assembly tier;
- a secretary general.

Two other issues—financing and payment of the secretariat and the possibility of executive and harmonising functions—had still to be discussed.

FitzGerald proposed that there should also be an Economic and Social Council as an advisory body representing vocational interests from north and south.

Faulkner suggested that when it was established the Council itself could discuss this idea.

Council of Ireland—functions

Discussion then turned to the proposal that the Council should have both executive and harmonisation functions. [These were discussed in rather general terms and there could be scope for differences in understanding when it came to defining them more precisely in practice.]

Hume said it would not be enough that the governmental level should simply meet or that it would be merely advisory—it should have specific executive authority in specified areas. A degree of harmonisation of laws etc., which is already proceeding anyway under the EEC, could be done more efficiently in Ireland if the Council were to be one of the agencies involved.

Heath, seeming to agree, asked if this [harmonisation of laws etc.] would relate to economic and social issues, as in in the EEC?

Hume thought there should be harmonisation wherever it was required. It could, for example, extend to laws dealing with violence—he would prefer to see exactly similar laws on either side of the border. There would of course be problems and the matter would need to be carefully handled.

Faulkner pointed out that there could not be complete harmonisation of laws since Northern Ireland was within the UK.

Cooper added that there should not simply be a blanket commitment to harmonisation in every field—it should be done only where it would be useful.

Heath and **Hume** both agreed.

FitzGerald said [it might be] we who would have to do the harmonisation!

Paddy Devlin (SDLP) suggested that there should be harmonisation in both directions. Harmonisation, however, should not be simply 'slapped down' on everything—it should be a gradual process.

Faulkner said the Council would not superimpose its views on the Dáil or the Northern assembly. It should not be able to do something either body disapproved of.

Fitt said that what was needed were institutions that would have a role in relation to the whole island of Ireland—and not merely a psychological influence. It might not be possible to lay down specific functions now. 'We will see that as it goes along.'

Napier said that the Council should be capable of handling executive powers given to it by the Dáil and the Northern assembly but he would hate to see any attempt made now to decide what these should be. Tourism could be one function that perhaps could be better handled by a single body.

Garret FitzGerald said there was no question of imposition. The Irish government envisaged that the Council would have both harmonising and executive functions but what those executive functions were to be had to be examined.

Austin Currie said it was agreed by the Northern parties in Belfast that the proposed Council would have executive functions.

FitzGerald added that the Council should not be merely a debating forum. There were some things that could be done better in common. Do we really need to have everything duplicated in a small island? Examples were animal health, management training etc. He regarded it as very important that they should agree at the conference on a small number of issues where executive functions would be delegated to the Council from the outset.

Roy Bradford agreed about animal health.

Currie, quoting a reference to executive functions from the document agreed by the Northern Ireland parties in Belfast on 21 November, asked whether or not that document could be taken as agreed?

FitzGerald—there must be *some* content [from the outset].

Faulkner replied that his party's attitude would depend to some extent on what specifically was proposed by way of executive functions. Perhaps the matter should be left over for the moment?

FitzGerald—until later in the conference?

Austin Currie—possibly until the formal session [i.e. the second more formal stage envisaged for the conference].

The taoiseach said that they should agree that the Council from the outset would have *certain* executive functions but he suggested leaving over specifying just what these functions should be until that evening or the following morning.

Faulkner thought it would be helpful if some could be specified now.

FitzGerald then suggested animal health, implementation of the EEC Common Agricultural Policy but not policy aspects, pollution issues, some aspects of road development and the concept of an open broadcasting area.

It was agreed that in informal group discussions the various parties could indicate more specifically which functions they considered suitable to become executive functions of the Council.

Hume then asked how they could ensure that the veto power retained by the British government under the provisions of the Constitution Act 1973 would not be used to block action by the Council of Ireland?

Taoiseach said there had to be a way to deal with a situation of deadlock on matters where the Council had been given executive functions. He said that, supposing there was discussion of a [single] nuclear power station, and agreement could not be reached, then there would have to be some way for each side to protect its position.

Hume said that even on transferred [i.e. devolved] matters there appeared to be a right by the British government to veto proposals. He would like to see a form of words to provide against this—he wanted to ensure that where executive functions are given to the Council the British government would not take them back using Section 4 of the 1973 Act.

Heath said that the British government could certainly examine the possibility of this.

Council of Ireland—location, frequency of meetings

FitzGerald suggested that the Council should meet once a month.

Heath nodded, but then said that it was primarily a matter for the Council itself to decide.

Faulkner agreed. Rather than argue about a venue for meetings he suggested that the Council meet alternately north and south.

Alliance [Napier?] agreed.

Austin Currie thought there should be a fixed site—Armagh, he said, had great symbolism.

The taoiseach commented that the secretariat would have to be situated somewhere. If the Northern Ireland executive thought Armagh would be suitable then that would be all right with the Irish government.

Bradford—there is a need to familiarise ourselves [with one another] as part of the exercise of reconciliation. He agreed that the secretariat must be in one place.

Faulkner agreed.
Break for afternoon tea.
After the break, discussion began on the 'status' issue.

The 'status' of Northern Ireland

The taoiseach read out the following text of the draft declaration which the Irish government was prepared to make.

> Whereas agreement has been reached as to the establishment and constitution of a Council of Ireland with functions in relation to policing, a common law enforcement area and human rights as well as other executive functions, the government of the republic declares:
>
> (i) that those who live on this island comprise different elements all of which contribute to the life and culture of Ireland, and that each has the right to pursue its legitimate ends by peaceful means;
> (ii) that, accordingly, the aspirations of a majority of the people of this island to its political unity shall be pursued through reconciliation alone;
> (iii) that for so long as a majority of the people of Northern Ireland maintain its present status, the government of the republic will work in friendship and cooperation with the institutions that are being established in Northern Ireland, with the full consent and participation of a majority comprising representatives elected by the votes of both sections of the Northern Ireland community; and
> (iv) that accordingly, the government of the republic have agreed to join in establishing a Council of Ireland within which representatives of that government and the Dáil will participate with the Northern Ireland executive.

He asked that there should be a corresponding declaration by the British government on the lines John Hume had asked for earlier.

Faulkner—how can there be credibility while the constitutional claim still exists? Would the Dublin government not be prepared to make a declaration of a will to change the Constitution? He hoped, in any case, that the wording [of the proposed declaration] would be more succinct.

Conor Cruise O'Brien said there were two separate issues. One was the question of a declaration, the second was the question of the Irish Constitution. Only the first of these was for discussion here. As to the second, the government of the republic should not be asked to say, without considerable preparation being made, that it would like to see a change in the Constitution—the answer would be no, and that would entrench Articles 2 and 3. He was very doubtful about what the outcome of a referendum in the republic on the issue would be.

FitzGerald said they had recognised that there were two legitimate aspirations. The taoiseach's proposal made a gesture towards the Northern majority. Political survival is a necessity for all. The Irish government could not get a constitutional amendment through. However, a formula for a declaration could be found, including a provision that if and when a majority want to change, the British government would facilitate it.

Faulkner, responding, appeared to be willing to accept the idea of reciprocal declarations.

Hume said there were two important points from the past. One was the failure of the minority to accept the institutions in Northern Ireland. However, he believed that in accepting the terms of the Constitution Act 1973 his party had given the greatest possible acceptance on the issue of status. But, second, 'we also have our own legitimate aspiration'; and both the Green Paper and the White Paper had spoken of the possibility of change.

Basil McIvor (Ulster Unionists) [apparently misunderstanding what Cruise O'Brien had said?] queried the word 'legitimate'.

Brendan Corish (Tánaiste and Labour Party leader) said that 1937, when the Constitution was drafted, was a different epoch. He recalled that the Irish All-Party Committee on the Constitution in the late 1960s had reached general agreement on the idea of changes to the Constitution, though not on how precisely it should be changed.[3] 'We would ask you to leave us to be the judge of when we might do something. We have no room for manoeuvre'.

Jim Tully (Irish Minister for Local Government) added that it would be disastrous to try to change the Constitution now.

Roy Bradford said that rhetoric and presentation were very important. He accepted the good faith of people in the south. The reality was, however, that while people in the north acquiesce in power-sharing—though not with great enthusiasm—'the Council of Ireland for us is deep and dangerous water'. One thing they must have was a declaration [on the 'status' of Northern Ireland]. It must be clear-cut and it would be undesirable to tie it to a reciprocal British declaration saying that the British government would welcome the unity of Ireland.

Bob Cooper (Alliance)—It is not *what is* which matters but *what people think it is*. There have been incredible changes in Ireland, although the 1937 Constitution remained a fixed point. 'You are not prepared to make changes—though I accept your *bona fides*.'

The taoiseach said 'if we get a proper package [as an outcome to the conference] then that would certainly convince people in Northern Ireland that we are taking effective action to deal with the situation. It will carry conviction.'

Faulkner suggested that the issue be left overnight—the taoiseach could produce another form of words. It would be unfortunate, however, in any press briefing, to go into what might be done on the 'status' issue—whatever was to emerge would have to be kept as 'the plum' [to be produced at the end of the conference].

Austin Currie said they should accept that there would be no victory and no defeat on the issue of 'status'. There were two different aspirations both within Northern Ireland and in Ireland as a whole. If the conference succeeded then some accommodation between them might emerge from the talks, but so far there had been no compromise. However, a situation had been reached where, for the first time, the minority in Northern Ireland were prepared to identify with the new institutions. That was considerable progress.

Napier said that it was not necessary to change the Constitution now but there must be a clear declaration by the Irish government.

Hume—we are talking about a new situation which supersedes the Constitution. The British Constitution applies a religious criterion for succession to the monarchy. Nobody in their right senses would try to change that at this point. We are in the same position [as regards changing the Irish Constitution].

Heath, summarising the discussion, said that the taoiseach had said it was not possible to change the Irish Constitution and Oliver Napier had said it was not necessary to do so. Brian Faulkner, he suggested, might consider accepting that it was not practical politics to get the Constitution changed. But there might be a suitable declaration. 'As far as her Majesty's government is concerned we have already made our declaration which has been endorsed by all parties in the House of Commons and expressed in speeches in the Guildhall and in the House of Commons. We could consider whether additional weight could be given by registration of a declaration with the United Nations. On all of this we are in private discussion here. As regards the press there is need for complete confidence.'

The taoiseach agreed, saying that there should be no leak from that day's session. He had wondered about an agreed briefing but he thought nobody had anything to gain and that it would be better to leave it until the end of the conference.

Common Law Enforcement Area proposals
Discussion then turned to the proposals of the Irish government in regard to a 'Common Law Enforcement Area'.

Declan Costello, the Irish attorney general, explained the difficulties which the government saw with extradition for political offences because of the commitment in the Constitution to the principles of international law. In 1965 the British government had passed an Extradition Act which was similar to ours in Ireland.

[This was a reference to the Backing of Warrants (Republic of Ireland) Act 1965 in the UK and the Extradition Act 1965 in the Republic.] As a way around the difficulty he outlined the idea of an all-Ireland Court to try scheduled terrorist offences. There were of course differences between the scheduled offences in the UK and Irish jurisdictions respectively, but if there were agreement in principle these could be ironed out.

Basil McIvor, however, saw this as an enormous problem. Not only were there different definitions of offences but also a different development in common and statute law, in the rules of evidence, in sentencing policy, in the constitutional implications, in rules for bail, and in the right to summon witnesses. It would be necessary to build up a new system of law and to work out what appellate court would be involved and so on. There were so many difficulties—he wondered if the attorney general [Declan Costello] had considered all of this?

Sir Peter Rawlinson, the British attorney general, said that in the UK system prosecution was a matter reserved ultimately to the attorney general. These were very complex matters. Lawyers had to act with certainty and precision. In principle the proposal could be examined. He would very much welcome very close study of the proposal for a 'Common Law Enforcement Area'—however, he was not at all clear as to the objective. They needed to look at the scale of the problem. There would be no more than about 25 persons involved in such cases. Was it worth doing what had been proposed for this? Would it not be better, for example, to change Irish law so that it would say that the reference to 'offences of a political character' did not extend to offences involving the use of explosives or firearms? He also referred to the [Council of Europe] Convention on Extradition of 1957 to which both the UK and Ireland were parties. The Irish government's proposals could of course be studied—there might perhaps be some solution—but not by a large conference such as this which could not create proper law in 48 hours. However, if a commission were set up it could study this matter.

Napier raised a number of problems. Where would people sentenced in these courts be locked up? Who would exercise the prerogative of mercy? What the attorney general [Rawlinson] said had struck a chord. They all hoped that violence could soon be brought to an end. There would be great difficulty for a few years— but there would be only about 25 cases and then the whole thing would be obsolete. So why propose this elaborate procedure when there were infinitely simpler ways of achieving the same end— simple extradition or trial in existing courts?

Currie said that they were 'non-lawyers'. They should agree on the principles and let the lawyers work out the details.

Hume (supported by **Devlin)** said 'our aim is to end politically-motivated violence in Ireland for all time.' They were agreed on the basic aim. The major difficulty was that one section of the population in Northern Ireland did not identify with the forces of law and order. A first essential was that they should feel able to do so. 'There are certain areas where this does not happen at present. We want the local community to be able to say to stone-throwers "this is our police force you are throwing stones at".'

Currie said that it had been accepted that the south had a consider-able role to play. There was now an executive-designate in Northern Ireland. But unless certain changes were made it would have author-ity without responsibility and would not be able to enforce law and order. If the executive was set up something could happen in the field of law and order which would put it under severe strain. 'We believe it would be far better not to go into the executive than to go in and have law and order erupt in our faces. Let no one say that we are not concerned about the lack of proper policing. It is our areas which have suffered most and it is in our interest that law and order be enforced. At an early stage we suggested that the name of the RUC be changed. That was not very popular. But we accepted that the British government was not amenable to this argument and in agreeing to the statement of 21 November about forming an execut-ive we accepted that the RUC will continue to provide policing. We have had to work for some alternative in the interest of ending polit-ically-motivated violence for all time on the island of Ireland. We believe that is the Council of Ireland' [i.e. the proposals on a role for the Council in matters of law and order].

Hume added that the British attorney general had suggested a study of the proposals. The former Northern Ireland secretary Willie Whitelaw had talked about a study on 19 October but with what result?

Rawlinson, in response to Hume, said that he had been talking about a study of legal aspects by the respective attorneys general.

Declan Costello, responding to the questions that had been raised, clarified some aspects of the Irish government's proposals. He said they envisaged that of the five judges for the proposed new court, two each would be drawn from the respective High or Supreme courts. He also touched on the human rights aspects of the proposals and said that the proposed 'defender of human rights' would be able to sieve out crank cases before they came to the courts.

Napier still questioned why a minor amendment could not be made to the extradition laws?

John Hume noted that the two extradition acts [north and south] were the same except for the reference in the Act in the republic to [an exception for] 'an offence connected with a political offence'.

Rawlinson said again that both countries were signatories to the 1957 Extradition Convention of the Council of Europe. He accepted that judges in the republic properly carried out their country's laws as they stood. But why not make a simple amendment to say that this does not cover 'firearms offences'? This would be preferable to creating a whole new framework of law to deal with the matter.

Fitt said that a study committee would take months to do its work but the situation was an emergency—policing was a vital matter.

Brian Faulkner said they should not get into arguing about 'political offences'. He returned to the idea of declaring that offences involving firearms should be subject to extradition. It was very hard to have to tell a mother grieving for her dead son [that extradition for the killing was not possible].

FitzGerald referred to the fact that we had a written Constitution and a Supreme Court to deal with. We wanted the IRA to know that they have no way out—we want them to be tried in a way which will not gain them popular sympathy. He was concerned about delay—it should be a matter of weeks, not months.

Heath proposed that the respective legal advisers be asked to get together first thing next morning to have a good go at the issue and then report back to the conference. 'If we are going to do this [i.e. the Common Law Area proposals] then we must have legislation'. The drafters would require precise instructions to draft a bill and there could be nine months of debate.

FitzGerald commented that it had been possible on a previous occasion in the House of Commons to get a bill through in one day.

Rawlinson said that drafting instructions for the study Heath had requested could be given that evening.

Policing

Patrick Cooney, the Irish minister for justice, then explained the Irish government's proposals on the issue of policing and the linkage with the Council of Ireland, one of the purposes of which was to help to end terrorism. As part of the proposed new arrangements the Irish government was prepared to set up, and cede some of their authority for policing to, a new police authority [with a relationship to the Council].

Faulkner—in what way would the two police authorities be responsible to the Council? Would they be appointed by the Council? Was the republic suggesting that it would delegate its authority for the policing function to the Council? Or only the right to approval of the members to be appointed?

Cooney replied that the powers to be delegated were a matter to be decided.

Faulkner said that he understood it as largely a political step to make the police force in Northern Ireland more acceptable throughout the community—but there could also be dangers to this approach.

John Hume said he lived in an area where there were no policemen. His windows had been smashed four times in the previous month and his colleague Austin Currie had been shot at. He could do nothing about it—in effect there was no police force in their areas. He believed that Unionist insistence on retaining the name RUC had been a fundamental error. People, notwithstanding their different aspirations, need to be able to identify with the police. The 'cement' of community is law and order. The proposals of the minister for justice would allow people from the minority community to join the police force, back the police force and support law and order. 'We are talking now about a crucial matter on which the whole thing hinges'.

Currie said he could speak from personal experience. 'In 1969, following the Hunt Report, we decided to ask Catholics to join the RUC. That took courage. But I am convinced that to do so now would be totally impossible unless there is some new way in which the Catholic community can identify with the police force or accept it at the very least'.

Francis Pym, the newly appointed secretary of state for Northern Ireland (reading from a text), said that the facts were unattractive. Most incidents since November 1970 had been near the border with the south—a total of 355. Nearly all emanated from [IRA] 'active service units' across the border, and 24 members of the security forces had been killed within ten miles of the border. Policing in Northern Ireland was a reserved matter and the RUC was funded entirely by monies voted by parliament. He could see the two police authorities being brought together to discuss policing in all of Ireland and he could see the Council of Ireland being consulted in regard to appointments. Handling complaints against police was an important matter and he was about to appoint a working party in Northern Ireland to consider a procedure for complaints. He wanted to see cooperation between the two police forces. The immediate issue, however, was cases occurring near the border.

Patrick Cooney, the Irish minister for justice, replied that 'active service units' were operating in complete safety on the northern side of the border. He was satisfied that there were large areas there which were not policed at all and that a person engaged in violence can go back into 'no man's land'. This highlighted the need for different approaches to two different situations.

Paddy Devlin said 'we are talking about *our* constituents. We are intelligent men. We believe that the approach you [the British and unionists] are pursuing is not right. What happened on the Shankhill and the Falls is symbolic. People feel these people [para-militaries] are patriots—in fact they are thugs and gangsters. During the ceasefire last year the Provos came on to the streets and acted as a police force. If you don't change the title, people will continue to see the RUC as a paramilitary force. The rumours and stories of 50 years are still in their minds. We feel that if it is iden-tified with the Council of Ireland people will switch this off and see it as a non-political thing—the common people will support it. There is no other alternative. Regardless of the reform in 1969 lead-ing to more diverse recruiting, people still see the police as "black bastards". We are talking about areas where violence is endemic'.

Fitt conceded to the Northern Ireland secretary that there were problems in border areas. But there had been over 200 assassina-tions in Northern Ireland and over 150 in Belfast. The police were very slow in dealing with these. There must be some reason for this—it must be that the police in Belfast were not effective. There were murderers living in every ghetto. People in the republic did not need a police authority—their police force was acting well. So he regarded it as a concession that the republic was prepared to cede some responsibility [to a police authority with some link to a Council of Ireland].

Currie said that the republic too had had a history of violence—in the Civil War for example. The IRA were not only dedicated to removing the northern state [i.e. they were also opposed to the gov-ernment and the state in the south]. Yet the IRA does not shoot at the police force in the south. They know that people there support and identify with the police and if they did [shoot at police] they [the IRA] would lose support. He would like to see a similar situ-ation in Northern Ireland.

Napier said that in his own constituency there had been dozens of murders. Slightly over 50 per cent of the entire Catholic population of the constituency had been intimidated out of their homes. The scheme proposed by the Irish government had been 'thrown at' them at the conference. However, he would like to look at it.

Bradford said he represented East Belfast, a Protestant area where UDA headquarters had issued a 'Declaration of War'. There had been a substantial reduction in the strength of the army there but the police were being 're-filtered' back in. The situation, which was already very delicate, would be more so if the police force were seen to be 'controlled'—even as to 50 per cent—by the government of the republic.

Hume said that in contrast to other discussions at the conference, which were rational, this discussion on policing had shown a high degree of feeling. Why did violent groups not get off the ground in the republic or in the UK? Because people would tell the police about them. 'There are problems in the border area. We are talking about detection and prevention through the proposals for a common-law enforcement area. The report of the chief constable for 1973 admitted that the police were getting no information from the public. You, secretary of state, are asking us to "sell" that force now. I would be less than honest if I did not say that that could bring the executive down around our ears within weeks. I am not being awkward or stating purely political points.'

Heath said that they had had a long and wide-ranging discussion and had taken on some tough points. This issue was different from the issue of the Common Law Enforcement Area. That was tough too, but policing went to the heart of government and required identification of the population with the police. It was because of these problems that Westminster in the Constitution Act had decided to keep to itself the arrangements to allow the secretary of state to make the appointments to the police authority. The problem now was how that should be linked with the new institutions.

He proposed that the conference meet again next day at 11.30 a.m. rather than 10.30 a.m. In the meantime, senior advisers should get together to see if they could work things out. At the end of the conference they would put out a simple statement but there should be no [individual] briefings after each session.

> At a meeting later in the Irish delegation room, Conor Cruise O'Brien told the taoiseach and the other ministers that a problem had arisen—word had got out to the press that there had been agreement on six points in relation to the Council of Ireland. It emerged shortly afterwards that the government press secretary, Muiris MacConghail, through a misunderstanding, had briefed the press to this effect. Cruise O'Brien said that Faulkner was 'as mad as a wet hen' but he thought he would simmer down. A joint statement had been put out immediately afterwards to say that nothing was agreed until everything was agreed.

Friday, 7 December 1973

[The discussions on Thursday 6 December, the opening day of the conference, as recounted above, took place in plenary session. From the morning of Friday, the second day, onwards, there were occasional short plenary meetings to hear of progress, or the lack of it, but a great deal of the most significant negotiation took place in smaller working groups attended for the most part by ministers and politicians only. My notes on the relatively brief plenary sessions that took place over these days, which were mainly to hear progress/drafting reports, are much shorter and more succinct than those on the early plenaries, at which there was substantial debate on the various issues.]

Friday, 7 December 1973, morning session

The conference began work on Friday morning with reports back to plenary on the state of play in the various smaller working groups. [I have numbered the groups for convenience.]

(1)   The 'status' of Northern Ireland

Work was still continuing on the drafting of a possible text.

Faulkner said there was no agreement as yet, but he was willing to continue discussion.

(2)   Possible executive functions for the Council of Ireland

There was broad agreement on a draft.

(3)   Common Law Enforcement Area

Costello (Irish attorney general)—we might need a little more time.

Faulkner—there has been very little progress. We are unhappy at the moment.

(4)   Policing

Hume—There has been no discussion with the Northern Ireland parties on policing—discussion should start there.

Devlin—all parties around this table ought to be represented at all [group] meetings.

Heath agreed.

(5)   Structures of a Council of Ireland (ministerial level)

Faulkner said it was unfortunate that there had been a leak about this on the previous day. For that reason they felt it necessary to change the number of core ministers who would sit on the Council from five as proposed initially.

There was general agreement to this. [The Agreed Communiqué issued at the end of the conference provides that 'The Council of Ministers would act by unanimity, and would comprise a core of seven members of the Irish government and an equal number of members of the Northern Ireland executive with provision for the participation of other non-voting members of the Irish government and the Northern Ireland Executive or Administration when matters within their departmental competence were discussed.']

Heath asked about discussions on 'status' between the Irish government and Brian Faulkner? **Alliance** and **SDLP** wanted to be involved. This was agreed.

The taoiseach said that a declaration by the British government would also be involved. There should also be discussion on financing the Council.

This was agreed. It was also accepted that everything depended on an overall agreement being reached on the various issues.

Currie hoped there would be an opportunity for delegations to get together to consider the overall position.

Faulkner—we know our mind on four or five issues.

Heath—since it looks as if progress is being made, group discussions should continue until lunchtime. After lunch there could be discussions between individual delegations.

It was agreed that there would be no briefing for the press at that stage.

[As the days and nights went on, the group negotiations focused more and more on the issue of policing in Northern Ireland, which was primarily an issue between the British government and the Northern Ireland parties. In later stages Prime Minister Heath made efforts to resolve it directly in bilateral meetings with the individual parties, particularly the Ulster Unionists and the SDLP. In the meantime officials, and also, indeed, Irish government ministers, were left to 'hang around' in delegation rooms or in the large central hall from which it was possible to see something of the comings and goings between meeting rooms and delegation rooms along the balcony at first-floor level.

I think that the best way to convey a flavour of these days and nights is to intersperse my summary accounts of the short plenary discussions with the more informal notes, marked with the date and time, that I made during those long hours of waiting for progress in working groups and bilateral meetings.]

Friday, 7 December 1973, 5.40 p.m.

We have been waiting around virtually all day. The whole matter is now very much in the hands of ministers. The morning session was very brief. It simply consisted of a roundup of progress, or lack of it, on various items which are being studied in subgroups. The main news of the day so far from our viewpoint has been the controversy over the leak by Muiris MacConghail yesterday afternoon when he gave a briefing to the journalists at which he mentioned that there had been agreement already on some points.

Friday, 7 December, 6.10 p.m.

The conference resumed on Friday at 6.10 p.m. in plenary session, its first since the morning.

Heath distributed a document that drew together in a single text all that he believed had been agreed so far.

A brief exchange took place that showed that there was disagreement about the wording of the proposed declarations [on 'status'] in paragraph 5. [**Faulkner** and his party wanted the Irish government declaration to refer explicitly not just to 'the status of Northern Ireland' but to 'the status of Northern Ireland as part of the United Kingdom'.]

Heath suggested meeting again in about an hour, after delegations had time to digest the document.

The plenary session resumed on Friday at 7.30 p.m.

Heath suggested they go through the text of the draft document to see where difficulties arose.

The main point of discussion was the text of the declarations of the British and Irish governments [these were eventually to become paragraph 5 of the Agreed Communiqué]. There was still disagreement on this.

FitzGerald asked to have the phrase 'government of the Republic of Ireland' changed to 'the Irish government'.

Faulkner said they should stick to the official designation.

There was still disagreement on paragraph 5.

Faulkner said the disagreement was so basic that they should try to resolve it before moving ahead. 'All we are asking is to add [acceptance of Northern Ireland] "as part of the United Kingdom".'

John Hume wanted to ensure that there was a reference to the possibility of change in the status of Northern Ireland. If Brian Faulkner's suggestion were accepted then the text in paragraph 5 would be [self-]contradictory. To meet Brian Faulkner's position he suggested adding 'at present those wishes are that Northern Ireland should remain part of the United Kingdom'.

Faulkner said that this was not adequate.

Heath said that they were dealing with both the present situation and future possibilities. It was not beyond possibility that the difficulties could be resolved by good drafting.

Faulkner asked what the government of Ireland understood the status of Northern Ireland to be?

Conor Cruise O'Brien replied 'what it is'. He went on, 'we have a written Constitution. We cannot enter into any legal commitment which would run contrary to that. It would be challenged in our courts. This requires a certain vagueness. In negotiation vagueness is sometimes useful'.

Heath commented, after some further discussion, that, after all, what they were mainly talking about was the declaration by Her Majesty's government. He thought it could say 'we recognise that that present wish is to remain part of the United Kingdom.'

Faulkner, in further discussion, said he was afraid of any text that would allow a gloss on the 'status' issue by different people in whatever way suited them. It had to be made clear to the world that the status of Northern Ireland is that it is part of the United Kingdom.

Hume said that they should agree to insert a sentence that would meet Brian Faulkner's position but also consider what would happen if there were to be a future change.

Heath—This is to be the declaration by HMG. He suggested they [the British side] would draft a form of words and then put it to the other participants.

Faulkner was reluctant to go any further until there was agreement on the point at issue.

Heath recalled that throughout the two days of discussions they had agreed that they were working on a package and that 'nothing was agreed until everything was agreed'.

Faulkner said he would rather clear the matter up now.

Heath said that they were now working in an orderly way to identify problems in the draft composite paper. He suggested that they move on for the moment—no one would be giving anything away by this.

Faulkner agreed to this proposal.

Discussion then turned for a short time to the question of registration of the outcome at the United Nations. There was some talk of registering the declarations to be made.

Garret FitzGerald clarified this. He said that his understanding was that what you register at the UN was not declarations but rather agreements. Of course an agreement could incorporate a declaration.

Rawlinson, the British attorney general, said that if an agreement were registered then it would be enforceable before the International Court of Justice.

Faulkner said he wanted to keep the discussion focused on the declaration and not on the whole agreement.

Declan Costello, the Irish attorney general, said that what was being worked on here was a communiqué. Later there would be a formal phase to the conference and a formal agreement. As he had explained to Brian Faulkner, it is that formal agreement that we envisaged would be registered at the UN. The formal agreement would recite the declaration and then go on with the other details of what had been agreed.

Faulkner seemed willing to accept this. However, he said he would like to come back to it later.

The meeting continued for another hour or more with drafting discussions and suggestions for other paragraphs in the combined document. [Note: in what follows the numbering relates to paragraphs in the draft document then under discussion. This may not correspond in all cases to the numbering of paragraphs in the final communiqué.]

The taoiseach noted that there were a lot of matters [in regard to the Council of Ireland] dealt with in paragraphs 8, 9 and 11 of the draft, and also some mistakes. He suggested they be pulled together and looked at by a working group.

FitzGerald (Irish Minister for Foreign Affairs) and **Devlin** (SDLP) saw the need for amendments to paragraphs 8, 9, 10 and 11.

Devlin raised questions about the terms 'executive' and 'harmonising' [functions].

Currie said that one of the six points Hume had made on the previous day had been omitted. This was that the Council should have executive and harmonising functions and not merely a consultative role.

Richard Ryan (Irish Minister for Finance) raised a question about paragraph 10 of the draft which dealt with financing the Council.

Hume said he would like some reference to a method of independent financing [i.e. not simply financing by governmental grants].

Heath—there is a reference to 'methods' [of financing] which includes 'all methods'.

Ivan Cooper (SDLP) joined in the discussion.

Ryan wanted to add another paragraph about financing after an initial period.

Heath suggested the Working Group on Financing should get together again to do further work.
This was agreed.

Discussion of the composite draft then turned to paragraphs 12–16 which dealt with the Common Law Enforcement Area proposals, policing and human rights.

Faulkner found paragraph 12 very unsatisfactory.

Currie had reservations about paragraph 12 and very considerable reservations about paragraph 13. In fact, he found the latter almost totally unacceptable. He had spelled out his party's position on policing on the previous day and again that morning. 'This does not go anywhere near the situation we want. If the executive got off the ground, it would fall apart at once.'

Cooney (Irish Minister for Justice)—paragraph 15 could cause some difficulties for us insofar as it involves the presence of HMG.

Cooper had grave doubts about acceptance by the Protestant population of some points though there must be some involvement of the Council in policing: 'Perhaps a subcommittee should meet on the whole package.'

Heath—the difficulty [about policing] goes to the heart of government. Willie Whitelaw [the former Northern Ireland secretary] arranged that policing would be kept as a reserved function. They were limited in what could be done because of this. The problem which faced them was how, with that reserved, there could be a link to the Council of Ireland.

Cooper suggested one committee to discuss paragraphs 12–15 instead of two.

Cooney was apprehensive that that would make the committee too big.

Devlin was uncomfortable about the role of committees. In some cases advisers had exercised a veto. The representatives on committees should be drawn from the elected members of delegations.

Cooper was disappointed at paragraph 16—there were no references to an all-Ireland Court or to an ombudsman.

Costello (Irish Attorney General)—could the CLEA committee also look at the human rights question and the ombudsman?

Rawlinson (British Attorney General) [referring back to Devlin's complaint about the role of advisers]—one problem is that the Alliance Party did not have enough people [to cover all the committees?].

Napier accepted this.

Devlin said he had no objection to advisers being present—'but not expressing views of that kind.'

Discussion continued on paragraphs 12, 16, 17, 18 and 19 in the draft document.

FitzGerald said slightly different wording would be needed if devolution of functions were to be deferred.

Costello thought devolution would be taken care of at the formal conference.

Heath clarified that there were two separate issues: (a) devolution of powers to the new executive and (b) devolution of functions to the proposed Council of Ireland, following the formal conference. Separate machinery would be required for each.

Costello—yes, but if, in three years' time, the Northern Ireland assembly and the Dáil decide that further powers should be given to the Council, HMG might have a role in this.

Arrangements were made for a number of working groups or committees to discuss various paragraphs further. It was then agreed to adjourn for supper. It was also agreed that there should be a formal announcement to the press that the conference had adjourned for supper and for consultations among the delegations and that there would be a formal session again later.

The plenary session resumed on Friday night at 11.20 p.m.

Heath chairing the meeting, suggested that the various subgroups report to that plenary session on how their respective discussions were going. The reports in summary were as follows.

Patrick Jenkin, Chief Secretary to the Treasury, reported that texts had been agreed in Group 1 which dealt with financing.

Rawlinson reported that Group 2, the legal advisory group, had made some progress but they would like to go on working.

Oliver Napier, **Bob Cooper** and **Basil McIvor** agreed.

Conor Cruise O'Brien, reporting on Group 3 (the 'status' of Northern Ireland) said that it had been exceptionally difficult for all of them. There had been some progress but there were still some difficulties of a legal character as he saw it. He suggested they might meet early in the morning to try to narrow the gap. He thought it possible but still quite difficult to achieve.

Faulkner said he would like to work at it that night to try to finalise it.

Cruise O'Brien agreed but added that it might be difficult to finalise it.

Pym, the Northern Ireland secretary, said that policing, which was discussed in Group 4, was very difficult. The facts were agreed. They were exploring various ways of improving cooperation and greater identification with the police but it was not possible to get any broad measure of agreement at the present time.

Austin Currie—there was total deadlock and disagreement on every section of the document.

Faulkner agreed that it was 'pretty well deadlocked' but he would hope that there might be seeds of hope within the document.

Bob Cooper said there was no point in continuing the discussion that night.

Devlin commented 'does this mean that Alliance surrender?'

Heath, as chair of the meeting, then summarised the reports as follows:

- Group 1 (financing) had reached agreement.
- Group 2 (the legal advisory group) would continue its work.
- Group 3 (the status of Northern Ireland) would also continue.

- Group 4 (policing) would start work early on the following morning.

Garret FitzGerald said that in Group 5 dealing with the functions and structures of the Council of Ireland there was, effectively, agreement.

Morrell (Ulster Unionist Party) appeared to agree.

Napier commented that, though there was some progress in Group 2 (legal), there had not been agreement.

There was talk of group discussion resuming at 9 a.m. the next morning.

Faulkner said they could not afford much more delay in telling the public in Northern Ireland what the position was. In that sense, they were at the point of a gun. He asked if they could agree tonight that 'whatever the hell happens' they would finalise something by noon on Saturday?

Currie said that he accepted the basic point but they should not be stampeded when they were involved in a difficult job.

Cooney, the Irish minister for justice, said that the Irish government was prepared to do what it could.

Heath said that the British government have responsibility for policing. 'We can defend our policy entirely. So can the Irish minister for justice. What we are trying to do now is to find a way to link policing in with the Council of Ireland in order to meet some of the points made with great sincerity in the discussion'.

FitzGerald said he hoped there could be flexibility shown by the British government also. As an outsider he had the impression that the British government too had some problems.

Heath agreed. They had reserved the policing function for that reason.

Fitt said it was essential that they agree on 'status' and policing at the same time. Otherwise there would be a leak about the 'status' text.

Liam Cosgrave, the taoiseach, responded that this would be part of a package.

Discussion resumed in the various working groups around midnight Friday.

The problem at this stage in regard to the issue of policing in Northern Ireland was summarised well years later in a sentence by Garret FitzGerald:

> The issue of policing seemed irretrievably stuck, however, with the SDLP requiring a major role for the Council, the Unionists resisting it and demanding transfer of policing to the power-sharing Executive, and the British refusing to contemplate transfer of control either to the Executive or to the Council.[4]

In the early hours of Saturday morning, as officials—and some of our ministers—waited around in the central lobby hoping for progress, I resumed my informal notes.

Friday/Saturday 7/8 December, 1.30 a.m.

> According to the secretary of foreign affairs [Hugh McCann], there has almost been a breakthrough on the status issue. The attorney general is still drafting.
>
> Discussion with Sean Donlon. Policing virtually deadlocked. SDLP believe that Heath will intervene on that issue and, therefore, their tactics will be to stall in the discussion. The minister for justice has been sitting in all day on the sub-group on policing with the secretary of the Department of Justice (Ward) and assistant secretary (Donnelly) and no one else from Dublin side until Sean himself sat in at 8 p.m. session. The attorney general and the minister for justice may have the same proposals but their respective presentations differ greatly. Ward does not

intervene—he does not greatly favour our proposals. Meanwhile the British delegation, comprising Pym [the Northern Ireland secretary], Frank Cooper (Permanent Secretary, Northern Ireland Office), Trevelyan (Deputy Secretary, NIO), Bampton (Assistant Secretary, NIO, a police expert), and others, tears shreds off the proposals. John Hume is a master strategist who will make use, somehow, of anything which may be said to him.

For me the day has been spent waiting around. It has been very much a day for ministers and not civil servants—even including secretary DFA [McCann], above whose level the line [for attendance at sub-groups] is often drawn. Conor Cruise O'Brien very active discussing with Brian Faulkner and others. At present we have a draft comprehensive statement drafted by the British side on the basis of their understanding to date. In it

(1) each of the parties states its position;
(2) there is a declaration by the Irish government and a declaration by the British government; and
(3) there is provision for a study which would examine what are to be the executive functions of the Council. Decisions to be taken at the next [that is the formal] session of the Conference.

CLEA [Common Law Enforcement Area proposal] is proving difficult.

Muiris [MacConghail] has apparently been forgiven by the taoiseach for [yesterday's] leak but appears rueful. He has been told now to go and leak in view of Faulkner's leak this evening. Sean Donlon, Sean Ó hUiginn and I consider that could be very damaging.

The general question in my mind is how far we really should *want* to get [in the negotiation]. Negotiation on these issues is very much more complex than in other multilateral negotiations such as EEC entry because here we must show sympathetic consideration for how far our opponents—if one could call the Unionists that insofar as the negotiation is concerned—could go. We must think the position through for them as well as for ourselves and pitch our case accordingly.

If our initial positions were to be the criterion we have slipped a bit. But did we, or should we, really want to go that far in the first place? If we did, then our negotiating team may not be doing too well? though they have shown goodwill. But I suspect Conor Cruise O'Brien is experienced enough to be playing his own view of the game.

As to the actual talks, our initial wish to take the chair alternately [with the British] has been virtually forgotten. It is said that Heath declined when the taoiseach asked for this arrangement after lunch on the first day. But this is actually a positive advantage inside [the conference], and it may not look too bad outside it either. Heath is a very good chairman and to date the conference has not been a direct Anglo-Irish adversarial negotiation at all. The question has been rather how to reach an accommodation between Faulkner Unionists, the SDLP, Alliance and the government in Dublin. The British, generally at least, are taking a benevolent, detached, and mildly encouraging, interest in this accommodation.

Beyond all expectations, Heath has stayed on personally guiding the conference for two whole days now. He is obviously interested and may hope to achieve the same success as Willie Whitelaw—something which, electorally, he badly needs. He is staying here tonight.

Pym has not yet mastered his brief. He was 'clobbered'

yesterday in a discussion in regard to cross-border incursions. Rawlinson, the British attorney general, is poor. Heath is obviously solicitous—even deferential—to the taoiseach, whenever the taoiseach wants to intervene.

AG quite good. Tánaiste [Corish] not participating, Tully not participating.

Other significant snippets. Heath [the prime minister] dunks his biscuit in his coffee! I sat beside the foreign secretary, Sir Alec Douglas Home, at lunch—he slurps his soup!

Friday/Saturday 7/8 December, 2.15 a.m.

The general atmosphere is fairly good and informal. We may agree about 3 or 4 p.m. tomorrow? But the question is how to agree on policing? Other points ok.

I haven't dared go near the press centre. I understand John Bowman thought well of the taoiseach's opening statement.

Saturday morning, 11.30 a.m.

Waiting around again! The subcommittee on policing met this morning for half an hour and there is deadlock. Pym and Cooper are to report back to the prime minister and a plenary session seems to be expected. Robin Haydon, the prime minister's press secretary, was at the subgroup meeting. This was unusual and perhaps significant?

The SDLP are stalling on policing, expecting a *deus ex machina* intervention from the prime minister.

However, if there is a breakdown they do not want it to be on policing alone but on several other issues too. This may not be possible. Brian Faulkner has virtually threatened to walk out if the Council of Ireland is given a role in relation to policing. The SDLP threaten deadlock if it is not. Our position is not particularly well presented in the sub-committee where there is heavy political representation on the British side. Our attitude, I think, is that our own police, and our general position on this, are alright—so as we see it, it is a matter for the Northern parties to agree. HMG position is that policing in Northern Ireland is a matter for them. What they may be willing to do further is unclear—to me at least. Heath is rumoured to have cancelled his afternoon engagements.

It seems we distributed this morning a slightly revised document strengthening the Council a bit in regard to structures? There is a rumour that the British may have gone back on something they had initially agreed yesterday—on 'status'?

Saturday, 3 p.m. (after lunch, waiting for a plenary meeting)

Apparently there is deadlock on policing. I understand that a delegation of the government and the SDLP were to see the British side about now. We have heard that the prime minister wants a plenary session shortly and also that he has to withdraw for a few hours. Probably he will call the plenary, explain this, hear formally if there is any progress and then fix a later meeting.

The question is, however, whether there might not be a breakdown on policing now, followed perhaps by a Unionist walkout. Could they then agree later?

Probably not, as their supporters would force them to harden their views in the interval.

Before lunch I did a quickly dictated paper on the question of the core group of ministers and the *ad hoc* ministers (for particular agenda items) on the Council of Ireland. A new concept has been added—that the *ad hoc* ministers should be non-voting. I also did a manuscript note on the draft paper about the Council of Ireland which, in its wording, may effectively rule out direct devolution to the Council. I discussed and showed both to the minister for foreign affairs, who will consider them—though the second point would be difficult to establish now as the emerging text is already agreed.

More than ever it has been a day for ministers and not for civil servants, though Hugh McCann, Charles Whelan [Head of the Anglo-Irish division in Foreign Affairs], and Dermot Nally are involved to some degree. CW appears more active than the others as a runner and fixer. The ministers' meetings are quasi—or full—government meetings?

The whole situation today reminds one of the kind of dramatic pre-birth scenes one sees in old movies, with shots of closed doors and calls for 'lots of hot water'. Finally the cry of an infant is heard from inside, and then the old family doctor emerges, rolling down his sleeves! Except that we have not yet reached the latter stage!

Saturday, 8 December, 4.10 p.m. (tea)

The prime minister has left until 6 p.m.[5] The SDLP and the [Irish] government are meeting separately. There is little hope of progress. Will there be a breakdown? If there is, there won't be an executive [since the agreement of 21 November by the Northern Ireland parties to form an executive was contingent on the success of the conference]. Then what? Who can stick it out longest? SDLP? Unionists? And if there were to be an agreement tonight, which seems unlikely, what would be the Saturday night consequences in Belfast?

Saturday, 4.25 p.m.

Charles Whelan tells us that there is to be a meeting of delegations on policing at 4.30 p.m. The ministerial team is now selecting our delegation—the minister for justice, the tánaiste [Brendan Corish] and the minister for foreign affairs?

Saturday, 8 December, 11.15 p.m.

I have just come from drafting a closing statement for the taoiseach. The plenary met for the first time today.

The prime minister read out the Communiqué as agreed to date. Some drafting errors were corrected. At the suggestion of **Declan Costello**, the Irish attorney general, paragraphs 10, 11 and 12 were made into a single paragraph. Space was left after paragraph 13 for the insertion of whatever might be agreed on policing.

Costello [?] noted that there was agreement otherwise over a wide field and it was incumbent now to reach agreement on policing. Ireland, the UK and the world would find it extraordinary that having reached agreement so far on such a wide range of issues there was no agreement on this last matter.

452

Saturday night/ Sunday morning, 8/9 December, 3.40 a.m.

We are all waiting around in the baronial hall like extras on a film set for Macbeth, Hamlet or Faust. There seems to be a deadlock on policing? Muiris [MacConghail] is worried about the overall package, and about the different views of the minister for justice and Conor Cruise O'Brien.

Saturday night/Sunday morning, 8/9 December, 5 a.m.

We are sitting around in the lobby/foyer. It looks like a railway terminal or an airline terminal.

Apparently the present situation is that there has been virtual deadlock on policing. We have tried to play honest broker but now we are leaving the whole thing to the SDLP and the Unionists to sort out. Some time ago we put forward a draft that made the SDLP a bit displeased and was rejected by the Unionists. So we dropped out of the honest broker game.

Sunday morning, 9 December, 5.25 a.m.

A short time ago John Hume rushed into the main hall and brought out Gerry Fitt who had been sprawled, apparently asleep, on a sofa in the centre of the hall.

Sunday, 9 December, 5.30 p.m.

[*Extracts from a lengthy note in which I tried to assess the emerging outcome.*] The *real* importance of the

Agreement, however, may be that it will allow the power-sharing executive to be appointed and it is the effect of this executive within Northern Ireland that may, in the long run, be more important than the *direct* effects of the Council itself—although, of course, the Council is an essential prop to the Northern structure…we are not [simply] negotiating…with Faulkner but rather negotiating *and* trying to sustain him at once in a complex five-sided conference.[6]

Sunday, 9 December, 6.15 p.m.

The long vigil seems to be still on—with alternating optimistic and pessimistic stories floating around. We finally abandoned last night's vigil at 8.15 a.m., went and had breakfast, and then went to bed at 9.30 a.m. until 2 p.m. (The conference was to resume at 3 p.m.). In fact, we are back to a similar situation to last night's—in the main lobby at least. The news on ITV just now said that we had had 24 hours yesterday and had broken for seven hours to change our clothes and get some rest!

Last night's scene here was fantastic—literally so. About 40 people sat around a baronial lobby-hall on deep chairs, or stood around, or sprawled. Others on the balcony looked down. Some slept—for example Gerry Fitt. Every so often the taoiseach, followed usually by a worried-looking Muiris at two paces, strode out and into another room on the balcony. Or Heath came up and down the stairs followed by attendants. Or Faulkner went off somewhere, or the SDLP— though it seems more likely that the SDLP had planned things and that Gerry Fitt's ostentatious sleeping stretched on a sofa while great things were afoot on policing was no accident.

The present situation is that something has been drafted (once again!) and it was being discussed between the SDLP and the Unionists in the conference hall. They came out with differences still to be resolved and went off to see their respective parties. Just now the party leaders—Faulkner, Currie, Bradford and Hume—went upstairs together to see Heath.

(Meanwhile Helen Gavigan has cancelled or postponed yet again our standby arrangements for special flights).

Sunday, 9 December, 7.45 p.m.
Agreement reached! *Habemus pacem?*

Sunday, 9 December, 8.25 p.m.

Plenary session resumes. All of the Communiqué except paragraphs 12 to 17 had already been agreed. These have now been agreed and the conference has been brought to a successful conclusion.

The taoiseach, Liam Cosgrave, thanked Prime Minister Heath and his fellow ministers and officials. It gave him great satisfaction, he said, to be able to agree with Brian Faulkner, Gerry Fitt and Oliver Napier. His firm hope now is that a new and better Ireland is emerging and that there will be further improved relations between Britain and Ireland.

Brian Faulkner (Ulster Unionist Party) thanked the prime minister for his painstaking work at the conference. He expressed appreciation to the taoiseach and his ministers for the way in which 'they had always been at personal pains to help us in discussion'. He also thanked Frank Cooper of the Northern Ireland Office. 'This is a historic moment. Everything we have done has been done with care. The prime minister and the taoiseach and I must now be sales-men—we have to be *super* salesmen. Thank God for what has been achieved'

Gerry Fitt (SDLP) said 'after the recent elections we realised we were entering a completely new era. The two communities facing one another were dealing with the problems of three centuries. We have had six weeks to bring about an executive designate. This was a very short time indeed'. He thanked William Whitelaw, the previous Northern Ireland secretary. The taoiseach, he said, had been very helpful in every political step they had taken to bring this about. 'Gladstone in the nineteenth century had said "my mission is to pacify Ireland." He did not succeed. I hope that [we have]' (applause).

Oliver Napier (Alliance) said that 'in six weeks of negotiations [to agree on the executive], and here at Sunningdale, the mem-bers of the executive got to know each other and they have a tremendous respect for each other's ability. The executive is likely to hold together. There is a new respect for fellow Ulstermen working together for the good of Northern Ireland. We are going back to sell the package. This will not be an easy job. We have a big task before us.' He thanked the prime minis-ter and his staff and the taoiseach for the assistance they had given in this task.

Ted Heath, the prime minister, thanked the taoiseach for 'the very full cooperation which he has given us' and also the leaders of the Northern Ireland parties. He said William Whitelaw had tele-phoned to convey his warmest congratulations. He also mentioned that there appeared to have been a leak about the successful conclu-sion. He congratulated Frank Cooper of the NIO ('hear, hear'). New relationships between north and south and between the United Kingdom and the south will now, he said, be placed on a permanent new basis. He also spoke about the press arrangements where the leaders of the five delegations were to give a joint press conference.

Final press conference

The press conference, which was to conclude the final plenary session of the conference, got under way eventually about 9.30 p.m. on that Sunday evening. Television cameras and press photographers were admitted. The text of the Communiqué was distributed to the waiting news media; and each of the leaders made a brief statement in which they expressed their satisfaction at the agreement reached and their hope for the future. I had been drafting and redrafting a text for the taoiseach as the situation changed—or did not change—while the conference dragged on through the long hours of Saturday night and Sunday morning.

The taoiseach, in his closing statement, said that there were no winners and no losers there at Sunningdale that day. They had reached accommodation with one another on many practical issues. But none of them had compromised or asked the others to compromise on basic aspirations.

However, the proposals they had agreed would work only if all concerned committed themselves wholeheartedly to them as a way of easing fears and resolving conflict in the island of Ireland. They had sought a settlement that would foster the growth of trust, and ease community fears, throughout the island of Ireland and benefit all its people. The agreement to establish a Council of Ireland was of primary importance because such a Council could establish trust between both parts of the island and all sections of the Irish people. Since the issue was complex, all parties had agreed to a review that would report to the second stage of the conference on areas where the Council would have executive functions. The Council would be financed, initially, by grants from the two administrations north and south and other possible methods of financing would be studied. 'We believe the formation of the Council will promote and encourage the growth of consensus politics throughout Ireland and the eventual elimination of violence.'

To ensure that those who seek by violent means to wreck the institutions of democracy would not find refuge in either part of the island, immediate legal steps would be taken so that persons accused of murder in either part of the island would be tried for the offence where they had been arrested. The Council itself would consider proposals on common measures to guarantee human rights in both parts of the island; and it could recommend whether additional legislation or new institutions, such as a Human Rights Court, or an ombudsman or commissioner for complaints for all Ireland, were desirable. The British government had committed itself again at the conference to bring internment to an end 'as soon as the security situation permits.' It had also 'expressed the hope that a number of detainees might be released before Christmas'.

The declarations made by each of the two governments, he said, 'give expression to a principle which those of us who aspire to a real unity of people in Ireland have always felt to be paramount—that unity can and should come only by consent.' In Northern Ireland, the executive-designate would now be formally appointed and powers would be devolved to it and to the assembly in the near future. The members of that executive and representatives of the two governments would attend the formal stage of the conference 'early in the New Year'. At that stage all of those taking part would sign a formal agreement that would be registered at the United Nations by the two governments.

******

Later that night the Irish government delegation returned home on a special Aer Lingus flight to Dublin, where they arrived in the early hours of the morning of Monday, 10 December 1973.

NOTES

[1] HMG is the usual British abbreviation for Her Majesty's Government.
[2] This was the term in general use at the time. As I noted earlier it meant some kind of common arrangements for law enforcement in the island of Ireland and not, as the term might seem to imply, 'enforcement of the common law' (as distinct from statute law).
[3] This was a reference to the *Report of the Committee on the Constitution*. For details see n. 9 in Chapter 18. Even though it did not reach agreement on all points, the committee did agree on a suggested wording that would have the effect of dropping

the so-called 'claim' to jurisdiction over the whole island in Article 3 and replacing it with a sentence that read 'The Irish Nation hereby proclaims its firm will that its territory be re-united in harmony and brotherly affection between all Irishmen'. However, its recommendation was not implemented.

[4] FitzGerald, *All in a life*, 216.

[5] Apparently, as I learned long afterwards, Heath went back to Downing Street to meet the Italian prime minister for a few hours. He then returned to Sunningdale.

[6] Copy of the full note is on NAI TSCH 2004/21/625 (folder 2).

Bibliography

Anderson, B., 1983 *Imagined communities: reflections on the origin and spread of nationalism.* London. Verso.

Bew, P., 1994 *Ideology and the Irish question: Ulster unionism and Irish nationalism, 1912–1916.* Oxford. Clarendon Press.

Bew, P. and Gillespie, G., 1999 *Northern Ireland: a chronology of the Troubles, 1968–1999.* Dublin. Gill and Macmillan.

Bloomfield, K., 1994 *Stormont in crisis: a memoir.* Belfast. Blackstaff Press.

Bloomfield, K., 2007 *A tragedy of errors: the government and misgovernment of Northern Ireland.* Liverpool. Liverpool University Press.

Buckland, P. (ed.) 1973 *Irish unionism, 1885–1923: a documentary history.* Belfast. The Historical Association.

Campbell, J., 1993 *Edward Heath: a biography.* London. Jonathan Cape.

Chambers, A., 2014 *T.K. Whitaker: portrait of a patriot.* London. Doubleday Ireland.

Corish, P.J., 1985 *The Irish Catholic experience: a historical survey.* Dublin. Gill and Macmillan.

Craig, A., 2010 *Crisis of confidence: Anglo-Irish relations in the early Troubles, 1966–1974.* Dublin and Portland, Oregon. Irish Academic Press.

Curtis, T.C. and McDowell, R.B (eds), 1943 *Irish historical documents, 1172–1922*. London. Methuen and Co. Ltd.

Dorr, N., 2010 *Ireland at the United Nations: memories of the early years*. Dublin. Institute of Public Administration.

Fanning, R., 2001 'Playing it cool: the response of the British and Irish governments to the crisis in Northern Ireland, 1968–69', *Irish Studies in International Affairs* (12), 57–85.

Fanning, R., 2013 *Fatal path: British government and Irish revolution, 1910–1922*. London. Faber & Faber.

Fanning, R., Kennedy, M., Keogh, D. and O'Halpin, E. (eds), 2000 *Documents on Irish foreign policy*, volume. II, *1923–1926*. Dublin. Royal Irish Academy.

Farren, S. and Haughey, D. (eds), 2015 *John Hume: Irish peacemaker*. Dublin. Four Courts Press.

Faulkner, B. (ed. by J. Houston), 1978 *Memoirs of a statesman*. London. Weidenfeld and Nicolson.

Feeney, B., 2014 *A short history of the Troubles*. Dublin. O'Brien Press.

Finn, T., 2012 *Tuairim, intellectual debate and policy formation: re-thinking Ireland, 1954–75*. Manchester. Manchester University Press.

FitzGerald, G., 1991 *All in a life: an autobiography*. Dublin. Gill and Macmillan.

FitzGerald, G., 2010 *Just Garret: tales from the political front line*. Dublin. Liberties Press.

Flackes, W.D., 1983 *Northern Ireland: a political directory*. London. Ariel Books.

Foster, R.F., 1988 *Modern Ireland, 1600–1972*. London. Allen Lane: The Penguin Press.

Hewitt, J., (ed. by F. Ormsby), 1991 *The collected poems of John Hewitt*. Belfast. Blackstaff Press.

Jackson, A., 2003 *Home Rule: an Irish history, 1800–2000*. London. Weidenfeld and Nicholson.

Jones, T., (ed. by Keith Middlemas), 1971 *Whitehall diary*, volume III. London. Oxford University Press.

Kendle, J., 1992 *Walter Long, Ireland, and the Union, 1905–1920*. Dublin and McGill. Glendale Publishing Ltd and Queen's University Press.

Kennedy, M., 2000 *Division and consensus: the politics of cross-border relations in Ireland, 1925–1969*. Dublin. Institute of Public Administration.

Kennedy, M. 2001 '"This tragic and most intractable problem": the reaction of the Department of External Affairs to the outbreak of the Troubles in Northern Ireland', *Irish Studies in International Affairs* 12, 87–95.

Kennedy, M. and McMahon, D. (eds), 2005 *Obligations and responsibilities: Ireland and the United Nations, 1955–2005*. Dublin. Institute of Public Administration.

Keogh, D., 2008 *Jack Lynch: a biography*. Dublin. Gill and Macmillan.

Laffan, M., 2014 *Judging W.T. Cosgrave: the foundation of the Irish state*. Dublin. Royal Irish Academy.

Larkin, E., 1972 'The devotional revolution in Ireland, 1850–75', *American Historical Review* 77 (June), 625–52.

Lynch, J.M., 1972 'The Anglo-Irish problem', *Foreign Affairs: An American Quarterly Review* 50 (4) (July), 601–17.

Maher, D.J., 1986 *The tortuous path: the course of Irish entry into the EEC, 1948–73*. Dublin. Institute of Public Administration.

Mansergh, N., 1975 *The Irish question, 1840–1921*. Toronto and Buffalo. University of Toronto Press.

Mansergh, N., 1991 *The unresolved question: the Anglo-Irish settlement and its undoing, 1912–72*. New Haven and London. Yale University Press.

Mansergh, N. (ed. by Diana Mansergh), 1997 *Nationalism and independence: selected Irish papers*. Cork. Cork University Press.

Mitchell, A. and Ó Snodaigh, P., 1985 *Irish political documents, 1916–1949*. Dublin. Irish Academic Press.

Moloney, E., 2007 *A secret history of the IRA*. London. Penguin Books.

Moloney, E. and Pollak, A. (eds), 1986 *Paisley*. Dublin. Poolbeg Press.

O'Brien, C.C., 1972 *States of Ireland*. London. Hutchinson.

O'Brien, C.C., 1998 *Memoir: my life and themes*. Dublin. Poolbeg Press.

O'Day, A. and Stevenson, J. (eds), 1992 *Irish historical documents since 1800*. Dublin. Gill and Macmillan.

O'Kane, E., 2004 'Anglo-Irish relations and the Northern Ireland peace process: from exclusion to inclusion', *Contemporary British History* 18 (1) (Spring), 78–99.

O'Donnell, C., 2007 *Fianna Fáil: Irish republicanism and the Northern Ireland Troubles, 1968–2005*. Dublin and Portland, Oregon. Irish Academic Press.

Peck, J., 1978 *Dublin from Downing Street*. Dublin. Gill and Macmillan.

Rees, M., 1985 *Northern Ireland: a personal perspective*. London. Methuen.

Santayana, G., 1905 *The life of reason: reason in common sense*. New York. Charles Scribner's Sons.

Stewart, A.T.Q., 1977 *The narrow ground: aspects of Ulster, 1609–1969*. London. Faber & Faber.

Taylor, P., 1998 *Provos: the IRA and Sinn Féin*. London. Bloomsbury Publishing.

Townshend, C., 1983 *Political violence in Ireland: government and resistance since 1848*. Oxford. Clarendon Press.

Walker, B.M., 2012 *A political history of the two Irelands: from partition to peace*. Palgrave Macmillan UK.

Walsh, J., 2008 *Patrick Hillery: the official biography*. Dublin. New Island.

Whitelaw, W., 1989 *The Whitelaw memoirs*. London. Aurum Press Ltd.

Whyte, J., *The reform of Stormont*. Belfast. A New Ulster Movement publication.

Zeigler, P., 2010 *Edward Heath: the authorised biography*. London. Harper Press.

Governmental publications

British and Northern Irish

Report of the enquiry into allegations against the security forces of physical brutality in Northern Ireland arising out of events on the 9th August 1971 (London, November 1971; HMSO, Cmnd. 4823).

Violence and civil disturbances in Northern Ireland in 1969: report of tribunal of inquiry (London, April 1972; HMSO, Cmnd. 566).

The future of Northern Ireland: a paper for discussion (London, 1972, HMSO).

Northern Ireland constitutional proposals (London, March 1973; HMSO, Cmnd. 5259).

Irish

Schedule to the Treaty (Confirmation of Amending Agreement) Act 1925 [No. 40].

Seanad Éireann Debates, vol. 48, no. 15, Wednesday, 29 February 1958 (accessed 27 September 2017 at: http://oireachtasdebates. oireachtas.ie/debates%20authoring/debateswebpack.nsf/takes/ seanad1958012900006).

Report of the Committee on the Constitution (Dublin, December 1967; Stationary Office, Prl. 9817).

The Taoiseach, John Lynch T.D., *Speeches and statements on Irish unity and Anglo-Irish relations, August 1969–October 1971* (Dublin, 1971).

Northern Ireland 1973/74: official documentation (Dublin, Government Information Service) [includes some of Taoiseach Liam Cosgrave's speeches, the Sunningdale Communiqué and the *Law Enforcement Commission Report*].

Joint British-Irish

Law Enforcement Commission Report (Dublin, 1974; Stationery Office, Prl. 3832).

Archival Sources

The National Archives (UK) (abbreviated here as TNA)

CAB 128/51/13
CAB 133 407

PREM 15/487
PREM 15/611
PREM 15/1004
PREM 15/1009
PREM 15/1685

FCO 33/757
FCO 33/758
FCO 33/759
FCO 33/760

Public Record Office of Northern Ireland (abbreviated here as PRONI)

DCR/1/126

The National Archives of Ireland (abbreviated here as NAI)

TSCH 2000/6/657
TSCH 2000/6/658

TSCH 2001/6/549
TSCH 2001/8/1
TSCH 2001/8/6
TSCH 2003/16/480-485
TSCH 2003/16/504
TSCH 2003/16/549
TSCH 2003/16/562
TSCH 2004/21/2
TSCH 2004/21/3
TSCH 2004/21/466
TSCH 2004/21/624
TSCH 2004/21/625
TSCH 2004/21/626
TSCH 2004/21/628
TSCH 2004/21/673
TSCH 2005/7/607
TSCH 2005/7/629

DFA 2000/5/38
DFA 2000/14/444
DFA 2002/19/500
DFA 2003/12/22
DFA 2003/13/7
DFA 2003/13/9
DFA 2003/13/10
DFA 2003/13/11
DFA 2003/13/16
DFA 2003/16/504
DFA 2003/17/30
DFA 2003/17/32
DFA 2004/7/665
DFA 2004/15/16
DFA 2004/15/25
DFA 2004/21/3
DFA 2007/58/36
DFA 2007/111/1863

Acknowledgements

This book evolved over two years. I should like to thank a number of people who helped and encouraged me over that period.

I owe very special thanks to Professor John Coakley who read an early version of the text—the first person to do so. He offered perceptive and helpful comments on what I had written and encouraged me to continue. He also, very generously, gave me some important archive material, which I have drawn on at several points in the book.

My former colleague in the Department of Foreign Affairs, Sean Donlon, who lived through the events I recount, and was with me at Sunningdale, also read an early draft and discussed it with me on several occasions. His comments and views, not just on Sunningdale but on the whole period, were very helpful—the more so because of the important part he played in relation to Northern Ireland not just before, during and after the Sunningdale conference, but also in subsequent years as ambassador to the USA and as my predecessor in the post of secretary general of the Department of Foreign Affairs. I know that my narrative offers just one view of the events I recount. I continue to encourage him to add at greater length to what he has already written about the central importance of John Hume's role and that of his colleagues in the SDLP, an aspect which I do no more than touch on, and acknowledge, in my account.

I am also very grateful to another former colleague from Foreign Affairs, Frank Sheridan, who read an earlier version of the text and also offered me some very helpful advice based on his own work on archival material in relation to Northern Ireland.

In the months before and after the Sunningdale conference, Muiris MacConghail, who was government press secretary at the time, and I cooperated well together in dealing with the news media and we remained friends. A stray remark he made to me many years later, which he could not now be expected to recall, stayed with me and played some part in my decision to try my hand at writing about these events. I am grateful to him for this.

I should like also to thank all of those who were involved in one way or another over the past year in bringing about the publication of this book by the Royal Irish Academy: Professor Mary Daly, the then president of the Academy and her colleagues on the Publication Committee who initially accepted it for publication; the two (unnamed) reviewers who recommended that the Academy should publish the text and then, when consulted further, offered additional helpful advice; Ruth Hegarty and her colleagues in the Publications Office—Helena King and Dr Valeria Cavalli; graphic designer Fidelma Slattery; and all of the other staff in the Academy who saw it through various stages in bringing it to print.

I owe particularly warm thanks to Maggie Armstrong who edited the text. She was very supportive, dealt expertly and well with various issues as they arose and was patient about late changes. I acknowledge, too, the role of her son, Frankie.

I thank the directors and the staff of both the National Archives of Ireland and The National Archives at Kew, in London. I have drawn heavily in the book on material from both these archival sources and, also, to a very limited extent, on the Public Record Office of Northern Ireland.

I am particularly grateful to my sister, Ben Kimmerling and my brothers, Donal and Frank for their continuing love and support. They regularly offered me encouragement to continue writing and, in Ben's words—to 'keep my nose to the grindstone'. The phrase suggests a somewhat uncomfortable way of working but I have tried as best I could to do as she said and this book is the result.

Throughout the two years of intermittent writing I have been able, as always, to count on the love, support—and patience—of my wife, Caitríona Doran. I know that I will always be able do so and I thank her, warmly and lovingly, for that.

Finally, I remember two successive taoisigh—Jack Lynch and Liam Cosgrave—a British prime minister, Ted Heath, ministers in both governments, the leaders and members of three political parties in Northern Ireland and the many officials in Dublin, Belfast and London, who, notwithstanding their differences, and the dangers and vicissitudes of the time, contributed in their various ways, over a number of years, to the effort to end a destructive conflict and bring peace to Northern Ireland. As I wrote about these events I had in mind particularly two former colleagues whose names recurred so often—Dermot Nally in the files in Dublin and Robert Armstrong in the London files. Both were to play a notable part in the negotiation of a later initiative, the Anglo-Irish Agreement of 1985, and both would become friends. I would have greatly wished to discuss what I have written about Sunningdale with Dermot, but, sadly—gone, as the Irish phrase has it, *ar shlí na fírinne*, 'on the way of truth'—he is no longer with us.

The Sunningdale conference, where the efforts of all of those involved culminated, did not succeed at the time but I believe that history will record it as a prelude to the settlement for peace in Northern Ireland achieved a generation later, and therefore that what they tried to do in their time will not have been in vain.

Index

T

Tass, 53
Taylor, John, 130, 369
Thatcher, Margaret, 307, 328
Thorn, Gaston, 262, 265
Thorpe, Jeremy, 128
torture, allegations of, 226, 297–8, 316
trade unions, 102
Trend, Sir Burke, 82, 92, 101, 104, 133,
     135–6, 170
Trevelyan, D.J., 364, 447
Troubles, the, 5, 6, 89, 232
     casualties of, 2, 35, 68, 85, 105, 125,
          130, 155–6, 169, 282, 374, 407,
          432, 433
     early phase of, 30, 33, 35, 52–3, 54,
          74, 77, 82, 85, 118, 182, 183,
          199, 309, 376
Tully, Jim, 292, 413, 426, 449

U

Ulster, 19, 20
Ulster Army Council, 324
Ulster Covenant, 20
Ulster Defence Association (UDA), 30, 125,
     149, 324, 367, 434
Ulster Defence Regiment (UDR), 102
Ulster Liberal Party, 187
Ulster Unionist Council, 20, 251, 259–60,
     330–1, 334
Ulster Unionist Party, 6–7, 27, 29, 92, 102,
     122–3, 156, 182, 185, 186–7, 191,
     243, 251, 256–9, 263, 284, 293,
     330, 334, 348, 349, 362, 413
     at Sunningdale, 274, 281, 294, 296, 319,
          400, 408, 437, 448, 452, 453, 455
Ulster Vanguard, 129, 138, 156, 251, 275,
     276, 328, 367
Ulster Volunteer Force (UVF) (founded
     1913), 20–1
Ulster Volunteer Force (UVF) (founded
     1965), 29, 125, 280n5, 324, 367
Ulster Workers' Council (UWC), 324,
     366–9, 380
UN General Assembly, 40–2, 77, 262
UN peacekeeping idea, 38–42
UN Security Council, 40–2
unionism, 20, 25, 27, 28, 77, 92, 129, 149,
     151, 166, 360

unionists, 12, 21–3, 28, 42, 46, 65,
     81, 104, 122, 125, 138, 147, 152,
     173, 176, 185–7, 191, 195, 201,
     215, 221, 224, 226, 232, 235,
     243–4, 246, 333, 336, 338, 355,
     357, 363, 378, 379, 381, 382,
     384–5, 390, 448
     power of, 92, 94–5, 106, 116, 147,
          305, 377
     rights of, 84, 290
united Ireland (as aspiration/objective), 48,
     73, 81–4, 90, 92, 95, 98, 104, 106,
     110, 122, 124–5, 133, 143–50, 152,
     153, 162–6, 170, 171, 177, 181,
     183, 186–9, 195, 219, 223–4, 228,
     230, 232, 240–1, 244, 252, 255,
     290, 305, 306–11, 321n4, 331–2,
     335, 377–8, 382, 387, 391, 424
United Ireland Association
     (Britain), 123–4
United Irishmen, 14, 18
United Ulster Unionist Council (UUUC),
     324, 328, 348

W

Waddell, Sir James, 44
War of Independence, 22, 23–4, 232
Ward, Andy, 365, 446–7
West, Harry, 328
Westminster parliamentary model, 26, 81,
     121, 122, 146, 150, 160, 164,
     183–4, 376
Whelan, Charles, 226, 260, 365, 451, 452
Whitaker, Ken, 36, 37, 67, 71–8, 81, 84,
     145, 152, 183, 309, 376
White, Kelvin, 43
White Paper (March 1973), 171, 201–3,
     206–8, 211, 217–18, 237–8, 251,
     255, 264, 276, 338, 376–7, 415
Whitelaw, William, 137, 138, 146, 148,
     149, 153–7, 161, 201, 202–3, 245,
     256, 258–61, 268–9, 275, 404, 430,
     442, 448, 456
Wilson, Harold, 5, 35, 44–5, 47, 82, 128,
     204, 347, 358, 359, 360, 364, 367,
     369, 380
Wolfe Tone, Theobald, 14
Woodfield, Philip, 153–4, 303, 364, 365
Wright, Oliver, 43